The BIOS Companion

Phil Croucher

Electrocution, Inc.

ADVICE Press
480 California Avenue, Suite 104
Palo Alto, CA 94306

The BIOS Companion

Printed in the United States of America.

Published by: ADVICE Press, 480 California Avenue, Suite 104, Palo Alto, CA 94306.
Phone: (650) 321-2198 Fax: (650) 321-2199 info@advice.com
http://www.advicepress.com

Printing History: December 1998
First Book Edition   1 2 3 4 5 6 7 8 9

Trademarks

ISBN: 1-889671-20-7   [12/98]

Sources

Which are gratefully acknowledged:

Experience.

Many conversations with technicians.

Hundreds of motherboard manuals, not all of which were helpful, which is why all this started in the first place!

AMI BIOS Tech Ref manual.

MR BIOS Tech Ref Manual. Thanks to Mike at Microid Research!

Readers, including Mick O'Donnell, Martyn Smith, Chris Crook, Chris Nicholson, Dart Computers, Pat Tan, John Dallman, Ulf Boehlau, Rick and Tilman at ProData, Adrian Clint of Samsung, Peter Farrow, Kerry and Toni at Award Software, Chuck French at Unicore, Ali Kiafar at ECS/TTX, John Dann at ProData and Mike Echlin.

amibios.txt, available from Jean-Paul Rodrigue at the University of Montreal, which had useful snippets, especially the explanation of Fast Decode. His BIOS Survival Guide is at **www.lemig.umontreal.ca**.

amisetup, a shareware program from Robert Muchsel, available from **ftp://194.163.64.1/pub/sanisoft/amisetup.zip**.

Table of Contents

Fixed Disk Parameter Tables. .365

The BIOS

The instructions that turn a PC into a useful machine come in three stages; *application programs*, which are loaded by an *operating system*, which is loaded by a bootstrap loader in the BIOS.

BIOS stands for *Basic Input/Output System*, of which there are several in a PC; a good example is the one on the video card that controls the interface between it and the computer. However, we are concerned with the *System BIOS*, which is a collection of assembly language routines that allow programs and the components of a PC to communicate with each other at the hardware level. It therefore works in two directions and is active all the time your computer is switched on. Software doesn't have to talk to a device directly; it calls a BIOS routine which does the job instead, but these days the BIOS is often bypassed by 32-bit software anyway. In fact, there are moves afoot to place the BIOS functions into the operating system, starting with Power Management (see *ACPI*).

For the moment, though, the BIOS will work in conjunction with the *chipset*, which is really what manages access to system resources such as memory, cache and the data buses, and actually is the subject of this book, as all those advanced settings relate to the chipset and not the BIOS as such.

On an IBM-compatible, you will find the BIOS embedded into a ROM on the motherboard, together with hard disk utilities and a CMOS setup program, although this will depend on the manufacturer. The ROM will usually occupy a 64K segment of upper memory at F000 if you have an ISA system, and a 128K segment starting at E000 with EISA.

Older machines, such as 286s, will have two ROMs, labelled *Odd* and *Even*, or *High* and *Low* (they must be in the right slots), because of the 16-bit bus, but these days there tends to be only one—look for one with a printed label (older 386s sometimes had 4). The reason for getting away with one is because BIOS code is now copied into *Shadow RAM* (explained later), and not actually executed from ROM, but extended memory.

A *Flash ROM* allows you to change the BIOS code without replacing the chip(s). Flash ROM, or *programmable read-only nonvolatile RAM*, if you want to be posh, is similar in concept to an EPROM, but doesn't need ultraviolet light to erase it; instead, a 12v pulse is used.

Including the ROM space, the BIOS takes 256 bytes of low memory as a *BIOS Data Area*, which contains details about the Num Lock state, keyboard buffer, etc. DOS loads higher than this, so it's quite safe.

There are several types of BIOS because so many computers need to be IBM-compatible and the companies don't allow to copying, for obvious reasons. The BIOS worries about all the differences and presents a standard frontage to DOS in the same way that DOS takes care of operating the computer and provides a standard interface for application programs. PC and motherboard manufacturers used to make their own BIOSes, and many still do, but most tend to be based on code supplied by third party companies, the most well-known of which are Phoenix Technologies, Award Software, Microid Research (MR) and American Megatrends (AMI). However, all is not what it seems! Award Software owns Unicore (the upgraders), which in turn owns MR, which does the customised stuff. Phoenix also owns Quadtel.

HOW OLD IS MY BIOS?

Microsoft says that any earlier than 1987 are "suspect" for running Windows, and there is a list of *Known BIOS Problems* see page -227 later on. For IDE systems, the AMI BIOS must be later than 04-09-90, and for SCSI 09-25-88, as long as the SCSI card is OS220 compatible. For RLL and MFM drives, try 9-25-88 or later. The keyboard BIOS for AMI systems must be revision 'F'. If you want to check how old your BIOS is, the date is on the start-up screen, usually buried in the *BIOS ID String*, which looks a bit like this (**121291** is the date in this AMI sample):

    40-0201-BY6379-01101111-**121291**-UMCAUTO-04

Try also using **debug**:

    -d f000:fff5 fffc

The AMI WinBIOS has a normal date on the startup screen. Otherwise, as you can see, you don't just get the date; many manufacturers include extras that identify the state of the chipset inside. For example, with the AMI Hi-Flex BIOS, there are two more strings, displayed by pressing **Ins** during bootup, or any other key to create an error condition.

ACER ID STRINGS

In the bottom left hand corner of the screen:

    ACR89xxxxxxxxxxxxxxxxR03-B6

The first 2 characters after ACR identify the motherboard:

The last few are the BIOS revision.

8F	M3 (SCSI)	Altos 9000
89	M5	Altos 7000P
07	M7	Altos 900/M and 9000/M
1A	M3A	Altos 300
2F	M11A	Altos 900/Pro
24	M9B	Altos 9000/Pro
46	M9N	Altos 920 and 9100
05	X1B	Altos 19000

AMI ID STRINGS

The BIOS release number is at the top left of the screen for AMI motherboards. The BIOS ID string is at the bottom left for theirs and any others. The AMI BIOS and BIOS Plus series (1986-1990) looks like this (for example):

DINT-1123-04990-K8

Or, in other words:

aaaa-**b**bbb-mmddyy-Kc

where:

aaaa	BIOS type
bbbb	Customer Number
mmddyy	Release date
Kc	Keyboard BIOS version number

If the first customer number (in bold above) is **1,2**, **8** or a **letter**, it is a non-AMI Taiwanese motherboard. If it is **3**, **4** or **5**, it is from AMI. **50** or **6** means a non-AMI US motherboard and **9** means an evaluation BIOS for a Taiwanese manufacturer.

Otherwise, there can be up to three lines (from 1991 onwards) at the bottom left of the screen. The first is displayed automatically, the other two can be seen by pressing the **Insert** key. Aside from version numbers, the 1s and 0s indicate the state of the settings inside. It might look like this:

41-0102-zz**5**123-00111111-101094-AMIS123-P

Again, check the bold number for the manufacturer.

ID STRING LINE 1

12_4-7_9-14_16-23_25-30_32-39_41 decodes as follows:

Byte	Description	
1	Processor Type	0 8086/8 2 80286 3 80386 80486 Pentium
2	Size of BIOS	0 64K 1 128K
4-5	Major Version Number	
6-7	Minor Version Number	
9-14	Reference Number	
16	Halt on Post Error	Set to 1 if On.
17	Initialize CMOS every boot	Set to 1 if On.
18	Block pins 22 & 23 of keyboard controller	Set to 1 if On.
19	Mouse support in BIOS/keyboard controller	Set to 1 if On.
20	Wait for if error found	Set to 1 if On.
21	Display Floppy error during POST	Set to 1 if On.
22	Display Video error during POST	Set to 1 if On.

3

23	Display Keyboard error during POST	Set to 1 if On.
25-26	BIOS Date	Month (1-12).
27-28	BIOS Date	Date (1-31).
29-30	BIOS Date	Year (0-99).
32-39	Chipset Identification	BIOS Name.
41	Keyboard controller version number	

ID String Line 2

123 5_7-10_12-13_15-16_18-21_23-24_26-27_29-31

Byte	Description	
1-2	Pin no for clock switching through keyboard controller	
3	High signal on pin switches clock to High(H) or Low (L)	
5	Clock switching through chipset registers	0=Off 1=On
7-10	Port address to switch clock high through special port	
12-13	Data value to switch clock high through special port	
15-16	Mask value to switch clock high through special port	
18-21	Port Address to switch clock low through special port	
23-24	Data value to switch clock low through special port	
26-27	Mask value to switch clock low through special port	
29-31	Turbo Sw Input Pin info (Pin no for Turbo Sw Input Pin)	

ID String Line 3

1-3 5 7-10 12-13 15-16 18-21 23-24 26-27 29-30 31 33

Byte	Description	
1y2	Keyboard Controller Pin number for cache control	Pin number for Cache Control
3	Keyboard Controller Pin number for cache control	Whether High signal on pin enables (H) or disables (L) cache.
5	High signal is used on the Keyboard Controller pin	
7-10	Cache Control through Chipset Registers	0=Cache control off 1=Cache Control on
12-13	Port Address to enable cache through special port	
15-16	Data value to enable cache through special port	
18-21	Mask value to enable cache through special port	
23-24	Port Address to disable cache through special port	
26-27	Data value to disable cache through special port	
29-30	Mask value to disable cache through special port	
31	Pin number for Resetting 82335 Memory controller.	
33	BIOS Modified Flag; Incremented each time the BIOS is modified from 1-9 then A-Z and reset to 1. If 0 the BIOS has not yet been modified.	

AMI WITH INTEL MOTHERBOARDS

The AMI version number looks like this when used on Intel motherboards:

1.00.XX.??Y

where :

1.00.07.DH0 would indicate a version 7 BIOS and a TC430HX (Tucson) motherboard.

XX	BIOS version number
??	Intel Motherboard model
Y	Usually 0 or 1

AWARD ID STRINGS

The date is at the front.:

05/31/94-OPTI-596/546/82-2A5UIM20-00

The next bit is the chipset and the next to last the BIOS Part Number, of which characters 6 and 7 identify the manufacturer (**M2** in the example – full decode overleaf). An *i* suffix after the part number means an Intel 12v Flash ROM, whereas *s* refers to an SST 5v (the difference lies in where ESCD data is stored in upper memory).

Code	Manufacturer	Code	Manufacturer
00	Unknown	J1	Jetway
A0	Asustek	J2	Jamicon
A1	Abit (Silicon Star)	J3	J-Bond
A2	A-Trend	J4	Jetta
A3	ASI	J6	Joss
A7	Arima Taiwan	K0	Kapok
AB	Aopen (Acer)	L1	Lucky Star
B0	Biostar	M0	Matra
B3	BCM	M2	Mycomp (TMC)
C1	Clevo	M3	Mitac
C2	Chicony	M4	Micro-Star (Achme)
C3	ChainTech	M8	Mustek
C5	Chaplet	M9	MLE
C9	Computrend	N5	NEC
D0	Dataexpert	O0	Ocean
D1	DTK	P1	PC-Chip
D2	Digital	PA	Pronix (Epox)
D3	Digicom	Q0	Quanta
D4	Diamond Flower	Q1	QDI
E1	ECS (Elite Group)	R0	Rise (Mtech)
E3	EFA	S2	Soyo
F0	FIC	S5	Shuttle (Holco)
F2	Freetech	S9	Spring Circle
F3	Full Yes	SN	Soltek
F5	Fugutech	T0	Twinhead

G3	Gemlight	T5	Tyan
G0	Gigabyte	T6	Trigem
H2	Holco (Shuttle)	U2	AIR (UHC)
H0	HsinTech	V3	Vtech (PC Partner)
H9	HsinTech	V5	Vision Top
I3	Iwill	V6	Vobis
I4	Inventa	W0	Wintec (Edom)
I5	Informtech	Z1	Zida

PHOENIX ID STRINGS

These start with a product family identifier (4A3NT0X in this example):

$$4A3NT0X0.86A.0047.P03.9704071222$$

It decodes to AN430TX (i.e. Anchorage). 4L3TT0X would be LT430TX (Lonetree). The number after the X is the revision. 86 is the BIOS OEM ID (Intel here), and the next letter indicates the type of motherboard:

A	Consumer Desktop
B	Corporate Desktop
C	Server Products

0047 is the BIOS build number. P is the BIOS release type:

P	Production (03 is the production release number)
D	Development
A	Alpha
B	Beta

9704071222 is the BIOS build date and time (here, 7 April 1997 at 12.22).

WHERE CAN I GET A NEW ONE?

In the early days, it was enough to be "IBM compatible" and you could literally swap BIOS ROMs between motherboards. It's not the case these days, as they are matched to a particular chipset *by the motherboard manufacturer* and are therefore specific to each other.

Before spending too much time on this, be aware that it's often easier (and cheaper) just to buy a new motherboard!

If you have a Flash BIOS, you may get one from:

MR BIOS	www.unicore.com
Award	www.unicore.com
AST	www.ast.com
AMI	www.megatrends.com

MR has many shareware versions, for as little as $15.

For Olivetti (and maybe others relatively less available): try *PC Care* in UK on 44 1992 462882. AMI BIOS and BIOS Plus series (with 16 character ID code) for cached motherboards are customised, and can only be obtained from the OEM, except:

> Those with E307 as the first 4 characters (**aaaa**), which can often be replaced with a standard type.

> Northgate or Motherboard Factory motherboards (except the Northgate slimline), which can take a standard type.

> Those with **aaaa** = DAMI, DAMX or EDAMI are usually for cached boards designed and/or built by AMI.

Gateway use Intel motherboards and modify the AMI BIOS, so don't expect an upgrade from Intel to work. A Gateway BIOS has a T suffix. Here are some others:

H	Vobis
K	NEC
L	Hewlett Packard
Q	AST
R	Packard Bell

Otherwise, call *Unicore* on (508) 686-6468 (for MR and Award Software). Phoenix resells through *Micro Firmware*, on (800) 767 5465. Try also *Silicon Pacific* in in UK on 44 1491 638275, who are AMI resellers. See "Useful Numbers" on page -405.

You need the proper information when you call; if you already have an AMI BIOS, for example, you will need the reference or part number in the ID string. If not, you must know what speed the board is and what chipset is on it (e.g. C&T, OPTi, etc).

FLASH BIOS UPGRADES

All the software you require will fit onto a boot floppy, which should naturally be checked for viruses. Aside from DOS, on the floppy you will need the upgrade utility and the data file for your particular motherboard. Both will be obtainable from the web site or BBS of either your motherboard or BIOS manufacturer (try the former first). It will usually be a self-extracting compressed file.

Take note of the *current* settings, so you can reinstall them after you have upgraded. In fact, it's a good idea to save your BIOS contents to a floppy as soon as you get your motherboard up and running. If updating a portable, run it from the mains, as a failure during the upgrade will cause severe problems. You may need to set a jumper or switch on the motherboard to allow the ROM to be written to, or to enable *Boot Block Programming*, if you want the official phrase.

Boot from the upgrade floppy, and run the utility. The command line will include the name of the utility and the file for the upgrade, typically:

> flash p5_aw.14g

In the above example, **flash** is the name of the utility (**flash.exe**) and **p5_aw.14g** is the file containing the code for the BIOS; in this case, it's for the P5 motherboard, which has an Award BIOS (aw), revision 14g.

DO NOT TURN THE MACHINE OFF DURING THE UPGRADE, even if there is a recovery procedure—just repeat the process. If the problem persists, reload the BIOS you saved earlier.

Once everything has finished, check for a successful upgrade with the BIOS identifier on the screen, turn the machine off, reset the jumper, reboot and enter all the previous settings (though you may have to accept the defaults). Reboot again.

NOTE: If you get problems after upgrading an AMI BIOS, press F5 in Setup to clear the CMOS.

Lots of good stuff about Flash BIOSes in **www.ping.be/bios**.

DMI

DMI (*Desktop Management Interface*) is a system which works with a Flash BIOS to keep a *Management Information Format* database up to date so you can find out what's inside a PC without opening it up, including device settings. Version 2.0 will allow remote network access, although this capability is unofficially available from some vendors with 1.1.

DMI can autodetect and record information concerning the computer, such as the CPU type and speed, and memory size—the BIOS stores the information in a 4K block in the Flash ROM, from where DMI can retrieve it. Plug and Play technology allows this to be updated by the operating system, which is better than having you update the whole BIOS every time. Indeed, NT occasionally flashes up a message that it's "updating DMI" as it boots.

Motherboards that can use DMI have a configuration utility that allows you to put other information in, like serial numbers, company addresses, etc.

FACILITIES PROVIDED

The BIOS ROM will include a bootstrap loader, Power On Self Test (POST), hardware initialisation, software interrupts and CMOS Setup routines, possibly with diagnostic or utility software and other facilities.

THE POWER ON SELF TEST

The POST verifies that:

The motherboard is working, and

The equipment in the machine is in the same condition (i.e. working) as when it was switched off. The testing is an exercising of the components; that is, it checks they are working, but not how well they are working.

THE BOOTSTRAP LOADER

Looks for an operating system, and hands over control to it, if found, on a floppy or a hard drive (Late Phoenix BIOSes will boot from a CD-ROM, and AMI from a Zip drive; Award BIOSes can boot from a CD-ROM, SCSI drive, Zip drive and LS-120 diskette). If an error is encountered before the display is initialized, a series of Nasty Noises will tell you what's wrong (see later). Otherwise, you will see an error message (again, later in the book).

A hard reset goes through the whole POST procedure. A soft reset (**ctrl-alt-del**) just runs a subset of POST and initialisation, after calling INT 19 from the BIOS.

CMOS SETTINGS

In AT-class computers, hardware setup information is kept in the CMOS RAM so the POST can refer to it. CMOS stands for *Complementary Metal Oxide Semiconductor*, which actually refers to a way of making chips with low power requirements, but has also come to mean the memory area which retains the information, because the clock chip that stored it was made that way. Back in the days of the 286, this may have been the only CMOS chip on a motherboard, so it became known as *the* CMOS chip. Anyway, the purpose of the CMOS is to remember what equipment the computer has, and the setup routine which initialises the CMOS must be run before you can use your computer for the first time. Some computers have this program separately on a disk, e.g. with early NEAT chipsets, Award v2.x or Samsungs, but now it's more commonly included as part of the System BIOS.

Every machine will have the Standard CMOS settings, but some will have *Advanced CMOS or Chipset Features* (the whole point of this), discussed later.

UTILITIES

Many helpful utilities come with the BIOS, particularly diagnostic and low-level format routines for the hard disk.

The main menu to the BIOS setup may contain the following heading:

> HARD DISK UTILITY

It allows you to low-level format the drive attached to your computer.

> DO NOT USE IT TO
>
> LOW LEVEL FORMAT
>
> AN IDE DISK!

Not that it will, anyway. Sorry for shouting, by the way, but that's quite important, because it will erase the head positioning tracks.

HARDWARE PERFORMANCE

A word about performance is necessary to understand the relevance of the settings discussed later. Although computers may have basic similarities, that is, they all look the same on the supermarket shelf, performance will differ markedly between them, just the same as it does with cars—it's all too easy to put a big engine in (or a fast processor) and forget to improve the brakes and suspension! Aside from that, you will never get a PC set up properly from the shop because there simply isn't enough incentive in terms of time or money for the builders to do so. They will just choose the safe settings to suit the widest variety of circumstances and leave you to it, which is where this book comes in. As an example, the default for some BIOSes is to have *both* internal and external CPU caches off, which is the slowest option! I suppose using "safe" settings at least reduces the number of tech support calls!

The PC contains several processes running at the same time, often at different speeds, so a fair amount of co-ordination is required to ensure that they don't work against each other.

9

Most performance problems arise from bottlenecks between components that are not necessarily the best for a job, but a result of compromise between price and performance. Usually, price wins out and you have to work around the problems this creates.

The trick to getting the most out of any machine is to make sure that each part is giving of its best, then eliminate potential bottlenecks between them. You can get a bottleneck simply by having an old piece of equipment that is not designed to work at modern high speeds (a computer is only as fast as its slowest component), but you might also have badly written software.

SYSTEM TIMING

The clock is responsible for the speed at which numbers are crunched and instructions executed. It results in an electrical signal that switches constantly between high and low voltage several million times a second.

The *System Clock*, or CLKIN, is the frequency used by the processor; on 286s and 386s, this will be half the speed of the main crystal on the motherboard (the CPU divides it by two), which is often called CLK2IN. 486 processors run at the same speed as the main crystal, because they use both edges of the timing signal, which is a square wave. A clock generator chip (82284 or similar) is used to synchronise timing signals around the computer, and the data bus would be run at a slower speed synchronously with the CPU, e.g. CLKIN/4 for an ISA bus with a 33 MHz CPU, resulting in the "standard" 8 MHz or so, although it was never properly established.

ATCLK is a separate clock for the bus, when it's run asynchronously, or not derived from CLK2IN. There is also a 14.138 MHz crystal which was used for all system timing on XTs. Now it's only used for the colour frequency of the video controller (6845). And talking of clocks....

THE YEAR 2000 (Y2K) PROBLEM

In a PC, the problem boils down to the date in the Real Time Clock not rolling over automatically, and not necessarily whether a date over 2000 can actually be coped with, because BIOS manufacturers appear to have solved that already and DOS has been able to cope with it for years (but see below about *Time Dilation*). If you set your system time and date to just before midnight 1999 and leave the machine running until the rollover happens, you will find that DOS (version 6.22, anyway) copes with the problem quite easily (boot the machine from a floppy, to make sure that date dependent software is not affected). Although it only shows two digits when you perform operations such as the **dir** command, four are used internally. As its official operating span is between 1980 and 2099, it can figure out that 00 equates to 2000, although it may cough and splutter a bit if the Real Time Clock specifically hands it a date of 1900, or any other date it can't cope with.

In practice, the BIOS converts it as well, so this shouldn't happen; some correct the time automatically at boot and others will supply DOS with 2000 instead of a hardware date of 1900, although many can't produce a date later than 1999 anyway—Award BIOS 4.5G prior to Nov 1995 can only accept dates between 1994-1999. Still others just add 20 years before passing the date to the operating system.

The official story from Microsoft about DOS (6.22) is that it will allow a date of up to 2099 to be input, but the operational range is actually up to 2035. 1980 is regarded as year 0. **msbackup** has other problems, but no-one uses that anyway. Windows 3.x depends on DOS, so it will react similarly, with the addition of setting the leap year from the keyboard.

The two main problems described here, such as the RTC not updating the century byte, and Time Dilation (see below) are both affected by the complex interaction between the POST and the hardware. For example, changing 99 to 00 takes the PC outside its operating envelope, so it returns a date of 01/04/1980, which is actually an error message indicating an out-of-range date, instead of the 01/01/1900 it gets from the Real Time Clock (RTC), which is inside its own specification. Also, changing the century byte from 19 to 20 causes the POST to use a different logic path and exceed the 244 microsecond grace period so that, occasionally, if the RTC is being read at just the wrong time (after Y2K), Time Dilation occurs. Incidentally, the date 01/01/1980 is set if your CMOS contents are lost, and 01/03/1980 means an invalid BCD, as mentioned below. And the 244 microsecond grace period?

Well, you can't read the RTC while it's updating, and the status is not checked after every read, so the designers set the status early and guaranteed the data for 244 microseconds, so it could be obtained even if it changed afterwards. Hence the problem if the POST takes a different logic path (which is because the RTC and PC keep the date in different formats and therefore need more conversion time if you now have to adjust for the new century and count the years since rollover on top of the normal calculations – more details below). Timing is important, too - if you read the RTC at the beginning of a second, you have almost the whole second minus about 600 microseconds (for updating) to do it in, but if you do it at the start of the grace period, you only have the 244 microseconds.

The Real Time Clock was introduced with the IBM AT, and it's ironic that anyone out there still using an XT-class machine (and there are many) won't have this problem, because it didn't have one. Instead, it used the DOS clock, which is set in motion every time the computer is switched on (it's actually a device driver called **clock$**, which is really a counter that increments at a known rate of about 18 times a second). It was never intended to be a precision time-keeping device, but for "operator convenience". There were certainly no specifications written down.

The DOS clock gets its starting information from the RTC, or from you typing it in, as was done with the XT. The RTC is then promptly ignored until the machine is switched on again. The date in the RTC is kept in second, minute, hour, day, month and year format, but is converted to the number of days since Jan 1 1980, plus the number of seconds since midnight on the current day. The latter is stored in the counter by the BIOS, and when DOS needs to read the clock, the BIOS is called to read the counter, and the number of ticks is converted back to seconds. This is to save going as far as the RTC for the time, which is a slower process, and explains why there is often a difference between your watch and your PC's clock at the end of the working day; the system clock has to compete for attention with other devices, and is often reprogrammed by games and other programs, that use it for their own timing purposes, mostly running the video faster. If they don't set it back, your DOS clock will be running very fast indeed! In short, being interrupt driven, the DOS clock's accuracy depends on system activity.

In all IBM PC/AT compatible systems, the current date and time are stored in internal CMOS memory in *Binary Coded Decimal* (BCD) format, with each component occupying one byte, such as second, minute, hour, day of week, month and year (the year uses up two bytes, one for the lower two digits, and one for the upper two). In case you were wondering what BCD means, I am indebted to Peter Farrow for the following…

> *In BCD each decimal digit is mapped to a 4-bit binary number. BCD is simply a binary sequence that terminates at the equivalent of decimal "9", so a sequence for 4 bits is:*

0000	0
0001	1
0010	2
0011	3
0100	4
0101	5
0110	6
0111	7
1000	8
1001	9

after which it returns to 0000, so any value above "9" is not valid. When the BIOS complains about an invalid BCD code, one of the 4-bit BCD numbers is carrying over to a value that would correspond to a decimal digit value of more than "9" (1001) which is, of course, invalid.

And to Mike Echlin for this:

> *It's just a decimal number stored in hex. i.e. BCD 12 is hex, but means decimal 12, and 0a in BCD is an error, but valid, that is, it's a valid hex number, but when converted to decimal is an error (Confused yet? ;-). In other words, a BCD number is just a hex number that when printed as hex, looks like decimal, and is read as if it was decimal. So it is stored as 0x12,printed in c as:*

x = 0x12;

printf("%x", x);

which looks like "12", and is interpreted as 12 decimal.

In summary, all BIOSes have the millenium bit problem, because it's a hangover from the IBM architecture, but Award Software, Phoenix and AMI seem to have sorted it out in all versions after 1994. However, whether the motherboard designer has sorted it out is another story! Here is the official chart of BIOS dates and the action you need to take, but after you've taken a quick look we will discuss what might happen in reality – we've already seen that some Award BIOSes after Nov 95, sorry, 1995, can only use a certain date range.

BIOS date	Action
Before 26 April 1994	Reset your system clock once, by turning the system off before midnight on 31 December 1999, and turning it on again after midnight (that is, on 1 Jan 2000), then reset the date manually in **setup**.
26 April 1994—31 May 1995	You either need an update or must be willing to reset the clock every day.
After 31 May 1995	Don't worry about it.

As of October 1997, all Compaqs are compatible—pre Y2K-compliant Presarios will read 1900 after the rollover. You can check out your machine and download a patch (if required) from their web site at **www.compaq.com**. For IBM products, you may just have to re-enter the date. Their web site is at **www.ibm.com/year2000**. All Toshiba computers manufactured after April 4, 1996 have Year 2000 compliance code written into the BIOS (version 5.0 or higher). All machines produced after 1992 will accept the date manually. Toshiba and its software partners have incorporated 4-digit dates into their products.

It may be of interest to note that the calendar for 2000 is the same as 1972, and from 2001-2027 the same as 1973-1999.

Time Dilation

Also known as the **Crouch-Echlin effect**, this refers to time and date instabilities that occur in and beyond 2000 on PCs and other embedded hardware. In other words, times and dates have been observed to intermittently and abruptly leap forward (or backward) when PCs are powered down and/or rebooted after 2000. In extreme cases, COM ports have ceased to work. For example, one produced a date in December after 2 weeks into 2000. See **www.intranet.ca/~mike.echlin/bestif/index.htm** (Mike Echlin's web page) or **www.nethawk.com/~jcrouch/dilation.htm** (Jace Crouch's) for more information.

TESTING THE HARDWARE

All this really takes is common sense. Although there is lots of test software out there, it all essentially uses the routine that follows. Again, making sure you boot the machine from a floppy, to protect any date dependent software you may have, set the time and date to a few minutes before midnight on 31 December 1999, and wait. As we have already seen, DOS will probably cope, but the acid test comes when you switch the machine off, then on again (if DOS can't handle it, change to a later version and try again to eliminate it from the equation). You might well see a system date starting at 01/01/1980, which is usually what you get if the machine has no other information, but if you see the correct figures, your hardware needs no further treatment, save to check for February 29th (2000 is a leap year), but some reports suggest that this is not a problem. You won't lose your hard drive details or other BIOS settings, which is what usually happens when you lose the CMOS. Repeat to make sure, but you might want to keep the machine running a little longer to check for Time Dilation (see above).

If your machine didn't pass the rollover test above, you might be able to reset it manually, in which case, set the time a few minutes *after* midnight, and switch off again (very important, that). If the date is still correct when you switch on, your hardware is useable. Otherwise, you will have to change the motherboard. You could try changing the BIOS, but that's often not cost-effective. If you feel the need to try, my web site (**www.electrocution.com**) has several links to BIOS and motherboard manufacturers who may have one you can use.

Replacement CMOS RAM/RTC chips can be obtained from Dallas Semiconductor for many machines; look at **www.resource800.com/dsfast.html**.

There appears to be some memory-resident software that takes up only 256K of memory. Presumably it traps any calls for the date and feeds back the correct one. However, once Windows '95 starts rearranging memory to its own liking, as it is wont to do, this might well become ineffective. A better solution is to use software that acts as a device driver, and which can therefore control interrupts.

Also, there are plug-in cards (e.g. from Unicore or Eurosoft – see *Useful Numbers*) that occupy an ISA slot.

For a list of Year 2000 web sites begin with Peter de Jager's *The Year 2000 Information Center* at **www.year2000.com**.

Try also:

> **www.rigel.co.nz**
> **www.everything2000.com**

The Motherboard

This is a large circuit board to which are fixed the Central Processor, the data bus, memory and various support chips, such as those that control speed and timing, the keyboard, etc. Below is a picture of a typical PC-compatible motherboard (although different computers may put the bits in different locations, the basic relationship between them is the same).

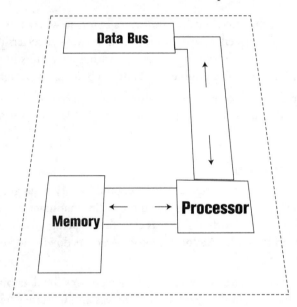

The Central Processor does all the thinking, and is told what to do by instructions contained in memory, so there will be a direct two-way bus connection between them. The bus width determines how much data can be read or written in a single operation.

Extra circuitry in the form of *expansion cards* is placed into *expansion slots* on the data bus, so the basic setup of the computer can be changed easily (for example, you can connect more disk drives or a screen here). To save you typing in the same old instructions every time, you buy software prepared earlier, copy it over the data bus into memory via the processor. There is a short cut, called DMA, which we will look at later.

Sometimes a math co-processor is fitted to work alongside the main processor, which is specially built to cope with floating point arithmetic (e.g. decimal points). Later CPUs have it integrated, so it's more correctly called a *floating point unit*, or FPU. The main processor has to convert decimals and fractions to whole numbers before calculating on them, and then convert them back again, and the size of the number it can cope with depends on the register width.

A maths coprocessor won't be used automatically—your software must be aware of how to use one, otherwise you won't get any benefit. Having said that, if you're only doing normal addition, multiplication, subtraction and division, you won't find much difference in performance.

BITS AND BYTES

Computers talk in *binary language*, which means that they count to a base of 2 (we use 10). When electrical signals are sent around the computer, they are either On or Off, which matches this perfectly. A state of On or Off is called a **B**inary Dig**it**, or **Bit** for short, and is represented on paper by a 1 for On or 0 for Off (the same as on power switches for electrical appliances).

To place one character on the screen takes eight bits (a byte), so when a machine is spoken of as being *eight-* or *sixteen-bit*, it's effectively dealing with one or two letters of the alphabet at the same time—a 32-bit computer can therefore cope with 4 characters in one go. 2 bytes are called a word, 4 bytes (32-bits) are a double word and 16 bytes are a paragraph.

Because it uses multiples of 8, a computer will also count to a base of 16, or *hexadecimal*, which uses letters as well as numbers, and the order is 0 1 2 3 4 5 6 7 8 9 A B C D E F (numbers run out after 9).

THE CENTRAL PROCESSOR

The chip that was the brains of the original IBM PC (and history has a great bearing on what we get up to today, as we will discover) was called the 8088, manufactured by Intel. No more need be said about it, except that although it was classified as being 16-bit, it spoke to the data bus and memory with 8 bits, which was both to keep the costs down and keep in line with the capabilities of the support chips.

Thus, when it wanted to send two characters to the screen over the data bus, they had to be sent one at a time, rather than both together, so there was an idle state where nothing was done every time data was sent (even at 4.77 MHz!).

In addition, it could only talk to 1 Mb of memory; the width of the address bus determines the amount of memory locations that can be addressed at any time (the *address range*) and there were 20 physical connections between memory and the Central Processor. Since computers work on the binary system, and therefore count with only two fingers, it's a simple calculation as to how much memory the CPU can talk to at once:

$$2^{20}=1048,576K$$

In fact, 8-bits, as supplied in the original PC can only represent 2^8, or 256 possible values, and the 16-bit word in the CPU could address 65,536 (or 64K), which still wasn't enough for serious work, so a **segment:offset** scheme of memory addressing was devised, where two numbers are used for an address to get a bigger total (see *Base Memory*, below, for more about this). The problem was to maintain compatibility with the 16-bit registers in the CPU while using 20 address lines. For the moment, just bear in mind that, although the CPU can see 1 Mb in total, it can only see it 64K at a time, because the offset is limited to 16 bits, and the largest number you can create with them is 65, 535.

THE 80286

The 80286 was introduced in response to those who were cloning the IBM PC. The connections between the various parts of the motherboard became 16-bit throughout, thus increasing efficiency—at the same clock speed, the throughput is 4 times more. It also had 24 memory address lines, so it could talk to 16 Mb of *physical* memory (1 Gb virtual). Having said that, DOS couldn't use it, since it had to be addressed in *protected mode*, using something like Xenix (or OS/2, which was created a little afterwards). DOS can only run in *real mode*, which is restricted to the 1 Mb that can be seen by the 8088.

Just to emphasise the point—when a 286 (or above) emulates an 8086 to run DOS, it is running in real mode—a Pentium running DOS is just a fast PC!

Protected mode is there to protect programs or running processes from each other, hence the name. The idea is that programs don't write to the wrong place in memory because a protected mode memory address is not the same as one used in real mode; that is, there is no guarantee to a program that an address used is the same as its equivalent in real mode.

A memory segment in real mode, or the first part of a segment:offset address becomes a *selector*, which refers to a *descriptor table*, which is the equivalent of a table of contents of what's in memory. The descriptor table's job is to relate sectors to real addresses in memory, so there is one more step to the process of memory addressing in protected mode as there is in real mode. A 286 descriptor can store addresses as large as 16,777,216 bytes (16 Mb).

As an aside, the first three bytes of a selector are used by Windows to check that the selector concerned relates to memory actually owned by the program you are using, and that memory can be written to, otherwise the program is shut down.

One problem was that the 286 went into protected mode easily, but found it difficult to get out again, and needed the chip level equivalent of **ctrl-alt-del** to do so. This used to be done with special codes that were interpreted by the keyboard controller (through an unused pin), but chips were later inserted to watch for these codes and reset the CPU immediately, rather than wait. This "fast decode" of the reset command allowed faster switching between real and protected mode (for 16-bit software), with resultant better performance, although the 286 is still ungainly at running Windows.

The 286 also began to be cloned, but legally, as Intel had to farm out manufacturing to keep up with the demand.

THE 80386

Compaq was the first company to use the 80386 (the DX version, as opposed to the SX—see below), which uses 32 bits between itself and memory, but 16 towards the data bus, which hasn't, until recently, been developed in tandem with the rest of the machine. This is partly to ensure backwards compatibility and partly due to the plumbing arrangements—because of its design (based on the technological knowledge of the time), if the data bus is run too fast, you get *electrical noise*, or extra voltages (extra 1s), which will look to the computer like extra data.

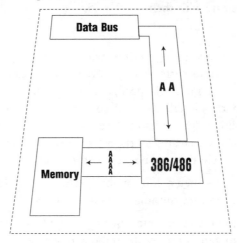

You also now have a speed problem..... The Central Processor may run at 33 Megahertz or so (think of it as miles per hour), but the data bus still runs at 8, because of the original design constraints. It is at once the busiest and slowest part of the computer, which is where your *Cache Scheme* helps.

Couple that with memory running at twice the speed of the CPU (so you can use cheap memory chips), not only do you have the equivalent of four-lane highways narrowing down to two-lane ones, you have to slow right down from anything up to 80 mph (or MHz) in the memory area, through 40 at the Central Processor, right down to 8 mph by the time you reach the data bus; more opportunities to waste processing cycles!

In view of the above, you can begin to see that processor speed alone is no guide to performance, and in some cases may even be irrelevant. A slow hard disk (on the data bus), for instance, will always make any processor wait for its data and waste cycles that could be used for serious work. In fact, as far as NetWare is concerned, a 486/33 is only noticeably better than a 386 when network loading is heavy.

The 386 can run multiple copies of real mode, that is, it can create several 8088s inside itself, called Virtual Machines, so that real mode programs, provided they are well behaved, can have some of the benefits of protected mode. It uses *paging* to remap memory so these machines are brought to the attention of the CPU when the programs in them need to be run; this is done on a *timeslice* basis, around 60 times a second, which is how we get multitasking in Windows, or Multiuser DOS (in '95, the slice is every 20 ns). It doesn't sound like much, but programmers tell me you can do a lot inside 60 ns.

Because of paging, these DOS sessions can be anywhere in memory, but, when used, they are made to look as if they are below 1 Mb, in real mode.

Virtual DOS machines can be created in extended memory because real mode programs under DOS (and/or Windows) don't write to real addresses, but selectors, and therefore have their calls redirected to the descriptor table. By changing the relationships in the descriptor table, programs can be moved around memory without them knowing anything about it; all a program needs to do is know how to work with selectors.

The 386 can also switch in and out of protected mode on the fly, or at least in a more elegant way than the 286; in order to get to the hard disk and other parts of the computer, protected-mode software, such as Windows, has to get DOS to perform *real mode services*, so the CPU has to switch in and out of protected mode continually (actually, on a 386 or above, the switching is to virtual 8086 mode rather than real mode). The goal is, therefore, to use real mode as little as possible and to run in protected mode. Windows does this by using *32-bit instructions.*

The 386 uses pipelining to help streamline memory accesses—they are done independently of each other (at the same time) while other units get on with their jobs, reducing intermediate steps and latency. Prefetching is where data is stored in CPU registers while spare cycles are used to fetch the next. The 386 has a *pre-fetch unit* for instructions, that tries to guess which ones you want next (a cache, sort of).

The 386 uses an externally generated clock frequency, and only the rising (positive) edge of it to calculate the output signal and the processor frequency, so the clock must run at twice the speed of the CPU. The bus interface operates with a two clock pulse cycle.

Although the 386 is 32-bit and has certain benefits, like the ability to manipulate memory and switch in and out of protected mode more readily, replacing a 286 with a 386 doesn't automatically give you performance benefits if you're running 16-bit 80286 code (i.e. most programs in DOS and sometimes Windows, which sits on top of it).

At the same clock speed, the 286 requires fewer clock cycles to execute many instructions, as well as executing some in the same number as the 386 (74 are faster, 66 the same speed, leaving 50 that actually run better in a 386). This is because the 386 has to emulate a 286 and needs more cycles to do it.

THE 80386SX

The 80386SX is a 32-bit chip internally, but 16-bit externally to both memory and the data bus, so you get bottlenecking, although it wasn't designed with that purpose in mind. It is a cut-down version of the 80386DX, created both to cut costs and give the impression that the 286 is out of date, because at the time other manufacturers could make the 286 under licence. Although it can run 386-specific software, it looks like a 286 to the machine it is in, so existing motherboards could be used, with a little redesigning, as the chips are not pin-compatible. At the same clock speed, a 386SX machine is around 25% slower than the 386DX.

THE 80486

To non-technical people, the 80486 is a fast 80386 (DX) with an on-board math co-processor and 8K of cache memory. It's not really newer technology as such (although it is second-generation), but better use is made of its facilities. For example, it takes fewer instruction cycles to do the same job, and is optimised to keep as many operations inside the chip as possible. The 386 prefetch unit was replaced by 8K of SRAM cache, and pipelining was replaced by *burst mode*, which works on the theory that most of the time spent getting data concerns getting its address; you don't need it again once you're there.

19

Burst allows a device to send large amounts of data in a short time without interruption. Pipelining on the 386 requires 2 clocks per transfer; only one is needed with 486 Burst Mode. Memory parity checks also take their own path at the same time as the data they relate to. The 486 has an on-board clock, and both edges of the square wave signal are used to calculate the clock signal, so the motherboard runs at the same speed as the CPU. In addition, the bus system uses a single pulse cycle.

The cache in the CPU (known as Level 1, or L1) is the fastest in the machine, as it runs at the same speed, and has no delays. It updates main memory only when the CPU hands over control to another device (e.g. a bus master), and so needs to know what changes have been made.

Generally speaking, at the same clock speed, a 486 will deliver between 2-3 times the performance of a 386.

THE 80486SX

The 486SX is as above, but with the maths co-processor facility disabled, therefore (generally speaking) you should find no significant difference between it and a 386; a 386/40 is broadly equivalent to a 486/25.

CLOCK DOUBLING

The DX/2 chip runs at double the speed of the original, but only inside itself; for example, the bus will still be running at "normal" speed. Unfortunately, high speed motherboards are more expensive for technical reasons.

Actual performance depends on how many accesses are satisfied from the chip's cache, which is how (in case you were wondering) the CPU is kept busy, rather than waiting for the rest of the machine. If the CPU has to go outside the cache, *effective speed* is the same as the motherboard or, more properly, the relevant bus (memory or data), so best performance is obtained when all the CPU's needs are satisfied from inside itself. The DX4 has a larger cache (16K) to cope with the higher speed.

Sadly, a cached DX2 system wastes exactly twice as many useable cycles as a normal one does! An Overdrive Chip and a DX2 are more or less the same thing, but the former can be fitted by the end-user (i.e. you), and the latter is intended for manufacturers.

The DX/4 is actually clock *tripled* (the 4 is to do with the 486 number; not the speed), but can be clock doubled with appropriate switching on the motherboard, so you could use a 50 MHz board and get better performance from the various buses.

THE PENTIUM

Essentially two 486s in parallel (or rather an SX and a DX), so more instructions are processed at the same time; typically two at once, assuming, of course, that software can take advantage of it, and get the timing of the binary code just right.

It has separate 8K caches, for instructions and data, split into banks which can be accessed alternately. It has a 64-bit external bus, but runs as 32-bit internally. Also, the data bus is not necessarily as large as the address bus. The core speed (inside the chip; not to be confused with *core voltage*, for MMX) will be more than the external, or memory bus, speed, so a 90 MHz one has the bus running at 60 MHz.

The multiplication is set by two external pins, BF0 and BF1, so you can run a 100 MHz Pentium at 1.5 rather than 2, and with a motherboard speed at 66 MHz, as opposed to 50. The PCI bus can be switched to match the rest of the machine (there's a chart in a couple of pages). *60 and 66 MHz versions are 5 volt—the remainder approx 3.3v.* 3.52 Volts is known as the VRE spec, also used by Cyrix.

On a newer Pentium, voltage information will be on the bottom, after the *s-spec* marking. The s-spec is a 3-digit number following SX, SK, SU, SY, or SZ, which includes such things as stepping, or version numbers, together with other characteristics. For voltages, there will be a slash mark followed by three letters, such as SK110 /ABC, for example:

> SX994/VMU
>
> iPP

It all decodes as follows (VMU=3.52v, Min valid timing and single processor only):

Pentium Markings

Spec	SX???, SY???
	SK???, Q0???
Vcc (A)	S=STD
	V=VRE (3.52, or 3.135-3.6v)
Timings(B)	S=STD
Timings(C)	S=STD
	M=Min valid MD timing
DP Support	S=STD
	U=Uniprocessor and multiprocessing; i.e. not for dual processing.
I75	For 75MHz
iPP	For 75/90/100/120/133MHz

There is more information available from **www.intel.com.**

PENTIUM PRO

This is a Socket 8 RISC chip with a 486 hardware emulator on it, running at 200 MHz or below (so far, but the technology for a 300 MHz version has been around for some time, if not the product itself). Several techniques are used by this chip to produce more performance than its predecessors; speed is achieved by dividing processing into more stages, and more work is done within each clock cycle; three instructions can be decoded in each one, as opposed to two for the Pentium. In addition, instruction decoding and execution are *decoupled*, which means that instructions can still be executed if one pipeline stops (such as when one is waiting for data from memory; the Pentium would stop all processing at this point). Instructions are sometimes therefore executed *out of order*, that is, not necessarily as written down in the program, but rather when information is available, although they won't be that much out of sequence; just enough to make things run smoother.

It has an 8K cache for programs and data, but has the processor and a 256K L2 cache in the same package, able to cache up to 64 Gb. The cache runs at full processor speed. The chip is optimised for 32-bit code, so will run 16-bit code no faster than a Pentium.

Pentium II

An MMX-enhanced Pentium Pro using Slot 1 technology with no L2 cache on board, but included on the daughtercard inside the Slot 1 cartridge, running at half the processor speed on its own bus. The II can be slower than the Pro for certain applications, as the Pro's FPU is better and the L2 cache is on board. It can also only cache up to 512 Mb of RAM, but it also has twice as much L1 and L2 cache. The Celeron, however, is a rehashed 266 MHz variant aimed at the lower end of the market with no L2 cache.

Up to 333 MHz, the P II only runs on a 66 MHz bus (even if you switch a BX chipset motherboard to 100 MHz, the chip can be autodetected and the bus speed reduced automatically. To get around this, see the instructions on Dr Thomas Pabst's Hardware Page at `www.sysdoc.pair.com`). Later versions, running above 350 MHz, can use a 100 MHz bus.

The L2 cache on the 333s and above only use 2 chips instead of 4, which your BIOS needs to be aware of to get the maximum benefit.

Cyrix Instead

The 6x86 is a Pentium-type chip with Pentium Pro characteristics, as it can execute faster instructions out of sequence, amongst other things. It is also made by IBM under licence. They use a *P-Rating* to determine performance relative to the Pentium, so a 6x86-166 is equivalent to a Pentium 166, even running at 133 MHz. The 233MHz version of the 6x86MX uses a 75 MHz bus, for which you should use a Cyrix-specific chipset, since no Intel chipset runs at that speed. Well, officially, anyway. These would include SiS, ALI and VIA, which all work with Intels, of course.

The MediaGX is based on the 5x86 and includes a graphics controller, DRAM controller and PCI bus interface.

AMD

For the K5, use the same settings as the equivalent Pentium. After the P-rating on the face of the chip are three letters. The first is the package type (A=SPGA 296 pins), the second refers to the voltage and the third to the case temperature. Voltages are listed in the first table and temperatures in degrees C in the second

K5 Letter	Voltage (Core/I/O)
B	3.45-3.6 (3.5)
C	3.3-3.465 (3.3)
F	3.135-3.465 (3.3)
G	x/y
H	2.86-3/3.3-3.465 (2.9/3.3)
J	2.57-2.84/3.3-3.465 (2.7/3.3)
K	2.38-2.63/3.3-3.465 (2.5/3.3)

Integrated Device Technology (IDT)

This company makes the *WinChip*, which was designed to run Windows business applications. The 200-speed version performs about 18% faster than the Intel 200 MMX and

Ltr	°C	Ltr	°C
Q	60	X	65
R	70	Y	75
W	55	Z	85

is approximately 25% cheaper. It is single-voltage, has a larger internal cache and disables the motherboard external cache when fitted, on the basis that a multitasking operating system tends not to benefit from it anyway.

MMX

This is an extension to x86 code to allow the better handling of the repetitive instructions typically found with multimedia applications, allowing parallel processing of many data items with only one instruction, or as many as will fit into a 64-bit register, so video, at least, will be smoother and faster. For example, normal Pentiums only process 1 pixel per clock cycle, where the 64-bit MMX registers will be able to handle 8, although a 32 K cache also has something to do with it. MMX also performs many of the functions of sound, video or modem cards. The MMX processor's core runs between 2.0-3.5 volts, but the output uses 3.1-3.6v (3.3), so motherboards need 2 voltage regulators. Talking of which, see the chart at the end of the chapter for chip voltages and other settings. MMX uses Socket 7 and above.

AGP

Standing for *Accelerated Graphics Port*, this is a system based on PCI, and used in Pentium II machines with the 440 LX chipset to allow graphic instructions to bypass the PCI bus, using the PCI 2.1 version (at 66 MHz) as a starting point; graphics processors will be able to directly access the chipset (and system memory) at the speed of the system bus (i.e. twice the PCI bus), which is where 3-D data will have been moved to, making room in the graphics controller memory for other functions. In effect, the graphics system acquires its own bus. Because it also uses both sides of the timing signal (that is, double-clocks, known as X2), you can move twice as much data and achieve an effective 133 MHz clock speed, allowing up to 533 Mb/sec, which is four times what PCI is allegedly capable of. There is also no arbitration to slow things down.

Aside from the 440 LX chipset, you also need DirectX 5.0, Windows '95 OSR 2.1 and **vgartd.vxd**, an Intel driver, not forgetting SDRAM for the bandwidth. Later VIA chipsets will support AGP on a Socket 7 motherboard.

SUMMING UP

In principle, the faster the CPU the better, but only if your applications do chip-centred work rather than writing to disk. For example, on a typical wordprocessing task, replacing a 16 MHz 386 with a 33 MHz one (that's double the speed) will only get you something like a 5-10% increase in practical performance, regardless of what the benchmarks might say. For a database, which accesses the hard disk a lot, spend the money on a faster hard disk.

Also, with only 8 Mb RAM, you won't see much performance increase from a DX2/66 until you get to a Pentium 90 (hardly any between a DX4/100 and a Pentium 75). With Windows, this is because the hard disk is used a lot for virtual memory (swap files), which means more activity over the data bus. Since the PCI bus runs at 33MHz (actually half the memory bus speed), the bottleneck is the disk I/O, running at much the same speed on them all. This is especially true if you use *Programmed I/O* (PIO), where the CPU must scrutinise every bit to and from the hard drive (although Multi-sector I/O or EIDE will improve things).

As the Pentium 90's motherboard runs faster (60 MHz), the I/O can proceed at a much faster pace (although a more sophisticated chipset helps). With 16 Mb of RAM, on the other hand, performance will be almost double anyway, because the need to go to the hard disk is so much reduced, and the processor can make a better contribution to performance. The biggest jump is from a DX2/66 to a DX/4, with the curve flattening out progressively up to the Pentium 90. There is also not a lot of difference between a 166-200 Mhz Pentium, the 200-233 MHz MMX and 266-300 MHz Pentium II, unless you speed up the I/O systems. Intel's competitors do relatively poorly with the MMX and FPU side of things, so maybe combine them with a good quality graphics accelerator to narrow the gap for 3D, though this won't help with image editing.

CHIP REFERENCE CHART

Overleaf are speeds of processors against the system clock. The PCI bus can run at *up to* 33MHz (officially), often switchable on the motherboard—the reason for the switch is to match the PCI bus to the CPU speed; for example, 33 MHz does not divide smoothly into the Pentium 120's memory bus speed of 60, so you're automatically introducing synchronization problems. Unofficially, the PCI bus can be run higher if the motherboard designer allows you to and your PCI cards can handle it. Although the PCI bus is not linked directly to the CPU, and can catch up here and there, switching properly does make a difference. Notice the motherboard speed of the P 150—slower than that of the 133!

Voltages are also included, but there might be slight differences from one motherboard manufacturer to another. For example, Asustek list the Cyrix/IBM 6x86MX as 2.9/3.3, where others might use 2.8/3.3. The difference will not do any harm other than a slight change in temperature or stability. Also, 3.3 or 3.5 volts for single plane processors refers to the STD or VRE settings, respectively. The higher voltage allows a cleaner detection between 0 and 1, hence more reliability at higher speeds, such as when overclocking.

Socket 7 is backwards compatible with Socket 5 processors, but doesn't have enough bandwidth for the high end of the market, hence Socket 8, for the Pentium Pro, with an extra (faster) 64-bit bus to talk directly to the L2 cache. Slot 1, for the Pentium II, is electrically identical to Socket 8, but an entirely different shape. It's actually a daughtercard inside a cartridge. Slot 2 is a larger version of Slot 1 that is meant for high-end machines.

Luckily, later chips, such as the Pentium Pro, support VID (Voltage ID) so voltage can be automatically regulated.

Maker	Designation	Socket	Voltage	Mem Bus	Clock X	PCI Bus
Intel	486DX (P24)		5	As CPU	1	As CPU
Intel	486DX2/50 (P24)		5	25	2	25
Intel	486DX2/66 (P24)		5	33	2	33
Intel	486SX (P23) (P24)		5	As CPU	1	As CPU
Intel	486 SL-Enhanced		5	As CPU	1	As CPU

Maker	Designation	Socket	Voltage	Mem Bus	Clock X	PCI Bus
Intel	486DX4/75		3.3	25	3	25
Intel	486DX4/100 (P24C)		3.45	33	3	33
Intel	P24D		5			
AMD	486DX2/80		3.45	40	2	
AMD	486DX4/120		3.45	40	3	
AMD	486DX4/133		3.45	33	4	33
AMD	486SX		5	As CPU	1	As CPU
AMD	486DX		5	As CPU	1	As CPU
Cyrix/IBM	486DX		5	As CPU	1	As CPU
Cyrix/IBM	486DX2-V50		3.3	25	2	
Cyrix/IBM	486DX2-V66		3.6	33	2	
Cyrix/IBM	486DX2-V80		4	40	2	
Cyrix/IBM	486DX4-100		3.45	33	3	33
Cyrix/IBM	5x86-100		3.45	33		
Cyrix/IBM	5x86-120		3.45	40		
Cyrix/IBM	5x86-133		3.45	33		
Intel	P 60		5	60	1	30
Intel	P 66		5	66	1	33
Intel	P 54C-75	5	3.52	50	1.5	25
Intel	P 54C-90	5	3.52	60	1.5	30
Intel	P 54C-100	5	3.52	66	1.5	33
Intel	P 54C-120	5	3.52	60	2	30
Intel	P 54C-133	5	3.52	66	2	33
Intel	P 54C-150	5	3.52	60	2.5	30
Intel	P 54C-166	5	3.52	66	2.5	33
Intel	P 54C-200	5	3.52	66	3	33
Intel	P54C-233	5	3.52	66	3.5	33
AMD	K5-PR75	5	3.52	50	1.5	25
AMD	K5-PR90	5	3.52	60	1.5	30
AMD	K5-PR100	5	3.52	66	1.5	33
AMD	K5-PR120	5	3.52	60	2	30
AMD	K5-PR133	5	3.52	66	2	33
AMD	K5-PR150	5	3.52	60	2.5	30
AMD	K5 PR166	5	3.52	66	2.5	33
Cyrix/IBM	6x86 P120+ (100)	5	3.52	50	2	25
Cyrix/IBM	6x86 P133+ (110)	5	3.52	55	2	
Cyrix/IBM	6x86 P150+ (120)	5	3.52	60	2	30
Cyrix/IBM	6x86 P166+ (133)	5	3.52	66	2	33
Cyrix/IBM	6x86 P200+ (150)	5	3.52	75	2	37.5
Intel	P55C-166 MMX	5	2.8/3.3	66	2.5	33
Intel	P55C-200 MMX	5	2.8/3.3	66	3	33
Intel	P55C-233 MMX	5	2.8/3.3	66	3.5	33
AMD	K6 166	7	2.9/3.3	66	2.5	33
AMD	K6 200	7	2.9/3.3	66	3	33
AMD	K6 233	7	2.1/3.3	66	3.5	33
AMD	K6 266	7	2.2/3.3	66	4	33
AMD	K6 300	7	2.1/3.3	66	4.5	33

The Motherboard

Maker	Designation	Socket	Voltage	Mem Bus	Clock X	PCI Bus
AMD	K6 PR233 (.35m)	7	3.2/3.3	66	3.5	33
AMD	K6 3D	7	2.2/3.3			
Cyrix/IBM	6x86MX PR150	7	2.9/3.3	60	2	30
Cyrix/IBM	6x86MX PR166	7	2.9/3.3	60	2.5	30
Cyrix/IBM	6x86MX PR200	7	2.9/3.3	66	2.5	33
Cyrix/IBM	6x86MX PR233	7	2.9/3.2	66	3	33
Cyrix/IBM	6x86MX PR266	7	2.9/3.2	66	3.5	37.5
IDT	C6	7	3.3			
Intel	Pro 150	8	3.1	60	2.5	30
Intel	Pro 180	8	3.3	60	3	30
Intel	Pro 200	8	3.3	66	3	33
Intel	Pentium II 233	Slot 1		66	3.5	33
Intel	Pentium II 266	Slot 1		66	4	33
Intel	Pentium II 300	Slot 1		66	4.5	33
Intel	Pentium II 333	Slot 1		66	5	33
Intel	Pentium II 350	Slot 1		100	3.5	33
Intel	Pentium II 400	Slot 1		100	4	33
Intel	Pentium II 450	Slot 1		100	4	33

NOTE: Because it controls I/O between all the major components on a motherboard, equally as important in your purchasing decisions must be the chipset. For example, VIA or SiS make Cyrix-specific chipsets that can run the bus at 75 MHz, while keeping the peripherals at 33 MHz, the PCI specification.

3   **Memory**

The memory contains the instructions that tell the Central Processor what to do, as well as the data created by its activities. Since the computer works with bits that are either on or off, memory chips work by keeping electronic switches in one state or the other for however long they are required. Where these states can be changed at will or, more properly, the operating system is able to reach every part of memory, it is called *Random Access Memory*, or RAM. The term comes from when magnetic tapes were used for data storage, and information could only be accessed sequentially; that is, not at random.

A ROM, on the other hand, has its electronic switches permanently on or off, so they can't be changed, hence *Read Only Memory.*

STATIC RAM

Static RAM (SRAM) is the fastest available, with a typical access time of 20 nanoseconds (the lower the number, the faster the chip can be accessed). It is expensive, however, and can only store a quarter of the data that Dynamic RAM (or DRAM) is able to, as it uses two transistors to store a bit against DRAM's one, although it does retain it for as long as the chip is powered (the transistors are connected so that only one is either in or out at any time; whichever one is in stands for a 1 bit). *Synchronous SRAM* allows a faster data stream to pass through it, which is needed for cacheing on fast Pentiums. Because of its expense, SRAM is used in caches in the CPU and between it and system memory, which is composed of *Dynamic RAM.*

DYNAMIC RAM

DRAM uses internal capacitors to store data (a single transistor turns one on or off) which lose their charge over time, so they need constant refreshing to retain information, otherwise 1s will turn into 0s. The result is that between every memory access is sent an electrical charge that refreshes the capacitors to keep data in a fit state, which cannot be reached whilst recharging is going on (like changing the batteries several million times a second). Normal bus operation is a 2-clock cycle external bus access; the first is called T1, and the second T2. Address and control signals are set up in the former, and the operation completed at the end of the latter.

Burst bus operation executes 4 consecutive external bus cycles. The first is the same setup and completion done in T1 and T2, and the next three operate without the setup cycle, by defining the sequence of addresses that follow the first. As the first takes the longest, burst timings look like 2-1-1-1 or similar. Memory addresses are found by a combination of row and column inside memory chips, with two strobe signals, *Row Address Strobe* (RAS) and *Column Address Strobe* (CAS), normally in that order. *Fast Page Mode* memory, for example, toggles CAS on and off as addresses change, that is, as columns are accessed within the row (further described under *Wait States*). FPM makes 60 ns RAM look like 40 ns, allowing you a 25 MHz CPU. Quick explanation:

Under normal circumstances, a 33MHz CPU takes about 30 ns per cycle:

Clock Speed (MHz)	Cycle Time (ns)
1	1000
5	200
8	125
12	83
16	63
20	50
25	40
33	30
40	25

At that speed, memory chips need to operate at something like 20 nanoseconds to keep up, assuming the CPU needs only 1 clock cycle per 1 from the memory bus; 1 internal cycle for each external one, in other words. Intel processors mostly use 2 for 1, so the 33 MHz CPU is actually ready to use memory every 60 ns, but you need a little more for overheads, such as data assembly and the like, so there's no point in using anything faster anyway.

With *Static Column* memory, CAS may be left low (or active) with only the addresses changing, assuming the addresses are valid throughout the cycle, so cycle time is shorter.

EDO (*Extended Data Output*) is an advanced version of fast page mode (often called *Hyper Page Mode*, but see below), which can be up to 30% better and only cost 5% more. *Single-cycle EDO* will carry out a complete memory transaction in 1 clock cycle by overlapping stages that otherwise would take place separately; for example, precharging can start while a word is still being read, and sequential RAM accesses inside the same page take 2 clock cycles instead of 3, once the page has been selected, because the data output buffer is kept open rather than being turned off, as it would be with Fast Page Mode Memory (see *Wait States*, below). It is assumed that if one address is needed, others nearby will be, too, so the location of the previous one is held open for a short while.

In other words, output is not turned off when CAS goes high (i.e. turned off, or has stopped allowing addresses to be moved to the device). In fact, data can still be output after CAS has gone high, then low again (and another cycle has therefore started), hence the name, *Extended Data Out*; data remains available until that from the next access begins to appear.

This means you can begin precharging CAS whilst waiting for data. The end result is that cycle time is cut by around 20% and data is available longer. The really neat thing is that CAS can go high before data appears (well, maybe not to you and me, but it is to a motherboard designer). Note that EDO is only faster with memory reads; writes take place at the same speed as Fast Page Mode. In any case, it effectively reduces 60 ns RAM to 25 ns, giving you a 40 MHz CPU, without wait states.

The combination of DRAM plus an external latch between it and the CPU (or other bus mastering device), would look like EDO DRAM because the external latch can hold the data valid while the DRAM CAS goes high and the address is changed. It is simpler and more convenient to have the latch inside the DRAM, hence EDO. As it replaces a level 2 cache and doesn't need a separate controller, space on the motherboard is saved, which is good for notebooks. It also saves on battery power. In short, EDO gives increased bandwidth due to shortening of the page mode cycle (and 3-2-2-2 bursts rather than 7-4-4-4). It appears to be able to run (unofficially) above 66 MHz. Don't get 70 ns EDO, as it will be difficult to upgrade the CPU.

BEDO, or *Burst Extended Data Out*, is as above, but has a pipeline stage and a 2-bit burst counter that can read and write large streams of data in 4-cycle bursts for increased performance, based on the addresses being dealt with in the first cycle. The pipelining system can save 3 cycles over EDO. It is designed to achieve 0 wait state performance at 66 MHz and upwards, as it brings your 60 ns RAM down to 15 ns (again, see chart above). The relevant speeds for Fast Page Mode and EDO are 25 and 40, respectively, and the increase in performance 100% and 40%.

Enhanced DRAM (**EDRAM**) replaces standard DRAM and the L2 cache on the motherboard, typically combining 15ns SRAM inside 35ns DRAM. Since the SRAM can take a whole 256 byte page of memory at once, it gives an effective 15ns access speed when you get a hit (35ns otherwise), so system performance is increased by around 40%. The L2 cache is replaced with an ASIC chip to sort out chipset/memory requirements (an ASIC chip is one specially made for the purpose). EDRAM has a separate write path that accepts and completes requests without affecting the rest of the chip. NEC is producing *RDRAM* which, they say, gives 2ns access speed. It interconnects with a system called RAMBUS, which is a narrow, but ultra high speed, local memory bus, made with CMOS technology. It also uses a packet technique for data transfer, rather than coping with individual bytes. BIOS support is needed in the chipset for this to work as system memory. Intel have licensed the design, so it looks as if it will be severely relevant in the future; with RAMBUS, they intend to bring out something called nDRAM.

WRAM (*Windows RAM*), created by Samsung, is dual ported, like VRAM, but costs about 20% less and is 50% faster with around 25% more bandwidth (dual porting means reading and writing takes place at the same time). It runs at 50 MHz and can transfer blocks and support text and pattern fills. In other words, some graphics functions are built in, so look for these on graphics cards. **VRAM**, by the way, is used on graphics cards that need to achieve high refresh rates; DRAM must use the same port as it does for data to do this, where VRAM uses one port to refresh the display and the other to change the data. Otherwise, it is generally the same speed as DRAM. **SGRAM**, or *Synchronised Graphics RAM*, is single ported, using dual banks where 2 pages can be opened at once. It has a block write system that is useful for 3D as it allows fast memory clearing.

Synchronous DRAM (**SDRAM**) is synchronised to the system clock, taking memory access away from the CPU's control; internal registers in the chips accept a request, and let the CPU do something else while the data requested is assembled for the next time it talks to the memory. As they work on their own clock (that is, special strobes such as CAS, RAS, etc are not required), the rest of the system can run faster (bus speeds up to 100). Data bursts are twice as fast as with EDO (above), but this is slightly offset by the organisation required. **SLDRAM** uses an even higher bus speed and a packet system. However, with a CPU running at 4 or 5 times the memory speed, even SDRAM is finding it hard to keep up.

The *cycle time* is the time it takes to read from and write to a memory cell, and it consists of two stages; precharge and access. *Precharge* is where the capacitor in the memory cell is able to recover from a previous access and stabilise. *Access* is where a data bit is actually moved between memory and the bus or the CPU. Total *access time* therefore includes the finding of data, data flow and recharge, and parts of it can be eliminated or overlapped to improve performance. The combination of Precharge and Access=Cycle Time, which is what you should use to calculate wait states from. Refresh is performed with the 8253/8254 timer and DMA controller circuit (Ch 0).

There are ways of making refreshes happen so that the CPU doesn't notice (i.e. *Concurrent* or *Hidden*), which is helped by the 486 being able to use its on-board cache and not needing to use memory so often anyway. Turn this off first if you get problems. In addition, you can tinker with the *Row Access Strobe*, or have *Column Access Strobe* before RAS, as described in *Advanced Chipset Setup*. The fastest DRAM commonly available is rated at 60 nanoseconds (a nanosecond is a billionth of a second). As these chips need alternate refresh cycles, under normal circumstances data will actually be obtained every 120 ns, giving you an *effective speed* of around 8 MHz for the *whole computer*, regardless of CPU speed, assuming no action is taken to compensate, which is a sobering thought when you're streaming audio through an ISA sound card.

One way of matching components with different speeds is to use wait states.

WAIT STATES

These indicate how many ticks of the system clock the CPU has to wait for other parts of the computer, typically for memory—it will generally be 0 or 1, but can be up to 3 if you're using slower memory chips. They are needed because there is no "data valid" signal from memory, so the system waits a bit to ensure it's OK. Ways of avoiding wait states include:

Page-mode memory. This uses cut-down address cycles to retrieve information from one general area, based on the fact that the second access to a memory location on the same page takes around half the time as the first; addresses are normally in two halves, with high bits (for row) and low bits (for column) being multiplexed onto one set of address pins. The page address of data is noted, and if the next data is in the same area, a second address cycle is eliminated as a whole row of memory cells can be read in one go; that is, once a row access has been made, you can get to subsequent column addresses in that row in the time available (you should therefore increase row access time for best performance). Otherwise, data is retrieved normally, taking twice as long.

Fast Page Mode is a quicker version of the above; the DRAMs concerned have a faster CAS (Column Access Strobe) access speed, and can anticipate access to the next column while the previous column is deactivating, and the data output buffer is turned off, assuming the data you need is in that location. Memory capable of running in page mode is different from the normal bit-by-bit type, and the two don't mix. It's unlikely that low capacity SIMMs are so capable. With banks of page mode DRAM in multiples of 2, you can combine it with ...

Interleaved memory, which divides memory into two or four portions that process data alternately; that is, the CPU sends information to one section while another goes through a refresh cycle; a typical installation will have odd addresses on one side and even on the other (you can have word or block interleave). If memory accesses are sequential, the precharge of one will overlap the access time of the other. To put interleaved memory to best use, fill every socket you've got (that is, eight 1 Mb SIMMs are better than two 4 Mb ones). The SIMM types must be the same. As an example, a machine in non-interleaved mode (say a 386SX/20) may need 60ns or faster DRAM for 0ws access, where 80ns chips could do if interleaving were enabled.

A **processor RAM cache**, which is a (level 2) bridge between the CPU and slower main memory; it consists of anywhere between 32-512K of (fast) Static RAM chips and is designed to retain the most frequently accessed code and data from main memory. It can make 1 wait state RAM look like that with 0 wait states, without physical adjustments, assuming that the data the CPU wants is in the cache when required (known as a *cache hit*). To minimise the penalty of a cache miss, cache and memory accesses are often made in parallel, with one being terminated when not required.

How much L2 cache you need really depends on the amount of system memory; according to Dell, jumping from 128K to 256K only increases the hit rate by around 5%, and Viglen think you only need more than 256K with more than 32 Mb RAM. L2 cache is not as important if you use Fast Page Mode DRAM, but once you start clock doubling, and increasing memory writes, the need for a writeback cache becomes more apparent. Several Intel chipset designs, such as the HX (for Socket 7) may need additional TAG RAM to cache more than 64 Mb (i.e. more than 8-bit). Pentium Pro/II boards aren't restricted this way.

A cache should be fast and capable of holding the contents of several different parts of main memory. Software plays a part as well, since cache operation is based on the assumption that programs access memory where they have done so already, or are likely to next, maybe through looping (where code is reused) or organising what's wanted to be next to other relevant parts. In other words, it works on the principle that code is sequential, and only a small proportion of it is used anyway. In fact, as cache is used for 80-90% of CPU memory accesses, and DRAM only 1-4% of the time, less errors result (actually a lower *Soft Error Rate*), hence the reduced need for parity; a side effect of a cache is that DRAM speed is not so critical.

Asynchronous SRAM is the cheapest solution, which needs wait states. A basic design will look up an address for the CPU and return the data inside one clock cycle, or 20 ns at 50 MHz, with an extra cycle at the start for the tag lookup. As the round trip from the CPU to cache and back again takes up a certain amount of time, there's less available to retrieve data, which total gets smaller as the motherboard speed is increased.

Memory

Synchronous SRAM is synchronised with the system clock, up to 66 MHz, using a buffer to keep the whole 2 or 3 cycle routine inside one. The address for data required by the CPU is stored, and while that for the next is coming in to the buffer, the *data* for the previous set is read by the CPU. It can also use burst timing to send data without decoding addresses.

Pipeline SRAM also uses buffers, but for data reads from memory locations, so the complete distance doesn't have to be travelled. *Pipeline Burst* SRAM will deliver 4 words (blocks of data) over four consecutive cycles, at bus speeds over 75 MHz.

In practice, it would appear that performance between synchronous and pipeline cache is similar. Asynchronous is not often found on fast motherboards, anyway, but should be about the same at or below 50 MHz. Note that level 2 cache can be unreliable, so be prepared to disable it in the interests of reliability, particularly with NT, but that defeats the object somewhat.

For maximum efficiency, or minimum access time, a cache may be subdivided into smaller blocks that can be separately loaded, so the chances of a different part of memory being requested and the time needed to replace a wrong section are minimised.

There are three mapping schemes that assist with this:

o **Fully Associative**, where the whole address is kept with each block of data in the cache (in tag RAM), needed because it is assumed there is no relationship between the blocks. This can be inefficient, as an address comparison needs to be made with every entry each time the CPU presents the address for its next instruction.

o **Direct Mapped**, also known as *1-way associative*, where a block can only be in one place in the cache, so only one address comparison is needed to see if the data required is there. Although simple, the cache controller must go to main memory more frequently if program code needs to jump between locations with the same index, which seems pointless, as alternate references to the same cache cell mean cache misses for other processes. The "index" comes from the lower order addresses presented by the CPU.

o **Set Associative**, a compromise between the above two. Here, an index can select several entries, so in a *2 Way Set Associative* cache, 2 entries can have the same index, so two comparisons are needed to see if the data required is in the cache. Also, the tag field is correspondingly wider and needs larger SRAMs to store address information.

As there are two locations for each index, the cache controller has to decide which one to update or overwrite, as the case may be. The most common methods used to make these decisions are *Random Replacement*, *First In First Out* (FIFO) and *Least Recently Used* (LRU). The latter is the most efficient. If the cache size is large enough (say, 64K), performance improvements from this over direct-mapping may not be much. Having said that, 2-way set can be better than doubling the size of a direct-mapped cache, even though it is more complex.

A Write *Thru Cache* means that every write access is saved to the cache and passed on to memory, so although cache and memory contents are identical, it is slow, as the CPU has to wait for DRAMs. Buffers can be used to provide a variation on this, where data is written into a temporary buffer to release the CPU quickly before main memory is updated (see *Posted Write Enable*).

A *Write Back Cache*, on the other hand, exists where changed data is temporarily stored in the cache and written to memory when the system is quiet, or when absolutely necessary. This will give better performance when main memory is slower than the cache, or when several writes are made in a very short space of time, but is more expensive. "Dirty words" are the differences between cache and main memory contents, and are kept track of with dirty bits. Some motherboards don't have the required SRAM for the dirty bit, but it's still faster than Write Thru.

Write Back becomes more important with clock doubling, where more memory writes are created in the course of a CPU's work, but not all motherboards, especially 486 ones, support it. *Early* Write cache exists where the address and data are both known and sent simultaneously to SRAM. A new address can be used once every clock. *Late Write* is where data follows the address by 1 clock cycle, so a new address can be written to every 2nd clock.

DOS-based software is happy with a 64K external cache because 64K is the largest chunk of memory that can be addressed, which is also true for Windows because it runs on top of DOS. You may need something like Windows '95, OS/2, Windows NT, Multiuser DOS 7, REAL/32 or NetWare 3/4 to get much out of a larger L2 cache. DOS has hit-rates of around 96% while multi-tasking operating systems tend to achieve 70% or so, because of the way that they jump around memory, so a cache can slow things down against a cache-less motherboard with efficient memory management. With multi-tasking, interleaving can often get more performance than a cache (check out Headland/ICL and OPTi chipsets, for example). Not only that, cache management often delays memory access by 1 to 2 clock cycles.

o **Refresh Bypass**, used by AMI on their 486-based motherboards.

o **Synchronous DRAM**, whose timing is linked directly to the PC's system clock, so you don't need wait states.

SHADOW RAM

ROMs are used by components that need their own instructions to work properly, such as a video card or cacheing disk controller; the alternative is loading the instructions from disk every time they are needed. ROMs are 8-bit devices, so only one byte is accessed at a time; also, they typically run between 150-400 ns, so using them will be slow relative to 32-bit memory at 60-80 ns, which is also capable of making four accesses at once (your effective hard disk interleave will drop if data is not picked up in time).

Shadow RAM is the process of copying the contents of a ROM directly into extended memory which is given the same address as the ROM, from where it will run much faster. The original ROM is then disabled, and the new location write protected. You may need to disable shadow RAM whilst installing Multiuser DOS.

If your applications execute ROM routines often enough, enabling Shadow RAM will increase performance by around 8 or 9%, assuming a program spends about 10% of its time using ROM instructions, but theoretically as high as 300%. The drawback is that the RAM set aside for shadowing cannot be used for anything else, and you will lose a corresponding amount of extended memory; this is why there is a shortfall in the memory count when you start your machine if shadowing is enabled. The remainder of Upper Memory, however, can usually be remapped to the end of extended memory and used there.

With some VGA cards, if video shadow is disabled, you might get DMA errors, because of timing when code is fetched from the VGA BIOS, when the CPU cannot accept DMA requests. Some programs don't make use of the video ROM, preferring to directly address the card's registers, so you may want to use the extended memory for something else.

If your machine hangs during the startup sequence for no apparent reason, check that you haven't shadowed an area of upper memory containing a ROM that doesn't like it—particularly one on a hard disk controller, or that you haven't got two in the same 128K segment. NetWare doesn't really benefit from Shadow RAM, and can make better use of the memory.

Flash ROM is now quicker than DRAM, so if you have a Flash BIOS you may find Shadow RAM is not required.

RANDOM ACCESS MEMORY

There are 6 types of Random Access Memory a program can use.

BASE (OR CONVENTIONAL) MEMORY

The first 640K available, which traditionally contains DOS, device drivers, TSRs and any programs to be run, plus their data, so the less room DOS takes up, the more there is for the rest. Different versions of DOS are better or worse in this respect. In fact, under normal circumstances, you can expect the first 90K or so to consist of:

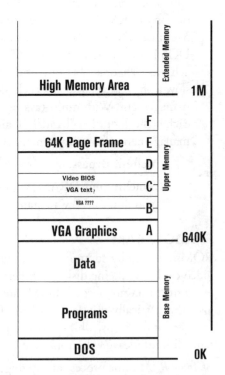

An **Interrupt Vector Table**, which is 1K in size, including the name and address of the program providing the interrupt service. Interrupt vectors point to routines in the BIOS or DOS that programs can use to perform low level hardware access. DOS uses **io.sys** and **msdos.sys** for the BIOS and DOS, respectively. This also include user-defined hard disk data (Type 47).

ROM BIOS tables, which are used by system ROMs to keep track of what's going on. This will include I/O addresses.

DOS itself, plus any associated data files it needs (e.g. buffers, etc).

DOS was written to run applications inside the bottom 640K block simply because the designers of the original IBM PC decided to—memory at the time was expensive, and most CP/M machines only used 64K anyway (the PC with 128K was $10,000!). Other machines of the same era used more; the Sirius allowed 896K for programs.

Contrary to popular belief, Windows uses memory below 1Mb, for administration purposes; although it pools all memory above and below 1 Mb (and calls it the *Global Heap*), certain essential Windows structures must live below 1 Mb, such as the *Task DataBase* (TDB) which is necessary for starting new tasks.

Every Windows application needs 512 bytes of memory below 1Mb to load, but some will take much more if they can, even all that's available, thus preventing others from loading, which is one source of "Out Of Memory" messages. There are programs that will purposely fragment base memory so it can't be hogged by any one program.

Rather than starting at 0 and counting upwards, memory addressing on the PC uses a two-step **segment:offset** addressing scheme. The *segment* specifies a 16-byte paragraph, or segment, of RAM; the *offset* identifies a specific byte within it.

The reason for using two numbers for an address is that using 16 bits by themselves will only give you 65536 bytes as the longest number you can write.

The CPU finds a particular byte in memory by using two registers. One contains the starting segment value and the other the offset, the maximum that can be stored in each one being 65,536 (FFFF in hex), as we said. The CPU calculates a physical address by taking the contents of the segment register, shifting it one character to the left, and adding the two together (see *High Memory*, below). To get a decimal number, multiply the segment by 16 and add the offset to the total.

Sometimes you'll see both values separated by a colon, as with FFFF:000F, meaning the sixteenth byte in memory segment FFFF; this can also be represented as the effective address 0FFFFFh. When referring only to 16-byte paragraph ranges, the offset value is often left out.

The 1024K of DOS memory is divided into 16 parts of 64K each. Conventional memory contains the ten from 0000h to 9FFFh (bytes 0 to 655,167), and Upper memory (below) contains the six ranging from A000h to FFFFh.

UPPER MEMORY

The next 384K is reserved for private use by the computer, so that any expansion cards with their own memory or ROMs can operate safely there without interfering with programs in base memory, and *vice versa*. Typical examples include Network Interface Cards or graphics adapters.

There is no memory in it; the space is simply reserved. This is why the memory count on older machines with only 1 Mb was 640 + 384K of *extended memory* (see below); the 384K was *remapped* above 1 Mb so it could be used. When upper memory blocks are needed, as when using **emm386.exe**, that memory is remapped back again, so you lose a bit of extended memory.

This area is split into regions, A-F, which in turn are split into areas numbered from 0000 to FFFF hexadecimally (64K each). With the right software, this area can be converted into

35

Upper Memory Blocks for use by TSRs (memory-resident programs) to make more room downstairs. The amount of upper memory available varies between computers, and depends on the amount of space taken up by the System BIOS and whether you have a separate VGA BIOS (on board video sometimes has its BIOS integrated in the system BIOS). It also depends on the number of add-in cards you have, e.g. disk controllers, that normally take up around 16K.

Some chipsets (such as Chips & Technologies) will always reserve this 384K area for shadowing, so it will not appear in the initial memory count on power-up, the system configuration screen, or when using **mem** (if you've ever wondered why you're missing 384K, this is the reason). Other chipsets have a *Memory Relocation* option which will re-address it above 1 Mb as extended memory.

Occasionally, some ROM space is not needed once the machine has booted, and you might be able to use it. A good example is the first 32K of the System BIOS, at F000 in ISA machines. It's only used in the initial stages of booting up, that is, before DOS gets to set up device drivers, so this area is often useable (the Stealth feature supplied with **qemm** takes advantage of this).

Note that many proprietary machines, such as Compaq or NEC, and particularly portables, have different arrangements; VGA ROMs sometimes turn up at E000!

If you have Plug and Play, you will lose another 4K for ESCD (*Extended System Configuration Data*), which is part of the specification and largely a superset of Extended ISA (EISA) that stores information on PnP or non-PnP EISA, ISA or PCI cards, so the operating system can reserve specific configurations. It occupies part of Upper Memory (from E000-EDFF), which is not available to memory managers. PC Cards, incidentally, like to use 4K at D000.

EXTENDED MEMORY

Memory above 1 Mb is known as *extended memory*, and is not normally useable under DOS, except to provide RAM disks or caches, because DOS runs in *real mode*, and it can't access extended memory in protected mode; you need something like OS/2 for that.

However, some programs, such as AutoCAD (and Windows!), are able to switch the CPU from one to the other by themselves, and some can use DPMI, the *DOS Protected Mode Interface*. DPMI is a method of allowing programs to run in protected mode, as is VCPI, another system promoted by Phar Lap Software (**win.com** starts a DPMI host, used to run the rest of Windows).

The difference between the two:

VCPI provides an interface between DOS Extenders and Expanded Memory Managers so they can run smoothly together by allowing them both access to extended memory with the same interrupt as that used for expanded memory (see below). It was originally designed for 386 systems and above, and doesn't support multitasking (or windowed DOS displays in Windows), hence.....

DPMI allows multitasking under similar circumstances as VCPI, but also works on a 286. It was designed by Microsoft, with the object of supporting Windows and controlling DOS software using 32-bit addressing in protected mode on any CPU.

Although extended memory first appeared on the 286, and some software was written to take advantage of it, the 286 was used mostly as a fast XT, because DOS wasn't rewritten (history again). It wasn't until the 386, with its memory paging capability, that extended memory came to be used properly.

HIGH MEMORY

The first 64K (less 16 bytes) of extended memory, which is useable only by 286, 386 or 486 based computers that have more than 1Mb of memory. It's a quirk in the chip design (or a bug!) that can be exploited by playing with certain I/O addresses to use that portion of extended memory as if it were below 1 Mb, leaving yet more available for programs in base memory. In other words, it is extended memory that can be accessed in real mode. It is activated with **himem.sys** (MS-DOS/ Novell DOS) or **hidos.sys** (DR DOS).

HMA access is possible because of the **segment:offset** addressing scheme of the PC, which can actually count to just under 64K more than 1 Mb, but the 20 address lines still restrict you. If you remember, memory addresses on a PC are 20 bits long, and are calculated by shifting the contents of a 16-bit register (a paragraph) one character to the left, and adding it to a 16-bit offset. For example, address 1234:5678 is interpreted like this:

1234	Segment Register
5678	Address Register
179B8	20-bit address

Shifting 1 to the left is the same as adding a zero to the right, thus multiplying by 16 to get the total byte count (like you do with decimals).

Address references near the last memory address in Upper Memory (FFFF:000F, or the sixteenth byte in segment FFFF) generate a "carry bit" when the 16-bit offset value (0FFFFh) is added to the 20-bit shifted segment value (FFFF0h):

FFFF	segment (FFFF0, or 1Mb-16bytes)
FFFF	offset (64K)
10FFEF	

The 8088, with only 20 address lines, cannot handle the address carry bit (1), so the processor simply wraps around to address 0000:0000 after FFFF:000F; in other words, the upper 4 bits are discarded (the number 1 above).

On a 286 or later, there is a 21st memory address which can be operated by software (see below), which gives you a carry bit. If the system activates this bit while in 8088 (real) mode, the wraparound doesn't happen, and the high memory area becomes available, as the 1 isn't discarded.

The reason for the HMA's size restriction is simply that it's impossible to create an address more than 64K above 1 Mb using standard real mode segments and offsets. Remember that segments in real mode become selectors in protected mode and don't have to follow the same rules; they can address more than 1 Mb.

Gate A20

So, the 8088 in the original PC would wrap around to lowest memory when it got to 1 Mb; the 286 would wrap around at 16 Mb. On some machines, an AND Gate was installed on

CPU address line 20 (the 21st address line) that could switch to allow either wraparound, or access to the 16 Mb address space, so the 286 could properly emulate the 8088 in real mode. A spare pin on the keyboard controller was used to control the gate, either through the BIOS or with software that knew about it.

Windows enters and leaves protected mode through the BIOS, so Gate A20 needs to be continually enabled and disabled, at the same time as the command to reset the CPU into the required mode is sent.

Programs in the HMA must be well behaved enough to disable the A20 line when they are not in use and enable it when they are. Only one program at a time can control A20, so only one can run in the HMA, which should do so as efficiently as possible.

DOS Extenders were one way of using this under DOS until something like OS/2 came along. Many were incorporated into applications, such as Lotus 123, v3 or AutoCAD. They typically intercept interrupts, save the processor state, switch the CPU into real mode, reissue the interrupt, switch back to protected mode, restore the CPU state and resume program execution. All very long-winded.

XMS

As there was originally no operating system to take advantage of extended memory, developers accessed it in their own way, often at the same time. Lotus, Intel and Microsoft, together with AST, came up with an eXtended Memory Specification that allowed real-mode programs to get to extended memory without interfering with each other. The software that provides XMS facilities in DOS is **himem.sys**.

EXPANDED MEMORY

This is the most confusing one of all, because it sounds so much like *expansion memory*, which was what extended memory was sometimes called! Also, it operates totally outside the address space of the CPU.

Once the PC was in the market, it wasn't long before 640K wasn't enough, particularly for people using *Lotus*, the top-selling application of the time, and the reason why many people bought PCs in the first place. They were creating large spreadsheets and not having enough memory to load them, especially when version 2 needed 60K more memory than the original. It wasn't entirely their fault; Lotus itself in its early days was very inefficient in its use of memory.

Users got onto Lotus, Intel and Microsoft for a workaround, and they came up with LIM memory, also known as *Expanded*. It's a system of physical bank-switching, where several extra banks of memory can be allocated to a program, but only one will be in the address space of the CPU at any time, as that bank is switched, or *paged*, in as required. In other words, the program code stays in the physical cells, but the electronic address of those cells is changed, either by software or circuitry.

You added a memory card to your PC that divided its memory into *pages* of 16K, up to 8 Mb. Four of those (contiguous) 16K pages were allocated space in upper memory, added to base memory and used to access the card. Software was used to map pages back and forward between the card and upper memory.

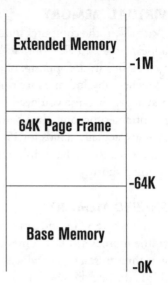

In effect, LIM (4.0) directly swaps the contents of any 16K block of expanded memory with a similar one inside upper memory; in fact, no swapping takes place, but the pages have their address changed to look as if it does; bank switching. Once the *page frame* is mapped to a page on the card, the data in that page can be seen by the CPU (imagine software using a torch through the page frame, and seeing the memory where the light falls):

Points to note about LIM:

It's normally only for data (not program code).

Programs need to be specially written to use it.

There are two LIM standards, 3.2 and 4, the latter incorporating standards from E(nhanced)EMS, which came from a memory card created by AST. Although, in theory, LIM 4 doesn't need a page frame, the programs you run may well expect to see one. In addition, there could be up to 64 pages, so you could bank switch up to a megabyte at a time, effectively doubling the address space of the CPU, and enabling program code to be run, so you could multitask for the first time (check out **desqview**). This was called *large-frame EMS*, but it still used only four pages in upper memory; the idea was to remove most of the memory on the motherboard. The memory card *backfilled* conventional memory and used the extra pages for banking.

On an 8086 or 286-based machine, expanded memory is usually provided by circuitry on an expansion card, but there are some (not altogether successful) software solutions. 386 (and 486) -based machines have memory management built in to the central processor, so all that's needed is the relevant software to emulate LIM (**emm386.exe** or similar).

At first this idea used the hard disk for the pages (on 286s), but later they were moved to extended memory; the extended memory is made to look like expanded memory to those programs that require it, helped by protected mode and the paging capabilities of the 386 and above.

When manually selecting a page frame, you will need 64K of contiguous upper, or non-banked, memory (that is, it needs to be all together in one place). Various programs (such as **msd**, which comes with Windows, or DOS 6) will inspect upper memory and tell you how it's being used, and help you place the page frame properly.

Try and place it directly next to a ROM, and not in the middle of a clear area, so what's left is as contiguous as possible for other programs. A good place is just under the system ROM, at E000, or above the video ROM, at C800 (its position in the diagram above is for illustration purposes only).

VIRTUAL MEMORY

"Virtual" in the computer industry is a word meaning that something is other than what it appears to be. In view of that, Virtual Memory isn't memory at all, but hard disk space made to look like it; the opposite of a RAM disk, in fact. Windows uses virtual memory for *swap files* when physical memory runs out (on the PC, you can only use virtual memory with 286s and above, because you need protected mode). Like disk cacheing, VM was used on mainframes for some time before migrating to the PC; VMS, the OS used on DEC VAX systems, actually stands for *Virtual Memory System*. There is a speed penalty, of course, as you have to access the hard disk to use it, but Virtual Memory is a good stopgap when you're running short.

SHARED MEMORY

This is where VGA and System memory share the same chips, and needs a BIOS to suit (and a little more RAM!). It comes under the name of *Unified Memory Architecture* (UMA) and uses three buses, two of which share memory address, data and control (CAS, RAS, WE). The third arbitrates between them all. There will be a buffer for the screen display, and you often have to set this in the BIOS.

Typically, the graphics controller has to wait its turn behind the CPU, PCI or ISA master.

Shared memory lives either at the top of overall system memory or the top of the first bank of DRAM. A *scramble table* is used to translate between the CPU host address and memory Row and Column address.

Timing is quite important, as you can imagine. The graphics controller must be able to get to as much data as possible in the short time it has access to its memory, often done while the CPU is accessing L2 cache.

4 **Bus Types**

A bus is a shared connection between devices, of which the PC has several; for example, the processor bus connects the CPU to its support chips, the memory bus connects it to memory, and the I/O (or expansion) bus (where expansion cards go) is an extension of the Central Processor, so when adding cards to it, you are extending the capabilities of the CPU itself. Each bus is made up in turn of an address bus and a data bus; the latter transfers data to a memory address located by the former; they are not necessarily the same size, but often are. CPU signals on them have an A or a D before the number, like A31, or D31, for *Address* and *Data*, respectively.

The I/O bus is what concerns us here, and the relevance of it with regard to the BIOS is that older cards are less able to cope with modern buses running at higher speeds than the original design of 8 or so MHz for the ISA bus. Also, when the bus is accessed, the *whole computer* slows down to the bus speed, so it's often worth altering the speed of the bus or the wait states between it and the CPU to speed things up.

> **NOTE:** The DMA clock is often coupled to the bus clock, and you run the risk of damaging it if it's run too fast. If you suddenly start having problems with your floppies, look here for a possible cause.

Although EISA, for example, has a peak bandwidth of 33 MB/s as opposed to PCI's 132, what you actually get is is a function of motherboard design and chipset, so the maximum *sustained* throughput becomes something more like 20 or 40, respectively, which is quite a reduction in the spread and gives less of an advantage to PCI for random access.

ISA

The eight-bit version came on the original PC, and the AT used an extension to make it 16-bit, so there is backwards compatibility. It has a *maximum* data transfer rate of about 8 megabits per second on an AT, which is actually well above the capability of disk drives, or most network and video cards. The *average* data throughput is around a quarter of that. Its design makes it difficult to mix 8- and 16-bit RAM or ROM within the same 128K block of upper memory; an 8-bit VGA card could force all other cards in the same (C000-DFFF) range to use 8 bits as well, which was a common source of inexplicable crashes where 16-bit network cards were involved.

Data movement between the ISA bus and memory is done 16 bits at a time with a block I/O instruction, which, even on a 486, involves a slow microcode loop, so the CPU will not use the bus at its maximum rate. With bus mastering, the controller itself takes over the bus, and blocks can be transferred 32 bits at a time, if the BIOS can cope (see *IDE 32-bit Transfer*). Bus masters can also transfer data between devices on the bus, rather than just to memory, like the DMA system. ISA only allows one bus master board, but the gains are not brilliant, and you can only access the first 16 Mb of RAM this way.

EISA

Extended Industry Standard Architecture is an evolution of ISA and (theoretically, anyway) backwards compatible with it, including the speed (8 MHz), so the increased data throughput is mainly due to the bus doubling in size—but you must use EISA expansion cards. It has its own DMA arrangements, which can use the complete address space. One advantage of EISA (and *Micro Channel*) is the relative ease of setting up expansion cards—plug them in and run configuration software which will automatically detect their settings.

MICRO CHANNEL ARCHITECTURE

A proprietary standard established by IBM to take over from ISA, and therefore incompatible with anything else. It comes in two versions, 16- and 32-bit and, in practical terms, is capable of transferring around 20 mbps. It runs at 10 MHz, and is technically well designed.

LOCAL BUS

The local bus is one more directly suited to the CPU; it's next door (hence local), has the same bandwidth and runs at the same speed, so the bottleneck is less (ISA was local in the early days!). Data is therefore moved along the bus at processor speeds. There are two varieties:

VL-BUS A 32-bit bus which allows bus mastering, and uses two cycles to transfer a 32-bit word, peaking at 66 Mb/sec. It also supports (486) burst mode, where a single address cycle precedes four data cycles, meaning that 4 32-bit words can move in only 5 cycles, as opposed to 8, giving 105 Mb/sec at 33 MHz. Up to 33 MHz, write accesses require no wait states, and read accesses require one.

Motherboards will have a switch marked <=33 or >33, which halves the VESA bus speed when switched to > (greater than) 33 MHz. The speed is mainly obtained by allowing VL-Bus adapter cards first choice at intercepting CPU cycles. It's not designed to cope with more than a certain number of cards at particular speeds; e.g. 3 at 33, 2 at 40 and only 1 at 50 MHz, and even that often needs a wait state inserted. VL-Bus 2 is 64-bit, yielding 320 Mb/sec at 50 MHz.

There are two types of slot; Master or Slave. Master boards, such as SCSI controllers, have their own CPUs which can do their own thing; slaves (i.e. video boards) don't. A slave board will work in a master slot, but not *vice versa*.

PCI, which is a mezzanine bus (meaning divorced from the CPU) with some independence and the ability to cope with more devices, so it's more suited to cross-platform work. It is time multiplexed, meaning that address and data (AD) lines share the same connections. It has its own burst mode that allows 1 address cycle to be followed by as many data cycles as system overheads allow. At nearly 1 word per cycle, the potential is 264 Mb/sec. It can operate *up to* 33 MHz, or 66 MHz with PCI 2.1, and can transfer data at 32 bits per clock cycle so you can get up to 132 Mbyte/sec (264 with 2.1). Being asynchronous, it can run at one speed (33, or 66 MHz) without worrying about coordination with the CPU, although matching them is still a good idea.

Each PCI card can perform up to 8 functions, and you can have more than one busmastering card on the bus. It should be noted, though, that many functions are not available on PCI cards, but are designed into motherboards instead, which is why PCI multi-I/O cards don't exist. Basic PCI bus transactions are controlled with the following signals:

FRAME	Driven by the master to indicate the beginning and end of a transaction.
IRDY	Driven by the master to force (add) wait states to a cycle.
TRDY	Driven by the target to force wait states.
STOP	Driven by the target to initiate retry cycles or disconnect sequences.
C/BE3..0	These determine, during the address phase, the type of bus transaction with a bus command, and during the data phase, which bytes will be transferred.

PCI is part of the *Plug and Play* standard, assuming your operating system and BIOS agree, so is auto configuring (though some cards use jumpers instead of storing information in a chip); it will also share interrupts under the same circumstances. More in *Plug and Play/PCI* see page -129.

The PCI chipset handles transactions between cards and the rest of the system, and allows other buses to be bridged to it (typically an ISA bus to allow older cards to be used). Not all of them are equal, though; certain features, such as *byte merging*, may be absent. It has its own internal interrupt system, which can be mapped to IRQs if required. The connector may vary according to the voltage the card uses (3.3 or 5v; some cards can cope with both).

PCMCIA

A 16-bit, 8 MHz *PC Memory Card International Association* standard originally for credit-card size flash memory additions to portable computers, as a replacement for floppies, but types 2 and 3 cover modems and hard disks, etc, each getting thicker in turn. Desk-top computers are beginning to use it for convenience. The cards are now called *PC-Cards*, and the current standard is 2.1. Most of version 5's standards have been implemented, but many haven't, so it's still not officially in force. It supports 32-bit bus mastering, multiple voltage (5/3.3) and DMA support, amongst others.

PC Cards usually need an area of 4K in upper memory to initialise themselves, which is not used afterwards. D000-D1FF seems to be popular. An enabler program is often supplied,

Bus Types

which is better than using the *Card and Socket Service* software that is supposed to provide compatibility, but is very cumbersome, consisting of up to 6 device drivers that take up nearly 60K of memory (Windows '95 has it built in).

The components of a PC Card system consist of hardware

Host Bus Adapter, the interface between a bus and the sockets into which the cards go.

Sockets, type I, II and III, each thicker in turn and usually come in pairs. A mechanical key prevents 3.3 volt cards being inserted into 5v sockets. Type IV are unofficial Toshiba hard disks.

Cards. These are credit-card size and have 68-pin connectors.

and software:

Socket Services tell your PC how to talk to its slots or, in other words, provide an interface between the BIOS and PCMCIA host chips, such as the Intel 82365SL PCIC and the DataBook TCIC-2/N (written for a specific controller). It might configure the socket for an I/O or memory interface and control socket power voltages.

Card Services tell the operating system or other software how to talk to the card that's in it, or provide an interface between the card and the socket.

The two above combine together to handle hot-swapping and resource allocation, and normally come with the computer, to suit the host bus that comes with it.

There may be a *Resource Initialisation Utility* that checks on I/O ports, IRQs and memory addressing and report to Card Services, as well as software to help Windows (3.x) to recognise cards after it has started, since it assumes a card is not present if it is not seen at start up. A *Card Installation Utility* detects the insertion and removal of PC Cards and automatically determines the card type so the socket can be configured properly. This is where the beeps come from.

The main suppliers of software are Phoenix, Award, Databook and SystemSoft. *CardSoft* comes from the latter. Here is a table that lists their device drivers:

Device Driver	SystemSoft (CardSoft)	Phoenix	CardWare (Award Software)	Databook (Cardtalk)
Socket Services	SS365SL.EXE SS365LP.EXE SSCIRRUS.EXE SSDBOOK.EXE SVADEM.EXE SSVLSI.EXE	PCMSS.EXE	SSPCIC.EXE, SSTCIC.EXE, SSTACT.EXE	SNOTEPV2.SYS
Card Services	CS.EXE	PCMCS.EXE	PCCS.EXE	CTALKCS
Resource Initialisation	CSALLOC.EXE	PCMRMAN.SYS	RCRM.EXE	
IDE/ATA Driver	S_IDE.EXE ATADRV.EXE	PCMATA.SYS	PCATA.EXE	

SRAM Card Driver	SRAMDRV.EXE MTSRAM.EXE	PCMFFCS.EXE PCFORMAT.EXE	PCSRAM.EXE	
Flash Card Support (files from Microsoft)	MTAA.EXE MTAB.EXE MTI1.EXE MT12P.EXE	PCMFFCS.EXE PCFORMAT.EXE MEMCARD.EXE	PCFLASH.EXE	
Memory Card Driver	SCARD29.EXE MEMDRV.EXE		PCDISK.EXE	
Card Installer/Client Driver	CIC.EXE CARDID.EXE	PCMSCD.EXE	PCENABLE.EXE	CARDTALK.SYS
Card Services Power Management	CS_APM.EXE		(inside PCCS.EXE)	

Cardbus is a new variation offering PCI-capable devices, so bus mastering can take place at 33 MHz to cope with 100 Mbps Ethernet, or later versions of SCSI. It uses the same protocol as PCI, and is 32-bit.

Client drivers work with the software described above, and tend to like their own cards; their purpose is to cover the card's resource requirements, as there are no switches to set IRQs, etc with. Generic enablers cover a variety of products.

Point enablers are specific; they don't need C&SS, but neither do they support hot swapping, and other facilities. Sometimes, you can only run one point enabler at a time, which is a problem if you have two cards.

USB

The *Universal Serial Bus* is a standard replacement for the antiquated connectors on the back of the average PC; computers will likely come with two USB ports as standard. It actually behaves more like a network, since one host (e.g. a PC) can support up to 127 devices, daisychained to each other, or connected in a star topology from a hub, but this depends on the bandwidth you need. Each device can only access up to about 6 Mbps, so Firewire (below) is a better choice for higher throughput, like DVD. A hub will have one input connector, from the host or an upstream device, and multiple downstream connectors. Otherwise, each device will have an upstream and downstream connection.

The maximum distance from one device to another is 5m, and the last device must be terminated. There are three types of device:

Low power, bus powered (100 mA).

High power, bus powered (500 mA).

Self powered, but may use bus power when in power save mode.

The bus complies with Plug and Play, so devices are hot-swappable, as they register automatically with the host when connected. More technically, USB is an external 4-wire serial bus with two 90 ohm twisted pairs in a token-based star network. Two lines carry signals based on *Differential Manchester NRZI*, one being for ground, and the other +5v. Zero/half amplitude pulses are used for control. Transmission speed is either 12Mbps with shielded wire or 1.5Mbps for unshielded. Data packets are up to 1023 bits in size, with an 8 bit synch pattern at the start of each frame.

Bus Types

45

A 1000msec frame is used, whose usage is allocated by the USB controller based on information provided by devices when logging in, which ensures that they all get bandwidth, and frequently. The controller sends data packets to the USB, from where the targeted device responds. A packet can either contain data or device control signals; the latter go one way only. When the transaction is complete, the next one in the *transfer queue* is executed. If more than one millisecond is needed, an extra transaction request is placed in the transfer queue for another time frame.

There is backward compatibility with ISA BIOS Code. The USB software is too much for an EPROM, so some space in the BIOS is used as well, because access to it is needed anyway (during POST, etc) for USB devices. Windows '98 has more robust USB support.

FIREWIRE

Similar to USB, but faster, originally developed by Apple, and now called IEEE 1394. It clocks in at a minimum speed of 100 Mbps, going up to somewhere near the bandwidth of PCI, whatever that is. Because it also guarantees bandwidth, isochronous data, that is, needing consistency to be effective, like digital video, can be transferred properly.

There are two more connections than USB, and it only supports up to 63 devices of varying speeds on the bus. It is also complex and expensive, and could be an alternative to SCSI for hard disks, etc.

5 Expansion Cards

Expansion cards use four ways of communicating with the rest of the computer; *Direct Memory Access* (DMA), *Base Memory Address*, *I/O address* and *Interrupt Setting* (IRQ).

DIRECT MEMORY ACCESS (DMA)

With this, high speed devices on the expansion bus can place data directly into memory over reserved *DMA channels* without having to involve the CPU for more than a minimum time; that is, enough for it to write the destination RAM address in the DMA controller along with the number of bytes to be transferred, so it can get on with something else. The DMA controller chip will be programmed by whatever software you're running, and is prone to burning out if run too fast (it's linked to bus speed, adjusted through your *Advanced Chipset Setup)*.

Typically, a hard drive controller might notify the DMA controller (over its request line) that it wants to move data to memory, whereupon the DMA controller will allocate a priority for that request according to its inbuilt logic and pass it on to the CPU. If the CPU accepts the request, the DMA controller is given control of the bus (the ALE, or *Address Latch Enable* signal helps here) so it can send a start signal to the hard disk controller.

The DMA Controller (8237A or equivalent) activates two lines at once; one to read and one to write. As the write line is open, data, when read, is moved directly to its destination. When DMA transfers are under way, the CPU executes programs, and the DMA Controller moves data, so it's primitive multitasking. DRQ lines, in case you're wondering, are used by the DMA controller to receive requests. You can transfer one byte per request, or a block. DMA Controllers need to know where the data to be moved is, where it has to go, and how much there is.

PCs and XTs use one DMA chip, and the standard setup is:

Channel	Device
0	Refresh (System Memory)
1	Available
2	Floppy controller
3	Hard Disk

ATs use 2 8237As to provide 8 channels, 0-7. Channel 4 joins the two controllers, so is unavailable. 0-3 are eight-bit (64K at a time), and 5-7 are 16-bit (128K); the controller for the former is known as DMA 1, and the one for the latter as DMA 2. Floppies use channel 2.

Don't count on channel 0, either, as it may be used for memory refresh (there's no harm in trying, though). PS/2s use 5 for hard disk transfers and XTs use 3.

If two devices try to use a channel at the same time, one or both will not work, though the channel can often be shared if only one uses it.

Channels available in AT compatibles are listed below:

Channel	Device	Notes
0	Memory Refresh	16-bit
1	Available	8-bit
2	Floppy	
3	Available	8-bit
4	DMA controller 1	
5	Available	16-bit
6	Available	16-bit
7	Available	16-bit

DMA transfers must take place within a 64K segment, and in the first 16 Mb, so memory problems can arise when remapping takes place and data is therefore moved around all over the place, particularly in extended memory. This is especially noticeable with ISA systems (you can use more than 16 Mb, provided it's not used or controlled by the operating system).

A program's request for memory access will be redirected by the CPU, but if it's not involved with the transfer (as with DMA), the DMA controller won't know the new location.

Memory managers trap the calls so they can be redirected properly; data is redirected to a buffer owned by the memory manager inside the proper address range.

Sometimes you can adjust the DMA buffer size (use **d=** with **emm386.exe**), but some systems don't use it, particularly Multiuser DOS (because there's no way of using interrupts to see if DMA transfers have finished, so the controller has to be polled, which is one more thing for the CPU to do when serious multitasking is taking place).

When the AT was made, DMA for hard disk transfers was given up in favour of Programmed I/O (PIO), where the CPU oversees the whole job by sending commands to the peripheral through I/O addresses. The reason is that the DMA controller had to run at 4.77 MHz for compatibility reasons and was too slow on later and faster machines, and with DOS/Windows, the CPU has to wait for the transfer to finish anyway.

Now that quicker buses exist, DMA is again used in the shape of *Fast MultiWord DMA*, which transfers multiple sets of data with only one set of overhead commands, for high performance, but PIO (especially with ATA) is still fast enough to give it a run for its money.

MultiWord DMA is used in EISA, VLB, and PCI systems, being capable of the very fast transfer rates, utilizing cycle times of 480ns or faster. Once the entire data transfer is complete, the drive issues an interrupt to tell the CPU the data is where it belongs.

Having said all that, Bus Master DMA is available for IDE, which helps with multimedia under a multithreaded operating system. Traditional DMA still uses the CPU, even if only for setting up data transfers in the first place.

A Bus Master DMA device can do its own setup and transfer, leaving the CPU (and the motherboard DMA controller) out of it. MultiWord DMA Mode 2 can transfer at the same rate as Mode 4 PIO, or 16.6 Mb/sec.

Many BIOSes support the following DMA transfer *modes*:

Single Transfer Mode, where only one transfer is made per cycle; the bus is released when the transfer is complete.

Block Transfer Mode, where multiple sequential transfers are generated per cycle. A DMA device using ISA compatible timing should not be programmed for this, as it can lock out other devices (including refresh) if the transfer count is programmed to a large number. Block mode can effectively be used with Type A, B or Burst DMA timing since the channel can be interrupted while other devices use the bus.

Demand Transfer Mode, as above, but used for peripherals with limited buffering capacity, where a group of transfers can be initiated and continued until the buffer is empty. DREQ can then be issued again by the peripheral.

A DMA device using ISA compatible timing should not be programmed for this unless it releases the bus periodically to allow other devices to use it. It is possible to lock out other devices (including refresh) if the transfer count is programmed to a large number. Demand mode can effectively be used with Type "A," Type "B," or Burst DMA timing since the channel can be interrupted while other devices use the bus.

Cascade Mode is used to connect more than one DMA controller together, for simple system expansion, through DMA Channel 4. As it is always programmed to cascade mode, it cannot be used for internal operations. Also, a 16 bit ISA bus master must use a DMA channel in Cascade Mode for bus arbitration.

You may come across these *types* of DMA transfer:

Read transfers, from memory to a peripheral.

Write transfers, from peripherals to memory.

Memory-Memory Transfer. What it says.

Verify transfers. Pseudo transfers, for diagnostics, where memory and I/O control lines remain inactive, so everything happens, except the command signal. Verify transfers are only allowed in ISA compatible timing mode.

BASE MEMORY ADDRESS

Expansion cards often contain small amounts of memory as buffers for temporary data storage when the computer is busy. The *Base Memory Address* indicates the starting point of a range of memory used by any card.

The following list indicates what may be used already:

A0000-AFFFF   EGA/VGA video memory (buffer)

Expansion Cards

49

B0000-B7FFF	Mono video memory (buffers)
B8000-BFFFF	RGB (CGA) and mono video
C0000-C7FFF	EGA/VGA BIOS ROM (EGA to C3FFF)
C8000-CFFFF	XT hard disk BIOS ROM (can vary)
D0000-DFFFF	LIM area (varies)
E0000-EFFFF	Some EISA BIOS/ESCD/32-bit BIOS
F0000-FFFFF	System BIOS-1st page available?

What address in Upper Memory to use for your card (that is, the *Lowest Free Address*) initially depends on the video card, e.g.

Video type	LFA
Hercules	C000
EGA	C400
VGA	C800

As an example, the video ROM typically occupies the area C000-C7FF, so the Lowest Free Address for another card is C800. However, C800 is also a good choice for (16K) hard disk controller ROMs in ISA or EISA machines, so if you have a VGA card as well, you wouldn't normally expect to use anything lower than CC00.

Using a base address of D0000 as an example, here are the ranges of memory occupied by a ROM or adapter RAM buffer:

ROM size	Range used
8 K	D0000-D1FFF
16 K	D0000-D3FFF
32 K	D0000-D7FFF

BASE I/O ADDRESS

I/O addresses (I/O = *Input/Output*) act as "mailboxes", where messages or data can be passed between programs and components, typically responses to IN or OUT instructions from the CPU; they are 1-byte wide openings in memory, also expressed in hexadecimal.

On a 386, there are 65,536, most of which are never used, because the ISA bus, which only implements 1024 of them, usually only decodes the lower 10 bits, thus using 0-3FF. To get more addresses, some boards, such as 8514/A compatible graphics boards, decode the upper 6 bits as well. When they use 2E8 and 2EA, you will get problems with COM 4, as it uses the former. Watch out for 3C0-3DA as well.

The bottom 256 I/O addresses (000-0FF) relate to the system board, so your expansion cards will only be able to use between 100-3FF. Hybrid motherboards (e.g. with EISA/PCI/VESA as well) will support up to address FFFFFFFF, and the ISA part may get confused if you use a card with an address higher than 3FF.

The Base I/O Address is the first of a *range* of addresses rather than a single one; for example, most network adapters use a range of 20h, so 360h really means 360h-37Fh (in which case watch for LPT 1, whose base is 378)—if you suddenly lose your printer when you plug in a network card, this is the reason.

Additionally, COM 1 reserves a range of addresses from 3F8h to 3FFh, which are used for various tasks, like setting up speed, parity, etc. The I/O address table is 00-FFFFh.

You can still get a conflict even when addresses appear to be different, because the cards may think in hexadecimal, when their drivers don't! They may resolve them in binary format, and from right to left (we read hex from left to right). Sound cards suffer from this in particular. Don't forget that most I/O cards only decode the lower 10 address lines, and few use all 16, which is why some video cards get confused with COM 4; as far as the lower 10 address lines are concerned, they're the same!

For example, 220h (standard Sound Blaster) converts to 10 0010 0000 in binary. If you have a card set at 2A20, the first 10 binary digits are the same as 220 (10 1010 0010 0000—right to left, remember), so it won't work. The same goes for the following:

Hex	Binary
220	10 0010 0000
0A20	1010 0010 0000
0E20	1110 0010 0000
1A20	1 1010 0010 0000
1E20	1 1110 0010 0000
2A20	10 1010 0010 0000
2E20	10 1110 0010 0000
3A20	11 1010 0010 0000

See also *Extended I/O Decode*. The Windows calculator can be used in binary mode to check this if you suspect a problem. Addresses can vary from machine to machine, but "standard" ones are used by convention. Here's a list of reserved I/O addresses:

000-01F	DMA controller 1
020-03F	Interrupt controller 1
040-05F	System timers
060-063	PPI (XT)
070-07F	CMOS Clock (AT)
080-087	DMA page registers
089-09F	DMA page registers
0A0-0BF	NMI (XT to 0AF); PIC 2 (AT & PS/2)
0C0-0DF	DMA controllers (AT & PS/2)
0E0-0EF	Real-time clock (PS/2 30)
0F0-0FF	Maths coprocessor
1F0-1F8	AT Hard disk controller
200-20F	Game port
210-217	XT Expansion Unit
220-22F	NetWare Key Card (old
230-23F	Bus mouse
258-25F	Intel Above Board
270-27F	LPT3 (278-27B; LPT 2 in the XT)
280-28F	LCD display on Wyse 2108 PC

Expansion Cards

51

2E0-2EF	COM 4 (2E8-2EF) GPIB adapter 0
2F0-2FF	COM 2 (2F8-2FF)
300-30F	Most NICs default setting/MIDI output
320-32F	Hard disk controller (XT)
370-37F	LPT 2 (AT-378-37B)
3B0-3BF	Mono display/printer adapter
3BC-3BF	LPT 1
3C0-3CF	EGA/VGA adapter
3D0-3DF	CGA/EGA/VGA adapter
3E0-3EF	COM 3 (3E8-3EF)
3F0-3F7	Floppy drive controller
3F8-3FF	COM 1

Some may vary according to your machine's architecture, especially COM 3 and COM 4.

INTERRUPT SETTING

If any part of the computer needs attention, it will have to interrupt the CPU, which is more efficient than having the CPU poll each device in turn, and wasting cycles when the device(s) are quite happy to be left alone, thank you very much. On a PC, a hardware interrupt, or IRQ, is a convenient way of calling subroutines from DOS or the BIOS, which are unfortunately also called interrupts!

In other words, the BIOS (and DOS) contains code which is allocated an *interrupt number* according to the service provided, which can be used by hardware or software. There are 256. Interrupt Vectors are loaded at boot time to create pointers to the appropriate handlers, in a table that is loaded into base memory.

This is so programs can use facilities whose actual address is unknown, so devices can be used regardless of where the software that drives them is located in memory.

Hardware interrupts (described more fully below), or IRQs, are translated into software interrupts, and they should naturally not be called by software. For example, IRQ 1 is used by the keyboard, which is translated to INT 09h. In fact, IRQs 0-7 relate to 08h-0Fh, and 8-15 (on ATs and above) to 70h-77h.

Each IRQ has a different priority, and each device must use a unique one. Classic symptoms of (hardware) interrupt conflicts include colour screens turning black and white, machines hanging up when certain programs load, and mouse problems.

In fact, there are three types of interrupt:

Internal, generated by the CPU.

External, generated by hardware other than the CPU, of which there are two variations; **NMI** (*Non-Maskable Interrupt Line*), which informs the CPU of catastrophic events, like memory parity errors or power failure, and **IRQ**, or *Interrupt ReQuest Line*, which is used by a device to grab the CPU's attention. IRQs are *maskable*, which means they can be turned off, or ignored by the CPU. NMIs need immediate attention and cannot be turned off, or worked around. XTs have eight IRQ levels; ATs and PS/2s have two sets of eight. A device will send an Interrupt Request (IRQ) to the 8259 PIC, which allocates priorities and passes interrupts on for translation one at a time, as the CPU only has one interrupt line.

Hardware interrupts can be *edge triggered*, by a sudden change in voltage, or *level triggered*, by a small change in voltage (which means they can be shared). ISA buses are edge triggered; EISA can be level triggered.

Software, initiated by INT and INTO instructions, and not the same as the above. An example is INT 13, used by Windows 32-bit Disk Access, which is an access point inside the BIOS code used for disk related requests. An operating system will hook into that point and run the code sitting there, rather than run its own; 32-bit disk access, of course, does run its own, hence the speed. These can be shared, otherwise the PC wouldn't run as fast. The clock tick, for instance, at 1Ch, is passed on from program to program in turn, known as being *chainable*.

The lower the IRQ level, the higher the priority the associated device is given. However, where a system has a dual interrupt controller (e.g. ATs, PS/2s, 386 and 486 machines) IRQ levels 8 to 15 have priority over levels 3 to 7, because the second controller's single output line is wired to IRQ 2 on the first chip. This makes IRQ 2 more complex to service and should be avoided for that reason. If you're using an EISA or Micro Channel machine, you may come across *arbitration levels*, which work in a similar way.

This table shows IRQ lines assigned (in the AT), in order of priority:

0	System timer
1	Keyboard
2	Slave interrupt controller
8	Real-time clock
9	Redirected to IRQ 2
10	
11	
12	PS/2 Mouse
13	Maths coprocessor
14	Hard disk controller/Primary IDE
15	Secondary IDE
3	COM 2/COM 4
4	COM 1/COM 3
5	LPT 2
6	Floppy controller
7	LPT 1

Many cards use IRQ 5 as a default (it's usually used for LPT 2:). As printing isn't interrupt-driven (in DOS, at least), you may be able to use IRQ 7, provided nothing strange is hanging off the parallel port (like a tape streamer).

Boards with 8-bit edge connectors are limited to IRQ 3-7 or 9 (in ATs) only.

With PCI machines, IRQs are allocated to ISA, Plug and Play and PCI cards in that order. The BIOS will automatically allocate an IRQ to a PCI card that requires one, mapping it to a PCI INT#. Leave all PCI Int assignments on A. PCI slot 1 automatically starts with A, 2 starts with B, 3 with C and so on.

6 Setting Up For Performance

Setting up the BIOS to get the best performance (or rate of data transfer around the machine, at least) involves quite a bit of tedious trial and error, rebooting your system time and again to check the results. For this reason, you want a quick and easily used diagnostic program (e.g. the Core hard disk performance test, or the Quake 1.06 benchmark) with which to check your hard disk data transfer rate, or whatever. It doesn't matter about the figures; they will only be used for comparison purposes. In fact, increases in performance will often not be indicated by the figures, but by your own judgments.

Performance between motherboards can be affected by the chipset, or who makes the support chips for the CPU; so much so that a 200 MHz Pentium with a slow chipset can be seriously outperformed by a 133 MHz one supported properly. The *Advanced Chipset Setup* helps you to tweak the settings provided if required. You want to concentrate on the following areas:

Burst Mode—used on 486s and above, where a single address cycle precedes four data cycles; 4 32-bit words can move in only 5 cycles, not 8. You need long bursts with low wait states; 1 wait state during a burst loses half the bandwidth.

Optimising Refresh Cycles—for example, *Concurrent Refresh* allows the CPU to read cache memory during a RAM refresh cycle. This should be the first to be turned off if you get a problem.

Interleaving—allows memory access whilst other blocks are being refreshed, though you don't have much control over this.

I/O recovery time—that is, the timing parameters of your main board (use *No, Disabled* or the lowest settings for best performance!). Use in preference to increasing bus speeds.

Shadow RAM—ROM contents are transferred to main memory, which is given the same electronic address as the original ROM, and run much faster. Not much good with NetWare, and possibly '95 or NT.

Take a note of all the settings in your *Advanced Chipset Setup* (you can use **PrtScrn**), and vary them one at a time, taking a note of the test results each time. You will probably find, perversely, that relatively high wait states and low bus clock speeds will actually result in better performance because the components are better matched. For example, a 60 MHz bus with a

120 MHz Pentium will run with zero wait states, whereas the 100 MHz version may need one.

Changing DMA settings often affects reliability rather than performance. Phoenix recommends that the first place to start if you have a problem is to turn off any *Hidden* or *Concurrent Refresh* options.

In any case, the notes that follow will at least give you a place to start, and the meaning of the various items you can adjust will (hopefully) become clear.

7 Open Sesame

The ways of getting into a BIOS are many and varied; if your PC doesn't actually need a setup disk, you could try any one of the following, in no particular order (of course, whether they work or not often depends on which keyboard driver you have loaded). Thanks to pellefsen, jfreeman, bruff, snafu, tankman, jdm17, sanity, pr, julesp, halftone, apel, and markjones, all on @cix.compulink.co.uk for some of the following:

Press **del** during boot (AMI, Award).

Press **Esc** during boot—Toshiba.

Press **F1** during boot (Toshiba; Phoenix; Late PS/1 Value Point and 330s).

Press **F2** during boot (NEC).

Press **F10** when square in top RH corner of screen (Compaq).

Press **Ins** during boot—IBM PS/2 with reference partition.

Press **reset** twice—some Dells.

Ctrl Alt Enter—Dell.

Ctrl Alt ?—some PS/2s, such as 75 and 90.

Ctrl-Esc

Ctrl Ins—some PS/2s when pointer at top right of screen.

Ctrl Alt Esc -AST Advantage, Award, Tandon.

Ctrl Alt +

Ctrl Alt S—Phoenix.

Ctrl Alt Ins (Zenith, Phoenix)

Ctrl S (Phoenix).

Ctrl Shift Esc—Tandon 386.

Shift Ctrl Alt + Num Pad **del**—Olivetti PC Pro.

Setup disk—Old Compaqs, Epson (Gemini), IBM, IBM PS/2, Toshiba, old 286s.

Fn+F2. AST Ascentia 950N

8

Standard CMOS Setup

This deals with the basic information, such as time of day, what disk drives and memory you have, etc. It is mostly self-explanatory, and will be found in every AT-class machine. Memory settings are usually dealt with automatically.

Date and Time

Speak for themselves, really, except the timekeeping won't be wonderful, due to variations in voltages, etc (see "The Year 2000 (Y2K) Problem" on page 10).

Daylight Saving

American for automatically adding an hour during Summer, at 0200 on the first Sunday in April; the clock chip is hardwired for it and activated by this setting. It resets to Standard Time on the first Sunday in October. Only relevant for North America, and Windows '95 does this by itself anyway.

Hard Disk (C and D).

Several types of hard disk are catered for (from *Not Installed* up to as many as 125). Choose a drive size *equal to or lower than* the one you propose to fit. User-defined fields are provided for anything strange you may want to fit, in which case you need to specify the following for each drive (see also the *Hard Disk Database*):

Cyln—number of cylinders.

Head—number of heads on the drive.

WPcom—The cylinder when compensation for timing differences between inner and outer edges of the disk is given. Not needed for most modern drives, but some manufacturers (e.g. Conner) specify 0. Be careful with this; what they really mean to say is "disabled", so set 65535 or 1 more than the last cylinder. Setting 0 may mean that WPC actually starts at 0 and confuses the drive.

LZone—the landing zone of the heads, which is where they will go when the system is shut down or they are deliberately parked. Not needed if your drive is autoparking (most are).

Sectors per Track—Usually 17 (MFM) or 26 (RLL), but otherwise varies (for ESDI, SCSI, IDE).

Capacity—the formatted capacity of the drive based on the formula below (the calculation is automatically made):

o Hds x Cyls x Secs/track x 512 bytes (per cyl)

o 1048,576

Mode type. That is, the *PIO Mode* (0, 1, 2, 3, 4), and only applies to IDE drives. Usually *Auto* does the trick, and allows you to change drives without entering setup, but if the drive responds incorrectly, you may have to set it manually. This may also be a *size selection* (with a different CMOS setting for each):

o **Normal**, through the BIOS, with only one translation step inside the drive (so is invisible) and a maximum drive size of 528 Mb, derived from 1024 cylinders, 16 heads and 63 sectors per track (see Large, below, for an explanation). Use if your drive is below 528 Mb, or your OS has a problem with translation.

o **Large**, using CHS translation for drives over 1024 cylinders, but without LBA support (see below). The number of cylinders is divided by 2 and the heads multiplied by 2 automatically, with the calculation reversed inside INT 13, so one translation is used between the drive and BIOS, and another between the BIOS and the rest of the machine, but not at the same time, which is the real trick. This is sometimes known as Extended CHS, and is often best for performance, if not for compatibility.

o **CHS** stands for *Cylinders, Heads, Sectors-per-track*. As Intel-based PC's use 16 bit registers, all processes must use them for compatibility purposes. In case you're interested:

o DX uses 8 bits for the head number and 8 for the drive.

o CX uses 10 bits for cylinder number and 6 for the sector.

o The largest 10-bit number you can have is 1024 (0-1023), which is where the limit on cylinder numbers comes from, and the largest 6 bit number is 63 (1-63), allowing 63 sectors per track, but as the DX register with 8 bits actually allows up to 256 heads (0-255), you can use translation for drives up to 8 Gb and still remain compatible. Although you would be forgiven for using the same logic to support up to 255 drives as well (8 bits for the drive number in DX), the Interrupt Vector Table only has pointers to two I/O addresses (104h and 118h) in the *BIOS Data Area*, where such data is stored as the machine boots.

o In addition, the WD 1003 controller, on which INT 13 is based, only allowed 4 bits for the head number and one for the drive (SCSI bypasses all this by setting the drive type as *Not Installed*, and including its own ROM on the controller).

o With translation, you end up with two levels of CHS—one for INT 13H and one for the device. The device CHS stops at 16 heads, hence 528 Mb.

o Operating Systems still have to check the drive types using INT 13 when they start, however much they may bypass them with their own code later, so everything you need to get things running in the first place should be inside the first 1024 cylinders.

o **LBA**, where CHS is internally translated into sequentially numbered blocks, a system stolen from SCSI. It allows drives larger than 528 Mb to be used (8.4 Gb), but only in conjunction with CHS and has nothing to do with performance. In fact, it can make things slower, as it only reduces CPU overhead in operating systems that use LBA themselves (more CPU cycles are used). Even then, they must still boot with CHS and not use any sectors beyond those allowed by it, so the drive size is the same in either case.

o It must be supported by the drive and the BIOS, and the BIOS in turn must support the INT 13 extensions, as must any operating system or application to get the best effect; for example, with Phoenix BIOS 4.03, if LBA is enabled with an appropriate drive, LBA will be used on all accesses to the drive. With 4.05, LBA will only be used if the INT 13 extensions are invoked, which saves an extra translation step by the BIOS.

o LBA can therefore be enabled, but not necessarily used. Windows '95 supports INT 13, but LBA calls will only be made if '95 's **fdisk** has been used and a new partition type (0E or 0F) created.

o **You may lose data** if LBA is enabled or disabled after the drive has been partitioned with it (or not), but it depends on the BIOS. Phoenix is OK in this respect.

o A Phoenix BIOS converts between the device CHS and INT 13, with LBA in the middle. Others use their own methods, and 32-bit drivers, such as those used in Windows, must be able to cope with all the variations, especially when they have to provide backwards compatibility for older drives, since most people insist on using their previous drive when they add a new one.

o As there so many variations, it is possible that LBA mode may be slower with your particular BIOS, in which case use the Large setting instead. Also, be aware that logical block 100 won't necessarily be in the same place on the same drive between different machines.

Large and *LBA* may not be supported by Unix, as it can already handle big drives. Also, if your OS replaces INT 13, the drive may not be accessed properly.

For Netware 286, you should shadow the system BIOS for user-defined settings. ESDI drives should be set to type 1, and SCSI to 0, or *not installed*, but some SCSI controllers, such as the Mylex DCE 376, require drive type 1.

When it comes to translation, later Phoenix, AMI, Award and MR BIOSes are based on the Microsoft/IBM specification, which is the standard. Others may use the WD EIDE system, which could mean problems when moving drives between machines.

Many new BIOSes can set all the above automatically by fetching the ID string from the (IDE) drive (with *Hard Disk Autodetect* on the main setup screen), so you would only set them manually if you are using a drive partitioned to something other than the standard.

Some PCI motherboards can cope with up to four drives (2 each for PCI and ISA). Drive letters will be assigned to primary partitions first, so logical drive names in extended partitions could be all over the place.

Some older AMI (pre 4-6-90) and Award BIOSes have compatibility problems with IDE and SCSI drives (see *Known BIOS Problems*).

AMI BIOSes dated 7-25-94 and later and support translation, as do some versions of Award 4.0G, which implies various versions of the same BIOS! Revision 1.41a is the latest I have seen, but if yours is earlier than 12/13/1994, the address translation table is faulty, so for drives with more than 1024 cylinders, you must use LBA rather than Large. MR have supported it since early 1990.

Only BIOSes conforming to the IBM/Microsoft/Phoenix standards allow access to disks larger than 8GB.

Two devices on the same channel should be configured as Master or Slave in relation to each other, and a device on its own should be a Master (some CD-ROMs come out of the box as Slaves). The hard drive should be the Master if it coexists with a CD-ROM on the same channel.

The configuration is usually done with jumpers or switches on the device itself, but increasingly, *Cable Selection* (CS) is used, where both are Masters, and the difference is resolved by the way the cable is made.

see "IDE Translation Mode" on page 88

Primary Master/Primary Slave, etc.

As above, for the primary and secondary EIDE channels.

Floppy Disks

Again, these speak for themselves. 360K drives can be automatically detected, but the BIOS can only tell whether others have 80 tracks or not, so you will get the default of 1.2 Mb. Sometimes you have to put the 360K drive as B: if used with another (on Vanilla PCs).

With the MR BIOS, you can also set the *step rate*, or the track to track speed of the recording heads.

Fast gives you improved performance on modern equipment.

Slow gives you backwards compatibility with anything older.

2.88 Mb drives need an i82077 or NSC8744 controller chip.

Keyboard Installed

Disables keyboard checking and is for fileservers, which don't need keyboards once they're up and running, mainly to discourage people from interfering with them.

Video Display

Mostly autodetects, since all screens except Mono can identify themselves to the system. If you have two monitors, you can assign the primary one from here.

Halt on

Whether the computer will stop if an error is detected on startup. Choices are:

All errors	Every time a non-fatal error is detected
No errors	System will not stop at all.
All but keyboard	System will not stop for a keyboard error.
All but diskette	System will not stop for a disk error.
All but Disk/Key	System will not stop for keyboard or disk errors

Disks and keyboards are excepted because the machine may be a server and not have them anyway.

Floppy 3 Mode Support

This is for the Japanese standard floppy, which gets 1.2 Mb onto a 3.5" diskette. Normally disable, unless you have one installed.

9

Advanced CMOS Setup

This allows you to tinker more deeply. Particularly important is the *Password* setting, which is often responsible for locking people out of their own computer.

Typematic Rate Programming

Concerns keyboard sensitivity, or the rate at which keystrokes are repeated, and subsequently the speed of the cursor.

The *Typematic Rate Delay* is the point at which characters are repeated when the key is continually pressed. Default is usually 250ns, or approx .25 secs.

The *Typematic Rate* is how many characters per second are generated (max 30 under DOS).

The **alt**, **shift**, **ctrl**, **numlock**, **caps lock** and **scroll lock** keys are excluded.

Possibly disable this for NetWare servers.

Above 1 Mb Memory test

Invokes test routines on extended memory (if you've got it), and is usually disabled in the interests of saving time during startup, but the drawback is that only the first 1Mb of memory is tested (the rest is just cleared). **himem.sys** does it better anyway!

Memory Priming

Found with the MR BIOS and similar to the above. The *Full Test* works at a rate of 1 Mb per second, and *Quick Scan* at 8, but the latter only primes memory by writing zeros to it. *Skip Test* means what it says.

Memory Test Tick Sound

Enable if you want to hear memory being tested.

Memory Parity Error Check

Tests for errors when data is read into memory. If disabled, only the first Mb is checked. If a parity error occurs, you get an error message:

> Parity Error
> System Halted
> Have A Nice Day

(only joking!) A lot of people find they get many more of these immediately after upgrading from Windows 3.x. They are usually caused by defective memory chips, but they could also be mismatched (in which case change the wait states), or the wrong ones for that motherboard.

Parity is a very basic check of information integrity, where each byte of data actually requires nine bits; the ninth is the parity bit, used for error checking (it was introduced in the early 80s because of doubts about the reliability of memory chips, but the problem was actually found to be emissions from the plastic packaging!). In fact, as cache is used for 80-90% of CPU memory accesses, and DRAM only 1-4% of the time, less errors now result (actually a lower *Soft Error Rate*), so the need for parity checking is reduced, but '95 uses much more 32-bit code. In Windows 3.x, 32-bit code lives at the low end of physical memory, inside the first 4 Mb, hence the increase in detection of parity errors on upgrading—very likely the memory with a problem has never been exercised properly.

Some memory checking programs use read/write cycles where Windows would use execute cycles, which are more vulnerable to parity errors, so memory would have to be extremely bad for memory checkers to actually find a problem. As it happens, parity is not checked during reads anyway.

Other machines, on the other hand, like the Mac, use only eight-bit RAM, and you can use it in motherboards with this option disabled (they are cheaper, after all). The Intel Triton chipset doesn't use parity.

Hit <Del> Message Display

Suppresses the instruction to hit **Del** to enter the setup routine during startup. You can still hit **Del** to get into it, but the message won't be there (helps keep ignoramuses out!).

Hard Disk Type 47 Data Area

Sometimes called an *Extended BIOS RAM Area*, or *Extended Data Segment Area*. Hard disk parameters (for the Standard CMOS Setup) are normally kept in the BIOS ROM, but you can also specify your own parameters for those not already catered for.

As the ROM can't be changed, these extra *Type 47* details are kept in a small area of reserved memory, normally in an unused area of interrupt vector address space in lower system RAM (at 0:300), or a 1Kb area at the top of base memory, using up DOS address space, in which case you go down to 639K. If using Multiuser DOS, select :300 to prevent fragmentation of memory used for the TPA, or if you find difficulties booting from the hard disk, especially SCSI. On the other hand, some network operating systems may object to :300 (ROM address :300 is *not* the same as I/O address 300!).

This is sometimes ignored if *Shadow RAM* or *PS/2 Mouse Support* is enabled because the memory it needs is already being used.

Scratch RAM Option

See *Hard Disk Type 47 Data Area.*

Wait For <F1> If Any Error

Stops the computer until the **F1** key is pressed when a *non-fatal* error is encountered during start up tests. In other words, if disabled, the system does not halt after this message is displayed.

System Boot Up <Num Lock>

Allows you to specify in what mode the calculator pad on the keyboard wakes up in. If you have a 102-key keyboard, and therefore have a separate cursor-control pad, you should keep this *On* (usually the default). With the 84-key version, you have the choice. If set to Off, both sets of arrow keys can be used.

Boot Up NumLock Status

See *System Boot Up <Num Lock>,* above.

Numeric co-processor

Whether you have one present or not (a 486SX doesn't).

Weitek Processor

Used to tell the computer if a Weitek maths co-processor (3167/4167) is present. The Weitek, beloved of scientists, and having 2-3 times the performance of Intel's version, uses memory address space which must be remapped, which is why the computer needs to know about it. Note that the Weitek processor needs to be the same speed as the CPU.

Floppy Drive Seek At Boot

Allows you to stop the computer checking if floppy drives are available for reading or writing when it starts, saving time on startup and possible wear and tear on the drive heads. It's also good for security as it stops people booting up with their own disks and giving you viruses.

Boot Up Floppy Seek

See *Floppy Drive Seek At Boot* above.

This one comes with the Award BIOS, and looks for a 360K drive—can't think why. Later versions determine whether the drive is 40 or 80 track. Can be disabled in the interests of speed and security, or if you don't have a 360K.

System Boot Up Sequence

Specifies in which order drives are searched for an operating system, assuming you haven't disabled the floppy drive search (above), in which case this setting will have no effect. The fastest (and least virus inducing) method is **C:, A:**, but if you have the MR BIOS, there may be other choices:

Auto Search	searches all floppies (you may have more than 2) before defaulting to drive C:, which is useful if you have a 5.25" boot disk and a 3.5" first drive!
Network 1st	lets you use a Boot ROM, whether your C: drive is bootable or not.
Screen Prompt	You can choose from a short menu.

With *Multiboot*, from Phoenix, the BIOS will identify all boot devices and prioritise them according to your choice (v4.0 of the Phoenix BIOS, and later AMI BIOSes will boot from a Zip drive, while Award's *Elite* BIOS supports CD-ROMs, SCSI, LS-120 and Zip drives). Multiboot is only relevant to Plug and Play, and devices that the BIOS is aware of. Your only adjustment is the boot priority.

Boot Up Sequence

See *System Boot Up Sequence*.

Boot Sequence

As for *Boot Up Sequence*, with a menu (Award Software).

Permit Boot from...

Allows you to stop the system seeking a boot sector on A: or C: (MR BIOS), for speed.

Drive C: Assignment

Whether to boot from a primary IDE drive or the first bootable SCSI drive, if you have both.

HDD Sequence SCSI/IDE First

Normally the IDE drive would be the boot disk where it coexists with SCSI in a system, but this option allows you to set the SCSI drive as the boot device instead.

Quick Power On Self Test

Skips retesting a second, third or fourth time.

Swap Floppy Drive

Changes floppy assignments, so the 1st and 2nd drives can exchange drive letters (Award BIOS). Useful if your system diskette is the wrong type for your first drive.

Floppy Disk Access Control

Allows reads from the floppy (*Read Only*), but not writes, for security purposes. *R/W* allows reads and writes.

System Boot Up CPU Speed

Sets the computer's operating speed during the POST, *High* or *Low*. Low= ∫ speed and should be set for 40 MHz CPUs or if you get problems booting. Bus timing is based on the CPU clock at boot time, and may be set low if your CPU speed is high.

Cold Boot Delay

Gives slow devices more time to get their act together; some IDE drives won't work if they're accessed too early. Some SCSI drives have a problem, too, because they may get a separate spin up signal. Usually disabled by selecting *None*. (MR BIOS).

System Warmup Delay

As above, between 0-30 seconds.

External Cache Memory

Sometimes called *Internal Cache Memory* on 386 boards (as 386s don't have internal cache), this refers to the level 2 static RAM on the motherboard used as a cache between the CPU and main memory, anywhere between 64-256K. Usually, you will want this *Enabled*, or *Present*, but disabling sometimes helps problem ROMs or interface cards to work. Don't enable this if you don't have cache memory, or when you see the

> Cache memory bad, do not enable

error message.

There are two types of cache, *write-back* or *write-through*, and there are cost/performance tradeoffs with each; write-back is a better choice for performance.

Talking of management, often you get better performance by using 1 bank of DRAM with only one bank of cache RAM, e.g. 128K with 4 Mb. This seems to provide better balance.

Internal Cache Memory

Refers to the 8K (or 1K if using a Cyrix) of cache memory found on 486 chips. This should be *Enabled* for best performance. Also known as *CPU Internal Cache* with Award.

Fast Gate A20 Option

Or *Turbo Switch Function*, determines how Gate A20 is used to access memory above 1 Mb, which is usually handled through the keyboard controller chip (the 8042 or 8742).

The 8088 in the original PC would wrap around to lowest memory when it got to 1 Mb. The problem was that some software addressed low memory by addressing high memory (Wordstar 3.3 would complain loudly if you had too much available!).

For older programs, an AND Gate was installed on CPU address line 20 that could switch to allow either wraparound to 1 Mb or access to the 16 Mb address space on the 286 by forcing A20 to zero. A convenient TTL signal from a spare pin on the keyboard controller was used to control the gate, either through the BIOS or with software that knew about it.

The keyboard controller is actually a computer in its own right; at least there is a PROM and a microcomputer in it (hence keyboard BIOS), and it had some spare programming space for code that was left out of the 286.

Programs such as Windows and OS/2 enter and leave protected mode through the BIOS, so Gate A20 needs to be continually enabled and disabled, at the same time as another command to reset the CPU into the required mode is sent.

Enabling this gives the best Windows performance, as a faster method of switching is used in place of using the (slower) keyboard controller, using I/O ports, to optimise the sending of the two commands required; the *Fast Gate A20* sequence is generated by writing D1h to port 64h, and data 02h to port 60h. The fast CPU warm reset is generated when a port 64h write cycle with data FEh is decoded (see *Gate A20 Emulation*). Some BIOSes use Port 92.

You will notice very little difference if all your programs operate inside conventional memory (that is, under DOS). However, this may cause Multiuser DOS not to boot. If you get keyboard errors, enable this, as the switching is probably going too fast.

One problem can occur with this option in AMI BIOSes dated 2/2/91 and later; it doesn't always work with the DOS 5.00 version of **himem.sys**. If you get an error message, disable this. If the error persists, there is a physical problem with the Gate A20 logic, part of which is contained in the keyboard BIOS chip, in which case try changing this chip.

This is nothing to do with the Turbo switch on the front of the computer (see below); The alternative heading could be *Turbo Switching Function*.

Turbo Switch Function

As above, but could also enable or disable the system Turbo Switch; that is, if this is disabled (*no*), computer speed is controlled through setup or the keyboard. On some machines the 486 internal cache is switched on or off; on others the CPU clock is altered as well. Others still extend the refresh duration of DRAM.

With power saving systems, you can set the turbo pin to place the system into a power management Suspend mode instead of changing the speed, in which case the other choice will be *Break Key*. Sometimes known as *Set Turbo Pin Function*.

Gate A20 Emulation

As for *Fast Gate A20 Option*, but you get the choice of *Keyboard Controller* (if disabled) or *Chipset*, which is faster. This is for programs that use BIOS calls or I/O ports 60/64H for A20 operations, where the chipset will intercept those commands and emulate the keyboard controller to allow the generation of the relevant signals (see above). The sequence is to write D1h to port 64h, followed by an I/O write to 60h with 00h. A fast reset is an I/O write to 64h with 1111XXX0b.

Fast means that the A20 gate is controlled by I/O port 92H where programs use BIOS calls. *Both* means Gate A20 is controlled by the keyboard controller and chipset where programs use I/O port 60/64H.

Gateway A20 Option

See *Gate A20 Emulation*.

Fast Reset Emulation

Enhances the speed of switching into and out of protected mode by delaying certain signals (INIT or CPURST) by a certain time and holding them for 25 CPUCLK. Switching from Protected to Real Mode requires a "reboot" at chip level, and this setting allows the BIOS to re-boot your system without having to re-initialize all of the hardware. In fact, a pulse is used to take the CPU out of protected mode, which is left set on a fast CPU reset, so is detectable by software. In a bootup, a bit is looked for which indicates whether this is a "boot-start" or a return to 8088. If the latter, the contents of the registers are kept. This setting helps solve problems caused by switching in and out of protected mode too fast.

See above and *Fast Reset Latency* (next).

Fast Reset Latency

The time in microseconds needed for software reset, between real and protected modes. The lower the figure, the better the performance, but this may affect reliability.

Keyboard Emulation

Enabling this allows the chipset to generate the signal normally provided by the keyboard controller. It also enables *Fast Reset Emulation*, above. See also *Gate A20 Emulation*, above.

Video ROM Shadow C000, 32K

Allows you to shadow (or electronically move) the contents of the Video ROM at the specified address, e.g. C000, into extended memory for better performance. The extended memory is then given the same address so the code thinks it's where it should be, and then write-protected (if you're programming or debugging you can sometimes set shadowed areas as Read/Write).

ROM instructions are 8-bit, and s-l-o-w—that is, accessed one bit at a time. Shadowing copies the contents of the ROM into 32-bit (or 16-bit on a 286 or 386SX) memory, disables the ROM and makes that memory look as if it's in the original location, so the code is executed faster. However, you will lose a corresponding amount of extended memory.

If your video card has 16K of ROM, shadow at C400 only. If it has 32K (most do), you should include C000 as well. Shadowed ROMs can also be cached in their new locations through the *Advanced Chipset Setup* , although this is not always adviseable (see below). Some video cards can't be shadowed because they use an EEPROM (or flash ROM) to store configuration data, and you won't be able to change the contents if this is enabled. Never mind! If you've got a large cache this setting may not be needed anyway.

C000 cacheing has one drawback, in that it's done *in the 486 internal cache*, which cannot be write-protected. Whenever a diagnostic test is done, the program sees there is a BIOS present, but has no knowledge of the cacheing, so it will treat the code as being a non-write-protected BIOS, which is regarded as an error condition. If you get failures in this area, disable this option.

Video BIOS Shadow

See *Video ROM Shadow C000, 32K*, above.

Adapter ROM Shadow C800, 16K

Together with others, this functions in the same way as *Video ROM Shadow*, above, but refers to 16K blocks of Upper Memory which cover ROMs on adapter cards, such as hard disk controllers. To use this item effectively, you need to know what memory addresses your expansion cards use (but you could enable them all if you don't know). However, some ROMs don't like being shadowed, particularly those on hard disk controllers, so the best you can do is experiment. Using this reduces available extended memory.

System ROM Shadow

Allows the 64K block of upper memory containing the system BIOS (starting at F000) to be shadowed for better performance, but only when using DOS or another single-user operating system. Disable for UNIX, XENIX or similar; they have their own arrangements.

C8000-CFFFF Shadow/D0000-DFFFF Shadow

See *System ROM Shadow*.

C8000-CFFFF Shadow/E0000-EFFFF Shadow

See *System ROM Shadow*.

Boot E000 Adapters

This works with *Drive C: Assignment* to let you boot from a ROM at E000 (usually SCSI).

Password Checking Option

Allows you to set up a password to be used during the computer's startup sequence. The options are:

> *Always*, which means every time the system is started.
>
> *Setup*, which only protects the BIOS routine from being tampered with, or
>
> *Disabled*.

You can still boot from a floppy and alter the settings with a diagnostic program, though.

You get three attempts to enter the correct password, after which the system will have to be rebooted. The default is usually the manufacturer's initials (try **ami**), or **biostar** or **AWARD_SW** for Award (before 19 Dec 96), but if this doesn't work, or you forget your own password, you must discharge the CMOS RAM.

One way to do this is simply to wait for five years until the battery discharges (ten if you've got a Dallas clock chip)! You could also remove the CMOS chip or the battery and just hang on for twenty minutes or so. Look for the chips mentioned below, under *Clearing Chips*.

> **NOTE:** Since 19 Dec 96, Award Software has not used a default password, leaving it for OEMs. Discharging the battery will not clear the OEM password.

> **NOTE:** When CMOS RAM loses power, a bit is set which indicates this to the BIOS during the POST test. As a result, you will normally get slightly more aggressive default values.

If your battery is soldered in, you could discharge it enough so the CMOS loses power, but make sure it is rechargeable so you can get it up to speed again. To discharge it, connect a small resistor (say 39 ohms) across the battery and leave it for about half an hour.

Some motherboards use a jumper for discharging the CMOS; it may be marked CMOS DRAIN. On the other hand, it may not! Sometimes (depending on the motherboard), you can connect P15 of the keyboard controller (pin 32, usually) to GND and switch the machine on. This makes the POST run, which deletes the password after one diagnostic test. Then reboot.

Very much a last resort is to get a multimeter and set it to a low resistance check (i.e. 4 ohms), place one probe on pin 1 of the chip concerned, and draw the other over the other pins. This will shock out the chip and scramble its brains. **This is not for the faint hearted, and only for the desperate**—use a paperclip or desolder the battery first! We assume no responsibility for damage!

Clearing Chips

The CMOS can mostly be cleared by shorting together appropriate pins with something like a bent paperclip (with the power off!). You could try a debug script if you are able to boot:

```
A:\DEBUG
- o 70 2E
- o 71 FF
- q
```

The CMOS RAM is often incorporated into larger chips:

P82C206 (Square). Also has 2 DMA controllers, 2 Interrupt controllers, a Timer, and RTC (Real-Time Clock). It's usually marked CHIPS, because it's made by Chips and Technologies. Clear by shorting together pins 12 and 32 on the bottom edge or pins 74 and 75 on the upper left corner.

F82C206 (Rectangular). Usually marked OPTi (the manufacturer). Has 2 DMA Controllers, 2 Interrupt Controllers, Timer, and Real-time Clock. Clear by shorting together pins 3 and 26 on the bottom edge (third pin in from left and 5th pin from right).

Dallas DS1287, DS1287A, Benchmarq bp3287MT, bq3287AMT. The DS1287 and DS1287A (and compatible Benchmarq bp3287MT and bq3287AMT chips) have a built-in battery, which should last up to 10 years. Clear the 1287A and 3287AMT chips by shorting pins 12 and 21—you cannot clear the 1287 (and 3287MT), so replace them (with a 1287A!). Although these are 24-pin chips, the Dallas chips may be missing 5, which are unused anyway.

Motorola MC146818AP or compatible. Rectangular 24-pin DIP chip, found on older machines. Compatibles are made by several manufacturers including Hitachi (HD146818AP) and Samsung (KS82C6818A), but the number on the chip should have 6818 in it somewhere. Although pin-compatible with the 1287/1287A, there is no built-in battery, which means it can be cleared by just removing it from the socket, but you can also short pins 12 and 24.

Dallas DS12885S or Benchmarq bq3258S. Clear by shorting pins 12 and 20, on diagonally opposite corners; lower right and upper left (try also pins 12 and 24).

For reference, the bytes in the CMOS of an AT with ISA bus are arranged thus:

00	Real Time Clock
10-2F	ISA Configuration Data
30-3F	BIOS-specific information
40-7F	Ext CMOS RAM/Advanced Chipset info

The AMI password is in 37h-3Fh, where the (encrypted) password is at 38h-3Fh. If byte 0Dh is set to 0, the BIOS will think the battery is dead and treat what's in the CMOS as invalid.

One other point, if you have a foreign keyboard (that is, outside the United States)—the computer expects to see a USA keyboard until your keyboard driver is loaded, so DON'T use anything in your password that is not in the USA keyboard!

Security Option

As for *Password Checking Option*, with two choices:

System, where the machine will not boot and access to setup will be denied without the correct password.

Setup, where access to setup is denied without the password.

This can be disabled by selecting *Supervisor/User Password Setting* at the main menu and pressing **Enter** without entering anything below).

Supervisor/User Password

Gives two levels of security; *Supervisor* has higher priority, so the other doesn't work if it is enabled. To disable, press **Enter** without entering anything.

Network Password Checking

When set to enabled, you are prompted for a password when connecting to a network. If disabled, password checking is left to the network. Best disabled.

Boot Sector Virus Protection

All it does is warn you when attempts are made to write to your boot sector or partition table, so it can be annoying when you see the error message every few seconds or so while trying to do something legitimate. Actually, it's useless for those drives that have their own BIOS in the controller (ESDI/SCSI). Disable when using Multiuser DOS, or installing software. Only available for operating systems such as DOS that do not trap INT 13.

Virus Warning

See *Boot Sector Virus Protection* (Award).

10 Advanced Chipset Setup

What you can do here depends on what facilities the motherboard manufacturer decides to supply you with when you want to program the chipset registers—it is not information used by the BIOS, but by the *chipset*. All the BIOS manufacturer has done is provide a screen so you can make your changes, if the motherboard designer allows you to use them. Bear in mind that the items in this area are actually provided for debugging purposes or to provide some level of tolerance for older expansion cards and slow memory chips; you alter the settings to help the machine cope with them. What one motherboard doesn't like is not necessarily wrong on another, so experiment! **For Pentiums**, it's usually best to set the defaults; what you might gain in performance, you often lose in floppy access!

There is a program called **amisetup**, written by Robert Muchsel, which interrogates your chipset settings at a very deep level, often allowing you to tweak settings not displayed. The shareware version can be downloaded from the MCCS BBS in Singen/Germany, on (49) 7731 69523 (use GAST as a username). It's on CIX or Compuserve as well. Try also **ftp://194.163.64.1/pub/sanisoft/amisetup.zip**. There's another one for other BIOSes, called **ctchip**-something, available from **www.sysdoc.pair.com**, but it doesn't work on all of them.

Highly recommended is **TweakBIOS**, which actually programs the chipset and the PCI bridges, etc on your motherboard. Available from **www.miro.pair.com/tweakbios/**.

Otherwise, you may find two sets of default settings, for convenience if you don't want to do too much tinkering; *Power-On* or *Setup Defaults* and *BIOS Defaults*. Power-On gives you the optimum (best case) settings for regular use, and BIOS Defaults are more conservative, being minimised for troubleshooting (that is, CPU in slow speed, no cache, etc).

For older AMI BIOSes (pre-1991), you can set the default values by holding down the **Ins** key and turning on the computer. An XCMOS Checksum Error will be generated. This can be corrected by entering XCMOS Setup, writing CMOS registers and exiting, and rebooting.

For newer versions, enter CMOS Setup and select:

LOAD DEFAULT VALUES

from the menu.

NOTE: If your machine hangs after changing anything, hold down the **Ins** key whilst switching the machine on, or the **Esc** key after rebooting—you can then load the default settings of your choice. Unfortunately, this takes you right back to the start, so take notes as you go along!

If you have a **green BIOS**, you might have *Auto Keyboard Lockout* set, in which case you need to press **Ctrl-Alt-Bksp**. The three keyboard lights will flash on and off and you will be prompted to enter the CMOS password.

Instructions for discharging the CMOS if you forget passwords are in the *Advanced CMOS Setup* section.

Automatic configuration

When this is *Enabled*, the BIOS sets its own values for some items, such as the Bus Clock Speed, Fast Cache Write Hit, Fast Cache Read Hit, Fast Page Mode DRAM, DRAM Wait State, DMA CAS Timing Delay, Keyboard Clock, etc (the items will vary between motherboards). The important thing to note is that *your own settings will be ignored*, so disable this one if you want to play, or have to change any of the above settings to accommodate a particular card, such as a Bus Logic BT-445S on a 50 MHz 486 system.

REFRESH

Memory is addressed by row and column, with two strobe signals, *Row Address Strobe* (RAS) and *Column Address Strobe* (CAS). Normally, when a DRAM controller refreshes DRAM, CAS is asserted before RAS, which needs a CPU cycle for each event (known as *cycle steal*), but some techniques allow a RAS signal to be kept active whilst a series of CAS signals can be sent, or delaying a cycle from the CPU (cycle stretch).

The charge in a DRAM cell can go up or down, because it is surrounded by electrically active conductors and other cells, which leak their charges. DRAM refreshes correct for this by reading the charge, deciding on its value (0 or 1) and restoring the bit to a full 0 or 1, if the charge level is above or below a certain threshold. Most DRAM can maintain an accurate charge for 16-128 milliseconds between refreshes, but data loss can result if it is too slow. Every time an address is read, the whole row is refreshed when the access is completed. As long as the cell hasn't leaked so much that it changes state, it begins from scratch after each refresh. Refreshes are sometimes staggered to spread out the current surges, but this takes more memory bandwidth and has some impact on performance.

The driver can only supply so much current, so adding DRAM can slow things down. In PCs, the DRAM voltage can be nearly 6 volts because of reflections and ringing driving the +5 up, which can make the memory run hotter.

A *burst refresh* consists of a series of refresh cycles one after the other until all rows have been accessed. A *distributed refresh* is most common, occurring every 15.6 ns when DRQ0 is called by the OUT1 timer. The controller allows the current cycle to be completed and holds all the instructions while a refresh is performed. A *RAS Only refresh* occurs when a row address is put on the address line, and RAS is dropped, whereupon that row is refreshed.

CAS-before-RAS (CBR) is for powersaving. CAS is dropped first, then RAS, with one refresh cycle being performed each time RAS falls. The powersaving occurs because an internal counter is used, not an external address, and the address buffers are powered down.

If using a Cyrix chip, you may need to increase the refresh interval or enable Hidden Refresh (below) if your BIOS has no special handling facilities.

If you don't have EMS, cacheing controllers or laser direct printing cards on the expansion bus, disabling refresh for the bus can improve throughput by 1-3%.

Hidden Refresh

When CAS is low, RAS is made high, then low. Since CAS is low before RAS, you get a CBR refresh. The "hidden" part comes from the fact that data out stays on the line while refresh is being carried out, otherwise this is the same as CBR.

If CAS is hidden, you can eliminate a CPU cycle, but the CPU can also maintain the cache status if the system starts power saving.

Best system performance is naturally obtained with this enabled, but expect to disable it if you are using 4Mb DRAMs (or certain SIMMs), or you get problems. Most of the effects of this setting are masked if you have a cache.

Hidden Refresh Control

See *Hidden Refresh*.

DRAM Refresh Mode

See *Hidden Refresh*.

AT Style Refresh

This happens when the refresh cycle starts with a process called *Hold Arbitration*, and proceeds when the CPU releases control of the memory, but since it holds the CPU up is now out of date. Disable.

Concurrent Refresh

If enabled, the CPU can read cache memory during a DRAM refresh cycle or, in other words, the CPU and refresh system have access to memory at the same time. Otherwise it is idle until refresh is complete, which is slower. Enable for Multiuser DOS on an Intel Express.

Decoupled Refresh Option

This is often called *Hidden Refresh*. Normally, motherboard DRAM and that on the data bus is refreshed separately. When this is disabled, the CPU sends refresh signals to both system RAM and the ISA bus; the latter takes longer because it's running slower. If enabled, the bus controller will perform arbitration between the CPU, DMA and memory refresh cycles on the bus, carrying them out in the background (i.e. hidden) so as not to hold the CPU up, and the DRAM controller will sort things out between the CPU and motherboard DRAM, thus the ISA bus refresh finishes while the CPU gets on with another instruction.

The problem is that some expansion cards (particularly video) need to have the CPU handle the first bus refresh cycle. Disable this if you get random characters or snowy pictures during high resolution graphics modes (you may need to disable *Memory Relocation* as well), albeit with the loss of a little performance. This is especially true with S3 801 boards (such as the SPEA V7 Mirage) coupled with Adaptec C cards and Bs fitted with enhanced ROMs for drives greater than 1 Gb.

Burst Refresh

Reduces overheads by performing several refresh cycles during a single Hold sequence.

Refresh When CPU Hold

Causes the CPU to pause whilst refreshing takes place. Slower.

DRAM Burst of 4 Refresh

Allows refreshes to occur in sets of four, at a quarter the frequency of normal, or in bursts occurring at quarter cycles. Enabling increases performance.

Fast DRAM Refresh

Two refresh modes are available here, Normal, and Hidden. CAS takes place before RAS in both, but in the latter a cycle can be eliminated by hiding CAS refresh, which is faster and more efficient, allows the CPU to maintain the status of the cache.

Divide for Refresh

As above, but you will have the choice of 1/1 or 1/4. 1/4 is best for performance.

Hi-speed Refresh

Affects system performance, except with some types of DRAM which cannot support it, in which case disable (especially for a 33MHz CPU). *Slow Refresh* (below) is preferred, since it gives longer between refresh cycles.

Slow Refresh

Enabled, makes refresh periods happen less often (typically 4 times slower than normal, at 64 rather than 16 ns, which is AT-compatible), so there is less conflict between refreshes and the CPU's activities, thus increasing performance (in other words, there is a longer time between refresh cycles, as modern memory chips can retain their contents better). You might use it if you were getting corruption because your DRAMs aren't fast enough. The timing is measured in microseconds.

Slow Refresh also saves power, which is useful on laptops. Not all DRAMs support this, so don't be surprised if you get parity errors! It requires proper DRAMs, and use 125ns if you get the option.

Staggered Refresh

Where memory banks are refreshed one after the other. This limits the current used and helps stop interference, or power noise, between banks. The RAS of odd banks will go active 1T after even banks.

Slow Memory Refresh Divider

Normally, in the AT, DRAM is refreshed every 16 ns. A higher setting, say 64 ns, will give best performance. Sometimes *4* sets *60 ns*.

DRAM Refresh Period

As for *Slow Memory Refresh Divider*; sets the time, in microseconds, between DRAM refresh cycles. The longer the interval, the better the performance because the CPU will not be interrupted as often, assuming your DRAM is capable.

If you lose data, knock this figure down a bit. Choices are:

15us	15 microseconds (default)
30us	30 microseconds
60us	60 microseconds
120us	120 microseconds

Refresh Value

Sets the refresh value for System RAM by programming the refresh timer (many shareware programs do this as well).

Refresh RAS active time

The time needed for the Row Address Strobe when DRAM is being refreshed, in T states. The lower the figure, the better the performance. Choices are:

6T	Six CPU cycles (default).
5T	Five CPU cycles.

Refresh RAS# Assertion

The number of clock ticks for which RAS# is asserted for refresh cycles. The lower the better for performance.

DRAM RAS Only Refresh

An older alternative to CBR. Leave disabled unless you know you need it for older DRAMs.

DRAM Refresh Queue

Enabled, permits queueing of up to 4 DRAM refresh requests so DRAM can refresh at the best time. Otherwise, all refreshes take priority as normal. Most DRAMs can support this.

DRAM Refresh Method

Specifies the timing pulse width where the Row Address Strobe (RAS) will be on the falling edge and followed by the Column Address Strobe (CAS). You get the choice of *RAS Only* or *CAS before RAS*. A *RAS Only refresh* occurs when a row address is put on the address line, and RAS is dropped, whereupon that row is refreshed.

CAS-before-RAS (CBR) is for powersaving. CAS is dropped first, then RAS, with one refresh cycle being performed each time RAS falls. The powersaving occurs because an internal counter is used, not an external address, and the address buffers are powered down.

DRAM Refresh Rate

Use 15.6 for SDRAM and EDO/FPM, and 31.2 for EDO/FPM only.

Refresh Cycle Time (187.2 us)

The default of 187.2 us is safest against data loss.

DATA BUS

AT Cycle Wait State

This figure represents the number of wait states inserted before an operation is performed on the AT bus. The effect is to lengthen the I/O cycle for expansion cards that have a tight tolerance on speed, such as high-end graphics cards, or you might be overclocking and the ISA bus is tied to the PCI bus speed and you can't change it. Again, for expansion cards with special requirements (you may get separate options for 16-bit and 8-bit transfers). The higher the delay in bus timing, the slower your system will run; 1 wait state can half the bus speed, and you will also need to set a higher DMA wait state.

To avoid confusion, a private message is sent along the data bus for 16-bit cards, before data is sent. The high part of the target address is sent out first, so that 16-bit cards are alerted as to where instructions are headed. As these are sent out over the extra 4 address lines on the extended bus (20-23), the only information the cards really get is which of the 16 possible megabytes is the destination, so three of the original 8-bit lines are duplicated (17-19), which narrows it down to the nearest 128K.

Once a card decides the message is for itself, it places a signal on **memcs16**, a line on the extended bus, which triggers a 16-bit signal transfer (without the signal, the message is sent as 8-bit). When the CPU sees **memcs16**, it assumes the current access will be to a 16-bit device, and begins to assemble data so any mismatches are transparent to the CPU and adapter card. The trouble is that there's no specification governing the amount of time between the advance notice and the actual transfer, and some cards don't request 16-bit transfers quickly enough, so it gets its data as 8-bit, hence confusion, and the need for wait states. VGA cards can switch into 8-bit mode automatically, but many others cannot. I/O operations on the bus generally have an extra wait state compared to memory.

Extra AT Cycle Wait State

See above.

16-bit Memory, I/O Wait State

The number of wait states inserted before 16-bit memory and I/O operations. You can often set this to the smallest value, since the device itself will activate the I/O-CHRDY signal, which allows it to extend the bus cycle by itself if required. If the bus is running faster than 8 MHz, 2 is generally safest. Try between 1-2 when running the bus slower.

8-bit Memory, I/O Wait State

If you get bus timing problems, this setting will insert wait states when accessing devices on the bus. You can often set this to the smallest value, since the device itself will activate the

I/O-CHRDY signal, allowing it to extend the bus cycle by itself if required. If the bus is running faster than 8 MHz, 1 is generally safest. Try 0 when running the bus slower.

Command Delay

The length of the *address phase* of 8- or 16-bit bus cycles (data phases are controlled elsewhere), expressed in wait states, typically 0-3.

AT Bus I/O Command Delay

See *16-bit I/O Recovery Time* (below).

16-bit I/O Recovery Time

Specifies the length of the additional delay inserted after 16-bit operations, for older ISA cards; in other words, the system allows more time for devices to respond before assuming a malfunction and stopping requests for I/O. There is usually an automatic minimum delay of four SYSCLKs between back-to-back I/O cycles to the ISA bus, so these are extra. SYSCLKs are complete machine clock cycles; get best performance with the lowest figure. On PCI systems, bus clock cycles are added between PCI-originated I/O to the ISA bus.

8-bit I/O Recovery Time

As for *16-bit I/O Recovery Time*.

ISA I/O Recovery

As for *16-bit I/O Recovery Time*.

ISA I/O wait state

Adds wait states to the bus so expansion cards can cope with higher speeds better. *Normal* is compatible with standard AT timing, and wait states are in addition to that.

ISA memory wait state

Adds wait states to the bus so memory on expansion cards can cope with higher speeds better. *Normal* is compatible with standard AT timing, and wait states are in addition to that.

ISA write insert w/s

If your ISA card doesn't like the write cycles on the bus, you can extend the timing here.

W/S in 32-bit ISA

Selects the 32-bit ISA cycle wait state. The lower the number the better the performance.

16 Bit ISA I/O Command

Determine the number of wait states between back-to-back I/O to 16-bit ISA devices.

16 Bit ISA Mem Command

The wait states between back-to-back memory reads or writes to 16-bit ISA devices.

AT Bus Clock Source

The AT bus clock is an output clock for the I/O channel. This allows you to change the *access speed* of the (ISA) bus, which should be between 6-8.33 MHz to be compatible with AT specifications (not that any were officially issued), so if your motherboard or PCI bus is running at 33 MHz, divide this by 4 (CLKIN/4, or PCI/4) for memory rated at 70 ns. Choosing *Autosync* sets this item based on the CPU clock speed. Only valid when *Auto Config* is disabled. A 16-bit card run too fast may revert to 8-bit mode.

ATCLK Stretch

Stops the I/O bus clock when there is no activity on the bus. ATCLK is used if the bus is asynchronous.

Bus Clock Selection

As for *ATCLK Stretch*.

ISA Bus Speed

As for *ATCLK Stretch*, but for PCI Pentiums. What speeds you get for the compatible and enhanced selections depends on the CPU speed:

CPU Speed	Compatible	Enhanced
60	7.5	10
66	8.25	16

Bus Mode

You can set the bus to run synchronously or asynchronously with the CPU. When synchronous, the bus will run at a speed in sympathy with the CPU clock, e.g. 33 MHz=CLKIN/4.Fast AT Cycle

Similar to *Bus Mode*, in that it affects wait states. It may speed up transfer rates if enabled.

ISA IRQ

To let PCI cards know which IRQs are in use by ISA cards so the Plug and Play system doesn't use them.

Master Mode Byte Swap

Only for bus mastering cards, such as SCSI controllers and fast network cards, and affects transfers from the bus master to 8-bit peripherals; *Low*, then *High* and back again. Normally disabled.

DMA clock source

The DMA controllers allow certain peripherals to access memory directly (hence *Direct Memory Access*). Usually, only the floppy controller uses it, but tape streamers, network cards and SCSI adapters might, amongst others. This setting selects the source for the DMA clock, which runs at ∫the bus clock speed (e.g. ATCLK/2). Maximum is usually 5 MHz.

DMA Wait States

Affects the number of wait states inserted before DMA commands are executed. Often appears separately for 8 and 16-bit transfers (as 8 is used for floppy transfers, adjusting the 16-bit variety doesn't affect them). In general, slower cards may require more DMA wait states. DMA settings often affect reliability rather than performance. For low CPU speeds (<= 25 MHz, this should be 0; otherwise set to 1).

DMA Command Width

You can compress the "normal" DMA transfer cycle of 4 clocks to 3 with this setting.

MEMR# Signal

Concerning DMA transfers, you can set the MEMORY READ control signal to start one clock cycle earlier than normal with this setting. Affects reliability.

MEMW# Signal

As above, but for the MEMORY WRITE signal.

DMA Address/Data Hold Time

"During the DMA/Master cycle, address and data from the X or S-buses are latched and held to local bus-DRAM/CACHE RAM operation". I haven't a clue what that means, but the X-bus is the peripheral bus where the support chips are located (e.g. 82C206 or equivalent), and the S-bus is the expansion bus. Perhaps it means that when DMA mode is operative, data in the local bus, cache or DRAM is held where it is. Latch is techie-speak for "read".

DMA MEMR Assertion Delay

Whether the signal to write to memory is delayed by a cycle from the signal to read the I/O port during DMA operations. This affects reliability and should normally be left alone.

I/O Recovery Time Delay

The AT Bus uses wait states to increase the width of an AT BUS cycle, for slower-reacting expansion cards, and this refers to the delay *before* starting Input/Output cycles. The lower the value, the better the performance, but you might have to change DMA settings as well.

I/O Recovery Select

As for *I/O Recovery Time Delay*.

AT Bus Precharge Wait State

Set to 0 for best performance, but you may need 1 for some devices, such as the AHA 1542B, at high speeds.

I/O Cmd Recovery Control

If enabled, a minimum of 7 bus clocks will be inserted *between* any 2 back-to-back I/O commands. This helps with problematic expansion cards and can affect ROM wait states, DMA and bus timing. Disable this, or set to *Normal* or the lowest figure available for best performance. Also known as *Timing Parameter Selection*.

Single ALE Enable

If enabled, single instead of multiple ALEs (see below) will be activated during data bus access cycles. *Yes* is compatible with AT bus specifications, with less performance. This sometimes appears in older BIOSes as *Quick Mode*, and you might see *Extended ALE* instead of *Multiple*. May slow the video if enabled, or you might get missing characters on screen.

ALE stands for *Address Latch Enable*, a signal used by 808x processors while moving data inside the memory map; it is used by DMA controllers to tell the CPU it can move data along the data bus, or that a valid address is posted. Conversely, they can stop this signal and make the CPU wait while data is moved by the controller, so set to *No* for normal use.

When the CPU wants data, it places the addresses it wants to look at on the bus, followed by a control signal to let the memory controller know the address is there, which then latches the address, decodes it and puts what the CPU wants on the bus, where it can be latched in turn by the CPU (*latch* means *read*).

E0000 ROM belongs to AT BUS

Officially, the E000 area of upper memory is reserved for System BIOS code, together with F000, but many machines don't use it, so E000 can often be used for other purposes (note, however, that this 64K is needed to run protected mode software, such as OS/2, or Multiuser DOS, which loads Advanced BIOS code into it). This will only tend to appear on older machines, as PCI needs it too.

This determines whether access to the E area of upper memory is directed to the system board, or to the AT bus. Set *Yes* if you want to use it for anything (e.g. a page frame or a Boot ROM), or if you're using Multiuser DOS and want the maximum TPA to be available. Can also turn up as *E000 ROM Addressable*.

Internal MUX Clock Source

Mux means *Multiplex*. Controls the frequency of polling the IRQ, DRQ and IOCHCK# signals. Sometimes this has an AUTO setting which sets the frequency according to CPU speed, but usually SCLK/1 is recommended. I don't think it refers to *Memory, Upper* and *XMS* specified in some operating systems, like Novell DOS 7.

Fast Decode Enable

According to one motherboard manual, DRAM access is speeded up if this is enabled. Possibly ignored if internal/external cache is present.

Fast CPU Reset

See *Fast Decode Enable*.

Extended I/O Decode

In (8-bit) ISA systems, ten address lines are normally used for I/O address decoding, that is, in ports 000-03FF. If your motherboard uses more, enable this for better performance to get 0000-FFFF. Some cards can use the same lower 10 bits by accident, in which case enable this. Otherwise, leave it (more in *Base I/O Address* in *Expansion Cards*).

Local Bus Ready Delay 1 Wait

Mostly disable this in systems running at 33 MHz or below, but some VL-bus devices may need 1 wait state anyway. You may need to enable this (i.e. insert 1 wait state) if running at 50 MHz.

Local Bus Ready

Selects the timing the system will use to exchange data with a VL-bus device after it has signalled that it is ready. The choices are:

Synchronize	Synchronize in the next clock (default).
Transparent	Enable the exchange immediately.

Local Bus Latch Timing

Specifies the time period in the AT machine cycle when the VL-bus is latched (read), so data can be transferred reliably, that is, to hold data stable during transactions with the local bus, the local bus will be latched after a read command and before the end of the AT cycle. This item allows you to determine how long the system will wait to latch the bus after the read command has gone inactive.

Use *T2* (2 clocks) for 25/33 MHz, or *T3* (3 clocks) for 40/50 MHz. T2 is earlier in the cycle than T3.

Latch Local Bus

See *Local Bus Latch Timing*.

ADS Delay

Concerns the local bus. If set to enabled, it affects performance; the default is disabled, or no delay. ADS# is a bus control signal, or an *Address Status* strobe driven by the CPU to indicate the start of a CPU bus cycle. It indicates that a valid command and address is stable on the bus. When enabled, more time will be allocated for ADS; you would only need this if a faster processor has been added.

CPU ADS# Delay 1T or Not

With a CPU clock is 50Mhz, choose *Delay 1T*. Otherwise, disable. Probably only for BIOSes that support PS/2 mice.

Fast Programmed I/O Mode

Controls the speed at which Programmed I/O (PIO) transfers occur on the PCI IDE interface. If disabled, Mode 0 (e.g. unoptimised) is used, so only use this if a device cannot function with advanced timings.

IDE Multi Block Mode

Enables suitably configured IDE hard drives to transfer multiple sectors per interrupt, as opposed to one (there may be an option to specify the number of sectors), using the ATA Read Multiple and Write Multiple commands. Setting 16 saves 1920 (2048-128) interrupts .

This is to avoid situations where the CPU can take some time to reply to an interrupt. There are several modes available, often dependent on the size of your hard disk cache.

The first three, 0-2, are from the old ATA standard. The others (3 and 4) are ATA-2 specific and use the IORDY line to slow the interface down if necessary. Interfaces without proper IORDY support may cause data corruption, so don't expect to mix two drives with different modes on the same channel.

If you must mix, and you get problems, force each drive to its proper mode.

Mode 0	Standard Mode; conforms to original PC standard and is compatible with all drives. Single sectors transferred with interrupts.
Mode 1	Polls the drive to see if it's ready to transfer data (no interrupts).
Mode 2	Groups of sectors are transferred in a single burst.
Mode 3	Uses 32-bit instructions, up to 11.1 Mb/sec.
Mode 4	Up to 16.7 Mb/sec. Two versions; the second supports 32-bit transfer, possibly to cope with 32-bit disk access.
Mode 5	Up to 20 Mb/sec, but now abandoned in favour of Ultra DMA, due to electrical noise.

This can mess up comms software when up- or downloading, because multi block transfers cannot be interrupted, and you may lose characters. For example, you need to run **telix** with the D option (e.g. drop DTR when writing to disk), or use buffered UARTS for terminals with Multiuser DOS. Consider disabling Smartdrive. The T I Chipset has problems with this as well, due to its plumbing arrangements; it gets its timing from the PCI clock, with a minimum (fastest) cycle of 5 clocks, so the maximum transfer rates achievable are:

PCI Clock (MHz)	Transfer Rate (Mb/sec)
25	10
30	12
33	13.3

There is also a reliability problem, and you will probably get data corruption if you try and get more than 11 Mb/sec or so with Mode 4, so the MR BIOS doesn't select rates beyond that automatically. If you're allowed to set block sizes, the FAT system seems to like them the same as the cluster size, and as what's best for the drive is not necessarily best for the system as a whole, check this with a high level benchmark, that is, at application level.

Quantum have a document called *ATA Signal Integrity Issues* that explains more.

IDE Block Mode Transfer

As for *IDE Multi Block Mode*.

Multi-Sector Transfers

As for *IDE Multi Block Mode*, allowing you the choice of 2, 4, 8 or 16 sectors. An *auto* setting queries the drive and allows it to set itself.

IDE Multiple Sector Mode

If *IDE Multi Block Mode* (or similar) is enabled, this sets the number of sectors per burst. Setting 64 gives the largest size your drive supports. Watch this with comms; when multiple sectors are being transferred, they can't be interrupted, so you may lose characters if you don't have buffered UARTS. see "IDE Multi Block Mode" on page 85

Multiple Sector Setting

As for *IDE Multi Block Mode*. The number of sectors transferred per interrupt. If disabled, an interrupt will be generated for each sector transferred. You get a choice of 4, 8 or AUTO.

IDE (HDD) Block Mode

Makes multi-sector transfers, as opposed to single-sector transfers, or reads and writes using large blocks of data rather than single bytes. It affects the number of sectors that can be transferred per interrupt. Only appears in BIOSes dated approximately 08/08/93 or later.

IDE Primary Master PIO

Enables PIO mode, as opposed to DMA.

IDE DMA Transfer Mode

The default is *Disabled* (=PIO), but you have the choice of:

> *Type B* (for EISA).

> *F* or *Standard* (PCI) as well (EIDE supports B/F, for 8.53-13.33 Mb/sec).

Type F is an 8.33 MHz EISA-style PCI DMA (normal is 5 MHz) for PCI/ISA, which replaces EISA type C, although A and B type transfers are supported. C is a burst mode that needs special controller logic. However, with F, you cannot DMA into ISA memory, only PCI, and neither does Type F apply to PCI bus mastering.

The Standard setting is the same as *Disabled*, but you can set the number of sectors per burst (see below). Type F is fastest, but there may be conflicts with multimedia. IDE CD ROM drives require Standard or Disabled.

Channel 0 DMA Type F

What DMA channel the *first drive* (0) in the system uses when set to F (see *IDE DMA Transfer Mode*). Choices are *Disabled* (no drive capable), *0, 1, 2,* or *3*.

Channel 1 DMA Type F

As for *Channel 0 DMA Type F,* but for the second drive.

ISA IRQ 9,10,11

These may be used by the PCI bus if they are available, so set them as *Used* if you want to reserve them.

Onboard CMD IDE Mode 3

Found where CMD Enhanced IDE chipsets are built in to the motherboard. The code is kept in a ROM at E800, and this setting allows access to it. Enable for best performance, as the code will still be used to optimise hard disk useage, with 32-bit I/O, even if it is not compatible with Mode 3.

> **NOTE:** There are considerable problems with many PCI motherboards and CMD controllers, especially with true 32-bit operating systems, where subtle changes are made to your files; that is, bytes are randomly changed once in a while. The problems also appear with Windows for Workgroups in 32-bit mode during floppy backup and restore.

More information from **http://tcp.ca/Nov95/PCIController.html.**

IDE Translation Mode

For using large IDE drives. Disable for smaller drives below 528 Mb. Choices are:

Standard CHS	(Cylinders, Heads, Sector)—limit is 528 Mb.
LBA	Logical Block Addressing; both BIOS and drive must support it. CHS addresses are used to create a 28-bit Logical Block Address rather than being mapped separately; in short, LBA sequentially assigns unique numbers to sectors, which are not necessarily in the same place if the drive is used on another machine.
Extended CHS	Similar to LBA, but not quite. Also known as *Large*. Can better performance of LBA.

Different systems cope with the above in different ways; Unix does its own thing anyway, OS/2 2.1 can support them all, as can DOS and Windows, but if you're running Windows' 32-bit Disk Access, select *Standard CHS*, unless you have a version of **wdcddrv.386** that supports advanced geometries. OS/2 2.0 and Netware cannot support LBA. If set to *Auto Detect*, the BIOS will detect what the drive is capable of, not what it is formatted with. Your hard drive may require different input to the CMOS for each method. See also *Hard Disk (C and D)*.

IDE LBA Translations

See *IDE Translation Mode*.

LBA Mode Control

See *IDE Translation Mode*. Turns LBA on or off.

Large Disk DOS Compatibility

For drives greater than 528 Mb *not* using LBA. This and LBA are not supported by all operating systems (e.g. UNIX R3.2.4).

IDE 32-bit Transfer

Many local bus interfaces can combine two 16-bit words into a 32-bit doubleword when reading data to and from the disk, particularly useful with bus mastering. This is often called *32-bit access*, though it's really 32-bit host bus transfers. Either way, more efficient use is made of the bus and CPU, so this may or may not make much difference if you don't actually have a bottleneck. This is not the same as Windows' 32-bit features, which are also misnamed as they just work in protected mode.

If disabled, 16-bit data transfers are used, so performance will be less. If enabled, hard disk data is read twice before request signals are sent to the CPU. This setting can only be enabled if *IDE Prefetch Mode* is also enabled. As far as AMI are concerned, the WinBIOS will initialise the hard disk firmware for 32-bit I/O, assuming your hard disk is capable—it refers to the new release of high performance Mode 4 drives.

Enhanced ISA Timing

Gives higher bus speeds, set by manufacturer.

Back To Back I/O Delay

Inserts a slight pause in between 2 processes talking to the same I/O port.

DMA FLOW THRU Mode

Enable this if you enable write buffers to avoid inconsistencies; this makes the DMA wait until all write buffers are empty.

You won't increase performance by increasing the DMA clock by itself but, since it's often linked to the bus clock, will increase in sympathy with it. Generally, only floppies use DMA anyway, but some tape streamers and sound cards do.

Extended DMA Registers

DMA normally takes place within the first 16 Mb of address space on an AT. This setting allows you to use the whole 4 Gb of address space of a 32-bit processor.

Hard Disk Pre-Delay

POST procedures are quite fast these days. This setting delays the BIOS's attempts to initialise the first IDE drive in the system, so slower devices can have a chance to get their act together; some drives may hang if they are accessed too soon. Set this in conjunction with *Initialisation Timeout*. See also *Cold Boot Delay*.

Initialisation Timeout

The number of seconds the BIOS will wait to see if an IDE drive is there before proceeding. Works with *Hard Disk Pre-Delay*. If your drive doesn't respond within the specified period, the system will not recognize it.

Fast Programmed I/O Modes

Controls the speed at which Programmed I/O (PIO) transfers occur over the PCI IDE interface:

Disabled	Mode 0
Autodetect	Rated maximum of the drive

Only set disabled if a drive incorrectly reports its capabilities. Do not use mixed mode drives on the same channel; at least, don't let the BIOS on a board with a Triton chipset make its own decision, as it seems unable to handle two drives with separate EIDE rates; they share a common timing register. The MR BIOS can handle this better than most.

DMA Channel Select

Helps you change IRQ and DMA channels of a built-in SCSI controller.

Data Transfer

You have the following choices:

PIO   Polling mode; the CPU controls everything and fetches each byte from the controller through I/O addresses.

DMA   Transfer is done by DMA, which is faster when multitasking, as the CPU can get on with something else whilst data is being transferred. With ISA, this only works below 16 Mb.

Don't switch on DMA mode with a PIO device installed.

DMA Frequency Select

Sets the frequency at which DMA (Direct Memory Access) data transfers take place as a function of the system clock. Choices are:

SYSCLK/1   Enable one full system clock cycles
SYSCLK/2   Enable one-half system clock cycle (default)

Hold PD Bus

Sets the timeout function of the processor data bus, presumably before it assumes a malfunction. The default is 1-2T.

Local Device Syn. Mode

This concerns *Synchronous* and *Bypass* mode for the CPU's signal to terminate Local Bus cycles. Bypass mode, or *transparent mode*, gives better performance, but is limited to at or below 33 MHz because it is not compatible with VL bus expansion cards.

CACHEING

Disabling cacheing often cures obscure memory problems; it may be because non-32-bit address cycles are redirected to the AT Bus. Certainly, with cacheing enabled, only 32-bit cycles are affected, but *Hidden Refresh* is often automatic as well. Also, Shadow RAM is cached here. Be aware that some chipsets do more than just disable the cache when you select *Disable*. Cache SRAM can be tested in the same way as DRAM, except for Tag RAM, which cannot be written to directly, so there is a special access channel for testing. Data is written, read and checked for consistency. If this can be done in a certain time, say by the end of T2, it is likely to be Burst SRAM.

SRAM chips share a common data bus with other memory processor devices which need to control the bus at some time or other. If you minimise the cycle times for each, you get the maximum performance. *Bus contention* occurs when 2 devices are trying to use the bus at the same time. Any settings with regard to this therefore affect reliability.

Certain cycles are non-cacheable anyway, such as I/O cycles, interrupt acknowledge cycles, halt/shutdown cycles and some memory areas.

Cacheable cycles come in four varieties:

Read Hit means the system reads the data from the cache, therefore not needing to go to system memory.

Read Miss means the data is not in the cache, so it goes to system memory and will copy the same data to the cache.

Write Hit means the system writes the data the cache and main memory.

Write Miss means the system only writes the data to system memory.

Cache RAM (SRAM) Types

Here you can tell the machine what sort of level 2 cache RAM it has to deal with, *Pipeline*, *Burst* or *Synchronous*. They are fully described in the *Memory* section.

Pipeline Cache Timing

Two choices, *Faster* and *Fastest*, to suit the speed of your memory.

F000 Shadow Cacheable

When enabled, accesses to the System BIOS between F0000H-FFFFFH are cached, if the cache controller is enabled.

Fast Cache Read/Write

Usually used if you have two banks of external SRAM cache chips, that is, 64 or 256K. It's similar to Page Mode for DRAM.

Flush 486 cache every cycle

Enabled, flushes the internal 8K cache of the 486 every cycle, which seems to defeat the object somewhat. Disable this.

Async SRAM Leadoff Time

Sets the number of CPU clock cycles your asynchronous SRAM needs before each read from or write to the cache.

Sync SRAM Leadoff Time

Sets the number of CPU clock cycles your asynchronous SRAM needs before each read from or write to the cache.

Async SRAM Burst Time

Sets the timing for burst mode cache operations. The fewer the faster.

SRAM WriteTiming

Sets the timing, in CPU wait states, for writes to the external cache. 0 WS is the default.

Cache Read Hit Burst

Burst Mode is a 486 function for optimising memory fetches if you need to go off-chip, which works by reading groups of four double-words in quick succession, hence *burst*. The first cycle has to cope with the start address as well as its data, so it takes the longest (the other three addresses are deduced). Once the transfer has been started, 4 32-bit words could therefore move in only 5 cycles, as opposed to 8, by interleaving the address and data cycles after the first one. For this, you need fast RAM capable of *Page Mode*.

This setting determines the number of cycle times to be inserted when the CPU reads data from the external (level 2) cache, when it can't catch up with the CPU (you may see similar figures allocated to L1 cache, on chip). The *Secondary Cache Read Hit* can be set to 2-1-1-1, 3-1-1-1, 2-2-2-2 or 3-2-2-2 (3-1-1-1 means the first 32-bit word needs three clock cycles and the remainder need one, giving a total of 6 clock cycles for the operation).

Performance is affected most by the first value; the lower the better; 2-1-1-1 is fastest. You can alter it with the *Cache Read Hit 1st Cycle WS* setting. This will have no effect if all the code executes inside the chip.

For example, the setting for 33 MHz may need to be changed to 3-2-2-2 if you only have 128K, or with Asynchronous SRAM.

The following settings may be useful as a starting point (1 bank cache/2 banks cache):

Item	20 MHz	25 MHz	33 MHz	50 MHz
SRAM Read Burst Control	3222/2111	3222/2111	3222/3111	3222
SRAM Write Wait States	0W	0W	1/0W	1W
DRAM Write Wait States	0W	0W	1W	1W
DRAM Read Wait States	1W	2W	2W	3W
RAS# to CAS# Delay	1 Sysclk	1 Sysclk	1 Sysclk	2 Sysclk

Pentiums can perform Burst Writes as well as Burst Reads, so you might have a separate selection for these. 4-1-1-1 is usually recommended.

Cache Burst Read Cycle Time

See *Cache Read Hit Burst*. Automatically set to 2T if only one bank of level 2 cache is available, that is, the whole cycle takes place inside 2 T-states.

SRAM Read Timing

Similar to *Cache Read Hit Burst*. Relates the number of cycles taken for the SRAM address signal to the number of cycles allocated for the actual read. 2-1-1-1 is the default.

Burst SRAM Burst Cycle

This sets the precise timing of the burst mode read and write cycles to and from the external cache. Choices are:

4-1-1-1	Slower.
3-1-1-1	Fastest (Default).

Cache Mapping

Direct mapping is where data is loaded in one block. *N-way* is divided into *n*-banks (2-way, 4-way, etc). Further explained in the *Memory* chapter.

Data Pipeline

With reference to cache mapping above, after accessing DRAM for the first time, the data is stored in a pipeline. Enabling this is best for performance.

Cache Wait State

0 for best performance, but 1 may be required for VL bus devices at higher speeds. SRAM used for cacheing has a minimum access time requirement, otherwise you will get malfunctions. The trick is to use the least number of wait states that don't cause failures.

Cache Read Burst Mode

An Award setting, for 486s. See *Cache Wait State*.

Cache Write Burst Mode

An Award setting. See *Cache Wait State*, but delete *Read* and insert *Write*.

Cache Read Cycle

As for *Cache Wait State*.

Cache Read Wait State

Sets the number of wait states to be added on reads from cache memory, just in case you're using slow cache chips, or you wish to preserve data integrity. 1 wait state should be used for 40 MHz systems, and you can use 0 wait states at 33 MHz. Some VL bus devices need 1 wait state on 50 MHz systems.

Cache Write (Hit) Wait State

Sets the wait states to be added on writes to cache memory. 1 should be used for 40 MHz systems, and you can use 0 at 33 MHz. Some VL bus devices need 1 on 50 MHz systems.

CPU Cycle Cache Hit WS.

Normal	Refresh with normal CPU cycles.
Fast	Refresh without CPU cycles for CAS.

The second option saves a CPU cycle; see also *Hidden Refresh*.

Fast Cache Read Hit

Should be enabled if you have 64 or 256K of cache memory installed; otherwise it should be disabled.

Fast Cache Write Hit

See *Fast Cache Read Hit*.

Cache Tag Hit Wait States

This is similar to *Cache Read Wait States*, in that it allows you to set the number of wait states, 0 or 1, used to test for a cache tag hit.

Cache Scheme

Concerns the level 2 cache on the motherboard, between the CPU and memory, and whether it is to be *Write Back* (WB) or *Write Thru* (WT). The latter means that memory is updated with cache data every time the CPU issues a write cycle. Write Back causes main memory updates only under certain conditions, such as read requests to memory locations with contents currently in the cache. This allows the CPU to operate with fewer interruptions, increasing efficiency, but is not as safe in the event of power loss.

HITMJ Timing

For a write-back L1 cache, you can select the HITM# signal as inactive to the timing relating to IOCHRDY inactive. The choices are 2, 3, 4 or 6t. With only write-through, this cannot be used. 1t is equal to 1 CPU clock.

Internal Cache WB/WT

See *Cache Scheme*.

External Cache WB/WT

See *Cache Scheme*.

Cache Write Back

See *Cache Scheme*.

L2 Cache Write Policy

See *Cache Scheme*.

L1 Cache Write Policy

As for *Cache Scheme*, for L1 (internal) cache on the CPU.

L1 Cache Update Mode

See *Cache Scheme*.

L2 Cache Enable

When disabled, any cache addresses are regarded as misses, so the CPU talks directly to main memory; the effect is the same as not having it, as the cache is not actually turned off, and you just can't read from it. This is so that if it does become enabled, you can get coherent data immediately, as it is still being updated.

L2 Cache Zero Wait State

If you have a slower cache, disable this to have one wait state when accessing the external cache controller. When enabled, the chipset will not wait.

L2 Cache Cacheable Size

The size of the system memory the L2 cache has to cope with, for those motherboards that can take it. Up to 64 Mb or 512 Mb.

Linear Mode SRAM Support

Enable if you have an IBM/Cyrix CPU and linear mode SRAM, to get slightly better performance. Disable for Intel CPUs, as they only support Toggle Mode.

Cache Write Cycle

Affects the data hold time for writes to DRAM.

Posted Write Enable

A Posted Write Cache has "write buffers" that buffer data and write when things are quiet or, rather, when they don't interfere with reads. It's somewhere in between a write thru and write back cache. With write back, if the CPU writes a single byte to memory, and that address is in the L1 cache, the cache line with the newly written data is marked 'dirty' to indicate there is a difference between it and main memory. When the dirty cache line needs to be overwritten with newer information, the cache management routine uploads the new line (16 bytes) from lower memory, from which it cannot tell the new data, so it first writes all 16 bytes to memory, which can use as many as 18 clocks (6-4-4-4). Once the dirty line is written, the upload of the new line can begin. A good posted write system can accept the CPU write operation in a single clock, write the data to main memory when the bus is otherwise not in use, and never have to suffer the 18 clock penalty.

Write Back cache is therefore best when most or all of a line is made dirty and writes occur to addresses inside the cache system, which is not usual with multi-tasking and large active memory windows. Posted Write Buffers are typically used between PCI bus and IDE interface by decoupling the wait states effect from the slower IDE side. Read-ahead buffers eliminate idle cycles.

Posted I/O Write

Disable if using Multiuser DOS on an Intel Express.

Tag Ram Includes Dirty

Enabling this tells the system that the SRAM needed for the machine to remember that the level 2 cache and main memory contents are different is actually present on the motherboard (not often the case). If you can enable this, you will get about 10% extra performance, because unnecessary line replacement cycles can be eliminated (e.g. when you have to flush the old data then replace it with the new).

Tag RAM is used as a directory between main memory and cache RAM, storing the addresses of whatever data is in cache memory. The CPU checks TAG Ram for the address of any data it requires, which is how it knows it has to go to main memory if it's not there.

Some cache controllers support two methods of determining the state of data in the cache. One separates the tag signal from the alter (or dirty) signal, which imposes a minimal performance decrease, since the system must assume that some cache lines have been altered.

When the dirty and tag bits are combined, the system performs more efficiently, but less cache will be available (default).

Alt Bit Tag RAM

Choices are *7+1* or *8+0*. 7+1 is recommended. The Alt Bit means *Alter Bit*, or dirty bit, which indicates the particular line in L2 cache that contains modified data, so it keeps a note of the state of data in the cache. If you have selected *Write Back* for the external (L2) cache, 7+1 bits (the default) provides better error detection. With 8+0 Bits, the Alt bit is always assumed active.

Tag Option

If you have WB (*Write Back*) for L2 cache, 7 + 1 provides better error detection.

Non-cacheable Block-1 Size

Depending on the chipset, this concerns memory regions (including ROMs) *not* within the 32-bit memory space, e.g. those on 16-bit expansion cards *on the expansion bus* (video cards, cacheing disk controllers, etc) that should not be cached because RAM on them is updated by the card itself, and the main board cache controller can't tell if the contents change. These devices communicate as if they were DRAM memory (that is, they are *memory-mapped*), which means they need to react in real time and would be seriously affected by cacheing. You would also use this to lock out any ROMs you can't otherwise disable cacheing for; certain cacheing IDE controllers use a space at the top end of base memory for hard disk details, and therefore cause timing problems if the information is cached; symptoms include consistent bad sectors when formatting floppies, or a scrambled hard disk.

Also, video cards sometimes use a 1 Mb area in the 16 Mb address space of the ISA bus so they don't have to bank switch through the usual 64K page (early Video Blaster cards are notable for this requirement; they won't work in a machine with more than 15 Mb RAM).

You might get a choice of *System Bus* or *Local DRAM*. The former produces a hole in Local DRAM. NCB areas can be separate, contiguous or overlapped. With Asustek cache controllers, include the video buffer at A000-BFFF. This setting is closely linked to the next.

> **NOTE:** Some chipsets (e.g. SiS) use this to define non-cacheable regions *only in local DRAM*; with them, memory on PCI or VESA add-ons is *always* non-cacheable. Where memory space is occupied by both local DRAM and an add-on card, the local DRAM will take priority (as does VESA over PCI), so disable this to allow access or give priority to the card.

Non-cacheable Block-1 Base

The base address of the above block must be a multiple number of its size; e.g. if 512K was selected above, the starting address should be a multiple of 512K. In other words, if the previous option has a number other than *Disable*, this option will increment by that number.

Non-cacheable Block-2 Size

Can be 64K-16 Mb; otherwise, as above.

Non-cacheable Block-2 Base

See *Non-cacheable Block-2 Size*.

Memory above 16 Mb Cacheable

See *Cacheable RAM Address Range*.

Cacheable RAM Address Range

Memory is cached only up to the 16 or 32 Mb boundaries to reduce the bits that need to be saved. The lower the setting here, the better, corresponding to your main memory; that is, if you have 4 Mb, set 4 Mb. This memory is cached into SRAM.

XXXX Memory Cacheable

Some shadowed memory segments (e.g. starting at address C800) can be cached (or not). However, cacheing certain code (video or ROM BIOS) is sometimes inefficient because it is constantly updated, and you may get "cache thrash", where data feeds on itself in a circular fashion as new data constantly replaces the old. Also, certain programs that depend on timing loops could run too fast. Where you can select Associativity, you can improve on the normal direct mapped cache, where alternating references are made to main memory cells that map to the same cache cell, and all attempts to use the cache therefore result in misses.

Associativity concerns the amount of blocks that the cache memory is split into. For example, a *4-Way Set Associative* cache is in four blocks, and is used as four locations in which different parts of main memory are cached at the same time; a lot to keep track of. Its performance yield is not normally enough over a 2 Way Set to justify its use. Direct mapping is known as 1-way Associativity. Non-cacheable regions set elsewhere (above) override this.

C000 Shadow Cacheable

See *XXXX Memory Cacheable*.

Video BIOS Area cacheable

See *XXXX Memory Cacheable*. Only valid when *Video BIOS Shadow* is enabled, in which case the shadowed BIOS code will be cacheable. Be prepared to say No for an accelerator card which does its own thing, as the CPU needs to be kept informed of its activities, and if you have write-back cacheing enabled, your video won't be updated properly because the data will not reach the video board until the cache line it's in needs flushing).

Video RAM Cacheable

See above.

Shadow RAM cacheable

Not often a good idea, this, as the data often ends up in the internal cache of the CPU. Disable for safety, though it might work.

SRAM Speed Option

The speed of standard SRAM cache during normal read/. Similar to *DRAM Speed*.

SRAM Burst R/W Cycle

The speed of the SRAM burst read/write cycles. The lower figure is fastest.

Cache Early Rising

Whether your computer wakes up before you do! Seriously, this allows you to select the fast write-pulse rising edge technique of writing to the external cache over the normal timing, which is faster. Use this to cope with older DRAMs.

Enable	Write pulse on the rising edge (Default)
Disabled	Normal write pulse to the cache

VESA L2 Cache Write

Allows you to set the timing of writes from the VESA bus to the external cache. Using a long cycle gives you greater system stability, but you lose some performance.

Normal	VESA to cache writes handled normally (Default)
Long	Longer timing used in VESA to cache writes

VESA L2 Cache Read

See *VESA L2 Cache Write.*

1MB Cache Memory

Informs the system that a larger than usual L2 cache is present.

L2 Cache Tag Bits

Cache tag bits report the status of data in the cache. Here, select the number of bits used.

8 Bits	Eight tag bits (Default)
7 Bits	Seven tag bits

L2 (WB) Tag Bit Length

See *L2 Cache Tag Bits.*

SRAM Type

Which type, *Async* or *Synchronous*, is installed.

SYNC SRAM Support

If synchronous cache memory is installed, this setting allows you to specify whether it is the standard synchronous or less expensive pipelined SRAM.

Tag/Dirty Implement

One way of checking the state of data in the cache separates the tag from the dirty signal, while the other combines them into a single 8- or 9-bit signal.

Combine	Tag and Dirty combined (default)
Separate	Tag and Dirty signals are separate

Dirty pin selection

When *Combine* is selected above, this lets you choose which pin the dirty data is tied to.

I/O means Bi-directional input/output (default)

IN means Input only

Shortened 1/2 CLK2 of L2 cache

Working on this.

Cache Memory Data Buffer

Activate half T state earlier when a cache hit is made during a read cycle. Enable if your system runs faster than 33 MHz.

Cache Cycle Check

L2 cache checkpoint for hit or miss.

MEMORY

RAM is organised into rows and columns, and is accessed by electrical signals called *strobes*, which are sent along rows to the columns; when data is needed, the CPU activates the RAS (*Row Access Strobe*) line to specify the row in memory where the data is to be found (high bits). Then the CAS, or *Column Access Strobe*, specifies the column (low bits). The combination of RAS and CAS therefore specifies a particular RAM location in a particular RAM chip, where they intersect. Unfortunately, a lot of time is taken up with transferring these values rather than data. Rather than have separate pins providing power and data for both, each pin does double duty, serving rows or columns according to whether the RAS or the CAS pin is being asserted (that is, receiving current). Your system will operate most efficiently when the RAS and CAS timings are optimized, but you lose stability as speed is gained. With *page mode*, any column of DRAMS in a row can be accessed any number of times within a short period; since the row is already specified, only the CAS needs to be applied on subsequent memory accesses, making things quicker.

RAS and CAS are measured in nanoseconds; the lower value, the faster the RAM can be accessed, so the T state delay is similar to wait states. The RAS access time is actually the speed rating marked on the chip; CAS access time is around 50% less. Generally, choose the same speed for DRAM reading and writing, with as few wait states as possible. Burst cycles work the same way as they do for SRAM, consisting of four figures, with the first being larger because that's where the address is read; the remaining figures indicate the clock cycles for the reading of data. They might look like this on the screen:

x222/x333

The first set would be for EDO and the second for Fast Page Mode RAM. The 430 HX chipset can use lower figures than the VX. The idea is to keep the figures as low as possible, consistent with your machine working properly. Note that EDO is only faster when being read from; writes take place at the same speed as FPM RAM.

RAS# To CAS# Delay

Adds a delay between the assertion of RAS# and CAS#. In other words, this allows you to set the time it takes to move between RAS and CAS, or insert a timing delay between them. Reads, writes or refreshes will therefore take slightly longer, but you get more reliability.

Add Extra Wait for RAS#

Same as above.

Add Extra Wait for CAS#

Same as above.

DRAM (Read/Write) Wait States

Sets the cycles the CPU should be idle for whilst memory is being refreshed, such as 1 W/S if using 80 nanosecond DRAMs (for 40 MHz machines, 2 is suggested). This won't affect performance with internal or external cache memory. A rule of thumb is :

$$\text{Wait States} = \frac{\text{ns} + 10 \times \text{Clock Speed}}{1000} - 2$$

So:

$$.97 = \frac{80 + 10 \times 33}{1000} - 2$$

gives you (almost) 1 wait state for 80 ns RAM at 33 MHz. For machines with clock-doubled CPUs, you should use the motherboard speed. This chart should be a useful starting point:

CPU	Write	Read	Speed (ns)
386DX-25/33/40	1	2	80
	0	1	70
	0	0	60
485-20/25	0	2	80
	0	1	70
	0	0	60
486DX-33/DX2-50	1	2	80
	0	1	70
	0	0	60
486DX-50/DX2-66	1	3	80
	0	2	70
	0	1	60

Actually, wait states are *additional* to those built in by the motherboard manufacturer. 0 wait states probably means 6, so 1 would mean you get 7. Each wait state adds about 30ns to the RAM access cycle here. Theoretically, 9-chip 30-pin SIMMs are faster, because it can be marginally longer getting data from the 4-bit chips on the 3-chip variety. Windows has been known to work with less GPFs when running on 9-chip SIMMs. Certainly, never mix them in the same bank.

Memory Read Wait State

You can use slower DRAMs by inserting wait states (e.g. use 1 wait state for chips rated at 80ns at 33 MHz). This setting concerns the number of wait states inserted between DRAM write operations.

Memory Write Wait State

As for *Memory Write Wait State*.

DRAM Burst Write Mode

Enabled is best for performance.

DRAM Read Burst Timing

Of burst data transfers to and from DRAM. Similar to *Cache Read Hit Burst*. With EDO, select x222 for best performance.

DRAM Read Burst (B/E/P)

The timing for burst mode reads from DRAM, depending on the type of DRAM on a per-row basis (Burst/EDO/Page) The lower the timing numbers, the faster the system addresses memory, so select higher numbers for slower memory. With EDO, select x222 for best performance.

DRAM Write Burst (B/E/P)

See DRAM Read Burst (B/E/P).

DRAM Read /FPM

Sets the timing for burst mode reads according to your type of memory, EDO or Fast Page Mode. With EDO, select x222 for best performance.

FP Mode DRAM Read WS

This configures the exact timing of the read cycle from Fast Page (FP) mode memory. The timing consists of an address cycle (leadoff), where the location of the read to take place is indicated, and three data cycles, where the data is actually read. The shorter each phase (or cycle) is, the better the performance, but you will lose data if you don't allow enough time for each cycle. Choices are:

7-3-3-3
7-2-2-2
6-3-3-3
6-2-2-2 Default

Try the lowest figures first till your machine is running successfully.

DRAM Write Burst Timing

See *FP Mode DRAM Read WS*.

DRAM Speed

Set CPU speed instead of tinkering with RAS/CAS timings (these are for 100ns chips; push it a bit with faster ones). There may also be a *Normal* setting, which seems to be automatic.

Fastest	25 MHz (25/33 with Award)
Faster	33 MHz (40/50 with Award)
Slower	40 MHz
Slowest	50 MHz

Here's a comparison chart that may give you a good start:

CPU	DRAM Speed	Write CAS Width	Cache Write	Cache Read	BUSCLK
486SX-20	Fastest	1T	2T	1T	1/5
486SX-25	Fastest	1T	2T	1T	1/3
486DX2-50	Fastest	1T	2T	1T	1/3
486DX-33	Faster	1T	3T	2T	1/4
486DX2-66	Faster	1T	3T	2T	1/4
486DX-50	Slowest	2T	3T	2T	1/6

Notice that the higher the chip speed is, the more the wait states.

DRAM Timing Option

See *DRAM Speed*.

DRAM Timing

The speed of the RAM in your system. With Award, the choices are 60 or 70 ns. What you set here affects the settings for *Auto Configuration*.

DRAM Post Write

An Award setting. Still working on it, but see *Posted Write Enable*.

Fast DRAM

The system expects memory to run at the fastest speed—if you have mixed speed SIMMs, you might experience data loss. Disable this to use slower timing for all access to DRAM.

DRAM Last Write to CAS#

Sets how much time (or how many cycles) will elapse between the time when the last data has been signalled to when CAS# is asserted. This time is used as setup time for the CAS signal. Choices are 2 (default), 3 or 4.

DRAM Write Page Mode

Enabled, RAS is not generated during a page hit in page mode, so a cycle is eliminated and makes things faster as more data is written at once.

DRAM Code Read Page Mode

Affects access speeds when program code is being executed, based on its sequential character, so enabling page mode here will be more efficient, to allow the CPU to access DRAM more efficiently during read cycles. If your code is not sequential, you may be better off without this enabled.

Page Code Read

See *DRAM Write Page Mode*.

DRAM RAS# Precharge Time

See *FP DRAM CAS Prec. Timing*.

FP DRAM CAS Prec. Timing

The number of CPU clock cycles for CAS to accumulate its charge before FP DRAM is allowed to recharge. The lower figure is best for performance, but if you don't allow enough time, you could lose data.

FP DRAM RAS Prec. Timing

See *FP DRAM CAS Prec. Timing*.

DRAM CAS# Hold Time

Sets the number of cycles between when RAS# is signalled and CAS# is asserted. Choices are 4, 5, 6 (default) and 7.

CAS Address Hold Time

Sets how long it will take to change the CAS address after CAS has been initiated (asserted) and aimed at a target address (location) in DRAM. Choices are 1 or 2 (default) cycles.

Read CAS# Pulse Width

How long the CAS remains asserted for a DRAM read cycle. Choices are 2, 3 (default), 4 or 5 cycles. The same effect as wait states.

Write CAS# Pulse Width

How long the CAS remains asserted for a DRAM write cycle. Choices are 2 (default), 3, 4 or 5 cycles. The same effect as wait states.

EDO CAS Pulse Width

The number of CPU cycles the CAS signal pulses during EDO DRAM reads and writes, when memory is not interleaved.

EDO CAS Precharge Time

See *FPDRAM CAS Prec. Time*.

EDO RAS Precharge Time

The number of CPU clock cycles for RAS to accumulate its charge before EDO DRAM is allowed to recharge. The lower figure is best for performance, but if you don't allow enough time, you could lose data.

EDO RAS# to CAS# Delay

Enabled, adds a delay between the assertion of RAS# and CAS# (slower but more stable).

EDO MDLE Timing

Memory Data Read Latch Enable timing when EDO is read. Sets the CPUCLK signal delay from the CAS pulse. 1 is fastest, but 2 is more stable.

EDO BRDY# Timing

When the *Burst Ready Active* signal is low, the presented data is valid during a burst cycle. 1 is fastest, 2 is more stable.

EDO RAMW# Power Setting

RAMW# is an active low output signal that enables local DRAM writes. This setting lets you enable RAMW# power-saving mode when an EDO bank is being accessed.

EDO DRAM Read Burst

The timing you set here depends on the type of DRAM you have in each row. Use slower rates (bigger numbers) for slower DRAM.

EDO DRAM Write Burst

The timing you set here depends on the type of DRAM you have in each row. Use slower rates (bigger numbers) for slower DRAM.

EDO Read Wait State

Use this only if your system has EDO (*Extended Data Out*) DRAM, to configure the exact timing of the read cycle. The timing is composed of an address cycle (leadoff), for the location of the read, and three cycles where the data is actually read.

The shorter each phase (or cycle) is, the faster the system is operating, but if not enough time is allowed for each cycle, data will be lost. Choices are 7-2-2-2 (default) and 6-2-2-2.

Fast EDO Path Select

When enabled, a fast path is selected for CPU-to-DRAM read cycles for the leadoff, assuming you have EDO RAM. It causes a 1-HCLK pull-in for all read leadoff latencies (that is, page hits, page and row misses). *Enabled* is best for performance.

DRAM CAS Timing Delay

Sets *No CAS delay* (default) or *1 T state delay*. Use this only if you're using slow DRAMs. It's often ignored anyway if cache is enabled.

DRAM RAS# Active

Controls whether RAS# is actually activated after CAS; *Deassert* means not, which increases performance by saving a CPU cycle. The latter makes each DRAM cycle a Row miss.

Assert will be asserted after every DRAM cycle

Deassert will be deasserted after every DRAM cycle

DRAM R/W Burst Timing

Allows DRAM read and write bursts to have their timings coordinated.

Burst read and write requests are generated by the CPU in four parts, the first (leadoff) providing the location, and the remainder providing the data. The lower the timing numbers, the faster memory is addressed.

X444/X444 read and write DRAM timings are X-4-4-4

X444/X333 Read timing = X-4-4-4, write timing = X-3-3-3

X333/X333 read and write DRAM timings are X-3-3-3

Try the lowest figures first, until your machine is running successfully.

RAS Precharge Time

The Row Access Strobe is used to refresh or write to DRAM. The precharge time is the time taken for internal recovery of the chip before the next access, or when the system gets up enough power to do the refresh, about the same as the RAM access time, so use that as an estimate to start off with. If there is not enough time, you won't get a proper refresh, and you may lose data.

This determines the number of CPU clocks for RAS to accumulate a charge before DRAM is refreshed. If you have a 33 MHz CPU or higher, set this to 4, but try a lower number if your CPU is slower (e.g. 2 for 25 MHz, so as not to waste time), reducing idle time, unless your DRAMs can't operate with a lower figure anyway. Often ignored if cache is enabled.

RAS Precharge In CLKS

An Award Setting. Sets the length of time required to build up enough charge to refresh RAS memory. Choices are 3, 4, 5 or 6. Lower figures are best for performance.

CAS Precharge In CLKS

An Award Setting. As above, but for CAS.

CAS# width to PCI master write

The pulse width of CAS# when the PCI master writes to DRAM. Lower figures are best for performance.

RAS Active Time

Controls the maximum time that DRAMs are kept activated by increasing the *Row Access Strobe* (RAS) cycle, meaning that a row can be kept open for more than one access, allowing more column access in that time. The higher the figure, the better the performance.

105

Row Address Hold In CLKS

An Award setting, for the length of time in CPU cycles to complete a RAS refresh. A CLK is a single CPU clock tick, so the more you use here, the slower your machine will perform.

RAS Pulse Width In CLKS

The length of the RAS pulse refresh. Choices are between 4-6 CLKs, and the higher the number, the slower your machine will be.

CAS Read Width In CLKS

An Award Setting. Sets the number of CPU cycles required to read from DRAM using Column Address Sequence (CAS) logic. Choices are 2 or 3.

CAS Write Width In CLKS

Award Setting. As above, for write cycles.

Late RAS Mode

Controls the generation of an earlier RAS signal during memory accesses, extending the length of the RAS signal so you can use slower TAG RAM. It could also mean *RAS after CAS* (see below).

RAS Timeout Feature

For DRAMs that need a 10 microsecond maximum RAS-active time. If timeout is enabled, RAS is not allowed to remain low for longer than about 9.5 microseconds. Otherwise, it is limited to a maximum of about 15 microseconds. Affects reliability; disabled is the default.

RAS to CAS delay time

The amount of time after which a CAS# will be succeeded by a RAS# signal, or the time delay between Row Address Strobe and Column Address Strobe, to allow for the transition. Performance is best with lower figures at the expense of stability.

RAS(#) To CAS(#) Delay

As for *RAS to CAS delay time*. When DRAM is refreshed, rows and columns are addressed separately. This allows you to set the time it takes to move between RAS and CAS, or insert a timing delay between them. The unit of measurement is a CPU cycle. The shorter the better for performance.

2T	Two cycles
4T	Four cycles (Default)
6T	Six cycles

DRAM write push to CAS delay

The number of cycles needed by DRAM to force the CAS to slow down (delay) to match DRAM timing specifications.

CAS Before RAS

A technique for reducing refresh cycles, to help the CPU along. Also good for power consumption. CAS is dropped first, then RAS, with one refresh cycle being performed each time RAS falls. The powersaving occurs because an internal counter is used, not an external address, and the address buffers are powered down.

DRAM Write CAS Pulse Width

See *DRAM Head Off Timing*.

DRAM Head Off Timing

7/5 or 8/6. See *DRAM Leadoff Timing*.

Turbo Read Leadoff

Sometimes needed for faster memory, and disabled by default. The book *Enabled* shortens the leadoff cycles and optimizes performance in cacheless, 50-60 MHz, or 1-bank EDO systems, but it is known to speed up those with a 512K Level 2 Cache and 2 banks of EDO (2X16, 2X32 Mb SIMMs), especially when copying data, such as when backing up a hard drive. However, after a few hours of use, errors started in applications and when loading data from the hard drive, especially when switching between applications. Suggest enable this for games, but disable for important work.

CAS Width in Read Cycle

Determines the number of wait states when the CPU reads data into the local DRAM, in T states. The lower the figure, the better the performance.

Read-Around-Write

For DRAM optimisation; if a memory read is addressed to a location whose latest write is being held in a buffer before being written to memory, the read is allowed to be satisfied from the buffer instead of memory, as the information will be more up to date.

Read Around Write

Similar to the above, enabling the Memory Controller on an Orion chipset to let read operations bypass writes as long as their memory addresses don't match. In other words, priority is given to reads, except when they have the same address as a write, in which case the write is done first so the read gets the most up to date information. Found on a Pentium Pro. Enabled increases performance slightly, but visibly, at the expense of some stability.

F000 UMB User Info

Found with MR, lets you know what's going on in the F000-FFFF range usually occupied by System ROM. The first 32K can often be used for UMBs as it is only used on startup.

BIOS	FC14-FFFF
UTILS	FBAA-FC13
POST	F787-FBA9
SETUP	F1C0-F786
AVAIL	F000-FBA9

The above is information you feed to your memory manager so it can make the best use of what's available. You can't reassign the BIOS area, and you should leave the UTILS section alone, because various hot key and cache functions are kept there. POST and SETUP only contain power up and boot code.

Interleave Mode

Controls how memory interleaving takes place, or how DRAM access is speeded up because succeeding memory accesses go to different DRAM banks, and take place while another is being refreshed (2- or 4-way interleave). Not always possible.

Fast Page Mode DRAM

Should be enabled with DRAM capable of Fast Page Mode on your motherboard (not 256K SIMMs). Page Mode speeds up memory accesses when they occur in the same area; the page address of data is noted, and if the next data is in the same area, page mode is invoked to reduce the access time to about half (that is, the row and column need not be specified again, so the RAS or CAS lines don't need to be reset). Otherwise data is retrieved normally from another page. *Fast page mode* is a quicker version of the same thing. This technique is not necessarily the best for the PC; you may be better off adjusting the RAS values and extending the signal's length so that a row can be kept open for as long as possible.

Pipelined CAS

When enabled, the DRAM controller will not provide time between two successive CAS cycles. Otherwise, one Host Bus clock between successive CAS cycles will be provided (default). The former is best for performance.

*00 Write Protect

Normally, when a ROM is shadowed, the original ROM is disabled and the RAM area where its contents goes is write protected. You can disable this for special reasons, such as debugging ROM code, but very little else. Normally, leave enabled.

Parity Checking Method

You can check parity for every double word, or only the last double word during cache line fill. The Triton chipset does not support parity.

Parity Check

On a Phoenix BIOS, an NMI interrupt is produced with a parity error when this is enabled.

F/E Segment Shadow RAM

How the E/F segments of Upper Memory are used (refers to cacheing). Choices are:

Disabled	(E segment default)
Enabled	(F segment default)
Cached	L2 cache?
Into-486	L1 cache

Disable Shadow Memory Base

Alters the location of non-shadowed memory. For example, if using a SCSI host adapter, set this to the address of the adapter and the size to 16K (see below).

Disable Shadow Memory Size

Sets a shadow memory size for *Disable Shadow Memory Base*, above.

Base Memory Size

You might want to disable on-board RAM (i.e. base memory) between 80000-9FFFF (512K-640K), so you can give 128KB of contiguous address space to cards that need it (it is not normally available in upper memory). Normally set at 640, but set 512K for such a card.

Memory Remapping (or Relocation/Rollover)

The memory between A000-FFFF (that is, the 384K of upper memory normally used for ROMs, etc) can be remapped above the 1 Mb boundary for use as extended memory—this is sometimes not available with more than 1 Mb installed. Thus, your memory will run from 0-640K and 1-1.384Mb if you have 1 Mb. You usually have the choice of moving 256K (areas A, B, D and E) or 384K (Areas A-F), if no ROMs are shadowed. Relocated memory blocks must not be used for Shadow RAM, so relocating the full 384K means no Video or System BIOS Shadow! What you get from this depends on the total memory you have, and whether you use DOS or Windows. Use mostly when memory is tight. More precise control may be obtained from a memory manager.

384 KB Memory Relocation

See *Memory Remapping*. Can solve problems if you have more than 16 Mb in your machine.

256 KB Remap Function

See *Memory Remapping*.

DRAM Relocate (2, 4 & 8 M)

Remaps 256K of upper memory to the top of DRAM size. Only applicable when the D and E segments are not shadowed, and when you have 2, 4 or 8 Mb of on-board memory.

Memory Reporting

You get the choice of *Standard* or *Windows NT*. It's to help get around the limitations imposed by the ISA bus on the amount of memory the CPU can address. The 16-bit ISA bus has 24 address lines, which means it can theoretically see only 16Mb.

Extended Memory Boundary

Where extended memory ends, and expanded memory begins. Possibly for use with an expanded memory card.

Global EMS Memory

Whether expanded memory is used or present. If disabled, these settings are ignored:

EMS I/O port access	Enable if using EMS.
EMS Page Registers	Accessed through 3 I/O ports at:
	EMS 0 (208, 209, 20Ah)—default
	EMS 1 (218, 219, 21A)

Shared Memory Size of VGA

The system memory to be allocated to VGA in a shared memory system (see *Memory*).

Shared Memory Enable

Enable or Disable.

RAM Wait State

Allows an additional T-state (2 PROCCLK cycles) to be inserted on local memory accesses during CAS active interval, extending the width of the CAS pulse, and slowing the machine.

Cycle Check Point

This allows you to select how much time is allocated for checking memory read/write cycles. In effect, each selection sets a predetermined wait state for decoding cycle commands.

Fast	0, 1 waits (Default)
Fastest	0, 0 waits
Normal	1, 2 waits
Slow	-, 3 waits

Cycle Early Start

Allows read/write cycles to start half a clock cycle early, assuming addresses and other control signals are stable. Enabling this *may* eliminate a wait state.

Special DRAM WR Mode

Enables a special inquiry filter for bus master attempts to write to DRAM; the system checks the address of the write cycle to see if it was previously detected in the preceding cycle, and if it was the transaction will pass directly to system memory without the overhead of an extra inquiry cycle. Enabling is therefore best for performance.

MA Timing Setting

MA = Memory Access. Set disabled with EDO RAM. Also set *CAS Pulse Width* and *precharge* to 1T.

MA Additional Wait State

Enabled, inserts an extra wait state before the assertion of the first MA (*Memory Address*) and CAS#/RAS# during DRAM read or write leadoff cycles. This affects page hit, row and page miss cases. Always use the default unless you are getting memory addressing errors.

MA Wait State

When set to *Slow*, as above.

MA Drive Capacity

Or *Memory Address Drive Strength*. Sets current draw of multiplexed DRAM chips. The smaller the number, the less power consumption, and therefore heat, but if set too low you need an extra wait state—too high and you get ringing and reflections, and errors (in PCs, the DRAM voltage can be nearly 6 volts because ringing and reflections can drive the +5 up, making the memory run hotter). If your SIMMs have a high loading, (that is, you have over 64 memory chips), select 16ma/16ma. The more chips, the higher the figure.

DRAM R/W Leadoff Timing

Sets the number of CPU clocks before reads and writes to DRAM are performed (Award). Similar to the cache burst timings, but reads 7-3-3-3 or similar for 50 MHz. The higher the first figure (leadoff), the less the performance. EDO RAM uses one less wait state. The 430 HX chipset can use lower figures than the VX.

8/7	8 clocks leadoff for reads and 7 for writes.
7/5	7 clocks leadoff for reads and 5 for writes.

DRAM Leadoff Timing

See *DRAM R/W Leadoff Timing*. This is the AMI version and the settings are:

8-6-3		7-5-3	8-6-4	7-5-4

DRAM Fast Leadoff

Select *Enabled* to shorten the leadoff cycles and optimize performance.

Fast EDO Leadoff

Select *Enabled* only for EDO RAM in systems with either a synchronous cache or which are cacheless. It causes a 1-HCLK pull-in for all read leadoff latencies for EDO memory (that is, page hits, page and row misses). Disable for FPM or SDRAM.

Speculative Leadoff

The T II chipset (430HX) can allow a DRAM read request to be generated slightly before the address has been fully decoded, which can reduce latencies. *Disabled* is the default, but with this enabled, the DRAM controller will issue the read command before fully decoding the address, thus speeding up the process. The "speculative" bit arises from the chipset's ability to process what might be needed in the future, or speculate on a DRAM read address, so as to keep the pipeline full.

SDRAM Speculative Read

As above.

Advanced Chipset Setup

SDRAM (CAS Lat/RAS-to-CAS)

You can select a combination of CAS latency and RAS-to-CAS delay in HCLKs of 2/2 or 3/3. This sets up the SDRAM CAS latency time or *RAS to CAS Delay*. You will only see this if you have SDRAM installed. Usually set by the system board designer, depending on the DRAM installed. Do not change this unless you change the DRAM or the CPU.

SDRAM CAS Latency Time

Defines the CAS latency time in 66 or 100 MHz clocks, depending on the memory bus speed. The lower the number, the faster the performance at the expense of stability.

SDRAM Cycle Length

Sets the length of the SDRAM cycle. The shorter the faster, at the expense of stability.

SDRAM Bank Interleave

Allows support for interleaving banks of SDRAM for better performance.

SDRAM Configuration

Either *Disabled* or *By SPD*. SPD refers to a little EPROM on the DIMM that reports information about it to the system.

Sustained 3T Write

Affects PBSRAM. Enabled is possibly best for performance.

2 Bank PBSRAM

Sets the burst cycle for PBSRAM.

Turn-Around Insertion

When this is enabled, the chipset will insert one extra clock to the turn-around of back-to-back DRAM cycles. *Disabled* is the default, and best for performance.

DRAM ECC/PARITY Select

Allows you to select between two methods of DRAM error checking, ECC and Parity (default). ECC memory can correct some errors, in addition to detecting them in the first place. Some redundancy is added to data bits to enable duplication of the information, typically used in servers for extra safety.

Single Bit Error Report

When a single bit error is detected, the offending DRAM row ID is latched, and the value held until the error status flag is explicitly cleared by software.

ECC Checking/Generation

Enable with ECC SIMMs *in all rows*.

Memory Parity/ECC Check

You can choose between methods of memory error checking. Auto, Enabled and Disabled.

Memory Parity SERR# (NMI)

The default of *Disabled* will not show memory errors. If you have parity chips, you can select *Parity* or *ECC* to correct 1 bit errors.

OMC Mem Address Permuting

Enable to allow the Orion Memory Controller to permute memory addresses to get alternate row selection bits. May hang the machine.

OMC DRAM Page Mode

Affects the Orion Memory Controller on a Pentium Pro motherboard.

Fast Strings

Possibly related to 4-way memory interleaving. Enabled is best for performance.

Fast MA to RAS# Delay

Set by the system board designer, according to the DRAM. Don't change this unless you change the DRAM or the CPU. MA means *Memory Access*. Lower is best for performance.

Fast RAS to CAS Delay

The lower the better for performance.

DRAM Quick Read Mode

For 386s only. Set to *Normal*.

386 DRAM Quick Write Mode

As above.

DRAM Page Idle Timer

The time in HCLKs that the DRAM controller waits to close a DRAM page after the CPU becomes idle. The shorter the better for performance.

DRAM Enhanced Paging

When enabled, the chipset keeps the page open until a page/row miss. When disabled, the chipset uses additional information to keep the DRAM page open when the host may be "right back." Your guess is as good as mine!

MISCELLANEOUS

CPU Low Speed Clock

Or *Low Speed CPU Clock Select* selects whatever speed you want to use as the slow speed when you select Turbo Off on the front panel of your computer, or via your keyboard. This will be CLKIN (CPU speed) divided by 1, 2, 3 or 4.

Co-processor Ready# Delay

Enabling this with a non-compatible processor delays the ready signal by 1 T state, giving you a wider tolerance range, but less performance.

Co-processor Wait States

Number of wait states for the ready signal from NPU to CPU for similar reasons to above.

Check ELBA# Pin

Sets when the ELBA# pin is checked, during T1 or T2. Should mostly be set to T2, that is, later in the cycle for better reliability, but this can depend on other settings. The *External Local Bus Access#* pin is active during local bus access cycles, so the CPU can communicate with devices on it without disturbing some support chips.

> **NOTE:** This can hang the machine—DO NOT CHANGE IT IF YOUR
> MACHINE IS WORKING!

C000 32K Early Shadow

Shadows the video BIOS before it initialises, assuming your VGA card agrees. As it happens before the POST you get reduced POST time and faster booting.

Video Shadow Before Video Init

See above.

Mouse Support Option

Used to support a PS/2 type mouse on the keyboard port. Takes up 1K of base memory for an Extended BIOS Data Area, so you only get 639K.

IRQ 12 used by ISA or PS/2 Mouse

If you're not using a PS/2 mouse, you can make its IRQ available for the ISA bus.

PS/2 Mouse Function Control

As above. *Enabled* allows the system to allocate IRQ 12 automatically.

Appian Controller

An advanced IDE controller. Aside from enabling this if you've got one, you need special software to activate it.

CPU Address Pipelining

An Award Setting found on Pentiums. Can be enabled if required by a multithreaded operating system.

Keyboard Reset Control

If enabled, CPU operations will be halted before the System Reset signal is actually sent. Put more technically, HALT is executed before SYSC generates CPU reset from **Ctrl-Alt-Del**.

Keyboard Clock Select

As with bus speed, this should end up as standard, in this case 7.25 MHz, so for a 40 MHz CPU, you want CPUCLK/5. You can often decouple the keyboard clock from the bus clock, so you can run one faster than the other. Some motherboards give you an option of running at 9.25 MHz, but this is not often a good idea. The keyboard controller is actually a computer in its own right; at least, it has a microprocessor, and its own BIOS inside.

Novell Keyboard Management

Normally set to *No*, but if you find the keyboard sluggish when using a Novell product, set it for the smallest number between 1-30 that gives you best performance.

Middle BIOS

Sets the System BIOS to appear at E000. It's only for some old software, so mostly disable.

Delay Internal ADSJ Feature

ADS# is a bus control signal, or an Address Status strobe driven by the CPU to indicate the start of a CPU bus cycle, showing that a valid command and address is stable on the bus. The J is a substitute for # stands for *signal*. See *Synch ADS* below. Enable at 50 Mhz for best compatibility for VL bus cards, but performance is reduced.

Synch ADS

If set *Disabled*, can improve the performance on low speed machines (e.g. 25 MHz). Enable for 50 MHz 486 and 386/40 systems. Disable *Auto Setup* to use this.

Internal ADS Delay

Enabled, allows an additional span of time for the Address Data Status. Only use this if you have a fast processor.

NMI Handling

DO NOT DISABLE THIS! (sorry for shouting). It's for engineering testing only. Your machine will hang without the right equipment attached to the board and you will need to discharge the CMOS (see *Password*). NMI stands for *Non Maskable Interrupt*, which is one that can't be worked around.

Power-On Delay

Specifies a short delay when power is turned on so the PSU can stabilise.

Software I/O Delay

Can be 0-255 units. Each increment adds a fixed delay based on the processor speed. Should be set to 10, 12, 14, 18 or higher for 16, 20, 25 or 33 MHz systems, respectively.

Sampling Activity Time

Selects the delay time when the chipset monitors and samples SMI (*System Management Interrupt*). You get a choice of *No Delay* or *Delay 1T*.

GAT Mode

Also known as *Guaranteed Access Timing Mode* on Acer motherboards. This setting guarantees the 2.1us CHRDY timeout spec from EISA/ISA buses, to allow their adapters the maximum time to respond to bus signals. *Disabled* takes advantage of PCI reponse time.

Advanced Chipset Setup

SIO GAT Mode

Found on a Pentium Pro motherboard, similar to the above. Disabling appears to improve performance slightly.

Chipset NA# Asserted

Allows you to choose between two methods of asserting the NA# signal during CPU line fills (maybe). NA# stands for *Next Address*. Enabled helps performance.

LOCAL ready syn mode

Whether VESA Ready signal is synchronized by the CPU clock's ready signal, or bypassed.

SYN	VESA ready synchronized by the CPU (default).
BYPASS	Synchronization bypassed.

LGNT# Synchronous to LCLK

When a VL bus is prepared to give a VL Bus Master access to the bus, it returns the LGNT# signal active, which acknowledges a request for control of the VL Bus; by default, the bus issues LGNT# as soon as the current bus master finishes with it. When this is enabled, the VL bus will also synchronize its response with the LCLK, the VL bus clock. Normally, disable.

Cyrix A20M Pin

Cyrix chips need special BIOS handling, if only because their 386 version has a cache (Intel's doesn't), and it may have trouble keeping the cache contents up to date if any part of the PC is allowed to operate by itself, in this case, the keyboard controller toggling the A20 gate. The *A20M* signal can be raised separately by the BIOS to tell the CPU the current state of the A20 gate.

This also allows the CPU's internal cache to cache the first 64K of each Mb in real mode (the gate is always open in protected mode), and is fastest.

Cyrix Pin Enabled

As above, but refers to DMA and the FLUSH pin on the CPU, which invalidates the cache after any DMA, so the contents are updated from main memory, for consistency. If you can't set the FLUSH pin, increase the refresh interval and use Hidden Refresh.

Cyrix LSSR bit

Or LSSER. LSSR stands for *Load Store Serialize Enable* (Reorder Disable). It was bit 7 of PCR0 in the 5x86 (index 0x20), but does not apply to the 6x86 or the 6x86MX, as they have no PCR0 or index 0x20.

Chipset Special Features

When disabled, the (TII) chipset behaves as if it were the earlier Intel 82430FX chipset.

Polling Clock Setting

Sets the rate at which the system polls all sub-systems (buses, memory, etc.) for service
requests. Choices are:

14.318 MHz
CLK2 (Default)
CLK2/2
CLK2/3
CLK2/4
28.636 MHz

Host Bus Slave Device

This allows you to use an Intel 486 Host Bus Slave (e.g. a graphics device).

Host Bus LDEV

When this is enabled, the chipset will monitor the LDEV (local device) signal on the host bus for attempts to access all memory and I/O ranges out of the chipset's range.

Assert LDEV0# for VL

Found on machines with PCI and VL Buses, this controls a signal (LDEV0#) that allows a VLB slave device to talk to the chipset when there is no master present, in which case Enable.

Host Bus LRDY

When this is enabled, the chipset will monitor the LRDY (local ready) signal on the host bus, returning RDY to the CPU.

Memory Hole At 512-640K

When enabled, certain space in memory is reserved for ISA cards to improve their performance.

LBD# Sample Point

Allows you to select the cycle check point, which is the point where memory decoding and cache hit/miss checking takes place. Doing it at the end of T3 rather than T2 gives you more time for checking, for greater stability.

486 Streaming

As well as burst mode, the 486 (and true compatibles) support a streaming mode where larger amounts of data are moved to/from memory during a single cycle. Enabling improves performance.

CHRDY for ISA Master

When enabled, this allows an ISA bus master device to assert CHRDY (*Channel Ready*), giving it immediate access to DRAM. The default is enabled.

Set Mouse Lock

You can lock the PS/2 Mouse as a security precaution.

NA (NAD) Disable for External Cache

Controls whether the chipset Next Address pin will be enabled, for early posting of the next address when making back to back accesses to L2 cache. Enabled is best for performance, but worse for stability.

ATA-Disc

This only appears (in the MR BIOS) if you have an ATA device installed (actually up to eight). The fields are mostly filled automatically on selection, and should only be changed if you know the settings (transfer rates) are not correct.

Disconnect Selection

Turns the SCSI Disconnect function on or off. On is best for performance, as the SCSI device can disconnect and allow the CPU to get on with something else, although your operating system must be able to support this.

P6 Microcode Updated

Disabled is best for reliability. Microcode is program instructions inserted into a chip. Found on Pentium Pros.

ChipAwayVirus

Helps the BIOS cope with a special virus detector card that checks on the boot sector.

OS Select For DRAM >64MB

Use with OS/2 (or NT) when you have more than 64 Mb. The maximum reportable size of memory is 64 Mb, due to the size of the register used. OS/2 and NT can get this reported as 16 Mb and convert it internally.

Verifying DMI Status

To do with the Intel-Microsoft *Desktop Management Interface*, which is for remote sensing of computer configurations over a network.

POST Testing

Found on AST machines, determines whether POST testing will be *normal*, or *in-depth*. Normal just checks the memory.

MPS 1.1 Mode

The version of the multiprocessor specification.

BIOS Update

Leave disabled unless actually updating the BIOS.

In Order Queue Depth

Determines the length of the queue of instructions that must be processed in sequence, as the Pentium Pro is able to execute out-of-order for smoother processing. Can be set to 1 or 8. 1 should be best for performance.

Large Disk Access Mode

Choices are *DOS*, or *Other*. This was found on a Packard Bell with A Phoenix BIOS. Select the appropriate operating system.

Assign IRQ for VGA

If enabled, the BIOS will assign an IRQ for the VGA card, but most VGA cards don't need one. It's for when your card is bus mastering, like the Matrox Mystique, for the 3D features. It may allow an AGP card to share the same IRQ resource with the PCI 1 slot. Disabling releases the IRQ for another device, or reserves it for the PCI 1 slot.

Monitor Mode

Interlaced or Non-Interlaced, according to whether the video system should output a full screen in sequence (NI) or lines in alternate passes (Interlaced). Cheap monitors won't support full interlace at higher resolutions.

Speed Model

Used for BIOSes that autodetect the CPU. Speedeasy does it for you. *Jumper emulation* is for the settings as taken from the manual, in terms of bus clock, multiplier, voltage and CPU speed.

S.M.A.R.T. for Hard Disks

Self-Monitoring Analysis & Reporting Technology. Allegedly allows a drive to monitor itself and report to the host (through management software) when it thinks it will fail, so network managers have time to order spares.

Advanced Chipset Setup

11 Power Management

This is for Green PCs, or those complying with the EPA *Energy Star* programs; the intention is to save unnecessary power usage if the system becomes inactive. Power is reduced automatically to the devices and restored as quickly as possible when activity is detected (that's the theory, anyway). This is usually done with idle timing and event monitoring techniques. A Power Management Unit (PMU) monitors interrupt signals through an interrupt events detector. If the PMU hears nothing for a while, the system is put gradually and progressively to sleep, in that the longer the time inactive, the more parts of the system will close down.

Choices available range from simple "dozing" to complete shutdown:

Dozing slows the CPU down only, to around half speed.

Standby shuts down hard disk and video, or just CPU and SCLK (depends on the chipset).

Suspend shuts down all devices except the CPU.

Inactive stops the CPU, slows the SCLK and powers down the L2 cache.

HDD Power Down just shuts down the hard disk.

As with anything, there are industry standards. For energy saving purposes, these include:

APM, or Advanced Power Management, devised by Intel/Microsoft. This must be active if you want to keep the time and date when the system is suspended, with **power.exe** for DOS (try **power.drv** for Windows) that coordinates BIOS, DOS and program activity. APM is responsible for shutting the system down on quitting the operating system, typically Windows '95, and other useful tricks.

ATA, or *AT Attachments Specification*, for IDE drives. Some ATA compliant devices provide Spindown facilities.

DPMS, or *Display Power Management Signalling*. Monitors and cards conforming to this are meant to be matched, as signals are sent between them to put the CRT into various low power states, which need instructions from the BIOS. There are recognized power management states: *Run, Standby, Suspend* and *Off*. Suspend is slower to return to the Run state than Standby, which is regarded as being temporarily idle. Disable Standby and Suspend if you don't want PM.

ACPI, or *Advanced Configuration and Power Interface*, hashed out mainly by Intel, Microsoft and Toshiba. This will allow desktop PCs to have instant on, and be better for voicemail and household device control, as peripherals can be turned off as well as the main system unit. It will work the other way, too.

Some BIOSes have their own maximum and minimum settings for the times allocated, but you may have a "User Defined" option for your own. More options may be available for SL (low power) CPUs.

SM Out, by the way, means the System Management Output control pin.

SMART BATTERY SYSTEM

This is where circuitry is added to a battery pack to allow better power management, battery life and information for the user, such as time remaining. The battery can talk to the system, and tell it what services are required (some charging systems depend on battery heat as an indication of charge status). All this has been formalized into the SBS system, which actually stems from five documents containing the specifications for the battery itself, host system hardware, BIOS and charging.

The SMBus is a separate bus allowing direct communication between the host and the battery. The Smart Charger allows a battery to control its own charge, while a Smart Battery Selector is used in multiple systems to determine which one is in use, which is charging, etc.

PM Control by APM

Or *Power Management Control by Advanced Power Management*. Switches APM on or off; choices are *Yes* or *No*. If *Yes*, combine DOS and Windows utilities for Green Mode (only with S-series CPUs). When enabled, an Advanced Power Management device will be activated to enhance the maximum Power Saving mode and stop the CPU internal clock. In other words, the BIOS will wait for a prompt from APM before going into any power management mode. If disabled, the BIOS will ignore APM. You need DOS and Windows utilities as well.

IDE Standby Power Down Mode

Also known as Hard Disk Timeout, or HDD Power Down (Award), allows automatic power down of IDE drives after a specified period of inactivity, but some don't like it (notebook drives are OK). 15 minutes is a suggested minimum, to avoid undue wear and tear on the drive. Probably doesn't affect SCSI drives.

Standby Mode Control

Sets the standby clock speed to fractions of the CPU speed, and enables/disables the video.

IDE Spindown

As for *Standby Mode Control*, from MR BIOS.

Doze Timer/System Doze

Certain parts of the machine are monitored, i.e. hard disk, keyboard, mouse, serial and parallel ports, interrupts and the like, and if they are inactive for a length of time determined here, the computer dozes off for a short while; that is, it reduces activity and use of power until any of the above items become active again. Gives 80% sleep, 20% work.

Power-down mode timers

From MR, sets a timeout before power saving mode is entered. *Standby* slows down the CPU and video clocks.. *Suspend* turns them off - set this for longer, to give more time to recover.

Video Off Method

How the video will be switched off. Choose:

DPMS, if your VGA card and monitor support it.

Blank Screen. The screen will only be blanked when video is disabled. Uses more power than *V/H Sync + Blank*.

V/H Sync + Blank. As well as *Blank Screen*, the Vertical and Horizontal Sync signals are turned off, but if your card is not compatible, use *Blank Screen* only. Green monitors detect the V/H-Sync signals to turn off the electron gun.

Video Off After

See also *Video Off Option*. Turns the video off after a system event.

N/A	Never turn screen off
Suspend	Off when system in Suspend Mode
Standby	Off when system in Standby Mode
Doze	Off when system in Doze Mode

Standby Timer

Used when the computer is thought to be temporarily idle. Power reduction measures include the monitor partially powering down, or the CPU speed slowing to 8 MHz. Gives 92% sleep, 8% work (like me).

Green Timer

Either Disable, or establish between 10 secs-3 hours.

Suspend Timer

Comes into force after the system has been idle for some time, say an hour, when the computer thinks it's unattended. The CPU can be stopped, and the monitor disabled to the extent of needing to warm it up. There may be a **CRT OFF** mode, which will need the on/off switch to get the monitor working again. You may also see an **8X Mode** for factory testing and demonstrations; all it does is make everything operate 8 times faster. 99% sleep, 1% work (no, this is more like me). May support a Suspend switch on the motherboard.

Suspend Mode Switch

Controls a hardware switch that puts the computer into Suspend Mode.

Auto Keyboard Lockout

If the keyboard powers down, use **Ctrl-Alt-Bksp** and wait for the keyboard lights to go on and off, then enter the CMOS password.

Power
Management

Monitor Power/Display Power Down

You must have a green power supply for this. After the specified time interval, the monitor power will be turned off. Monitors with the circuitry to cope with this can be a pain if it goes wrong and keeps powering down anyway.

CPU Clock (System Slow Down)

After the specified time interval, the CPU will be slowed down to 8 MHz.

Event Monitoring

As Individual IRQ Wake Up Events (System IRQ Monitor Events), from MR.

Local monitoring checks only the keyboard, PS/2 mouse and two serial port interrupts.

Global monitoring checks all interrupts.

Individual IRQ Wake Up Events (System IRQ Monitor Events)

IRQs are monitored as an indirect method of watching the CPU, since it cannot be checked directly. The system can be woken up or sent to sleep if one is generated, or not, typically by a mouse (PS/2 mice use IRQ 12, but see *Expansion Cards* for a full list of IRQs).

IRQ 1(-15) Monitor

As for *Event Monitoring*.

DRQ 0 (-7) Monitor

As *IRQ 1(-15) Monitor*, but for DMA input monitoring. See *Expansion Cards* for a full list of DMA Channels.

System Events I/O Port Settings

Wakes the system up if one of these is accessed.

Keyboard IO Port Monitor

Allows ports 60 and 64h to be monitored for system activity (or not).

Floppy IO Port Monitor

As for *Keyboard IO Port Monitor*, but for port 3F5h.

Hard Disk IO Port Monitor

As *Keyboard IO Port Monitor*, but for ports 1F0h-3F6h.

Video Port IO Monitor

As Keyboard IO Port Monitor, but for video ports.

Video Memory Monitor

As Keyboard IO Port Monitor, but for accesses to A000-BFFF areas of upper memory.

VGA Adapter Type

If your card supports Green features, Vertical/Horizontal scanning will be stopped when the CRT is blanked. If *Green*, BIOS will turn off HSYNC/VSYNC when in Green mode. Otherwise, just the screen will be blanked.

Low CPU Clock Speed

What speed to use when at slow speed.

APM BIOS Data Area

Where to keep data relating to PM, F000 or DOS 1 K.

Power Management Control

Enabled, turns power management on.

Power Management RAM Select

Where the 32K required for power management is located in Upper Memory (def E000).

O.S

So you can use Non-S and AMD/Cyrix chips to shut down the monitor. Select *All O.S.* for non-DOS systems. Otherwise you can select the IRQ (e.g. DOS ONLY15).

Factory Test Mode

Do not enable this (if you see it).

Device Power Management

Has the following headings:

> *Display Type Support.* Set to *Green PC* if you have an EPA compatible monitor. Otherwise set *Standard.*

> *Video Off in Suspend Mode.* Permits the BIOS to power down the video display when the computer is in suspend mode.

> *IDD HDD Off in Suspend Mode.* As above, for hard drive.

> *Ser Prt Off in Suspend Mode.* As above, for serial ports.

> *Par Prt Off in Suspend Mode.* As above, for the parallel port.

> *Prog I/O Off in Suspend Mode.* As above, for Prog I/O.

System Power Management

Has the following headings:

> *System Cache Off in Suspend Mode.*

> *Slow Refresh in Suspend Mode.* Refreshes DRAM every 45 instead of 16 ns.

Power
Management

Power Button Override

Generates a hardware event so the system will transition into the self-off state if the power button is pressed for more than 4 seconds. Disabled, the machine powers off immediately the power button is pressed. Needs an ATX power supply.

System Monitor Events

The following are monitored for inactivity:

Video ROM Access C000h, 32K. Permits local bus access to Video ROM at C000-C7FF.

Video RAM Access A000-C7FF. Permits local bus access to this area.

Video Access A000-C7FF. Combines the previous two options.

Local Bus Device Access. Enabled, permits local bus device access.

Local Bus Master Access. Enabled, permits local bus master device access.

Local Bus Access. Combines previous two options.

DMA Request

Enabled, permits local bus DMA requests.

NON-SMI CPU Support

Selects IRQ to replace System Management Interrupt (SMI) events when the CPU doesn't support SMI.

Inactive Mode Control

(Award-UMC82C498 Chipset). Allows *Inactive Mode Clock* speed to be set to fractions of normal CPU speed or turned off. Also permits the VGA Display to be enabled or disabled. These apply only when the computer has entered Inactive Mode, which is a power suspend mode that involves both a chipset and an SMM capable CPU. If 0 Clock Speed (STOP CLK) is selected, the computer CPU cannot monitor external activities and cannot automatically bring the computer back to normal mode based on actions such as entry of a keystroke.

Video Off Option

Choices are:

Always On	Screen is never turned off
Suspend -> Off	Screen off when system in Suspend mode
Susp, Stby -> Off	Screen off when system in Standby or Suspend mode
All modes -> Off	As above (so why have it?)

Throttle Duty Cycle

The percentage by which CPU speed is cut back during power saving. Settings are in multiples of 12.5%.

Soft-off by PWR-BTTN

Instant-Off allows the system to switch off immediately the power button is pressed. Otherwise, it will only do so after you press the power switch for more than 4 seconds.

Resume By Ring

Powers the system on when the Ring Indicator signal is received in UART 1 or 2 from an external modem. Needs an ATX power supply and *IRQ8 Clock Event* to be enabled.

Resume By LAN/Ring

Allows the system to wake up in response to a Ring Indicator signal from an external modem through UART 1 or 2, or a wake-up signal through the network card from a server. Resume By Ring needs *IRQ8 Clock Event* to be enabled. *Wake on LAN* gives you the ability to remotely boot a PC from across a network even if it has been powered down.

Ring Power Up Act

Powers the system on when the Ring Indicator signal is received in UART 1 or 2 from an external modem. Needs an ATX power supply.

Resume By Alarm

Uses an RTC alarm to generate a work event or, in other words, an alarm from the Real Time Clock can be used to wake the system up from sleeping.. Needs an ATX power supply and *IRQ8 Clock Event* to be enabled.

IRQ 8 Clock event

Generates a clock event on IRQ8 being activated.

Thermal Duty Cycle

Slows down the CPU by the specifications listed here when it overheats.

CPU Warning Temperature

Sets an alarm when the CPU reaches a specified temperature.

Fan Failure Control

What happens if the CPU fan fails.

Automatic Power Up

For unattended or automatic power up of your system, such as *Everyday*, or *By Date*.

Instant On Support

Enable to allow the computer to go to full power on mode when leaving a power-conserving state. *Only available if supported by the hardware.* The AMI BIOS uses the RTC Alarm function to wake the computer at a prespecified time.

ZZ Active in Suspend

Version 1: Puts cache controller into sleep mode when system is in Suspend mode.

Version 2: When enabled, PB SRAM (cache) will consume power in power management mode.

Power Management

12 Plug And Play/PCI

A system intended to make fitting of expansion cards easier (yes, really!). In this context, ISA cards not compatible with PnP are known as *Legacy Cards*, and are switched as normal to make them fit in ("legacy" is a polite word used to describe something that's basically out of date but is tolerated in modern equipment because there would be an almighty fuss otherwise). Have as few of these as possible, as accesses to them are slow.

With *Concurrent PCI*, The T II (or 430HX/VX) chipset's *Multi Transaction Timer* allows multiple transfers in one PCI request, by reducing re-arbitration when several PCI processes can take place at once; with more than one CPU and PCI bus, both PCI buses can be accessed simultaneously. *Passive Release* allows the PCI bus to continue working when it's receiving data from ISA devices, which would normally hog the bus. *Delayed Transaction* allows PCI bus masters to work by delaying transmissions to ISA cards. *Write merging* combines byte, word and Dword cycles into a single write to memory.

The idea is that plug and play cards get interrogated by the system they are plugged into, and their requirements checked against those of the cards already in there. The BIOS will feed the data as required to the Operating System, typically Windows '95. Inside the BIOS, the POST is enhanced to include automatic resource allocation.

Here you will be able to assign IRQs, etc to PCI slots and map PCI INT#s to them. Although Windows '95 or a PnP BIOS can do a lot by themselves, you really need the lot, e.g. a Plug and Play BIOS, with compatible devices and an Operating System for the best performance.

Be aware that not all PCI (2.0) cards are PnP, and that although PC (PCMCIA) cards are "Plug and Play", they are not considered here.

PnP itself was originally devised by Compaq, Intel and Phoenix. Your chipset settings may allow you to choose of two methods of operation (with the *Plug and Play OS* setting):

All PnP devices are configured and activated.

All PnP ISA cards are isolated and checked, but only those needed to boot the machine are activated. The ISA system cannot produce specific information about a card, so the BIOS has to isolate each one and give it a temporary handle so its requirements can be read. Resources can be allocated once all cards have been dealt with (recommended for Windows '95, as it can use the Registry and its own procedures to use the same information every time you boot). This leads to....

ESCD (*Extended System Configuration Data*), a system which is part of PnP (actually a superset of EISA), that can store data on PnP or non-PnP EISA, ISA or PCI cards to perform the same function as the Windows '95 Registry above, that is, provide consistency between sessions by reserving specific configurations.

It occupies part of Upper Memory (E000-EDFF), which is not available to memory managers. The default length is 4K, and problems have been reported with EMS buffer addressing when this area has been used.

PCI SLOT CONFIGURATION

Although an unlimited number of PCI slots is allowed, in practice 4 is the maximum, due to the capabilities of the *host controller*, which connects the bus to the CPU and DRAM, so *bridge devices* are used to connect more buses downstream from the first, known as the *root*, up to 255. These extra buses don't have to be PCI; they can be EISA or ISA as well.

PCI cards and slots use an internal interrupt system, with each slot being able to activate up to 4, labelled either INT#A-INT#D, or INT#1-INT#4. These are nothing to do with IRQs, although they can be mapped (that is, *steered*) to them if the card concerned needs it. Typically IRQs 9 and 10 are reserved for this, but any available can be used. There are various ways of implementing this, so don't expect consistency!

Four registers control the routing of PCI Interrupts to IRQs. Two or more can be steered into the same IRQ signal, each of which must be set to *level sensitive* (see *Edge/Level Select*). The IRQs affected are IRQs 3-7, 9-12, and 14-15.

With PCI or IRQ Steering, multiple devices can share IRQs by intercepting requests and routing them to the next available ones. It is supported by Windows 95 OSR2, but not enabled (Error Code 29 in Device Manager, for the PCI bus under *System Devices*).

x86 chips generate two interrupt acknowledge cycles per interrupt; both are converted to one for PCI. As the PCI interrupt system finds it difficult to cope with expansion cards requiring IRQs for each device on them, I/O devices tend to be on the motherboard.

The system must know which bus is using a particular IRQ; remember, there are 16 available, though some are used up by the system already (see *Expansion Cards*). Those used by non-PnP Legacy cards can be allocated for *those cards only* in the *PCI/PnP Configuration* section of your Setup, after which they cannot be used elsewhere. Unfortunately, ISA and PCI buses use IRQs differently. With ISA, they are edge triggered and available to every slot, and once the card is set up it can be used in any slot. With PCI, an IRQ is allocated to a slot, and the card concerned must go into it. They are mainly level triggered, which means that IRQs can be shared (the "level" refers to a measure of voltage). For the card, all you need to do is set it to an INT assignment, which typically is INT #A (or INT #1) for each slot on a motherboard by default. If you have an edge triggered PCI card (rare), allocate an IRQ through the BIOS. *You don't need to assign an IRQ to a PCI card unless it requires one!*

In the BIOS setup, you may see each slot listed with these subheadings:

> Slot 1
> Latency Timer
> Using IRQ
> Trigger Method

A PCI Master can burst as long as the target can send or receive data, and no other device requests the bus. PCI specifies two ways of disconnecting a Master during a long burst cycle so others can get a look in; *Master Latency Timer* and *Target Initiated Termination*.

Resources Controlled By

Whether you let the BIOS assign resources (Auto), or do it yourself (Manual).

Force Updating ESCD

If enabled, the ESCD area in Upper Memory (for PnP information) will be updated once, then this setting will be disabled automatically.

Latency Timer (PCI Clocks)

Controls the length of time an agent can hold the PCI bus when another has requested it, so it guarantees a PCI card access within a specified number of clocks.

Since the PCI bus runs faster than ISA, the PCI bus must be slowed during interactions with it, so here you can define how long the PCI bus will delay for a transaction between the given PCI slot and the ISA bus. This number is dependent on the PCI master device in use and varies from 0 to 255.

AMI defaults to 66, but 40 clocks is a good place to start at 33MHz (Phoenix). The shorter the value, the more rapid access to the bus a device gets, with better response times, but the lower becomes the effective bandwidth and hence data throughput. Normally, leave this alone, but you could set it to a lower value if you have latency sensitive cards (e.g. audio cards and/or network cards with small buffers). Increase slightly if I/O sensitive applications are being run.

PCI Latency Timer

As above. The default of *32 PCI Clock* (80 sometimes) mostly gives maximum performance.

Reset Configuration Data

Normally, leave disabled, which retains PnP data in the BIOS. Otherwise, this resets ESCD when you exit setup after installing a new card and you cannot boot.

Using IRQ

Affected by the Trigger method. There are two methods of IRQ usage, *Level* or *Edge* triggered (see *Expansion Cards*). Most PCI cards use the former, and ISA the latter. If you select *Edge* for the slot concerned, you may also need to set jumpers on the motherboard.

Plug And Play/PCI

Slot PIRQ

A PIRQ (PCI IRQ) is signalled to and handled by the PCI bus. Not the same as a normal IRQ.

PCI Slot x INTx

Assigns IRQs to PCI INT#s in slot x (or whatever). See *Slot X using INT#* (below).

Slot x INT# Map To

See *Slot X using INT#* (below).

Slot X Using INT#

Selects an INT# channel for a PCI Slot, and there are four (A, B, C & D) for each one, that is, each PCI bus slot supports interrupts A, B, C and D.

#A is allocated automatically, and you would only use #B, #C, etc if the card needs to use more than one (PCI) interrupt service. For example, select up to #D if your card needs four; a typical situation would be an IDE card with two channels, each requiring an IRQ. However, using *Auto* is simplest. Most graphics cards don't need this.

Edge/Level Select

Programs PCI interrupts to single-edge or logic level. Select *Edge* for PCI IDE. IRQ 14 is used for Primary and 15 for Secondary. Some motherboards provide a particular slot for edge-triggered cards.

As the interrupts are level sensitive and can be shared, two or more PCI interrupts can be steered into the same IRQ signal.

PCI Device, Slot 1/2/3

Enables I/O and memory cycle decoding.

Enable Device

Enable PCI device as a slave.

Xth Available IRQ

Selects (or maps) an IRQ for one of the available PCI INT#s above. There are ten selections (3, 4, 5, 6, 7, 9, 10, 11, 12, 14, 15). *1st available IRQ* (below) means the BIOS will assign this IRQ to the first PCI slots (order is 1, 2, 3, 4).

NA means the IRQ is assigned to the ISA bus and is therefore not available to a PCI slot.

1st-6th Available IRQ

See *Xth Available IRQ.*0

PCI IRQ Activated by

The method by which the PCI bus recognises an IRQ request; *Level* or *Edge* (see *Expansion Cards*). Use the default unless advised otherwise, or if you have a PCI device which only recognizes one of them.

IRQ Assigned To

Specifies the type of device using the interrupt; *Legacy ISA*, which needs a specific interrupt, or *PCI/ISA PnP*, which complies with the Plug and Play standard, and will be set up automatically.

DMA Assigned To

Similar to *IRQ Assigned To*, for DMA channels.

Configuration Mode

Sets the method by which information about legacy cards is conveyed to the system:

Use ICU—the BIOS depends on information provided by Plug and Play software (e.g. *Configuration Manager* or *ISA Configuration Utility*). Only set this if you have the utilities. If you select this, you will see....

o **Boot to PnP Operating System**. When enabled, the BIOS will activate only those Plug and Play cards necessary to boot the system, and hand over to an operating system that can manage Plug and Play cards for the rest. Otherwise, the remaining Plug and Play cards will not be configured, but Legacy cards will operate fine.

Use Setup Utility. The BIOS depends on information provided by you as follows. *Don't use the above utilities.*

o **ISA Shared Memory Size**. Specifies a range of memory addresses that will be directed to the ISA bus rather than onboard memory. Enable only for a Legacy card that requires non-ROM memory space (such as a LAN card with onboard memory buffers). Normally, the BIOS will scan C8000-DFFFFh for any BIOSes, note their location and size, then autoconfigure the PCI and Plug and Play expansion cards, shadowing the area above E0000h (other than video) until it is full. Next, the BIOS will assign additional PCI and Plug and Play cards to the area between C8000h and DFFFFh. If a Legacy ISA card has non-BIOS memory requirements, Autoconfigure could write into an area needed by the card, so this setting tells Autoconfigure that the block of memory is reserved, and should not be shadowed. If you set this, you will get this:

o **ISA Shared Memory Base Address**. If you select the 96 KB setting, this can only be set to C8000h; If the 80 KB setting is selected, the address can only be set to C8000h or CC000h, and so on. With 64K, you can only choose D000 or below.

o **IRQ 3-IRQ 15**. The IRQs in use by ISA Legacy cards. If not used, set to *Available*. Otherwise, set *Used by ISA Card*, which means that nothing else can use it.

PCI IDE Prefetch Buffers

Disables prefetch buffers in the PCI IDE controller. You may need this with an operating system (like NT) that doesn't use the BIOS to access the hard disk and doesn't disable interrupts when completing a programmed I/O operation.

Disabling also prevents errors with faulty PCI-IDE interface chips that can corrupt data on the hard disk (with true 32-bit operating systems). Check if you've got a PC-Tech RZ1000 or a CMD PCIO 640, but disabling is done automatically with later boards.

Plug And Play/PCI

133

PCI IDE 2nd Channel

Use if your second IDE channel is PCI based, but disable if you're not using the 2nd channel, or you will lose IRQ 15 on the ISA slots.

PCI Slot IDE 2nd Channel

Enable if your secondary IDE controller is in a slot as opposed to being on the motherboard.

PCI IDE IRQ Map to

Used for assigning IRQs 14 (Primary) and 15 (Secondary) to particular slots and INT#s, so is mostly for when you don't have IDE on the system board, but use a card in a slot. You can define the IRQ routing to make them work properly and configure your system to the type of IDE disk controller (an ISA device is assumed; the ISA setting does not assign IRQs).

Here, you specify the PCI slot and interrupt (A, B, C or D) associated with the connected hard drives (not the partitions). Since each IDE controller (primary or secondary) supports two drives, you can select the PCI INT# (not IRQ) for each. You will need to map an IRQ to each if you are using two channels.

PCI-Auto

If the IDE is detected by the BIOS in a PCI slot, then the appropriate INT# channel will be assigned to IRQ 14.

PCI-Slot X

If the IDE is not detected, you can manually select the slot.

Primary IDE INT#, Secondary IDE INT#

Assigns 2 INT channels for primary and secondary channels, if supported. This screen is not displayed if *ISA* is selected:

ISA. Assigns no IRQs to PCI slots. Use for PCI IDE cards that connect IRQs 14 and 15 directly from an ISA slot using a table from a legacy paddleboard.

PCI Bus Parking

Sort of bus mastering; a device parking on the PCI Bus has full control of it for a short time. Improves performance when that device is being used, but excludes others.

IDE Buffer for DOS & Win

For IDE read ahead and posted write buffers, so you can increase throughput to and from IDE devices by buffering reads and writes. Slower IDE devices could end up slower, though. Award BIOS.

IDE Master (Slave) PIO Mode

Changes IDE data transfer speed; *Mode 0-4*, or *Auto*. PIO means *Programmed Input/Output*.

Rather than have the BIOS issue commands to effect transfers to or from the disk drive, PIO allows the BIOS to tell the controller what it wants, and then lets the controller and the CPU perform the complete task by themselves. Modes 1-4 are available.

Host Clock/PCI Clock

Determines the speed of the PCI bus relative to the CPU internal clock, which is assumed to have the value of 1.

HCLK PCICLK

Similar to above. Host CLK vs PCI CLK divider; AUTO, 1-1, 1-1.5.

PCI-ISA BCLK Divider

PCI Bus CLK vs ISA Bus CLK divider; the difference between the PCI and the ISA bus: Assuming 33 MHz, you have:

AUTO	
PCICLK1/3	11 MHz
PCICLK1/2	16 and a bit
PCICLK1/4	8 ish

ISA Bus Clock Frequency

Allows you to set the speed of the ISA bus in fractions of the PCI bus speed, so if the PCI bus is operating at its theoretical maximum, 33 MHz, PCICLK/3 would yield an ISA speed of 11 Mhz. Avoid the asynchronous speed of 7.159 because of its overheads. Remember the PCI clock runs at half the speed of the memory bus.

7.159 MHz	(default)
PCICLK/4	A quarter speed of the PCI bus
PCICLK/3	One third speed of the PCI bus

PCI Write-byte-Merge

When enabled, this allows data sent from the CPU to the PCI bus to be held in a buffer. The chipset will then write the data to the PCI bus when appropriate.

CPU-to-PCI Read Buffer

When enabled, up to four Dwords can be read from the PCI bus without interrupting the CPU. When disabled, a write buffer is not used and the CPU read cycle will not be completed until the bus signals its readiness to receive the data. The former is best for performance.

PCI-to-CPU Write Buffer

See *CPU-to-PCI Read Buffer.*

PCI Write Buffer

As for *CPU-to-PCI Read Buffer,* but you can choose 2, 4 or 8 deep (Phoenix).

CPU-to-PCI Read-Line

When On, more time will be allocated for data setup with faster CPUs. This may only be required if you add an Intel OverDrive processor to your system.

CPU-to-PCI Read-Burst

When enabled, the PCI bus will interpret CPU read cycles as the PCI burst protocol, meaning that "back-to-back sequential CPU memory read cycles addressed to the PCI will be translated into fast PCI burst memory cycles". Performance is improved, but some non-standard PCI adapters (e.g. VGA) may have problems.

Byte Merging

This exists where multiple writes to non-contiguous memory addresses are merged into one PCI-to-memory operation by the host controller, letting the device concerned sort out which ones it wants, which increases bus throughput and hence performance for devices that support it—not all PCI video cards do, so enable unless you get bad graphics. See also *Byte Merge Support* (next) and *CPU-PCI Byte Merge* (after that).

Byte Merge Support

In this case, enabling means that CPU-PCI writes are buffered (Award).

CPU to PCI Byte Merge

Consecutive 8- or 16-bit writes inside the same double word address en route from the CPU to the PCI bus are held in a posted write buffer from where they are sent as a single double-word, giving faster video performance, as byte merging is performed in the compatible VGA range only (0A0000-0BFFFFh. Enabled is best for performance.

PCI to DRAM Buffer

Improves PCI to DRAM performance by allowing data to be stored if a destination is busy. Buffers are needed because the PCI bus is divorced from the CPU. If enabled, two buffers, capable of holding 4 Dwords each, store data written from the PCI bus to memory. When disabled, PCI writes to DRAM are limited to a single transfer.

Latency for CPU to PCI write

The delay time before the CPU writes data to the PCI bus.

PCI Cycle Cache Hit WS

Similar to *Latency for CPU to PCI Write*. With *Fast*, the CPU has less to do, so performance is better.

Normal	Cache refresh during normal PCI cycles.
Fast	Cahe refresh without PCI cycle for CAS.

Use Default Latency Timer Value

Whether or not the default value for the Latency Timer will be loaded, or the succeeding Latency Timer Value will be used. If *Yes* is selected (default), you don't need *Latency Timer Value* (below).

Latency Timer Value

The maximum number of PCI bus clocks that the master may burst, or the time the bus master will occupy the PCI bus. A longer latency time gives it more of a chance. See also *Latency Timer (PCI Clocks)*.

Latency from ADS# status

This allows you to configure how long the CPU waits for the *Address Data Status* (ADS) signal; it determines the CPU to PCI Post write speed.

When set to 3T, this is 5T for each double word. With 2T (default), it is 4T per double word. For a Qword PCI memory write, the rate is 7T (2T) or 8T (3T).

The default should be fine, but if you add a faster CPU to your system, you may need to increase it. The choices are:

3T	Three CPU clocks
2T	Two CPU clocks (Default)

PCI Master Latency

If your PCI Master cards control the bus for too long, there is less time for the CPU to control it. A longer latency time gives the CPU more of a chance. Don't use zero.

Max burstable range

The maximum bursting length for each FRAME# asserting. FRAME# is an electrical signal, so this appears to set the size of the maximum range of contiguous memory which can be addressed by a burst from the PCI bus, a half or one K.

CPU to PCI burst memory write

If enabled, back-to-back sequential CPU memory write cycles to PCI are translated to PCI burst memory write cycles. Otherwise, each single write to PCI will have an associated FRAME# sequence. Enabled is best for performance, but some non-standard PCI cards (e.g. VGA) may have problems.

CPU to PCI Bursting

Enables or disables PCI burst cycles for CPU-PCI write cycles where back-to-back sequential CPU memory writes are sent out on the PCI bus as a burst cycle, which may help improve video performance significantly.

CPU to PCI post memory write

Enabling allows up to 4 Dwords of data to be posted to PCI at once, increasing efficiency. Otherwise, not only is buffering disabled, completion of CPU writes is limited (e.g. not complete until the PCI transaction completes). Enabled is best for performance.

CPU to PCI Write Buffer

As above. Buffers are needed because the PCI bus is divorced from the CPU; they improve overall system performance by allowing the processor (or bus master) to do what it needs without writing data to its final destination; the data is temporarily stored in fast buffers.

PCI to ISA Write Buffer

When enabled, the system will temporarily write data to a buffer so the CPU is not interrupted. When disabled, the memory write cycle for the PCI bus will be direct to the slower ISA bus. The former is best for performance.

DMA Line Buffer

Allows DMA data to be stored in a buffer so PCI bus operations are not interrupted. *Disabled* means that the line buffer for DMA is in single transaction mode. *Enabled* allows it to operate in an 8-byte transaction mode for greater efficiency.

ISA Master Line Buffer

ISA master buffers are designed to isolate slower ISA I/O operations from the PCI bus for better performance. *Disabled* means the buffer for ISA master transaction is in single mode. *Enabled* means it is in 8-byte mode, increasing the ISA master's performance.

SIO Master Line Buffer

As above, found on Pentium Pro machines.

CPU/PCI Post Write Delay

The delay time before the CPU writes data into the PCI bus.

SIO PCI Post Write Buffer

Something to do with buffering data between the CPU and an Orion Memory Controller.

Post Write CAS Active

Pulse width of CAS# after the PCI master writes to DRAM.

PCI master accesses shadow RAM

Enables the shadowing of a ROM on a PCI master for better performance.

Enable Master

Enables the selected device as a PCI bus master and checks whether the card is so capable.

AT bus clock frequency

Access speed for the AT bus in a PCI system, actually used for memory access instead of wait states. Choose whatever divisor gives you a speed of 6-8.33 MHz, for 70 ns memory, depending on the speed of the PCI bus (e.g. PCI/4 at 33 MHz).

Base I/O Address

The base of the I/O address range from which the PCI device resource requests are satisfied.

Base Memory Address

The base of the 32-bit memory address range from which the PCI device resource requests are satisfied.

Parity

Allows parity checking of PCI devices.

ISA Linear Frame Buffer

Set to the appropriate size if you use an ISA card that features a linear frame buffer (e.g. a second video card for ACAD). The address will be set automatically.

Residence of VGA Card

Whether on PCI or VL Bus.

ISA LFB Size

LFB = *Linear Frame Buffer.* This creates a hole in the system memory map when there is more than 16Mb of RAM, so accesses made to addresses within the hole are directed to the ISA Bus instead of Main Memory. Leave *Disabled*, unless you're using an ISA card with a linear frame buffer that must be accessed by the CPU, and you aren't using Plug and Play's Configuration Manager or ISA Configuration Utility. If you choose 1 Mb, the *ISA LFB Base Address* field will appear (see below).

ISA LFB Base Address

The starting address for the ISA memory hole if 1 Mb has been set for the *ISA LFB Size* (above).

ISA VGA Frame Buffer Size

This is to help you use a VGA frame buffer and 16 Mb of RAM at the same time; the system will allow access to the graphics card through a hole in its own memory map; accesses to addresses within this hole will be directed to the ISA bus instead of main memory. Should be set to *Disabled*, unless you are using an ISA card with more than 64K of memory that needs to be accessed by the CPU, and you are not using the Plug and Play utilities. If you have less than 8 Mb memory, or use MS-DOS, this will be ignored.

Memory Hole

Enables a memory hole at either 512K-640K or 15M-16M to support adapters that require linear frame buffer memory space.

Memory Map Hole; Memory Map Hole Start/End Address

See *ISA VGA Frame Buffer Size*, above. Where the hole starts depends on *ISA LFB Size*. Sometimes this is for information only. If you can change it, base address should be 16Mb, less buffer size. Only one memory hole is allowed with the Triton chipset.

Memory Hole Size

Enables a memory hole in DRAM space. CPU cycles matching an enabled hole are passed on to PCI. Options include *1 Mb, 2 Mb, 4 Mb, 8 Mb, Disabled*. These are the amounts below 1 Mb assigned to the AT Bus, and reserved for ISA cards.

Plug And Play/PCI

Memory Hole Start Address

To improve performance, certain parts of system memory may be reserved for ISA cards which must be mapped into the memory space below 16 Mb for DMA reasons (check the documents). The chipset can then access any code or data directly from the ISA bus. The selections are from 1-15 with each number in Mb. This is irrelevant if the memory hole is disabled (see above). Areas reserved in this way cannot be cached.

Memory Hole at 15M-16M

See *Memory Hole Start Address*, but the area above 15 Mb becomes unavailable to the system. Sometimes this is reserved for expanded PCI commands.

Local Memory 15-16M

To increase performance, you can map slower device memory (e.g. on the ISA bus) into much faster local bus memory.

Local memory is set aside and the start point transferred from the device memory to local memory. The default is enabled.

15-16M Memory Location

The area in the memory map allocated for ISA option ROMs. Choices are *Local* (default) or *Non-local*.

Multimedia Mode

Enables or disables palette snooping for multimedia cards.

Palette Snooping

Enable when using a Multimedia video card, so the address space of the PCI VGA palette can be snooped for the colour information from the video processor and overlay.

Video Palette Snoop

This allows multiple VGA cards to be used on multiple buses. It controls how a PCI graphics card can "snoop" write cycles to an ISA video card's colour palette registers (snooping essentially means interfering with a device).

Only set to *Disabled* if:

> An ISA card connects to a PCI graphics card through a VESA connector

> The ISA card connects to a colour monitor, and

> The ISA card uses the RAMDAC on the PCI card, and

> Palette Snooping (RAMDAC shadowing) not operative on PCI card.

PCI/VGA Palette Snoop

VGA snooping is used by multimedia video devices (e.g. video capture boards) to look ahead at the video controller (VGA device) and see what colour palette is currently in use.

Where you have multiple graphics cards, such as an MPEG board attached to the feature connector of your video card, this alters the VGA palette setting. Enable if you have ISA

MPEG connections through the PCI VGA feature connector, so you can adjust PCI/VGA palettes, and solve situations where the colours in Windows are wrong. For example, you may get a black and white display while booting.

However, you should only need this in exceptional circumstances, so disable for ordinary systems. (Award BIOS).

Snoop Filter

Saves the need for multiple enquiries to the same line if it was inquired previously. When enabled, cache snoop filters ensure data integrity (cache coherency) while reducing the snoop frequency to a minimum. Bus snooping is a technique for checking if cached memory locations have been changed through DMA or another processor; it compares the address being written to by a DMA device with the cache Tag RAM. If a match occurs, the location is marked. If the CPU tries to read that location later it must get the data from main memory, which contains what has been written by DMA. In other words, bus snooping invalidates cached locations modified by anything other than the CPU, to prevent old data being read.

Bus snooping must access L1 and L2 caches, involving using the processor bus in the case of the former. Nine bus clocks are used to perform the snoop, so it involves a loss of performance, particularly as the CPU cycle is delayed if the snoop starts just before a CPU memory access cycle. For these reasons, it is pipelined in the HX chipset.

PCI VGA Buffering

Enabled is best for performance.

E8000 32K Accessible

The 64K E area of upper memory is used for BIOS purposes on PS/2s, 32 bit operating systems and Plug and Play. This setting allows the second 32K page to be used for other purposes when not needed, in the same way that the first 32K page of the F range is useable after boot up has finished.

P5 Piped Address

Default is Disabled.

PCI Arbiter Mode

Devices gain access to the PCI bus through arbitration (similar to interrupts). There are two modes, 1 (the default) and 2. The idea is to minimize the time it takes to gain control of the bus and move data. Generally, Mode 1 should be sufficient, but try mode 2 if you get problems.

PCI Arbitration Rotate Priority

Typically, access is given to the PCI bus on a first-come-first-served basis. When priority is rotated, once a device gains control of the bus it is assigned the lowest priority and all others moved up one in the queue. When enabled, PCI masters arbitrates for PCI bus ownership using rotate priority. Otherwise, fixed priority is used.

Plug And Play/PCI

Stop CPU When Flush Assert

See *Stop CPU when PC Flush*.

Stop CPU when PC Flush

When enabled, the CPU will be stopped when the PCI bus is being flushed of data. Disabling (default) allows the CPU to continue processing, giving greater efficiency.

Stop CPU at PCI Master

When enabled, the CPU will be stopped when the PCI bus master is operating on the bus. Disabling (default) allows the CPU to carry on, giving greater efficiency.

Preempt PCI Master Option

Enabling allows PCI bus operations to be pre-empted by certain activities, such as DRAM refresh. Otherwise, everything takes place concurrently.

I/O Cycle Recovery

When enabled, the PCI bus will be allowed a recovery period for back-to-back I/O, which is like adding wait states, so disable (default) for best performance.

I/O Recovery Period

Sets the length of time of the recovery cycle used above. The range is from 0-1.75 microseconds in 0.25 microsecond intervals.

Action When W_Buffer Full

Sets the behaviour of the system when the write buffer is full. By default, the system will immediately retry, rather than wait for it to be emptied.

Fast Back-to-Back

When enabled, the PCI bus will interpret CPU read cycles as the PCI burst protocol, meaning that back-to-back sequential CPU memory read cycles addressed to the PCI will be translated into the fast PCI burst memory cycles. Default is enabled.

CPU-to-PCI Fast Back to Back

As above, found on the Phoenix BIOS. *Disabled* is recommended unless your expansion cards support it.

CPU Pipelined Function

This allows the system controller to signal the CPU for a new memory address, before all data transfers for the current cycle are complete, resulting in increased throughput. The default is *Disabled*, that is, pipelining off.

Primary Frame Buffer

When enabled, this allows the system to use unreserved memory as a primary frame buffer. Unlike the VGA frame buffer, this would reduce overall available RAM for applications.

M1445RDYJ to CPURDYJ

Whether the PCI Ready signal is to be synchronized by the CPU clock's ready signal or bypassed (default).

VESA Master Cycle ADSJ

Allows you to increase the length of time the VESA Master has to decode bus commands. Choices are *Normal* (default and fastest) and *Long*. Increasing the delay increases stability. On the Phoenix BIOS, when the VESA Master Speed is less than or equal to 33 MHz, you can set *Non-Delay ADSJ*. Above that, you can use *Delay ADSJ* if you get a problem with VESA Master cards running too fast.

LDEVJ Check Point Delay

Selects the time allocated for checking bus cycle commands, which must be decoded to see whether a *Local Bus Device Access Signal* (LDEVJ) is being sent, or an ISA device is being addressed or, in other words, when the chipset checks if the current CPU cycle relates to the VL or ISA bus. Increasing the delay increases stability, especially of the VESA sub-system, while very slightly degrading the performance of ISA. Settings are in terms of the feedback clock rate (FBCLK2) used in the cache/memory control interface.

1 FBCLK2	One clock
2 FBCLK2	Two clocks (Default)
3 FBCLK2	Three clocks

Delay ISA/LDEVJ check in CLK2

See *LDEVJ Check Point Delay*. Settings are in terms of *Standard* + a number of CLK2 periods.

CPU Dynamic-Fast-Cycle

Gives you faster access to the ISA bus. When the CPU issues a bus cycle, the PCI bus examines the command to see if a PCI agent claims it. If not, an ISA bus cycle is initiated.

The Dynamic-Fast-Access then allows for faster access to the ISA bus by decreasing the latency (or delay) between the original CPU command and the beginning of the ISA cycle.

CPU Memory sample point

This allows you to select the *cycle check point*, which is where memory decoding and cache hit/miss checking takes place.

Each selection indicates that the check takes place at the end of a CPU cycle, with one wait state indicating more time for checking to take place than with zero wait states. A longer check time allows for greater stability at the expense of some speed.

Memory Sample Point

Concerns when the chipset checks if the current CPU cycle is at the memory cycle. 0 wait states means at the first T2 rising edge, 1 wait state means at the second. The former is the best for performance.

143

LDEV# Check point

The VESA local device (LDEV#) check point is where the VL-bus device decodes the bus commands and error checks, within the bus cycle itself.

0	Bus cycle point T1 (Default and fastest)
1	During the first T2
2	During second T2
3	During third T2

The slower the motherboard, the lower the number you can use here. Your VL-bus card must be fast enough to produce an LDEV# signal.

Local Memory Detect Point

Selects the cycle check point, or where memory decoding and cache hit/miss checking takes place. More wait states gives greater stability.

Local memory check point

Selects between two techniques for decoding and error checking local bus writes to DRAM during a memory cycle.

Slow	Extra wait state; better checking (default)
Fast	No extra wait state used

FRAMEJ generation

When the PCI-VL bus bridge is acting as a PCI Master and receiving data from the CPU, this enables a fast CPU-to-PCI buffer that allows the CPU to complete a write, before the data has been delivered, reducing the CPU cycles involved and speeding overall processing.

Normal	Buffering not employed (Default)
Fast	Buffer used for CPU-to-PCI writes

PCI to CPU Write Pending

Sets the behaviour of the system when the write buffer is full. By default, the system will immediately retry, but you can set it to wait for the buffer to be emptied before retrying, which is slower.

Delay for SCSI/HDD (Secs)

The length of time in seconds the BIOS will wait for the SCSI hard disk to be ready for operation. If the hard drive is not ready, the PCI SCSI BIOS might not detect the hard drive correctly. The range is from 0-60 seconds.

Master IOCHRDY

Enabled, allows the system to monitor for a VESA master request to generate an I/O channel ready (IOCHRDY) signal.

Busmaster IDE on PCI

This reduces the CPU and PCI overhead. As the CPU-PCI bridge generates several wait states per bus command, the busmaster can give a greater bandwidth by only reading 1 memory cycle (PIO needs 2).

VGA Type

The BIOS uses this information to determine which bus to use when the video BIOS is being shadowed. Choices are *Standard* (default), *PCI, ISA/VESA*.

PCI Mstr Timing Mode

This system supports two timing modes, 0 (default) and 1.

PCI Arbit. Rotate Priority

See *PCI Arbitration Rotate Priority*.

I/O Cycle Post-Write

When Enabled (default), data being written during an I/O cycle will be buffered for faster performance. Posted Write Buffers are used when write-thru cacheing is enabled, to reduce the time the CPU has to wait. Intel CPUs have 4 internal posted write buffers.

PCI Post-Write Fast

As in the above *I/O Cycle Post-Write*, enabling this will allow the system to use a fast memory buffer for writes to the PCI bus.

CPU Mstr Post-WR Buffer

When the CPU operates as a bus master for either memory access or I/O, this controls its use of a high speed posted write buffer. Choices are NA, 1, 2 and 4 (default).

PCI Mstr Post-WR Buffer

As above, for PCI devices.

CPU Mstr Post-WR Burst Mode

When the CPU operates as a bus master for either memory access or I/O, this allows it to use burst mode for posted writes to a buffer.

PCI Mstr Burst Mode

As above, for PCI devices.

CPU Mstr Fast Interface

Enables or disables a fast back-to-back interface when the CPU operates as a bus master. Enabled, consecutive reads/writes are interpreted as the CPU high-performance burst mode.

PCI Mstr Fast Interface

As above, for PCI devices.

Plug And Play/PCI

CAS Delay in Posted-WR

Select the number of CPU cycles for CAS to remain active after a posted write is complete. The fewer, the faster.

CPU Mstr DEVSEL# Time-out

When the CPU initiates a master cycle using an address (target) which has not been mapped to PCI/VESA or ISA space, the system will monitor the DEVSEL (device select) pin to see if any device claims the cycle. Here, you can determine how long the system will wait before timing-out. Choices are 3 PCICLK, 4 PCICLK, 5 PCICLK and 6 PCICLK (default).

PCI Mstr DEVSEL# Time-out

As above, for PCI devices.

IRQ Line

If you have a device requiring an IRQ service into the given PCI slot, use this to inform the PCI bus which IRQ it should initiate. Choices range from IRQ 3-15.

Fast Back-to-Back Cycle

When enabled, the PCI bus will interpret CPU read or write cycles as PCI burst protocol, meaning that back-to-back sequential (e.g. fast) CPU memory read/write cycles addressed to the PCI will be translated into fast PCI burst memory cycles.

State Machines

The chipset uses four *state machines* to manage specific CPU and/or PCI operations, which can be thought of as highly optimized process centres for specific operations. Generally, each operation involves a master device and the bus it wishes to employ. The four state machines are:

> CPU master to CPU bus (CC)
>
> CPU master to PCI bus (CP)
>
> PCI master to PCI bus (PP)
>
> PCI master to CPU bus (PC)

Each have the following settings:

> **Address 0 WS**. The time the system will delay while the transaction address is decoded. Enabled=no delay (fastest).
>
> **Data Write 0 WS**. The time the system will delay while data is being written to the target address. Enabled=no delay (fastest).
>
> **Data Read 0 WS**. The time the system will delay while data is being read from the target address. Enabled=no delay (fastest).

On Board PCI/SCSI BIOS

You would enable this if your system motherboard had a built-in SCSI controller attached to the PCI bus, and you wanted to boot from it.

PCI I/O Start Address

Allows you to make *additional* room for older ISA devices by defining I/O start addresses for the PCI devices, thus overriding the PCI controller.

PCI Memory Start Address

For devices with their own memory which use part of the CPU's memory address space. You can determine the starting point in memory where PCI device memory will be mapped.

VGA 128k Range Attribute

When enabled, this allows the chipset to apply features like *CPU-TO-PCI Byte Merge*, *CPU-TO-PCI Prefetch* to be applied to VGA memory range A0000H-BFFFFH.

Enabled	VGA receives CPU-TO-PCI functions
Disabled	Retain standard VGA interface

CPU-To-PCI Write Posting

The Orion chipset has internal read and write buffers which compensate for the speed differences between the CPU and the PCI bus. When enabled, writes from the CPU to the PCI bus will be buffered. When disabled (default), the CPU will be forced to wait until the write is completed before starting another write cycle.

OPB P6 to PCI Write Posting

As above, but found on Pentium Pro machines.

OPB PCI to P6 Write Posting

As above, but in reverse.

CPU-To-PCI IDE Posting

Enabled, IDE accesses are buffered in the CPU-PCI buffers, which is best for performance.

CPU-PCI Burst Memory Write

Enabling is best for performance.

CPU-PCI Post Memory Write

Enabling is best for performance.

CPU Read Multiple Prefetch

A prefetch occurs during a process such as reading from the PCI or memory, when the chipset peeks at the next instruction and actually begins the next read. The Orion chipset has four read lines, and a multiple prefetch means the chipset can initiate more than one prefetch during a process. Default is *Disabled* (slowest).

CPU Line Read Multiple

A line read means that the CPU is reading a full cache line, which means 32 bytes (eight DWORDS) of data. Because the line is full, the system knows exactly how much data it will be reading and doesn't need to wait for an end-of-data signal, so blocks of data can be read without pausing every 4 cycles to specify a new address. When this is enabled, the system can to read more than one full cache line at a time. The default is disabled.

OPB P6 Line Read

As above, but found on Pentium Pro machines, possibly with the Orion Chipset.

CPU Line Read Prefetch

See also *CPU Line Read Multiple* (above). When this is enabled, the system is allowed to prefetch the next read instruction and initiate the next process.

OPB Line Read Prefetch

As above, but found on Pentium Pros, possibly with the Orion chipset.

CPU Line Read

Enables or Disables (default) full CPU line reads. See *CPU Line Read Multiple*, above.

CPU Burst Write Assembly

The (Orion) chipset maintains four posted write buffers. When this is enabled, the chipset can assemble long PCI bursts from the data held in them. Default is *Disabled*.

OPB Burst Write Assembly

Similar to the above, found on a Pentium Pro machine. It relates to USWC (see below), which affects video cards. OPB may stand for *Orion Post Buffers*. Then again, it may not.

USWC Write Posting

Un-cacheable Speculative Write Combination. Improves display performance for graphic cards with Linear Frame Buffers.

VGA Performance Mode

If enabled, the VGA memory range of A_0000-B_0000 will use a special set of performance features. This has little or no effect using video modes beyond those commonly used for Windows, OS/2, UNIX, etc, but this memory range is heavily used by games.

Snoop Ahead

This is only applicable if the cache is enabled. When enabled, PCI bus masters can monitor the VGA palette registers for direct writes and translate them into PCI burst protocol for greater speed, to enhance the performance of multimedia video.

DMA Line Buffer Mode

This allows DMA data to be stored in a buffer so as not to interrupt the PCI bus. *Standard* is equal to single transaction mode. *Enhanced* means 8-byte transaction mode.

Master Arbitration Protocol

The method by which the PCI bus determines which bus master device gains access to it.

Host—to—PCI Wait State

1, 0 or Auto.

PCI Parity Check

Enables/disables PCI Parity checking. The latter is default and slower due to extra overhead.

PCI Memory Burst Write

When enabled, CPU write cycles are interpreted as the PCI burst protocol (by the PCI bus), meaning that back-to-back sequential CPU memory write cycles addressed to PCI will be translated into (fast) PCI burst memory write cycles. This directly improves video performance when consecutive writes are initiated to a linear graphics frame buffer.

PCI Clock Frequency

Set the clock rate for the PCI bus, which can operate between 0-33 MHz, relative to the CPU, e.g. CPUCLK/2, or half the CPU speed.

CPUCLK/1.5	CPU speed / 1.5 (Default)
CPUCLK/3	CPU speed/3
14 MHz	14 MHz
CPUCLK/2	CPU speed/2

8 Bit I/O Recovery Time

The recovery time is the length of time, measured in CPU clocks, that the system will delay after the completion of an input/output request to the ISA bus, needed because the CPU is running faster than the bus, and needs to be slowed down. Clock cycles are added to a minimum delay (usually 5) between PCI-originated I/O cycles to the ISA bus.

Choices are from 1 to 7 or 8 CPU clocks. 1 is the default.

16 Bit I/O Recovery Time

As above, for 16 bit I/O. Choices between 1 to 4 CPU clocks.

I/O Recovery Time

As for *I/O Recovery Time Delay*, but concerns refreshing *between* cycles, so the lower the number the better. Set to *Enhanced* with Multiuser DOS on an Intel Express. If you get two numbers, the first is for 8-bit cycles, and the second 16-bit. In other words, this is a programmed delay which allows the PCI bus to exchange data with the slower ISA bus without data errors.

Settings are in fractions of the PCI BCLK:

2 BCLK	Two BCLKS (default)
4 BCLK	Four BCLKS
8 BCLK	Eight BCLKS
12 BCLK	Twelve BCLKS

IO Recovery (BCLK)

As for *I/O Recovery Time*.

PCI Concurrency

Enabled (default) means that more than one PCI device can be active at a time (Award). With Intel Chipsets, it allocates memory bus cycles to a PCI controller while an ISA operation, such as bus mastered DMA, is taking place, which normally requires constant attention. This involves turning on additional read and write buffering in the chipset.

The PCI bus can also obtain access cycles for small data transfers without the delays caused by renegotiating bus access for each part of the transfer, so is meant to improve performance and consistency.

Peer Concurrency

Whether or not the CPU is allowed to run DRAM/L2 cycles when non-PHLD PCI master devices are targeting the peer device. That is, whether the CPU can use cache or system memory when something else is going on.

This speeds things by allowing PCI devices to operate at the same time, or as near to it as possible. Some might not like it.

PCI Streaming

Data is typically moved to and from memory and between devices in chunks of limited size, because the CPU is involved.

On the PCI bus, however, data can be streamed, that is, much larger chunks can be moved without the CPU being bothered. Enable for best performance.

PCI Bursting

Consecutive writes from CPU are regarded as a PCI Burst cycle, so allows multiple data bytes to cross the PCI bus in one go.

When enabled (default), one address cycle is combined with several data cycles before being sent across the PCI bus; the receiving agent increments the addresses itself (when disabled, data moves across the PCI bus in a single cycle/data cycle pair). You may need to change this for slower PCI Video cards.

PCI (IDE) Bursting

As above, but this one enables burst mode access to video memory over the PCI bus. The CPU provides the first address, and consecutive data is transferred at one word per clock. The device must support burst mode.

PCI Dynamic Bursting

Combines several PCI cycles into one.

PCI Burst Write Combine

When enabled, the chipset assembles large PCI bursts from data in burst buffers.

PCI-To-DRAM Pipeline

If enabled, full PCI-DRAM write pipelining is used, where buffers in the chipset store data written from the PCI bus to memory. Otherwise, PCI writes to DRAM are limited to a single transfer per write cycle.

Burst Copy-Back Option

If a cache miss occurs with this enabled, the chipset will initiate a second, burst cache line fill from main memory to the cache, to maintain the status of the cache.

IBC DEVSEL# Decoding

Sets the type of decoding used by the ISA Bridge Controller (IBC) to determine which device to select. The longer the decoding cycle, the better chance the IBC has to correctly decode the commands. Choices are *Fast*, *Medium* and *Slow* (default). *Fast* is less stable and may possibly trash a hard disk.

PCI Preempt Timer

Sets the length of time before one PCI master preempts another when a service request has been pending.

Disabled	No preemption (default).
260 LCLKs	Preempt after 260 LCLKs
132 LCLKs	Preempt after 132 LCLKs
68 LCLKs	Preempt after 68 LCLKs
36 LCLKs	Preempt after 36 LCLKs
20 LCLKs	Preempt after 20 LCLKs
12 LCLKs	Preempt after 12 LCLKs
5 LCLKs	Preempt after 5 LCLKs

Arbiter timer timeout (PC CLK) 2 x 32

Working on this.

Keyboard Controller Clock

Sets the speed of the keyboard controller (PCICLKI = PCI bus speed).

7.16 MHz	Default
PCICLKI/2	1/2 PCICLKI
PCICLKI/3	1/3 PCICLKI
PCICLKI/4	1/4 PCICLKI

CPU Pipeline Function

This allows the system controller to signal the CPU for a new memory address, even before all data transfers for the current cycle are complete, resulting in increased throughput. Enabled means that address pipelining is active.

Plug And Play/PCI

151

PCI Dynamic Decoding

When enabled, this setting allows the system to remember the PCI command which has just been requested. If subsequent commands fall within the same address space, the cycle will be automatically interpreted as a PCI command.

Master Retry Timer

Sets how long the CPU master will attempt a PCI cycle before the cycle is unmasked (terminated). The choices are measured in PCICLKs. Values are 10 (default), 18, 34 or 66 PCICLKs.

PCI Pre-Snoop

Pre-snooping is a technique by which a PCI master can continue to burst to the local memory until a 4K page boundary is reached rather than just a line boundary. Enabled is best for performance.

CPU/PCI Write Phase

Determines the turnaround between the address and data phases of the CPU master to PCI slave writes. choices are 1 LCLK (default) or 0 LCLK.

CPU to PCI POST/BURST

Data from the CPU to the PCI bus can be posted (buffered by the controller) and/or burst. This sets the methods.

POST/CON.BURST	Posting and bursting supported (default)
NONE/NONE	Neither supported
POST/NONE	Posting but not bursting supported

PCI CLK

Whether the PCI clock is tightly synchronized with the CPU clock, or is asynchronous. If your CPU, motherboard and PCI bus are running at multiple speeds of each other, e.g. Pentium 120, 60 MHz m/b and 30 MHz PCI bus, choose synchronise.

PCI Master Cycle

Where the chipset checks for the PCI Master Cycle in local memory. *Fast* means in the address phase, which is earlier, and *Slow* refers to the first data phase.

IRQ 15 Routing Selection

MISA=*Multiplexed ISA* for asynchronously interrupting the CPU. IRQ 15 is usually used for Secondary IDE channels or CD-ROMs.

Secondary CTRL Drives Present

Allows you to manually set the number of drives on your secondary channel.

CPU cycle cache hit sam point

Working on this.

PCI cycle cache hit sam point

Working on this.

Plug and Play OS

Whether you have one or not. *No* means the BIOS will allocate interrupt settings. *Yes* means that they may be reassigned by the operating system, or that the BIOS will only initialise PnP PCI boot devices – others will be sorted out by the operating system.

PnP OS

See above.

PCI Passive Release

This item concerns the PIIX3 PCI-ISA bridge, and the latency of ISA cards. When enabled, CPU-PCI bus accesses are allowed during passive release. Otherwise, the arbiter only accepts another PCI master access to local DRAM. If you have a problem with an ISA card, set it to the opposite of the current setting.

Delayed Transaction

PCI 2.1 is tight on target and master latency, and PCI cycles to and from ISA generally take longer to perform. When *enabled,* the chipset provides a programmable delayed completion mechanism, where the PCI bus is freed during CPU access to 8-bit ISA cards, which normally consume about 50-60 PCI clocks without this. Disable for bus mastering PCI cards that cannot use the PCI bus, or some ISA cards that are not PCI 2.1 compliant.

Multi Transaction Timer

Allows PCI cards to hold their request lines high and receive PCI bursts without rearbitration delays and without locking others out of the bus (the Multi Transaction Timer controls the minimum burst size). May improve data transfer for devices needing uninterrupted high data transfer rates (anything to do with video), but may also cause problems.

FDD IRQ Can Be Free

Allows it to be used by the PnP system.

Multi-function INTB#

Enables or disables multi-function PCI cards using INTA# and INTB#.

AGP Aperture Size (64 Mb)

The AGP memory aperture is the amount of system memory for an AGP card, so host cycles hitting that area are forwarded to the card without translation. The default is usually 64 Mb, and it's only used if you have such a card.

AGP 2X Mode

Allows your AGP VGA card to switch to 133 MHz transfer mode, if it supports it. otherwise the card operates in 1X mode (66 MHz).

PCI Master 0 WS Write

Increasesthe write cycle speed when enabled.

PCI Master 1 WS Write

Writes to the PCI bus are executed with an extra wait state if enabled. Normally disabled.

PCI Master 1 WS Read

Reads to the PCI bus are executed with an extra wait state if enabled. Normally disabled

PCI Delay Transaction

When enabled, delays PCI data transactions, so disabled is best for performance.

PCI Master Read Prefetch

Enabled, allows the system to prefetch the next read and initiate the next process, so enabled is best for performance.

PCI#2 Access #1 Retry

Enables PCI #2 Access in #1 attempts.

PERIPHERAL SETUP

Mainly concerns all-in-one motherboards; the on board equipment is often not as good as other products, so you may want to disable some of them. *Onboard IDE*, for example, has been known to operate through the ISA interface rather than PCI.

Programming Option

Auto—the BIOS detects and sets up expansion cards and I/O ports automatically. On board I/O is dealt with last.

On Chip IDE Buffer (DOS/Windows)

See *IDE Buffer for DOS & Win*.

On Chip IDE Mode

Selects PIO Mode for your drive.

IDE 0 Master/Slave Mode, IDE 1 Master/Slave Mode

Sets independent timing modes for IDE devices on both channels, to stop the slowest interfering with the faster.

On Chip Local Bus IDE

Disable if you add another.

On-Chip Primary PCI IDE

Enables or disables onboard PCI IDE.

On-Chip Secondary PCI IDE

Enables or disables onboard PCI IDE.

PCI IDE Card Present

Use if secondary IDE card installed.

Onboard Floppy Drive

Disable if you want to use a floppy controller on an expansion card.

Onboard FDC Controller

See above.

Onboard FDC Swap A: B:

For swapping drive assignments through the onboard floppy controller, if it is enabled..

Onboard IDE

Enable/Disable. This often goes through the ISA interface.

Onboard Serial Port 1

(or 2). Sets IRQs and I/O addresses.

Onboard Parallel Port

Enable/Disable.

First Serial Port

(or 2). Sets IRQs and I/O addresses.

Parallel Port Address

What I/O address is used.

LPT Extended Mode

Standard Parallel Port (SPP)
Enhanced Parallel Port (EPP)
Extended Capability Port (ECP)
EPP + ECP

The SPP is unidirectional, as it was designed for printers, and only 5 of its wires are for input; bidirectional communications actually use printer status signals. SPP does not need interrupts, so they can be used for other devices.

EPP and ECP have more wires for input, so are bidirectional and do need interrupts. ECP defines register formats, allows RLL compression, is fast and buffered, and allows better communication between the device concerned and the PC. Expect ECP to use DMA 3. EPP allows devices to be connected in a chain, and was designed more as a high speed bus.

ECP was developed by HP and Microsoft in advance of the IEEE specification defining advanced parallel ports, so EPP is "more compatible". Both have approximately the same performance, but ECP can run faster than the maximum data transfer rate.

ECP+EPP (default) allows normal speed operation in two-way mode. SPP may be helpful if you have printing problems with Windows '95.

Plug And Play/PCI

155

IRQ Active State

Whether parallel/serial IRQs are active high or low.

ECP DMA Select

Available only if you select ECP or ECP+EPP above. Channels 1 or 3 (default) are available.

Parallel Port EPP Type

Sets one of two versions of EPP, 1.7 and 1.9. Try the latter first, but be prepared to use the former if you get problems. See also *LPT Extended Mode*.

Parallel Port Mode

Sets one of two versions of EPP, 1.7 and 1.9. Try the latter first, but be prepared to use the former if you get problems. See also *LPT Extended Mode*.

Floppy DMA Burst Mode

Enabled is best for performance.

Serial Port 1 MIDI

Allows you to configure serial port 1 as a MIDI interface. Or not.

USB Controller

Enabled or not.

USB Function

As above.

Infrared Duplex

If you've got it, whether disabled, half-duplex or full-duplex.

UART2 Use Infrared

Allocates the onboard infrared feature to the second serial UART. The default is *Disabled*, which allows it to be used for COM2.

NCR SCSI BIOS

Enables or disables the onboard NCR SCSI BIOS.

Onboard VGA Memory Size (iMb)

For allocating the total of VGA memory from shared memory. Choices are 1, 2 or 4 Mb.

Onboard VGA Memory Clock

Onboard Video speed. *Normal* is 50 MHz, *Fast* is 60 and *Fastest* is 66. Decrease this to match the monitor's frequency rate if your screen is unreadable.

Write Buffer Level

Select between 4 or 8 level write buffers for the PCI bridge.

Offboard PCI IDE Card

Whether an offboard PCI IDE controller is used, but you must also specify the slot, because it will not have a built-in configuration EPROM as required by PCI specification. The onboard IDE controller on the motherboard is automatically disabled. The settings are *Disabled, Auto, Slot1, Slot2, Slot3,* or *Slot4.* If *Auto* is selected, the AMI BIOS automatically determines the correct setting.

SYSTEM MONITOR SETUP

Fan Speed

The speed of the fan connected to the headers listed here. The value assumes 2 pulses per revolution and should therefore be used as a relative figure.

Voltage Values

Shows the current values on the motherboard. +3.3v, +5v, +12v, -12v and −5v come from the ATX power supply. VTT (+1.5) is GTL Termination Voltage from the on-board regulator and VCCVID (CPU) is the CPU core voltage from the on-board switching power supply.

Plug And Play/PCI

13 Nasty Noises

These are for error conditions that occur before the screen is initialised, or for troubleshooting without a monitor. A text message is often sent to mono and CGA CRTs; EGA/VGA cards may not yet be initialised. Beep codes occur after the fact.

ALR

See "Phoenix" on page -170.

AMBRA

See "Phoenix" on page -170

AMI

Beeps	What they mean	What to do
1	The memory refresh circuitry is faulty.	Reseat/replace memory.
2	Parity Errors in first 64K memory (parity detection may be defective).	
3	Failure within the first 64K of memory (could be address line error).	
4	System Timer failure; Timer #1 on the motherboard isn't working properly (an error with Timer #2 is non-fatal).	Repair motherboard.
5	CPU has generated an undetectable error.	
6	8042-Gate A20 Failure. The BIOS cannot switch the CPU into protected mode.	Reseat or replace the keyboard controller. Try another keyboard.
7	The CPU has generated an exception eOPDOPDrror.	Repair motherboard.
8	Video adapter is missing or has faulty memory (non-fatal).	Replace memory on the card or the card itself.
9	The ROM checksum does not match that in the BIOS.	Reseat/replace BIOS.
10	The shutdown register for the CMOS Interrupt channel #2 has failed the so the system board can't retrieve CMOS contents during POST.	Repair motherboard.
11	Ext (L2) cache memory has failed testing and has been disabled.	
2 short	POST failed; failure of one of the hardware testing procedures.	

1 long 2 short	Video failure;Video BIOS ROM failure where a checksum error was encountered or the video adapter has a horizontal retrace failure.
1 long, 3 short	Video failure;The video DAC the monitor detection process or the video RAM has failed.
1 long, 3 short	Conventional/extended memory test failure (older BIOSes)
1 long, 8 short	Display test and display vertical and horizontal retrace test failed
1 long	POST passed.

AST

Long	Short	Problem
0	1	Failed POST 1; Low level processor verification test.
0	2	Failed POST 2; Clears keyboard controller buffers.
0	3	Failed POST 3; Keyboard controller reset.
0	4	Failed POST 4; Low level keyboard controller interface test.
0	5	Failed POST 5; Reading data from keyboard controller.
0	6	Failed POST 6; System board support chip initialisation.
0	7	Failed POST 7; Processor register r/w verify test.
0	8	Failed POST 8; CMOS timer initialisation.
0	9	Failed POST 9; ROM BIOS Checksum test.
0	10	POST 10; Initialise primary video (never fails).
0	11	Failed POST 11; 8254 timer channel 0 test.
0	12	Failed POST 12; 8254 timer channel 1 test.
0	13	Failed POST 13; 8254 timer channel 2 test.
0	14	Failed POST 14; CMOS power on and time test.
0	15	Failed POST 15; CMOS shutdown byte test.
1	0	Failed POST 16; DMA channel 0 test.
1	1	Failed POST 17; DMA channel 1 test.
1	2	Failed POST 18; DMA page register test.
1	3	Failed POST 19; Keyboard controller interface test.
1	4	Failed POST 20; Memory refresh toggle test.
1	5	Failed POST 21; First 64K memory test.
1	6	Failed POST 22; Setup interrupt vector table.
1	7	Failed POST 23; Video initialisation.
1	8	Failed POST 24; Video memory test.

Advantage/Bravo/Manhattan/Ascentia/Premium/Premmia

Short	Long	Short	Replaceable Unit
3	1	X	System board
3	2	X	System board
3	3	X	System board
3	4	X	System board
3	5	X	SIMM memory
3	6	X	Integrated VGA or video board

Advantage/Bravo

Beeps	Replaceable Unit
1	System board
2	SIMM memory; System board
3	SIMM memory; System board
4	SIMM memory; System board
5	Processor; System board
6	Keyboard controller; System board
7	Processor; System board
8	Video adapter; Video RAM; System board
9	BIOS; System board
10	System board
11	External cache; System board

Manhattan

Beeps	Error Type	Replaceable Unit
1	Memory Refresh	DIMMs
2	Parity	DIMMs
3	Base 64KB Memory	DIMMs
4	Timer Not Operational	Processor board
5	Processor	Microprocessor or processor board
6	Gate A20	Keyboard or system board
7	Processor Interrupt	microprocessor or processor board
8	Video Memory	Add-in video/system board (not fatal)
9	ROM Checksum	System board
10	CMOS Register	System board
11	Cache Memory Bad	Processor or processor board

Beeps	Replaceable Unit
2-2-3	System Board
3-1-1	SIMMs; Processor board
3-1-3	System board
3-4-1	SIMMs; Processor board
3-4-3	SIMMs, Processor board
2-1-2-3	Flash BIOS; System board
2-2-3-1	System board; Processor board

Ascentia J

Beeps	Replaceable Unit
2-2-3	System Board
3-1-1	SIMMs; Processor board
3-1-3	System board
3-4-1	SIMMs; Processor board
3-4-3	SIMMs, Processor board
2-1-2-3	Flash BIOS; System board
2-2-3-1	System board; Processor board

Ascentia 810/800/Explorer/Bravo

Short	Long	Short	Replaceable Unit
1	1	X	Processor board
1	2	X	System board
1	3	X	Processor board memory
1	4	X	Processor board
2	X	X	Processor board memory
3	1	X	System board
3	2	X	System board
3	3	X	Video (Processor board, LCD)
3	4	X	Video (Processor board, LCD)
4	2	X	Processor board
4	3	X	Processor board
4	4	1	Serial port / System board
4	4	2	Parallel port / System board
4	4	3	Processor board

BIOS Update Beep Codes

Long	Short	Description
2	0	Update Successful.
2	2	CMOS Checksum failure; try again, but be prepared to replace the system board.
2	3	Floppy disk adapter. Reinsert the disk.
2	4	Disk belongs to another machine.
2	5	Not a BIOS update disk.
2	7	Flash programming error.
2	8	Flash programming error.
2	9	Flash programming error.
2	10	Flash programming error.
2	11	Flash programming error.
2	12	Flash programming error.
2	13	Flash programming error.
2	14	Flash programming error.

AST Enhanced

Short	Long	Short	Processor failure
3	1	X	Flash Loader failure (BIOS)
3	2	X	System Board component failure
3	3	X	System Board component failure
3	4	X	Memory failure
3	5	X	Video failure
0	6	X	Flash BIOS update error. Not early POST failure
	2	Any	Used by AST for low level diagnostics.

Early Premium 286

Short	Long	Meaning
1	2	Video Error
1	3	Keyboard Error
2	0	Any Fatal Error
1	0	No errors during POST

Early POSTBeep Codes

Beeps	Meaning
1	System Board
2	SIMM Memory; System Board
3	SIMM Memory; System Board
4	SIMM Memory; System Board
5	Processor; System Board
6	Keyboard Controller; System Board
7	Processor; System Board
8	Video Adapter;Video RAM; System Board
9	BIOS; System Board
10	System Board
11	External cache; System Board

AST Phoenix

Beeps	Meaning
1-1-3	CMOS read/write error. Fatal.
1-1-4	ROM BIOS Checksum failure. Fatal.
1-2-1	Programmable interval timer failure. Fatal.
1-2-2	DMA Initialisation failure. Fatal.
1-2-3	DMA Page Register r/w failure. Fatal.
1-3-1	RAM refresh verification error. Fatal.
1-3-3	First 64K RAM chip or data or data line failure multibit. Fatal.
1-3-4	First 64K RAM odd/even logic failure. Fatal.
1-4-1	Address line failure first 64K RAM. Fatal.
1-4-2	Parity failure first 64K RAM. Fatal.
2-1-1	First 64K RAM failure bit 0. Fatal.
2-1-2	First 64K RAM failure bit 1. Fatal.
2-1-3	First 64K RAM failure bit 2. Fatal.
2-1-4	First 64K RAM failure bit 3. Fatal.
2-2-1	First 64K RAM failure bit 4. Fatal.
2-2-2	First 64K RAM failure bit 5. Fatal.
2-2-3	First 64K RAM failure bit 6. Fatal.
2-2-4	First 64K RAM failure bit 7. Fatal.
2-3-1	First 64K RAM failure bit 8. Fatal.
2-3-2	First 64K RAM failure bit 9. Fatal.
2-3-3	First 64K RAM failure bit A. Fatal.
2-3-4	First 64K RAM failure bit B. Fatal.
2-4-1	First 64K RAM failure bit C. Fatal.
2-4-2	First 64K RAM failure bit D. Fatal.

2-4-3	First 64K RAM failure bit E. Fatal.
2-4-4	First 64K RAM failure bit F. Fatal.
3-1-1	Slave DMA register failure. Fatal.
3-1-2	Master DMA register failure. Fatal.
3-1-3	Slave interrupt mask register failure. Fatal.
3-1-4	Slave interrupt mask failure. Fatal.
3-2-4	Keyboard controller test failure. Fatal.
3-3-4	Screen memory test failure. Fatal.
3-4-1	Screen initialisation failure. Fatal.
3-4-2	Screen retrace test failure. Fatal.
3-4-3	Search for video ROM failure
4-2-1	No timer tick. Non-fatal.
4-2-3	Gate A20 failure. Non-fatal.
4-2-4	Unexpected interrupt in protected mode. Non-fatal.

AWARD

v4.5

Beeps	Meaning
1 long 3 short	Video error

XT 8086/88 v3.0

Beeps	Meaning
1 long, 2 short	Video error
2 short with PRESS F1 KEY TO CONTINUE	Any non-fatal error
1 short	No error during POST

286/386 v3.03

Beeps	Meaning
1 long, 2 short	Video error
2 short with PRESS F1 KEY TO CONTINUE	Any non-fatal error
1 short	No error during POST
1 long, 3 short, with system halt.	Keyboard controller error

EGA BIOS v1.6

Beeps	Meaning
1 long, 2 short	Video error
1 long, 3 short	EGA memory error

COMPAQ

General

Message	Beeps	What they mean
163 Time and date not set	2 Short	Invalid time or date
	2 V Short	Power-on successful
RESUME "F1" key	None	Any failure
	3 Long	Processor Self-test

	2 Long	Memory map failure
101—I/O ROM error	1 Long 1 Short	Option ROM checksum
101—ROM error	1 Long 1 Short	System ROM checksum
102—System Board Failure	None	DMA or timers
102—System or Memory Board Failure	None	High-order addresses
162—System Options Error	2 Short	No diskette drives/mismatched types
162—System Options Not Set (Run SETUP)	2 Short	System SETUP
163—Time and Date Not Set	2 Short	Invalid time or date in CMOS
164—Memory Size Error	2 Short	Memory size discrepancy
170—Expansion Device not Responding (Run SETUP)	1 Short	Expansion device not responding
172—EISA Configuration Memory Corrupt	1 Short	CMOS Corrupt
173—PCI Slot ID Mismatch	1 Short	CMOS not Updated
174—ISA/PCI Configuration Slot Mismatch	1 Short	Plug & Play board not found
175—ISA/PCI Configuration Slot Mismatch	1 Short	CMOS not updated (Plug & Play)
176—Slot with No Readable ID (Run SETUP)	1 Short	CMOS not updated (Plug & Play)
177—SETUP Not Complete (Run SETUP)	1 Short	EISA Configuration not complete
178—Processor SETUP Invalid (Run setup)	None	Processor SETUP invalid
201—Memory Error	None	RAM failure
203—Memory Error	None	RAM failure
205—Cache Memory Failure	None	Cache Memory Error
206—Secondary Cache Controller Failure	None	Cache Memory Controller Failure
301—Keyboard Error	None	Keyboard failure
301—Keyboard Error or Test Fixture Installed	None	Keyboard test fixture
303—Keyboard Controller Error	None	Keyboard controller
304—Keyboard or System Unit Error	None	Keyboard interface
401—Printer Error	None	Printer controller
401—Port 1 Address Assignment conflict	2 Short	Ext/Internal Port assignments to Port 1
402—Monochrome Adapter Failure	1 Long 2 short	Monochrome display controller
501—Display Adapter Failure	1 Long 2 short	Video display controller
601—Diskette Drive Controller Error	None	Diskette drive controller
602—Diskette Drive Boot Record Error	None	Diskette media not bootable
605—Diskette Drive Type Error	2 Short	Wrong drive type used in setup
607—Diskette Drive Controller Error	2 Short	Configuration error
611—Primary Diskette Drive Assignment Conflict	2 Short	Configuration error
612—Secondary Diskette Drive Assignment Conflict	2 Short	Configuration error
702—A-Coprocessor Detection Error	2 Short	Add coprocessor or configuration error
703—Coprocessor Detection Error	2 Short	Add coprocessor or configuration error
1125—Internal Serial Port Failure	2 Short	Defective internal serial port
1150—xx Comm Port Setup Error	2 Short	Setup not correct (run SETUP)
1151—COM1 Address Assignment Conflict	2 Short	Ext/internal port assignments to COM1

1152—COM2 Address Assignment Conflict	2 Short	Ext/internal port assignments to COM2
1153—COM3 Address Assignment Conflict	2 Short	Ext/internal port assignments to COM3
1153—COM 4 Address Assignment Conflict	2 Short	Ext/internal port assignments to COM4
1154—Port 4 Address Assignment Conflict	2 Short	Incorrect COM 4 assignment
1600—32-Bit System Manager Board Failure	2 Short	Configuration mismatch
1730—HD 0 Does Not Support DMA Mode	2 Short	Configuration mismatch
1731—HD 1 Does Not Support DMA Mode	2 Short	Configuration mismatch
1740—HD 0 Failed Set Block Mode Command	2 Short	Configuration mismatch
1741—HD 1 Failed Set Block Mode Command	None	Wrong drive type
1750—Hard Drive 0 Failed Identify Command	None	Wrong drive type
1751—Hard Drive 0 Failed Identify Command	None	Wrong drive type
1760—Hard Drive 0 Does Not Support Block Mode	2 Short	Configuration mismatch
1761—Hard Drive 1 Does Not Support Block Mode	2 Short	Configuration mismatch
1771—Primary Drive Port Address Assignment Conflict	2 Short	Internal and external hard drive controllers assigned to primary address
1772—Secondary Disk Port Address Assignment Conflict		Internal and external hard drive controllers assigned to sec address
1780—Hard Drive 0 Failure	None	Hard drive/format error
1781—Hard Drive 1 Failure	None	Hard drive/format error
1782—Hard Drive Controller Failure	None	Hard drive controller
1790—Hard Drive 0 Error	None	Wrong drive type used in SETUP
1791—Hard Drive 1 Error	None	Wrong drive type used in SETUP
1792—Secondary Drive Controller Error	None	Hard drive error or wrong drive type
1793—Secondary Controller or Drive Failure	None	Hard drive error or wrong drive type
XX000Y ZZ Parity Check 2	None	RAM parity failure NOTE: XX000Y ZZ Address (XX), byte (Y), data bit (ZZ) of failed memory test
Hard Drive Parameter Table or BIOS Error	3 Long	Configuration or hardware failure
IOCHECK Active, Slot X	None	Defective board in slot x
Bus Master Timeout Slot X	None	Defective board in slot x
Audible	1 Short	Power-On successful
Audible	2 Short	Power-On successful
(RESUME "F1" KEY)	None	As indicated to continue

Contura 400 Family

Message on Screen	Beeps	What They Mean
101 System ROM Error	1 L 1 S	System ROM Checksum
101 I/0 ROM Error	None	Option ROM Checksum
102 System Board Failure	None	DMA, timers, etc or unsupported processor
162 System Options Error	2 Short	No diskette drive or drive type mismatch
162 System Options Not Set	2 Short	Configuration incorrect
163 Time & date Not Set	2 Short	Invalid time or date in CMOS
164 Memory Increase Detected	2 Short	CMOS incorrect
164 Memory Decrease Detected	2 Short	CMOS incorrect

168 CMOS Checksum invalid		
201 Memory Error	None	RAM failure
203 Memory Address Error	None	RAM failure
205 Memory Error	None	Cache memory error
207 Invalid Memory Configuration Module	None	Memory module installed incorrectly
209 NCA RAM Error	None	RAM Failure Error
211 Memory Failure	None	RAM Failure
301 Keyboard Error	None	Keyboard Failure
303 Keyboard Controller Error	None	System board keyboard controller
304 Keyboard or System Unit Error	None	Keyboard or System Unit Error
401 Printer Error	None	Printer controller
402 Monochrome Adapter Failure	1 L 2 S	Monochrome display controller.
501 Display Adapter Failure	1 L 2 S	Video display controller
601 Diskette Controller Error	None	Diskette controller circuitry
602 Diskette Boot	None	Diskette in drive A not
605 Diskette Drive Error	2 Short	Mismatch in drive type
702 Coprocessor Detection Error	None	Coprocessor upgrade detection error
702A Coprocessor Detection Error	2 Short	Coprocessor upgrade detection error
703 A Coprocessor Detected by POST	2 Short	Coprocessor or CMOS Error
1125 Internal Serial Port Failure	2 Short	Defective internal serial port
1780 Disk 0 failure	None	Hard drive/format error
1782 Disk Controller	None	Hard drive circuitry error
1790 Disk 0 Failure	None	Hard drive error or wrong drive type
Audible	1 Short	Poweron successful
Audible	2 Short	Poweron successful

DELL (PHOENIX)

Beeps	Meaning
1-1-2	Microprocessor register failure
1-1-3	Non-volatile RAM
1-1-4	ROM BIOS Checksum failure
1-2-1	Programmable interval timer
1-2-2	DMA Initialisation failure
1-2-3	DMA Page Register r/w failure
1-3	Video memory test failure
1-3-1/2-4-4	SIMMs not properly identified or used
3-1-1	Slave DMA register failure
3-1-2	Master DMA register failure
3-1-3	Master interrupt mask register failure
3-1-4	Slave interrupt mask register failure
3-2-2	Interrupt vector loading failure
3-2-4	Keyboard controller test failure
3-3-1	Non-volatile RAM power loss
3-3-2	Non-volatile RAM configuration
3-3-4	Video memory test failure
3-4-1	Screen initialisation failure
3-4-2	Screen retrace failure
3-4-3	Search for video ROM failure

4-2-1	No time tick
4-2-2	Shutdown failure
4-2-3	Gate A20 failure
4-2-4	Unexpected interrupt in protected mode
4-3-1	Memory failure above address
4-3-3	Timer chip counter 2 failure
4-3-4	Time-of-day clock stopped
4-4-1	Serial port test failure
4-4-2	Parallel port test failure
4-4-3/4-4-4	Maths coprocessor test failure/Cache test failure

IBM

Beeps	Meaning
1-1-3	CMOS Read/Write Error
1-1-4	ROM BIOS Check Error
1-2-X	DMA Error
1-3-X	Memory Module
1-4-4	Keyboard
1-4-X	Error in first 64K RAM
2-1-1	Run Setup
2-1-2	Run Setup
2-1-X	1st 64K RAM failed
2-2-2	Video Adapter
2-2-X	1st 64K RAM failed
2-3-X	Memory Module
2-4-X	Run Setup
3-1-X	DMA Register failed
3-2-4	Keyboard controller failed
3-3-4	Screen initialisation failed
3-4-1	Screen retrace test detected an error
3-4-2	POST searching for video ROM
4	Video adapter
All others	System board
1 long, 1 Short	Base 640K or Shadow RAM error
1 Long, 2-3 short	Video adapter
3 Short	System Board Memory
Continuous	System Board
Repeating Short	Keyboard stuck
None	System Board

AT

Beeps	Meaning
1 short	Normal POST, OK
2 short	POST error—check messages on display
None	Power supply, system board
Continuous	Power supply, system board

Repeating short beeps	Power supply, system board
1 long, 1 short	System board
1 long, 2 short	Display adapter (MDA, CGA)
1 long, 3 short	EGA adapter
3 long	3270 keyboard cardvt

MR BIOS

More under *"POST Codes" on page 233*.

Long	Short	Problem
0	1	Failed POST 1; Low level processor verification test.
0	2	Failed POST 2; Clears keyboard controller buffers.
0	3	Failed POST 3; Keyboard controller reset.
0	4	Failed POST 4; Low level keyboard controller i/f test.
0	5	Failed POST 5; Reading data from keyboard controller.
0	6	Failed POST 6; System board support chip initialisation.
0	9	Failed POST 9; ROM BIOS Checksum test.
0	13	Failed POST 13; 8254 timer channel 2 test.
0	15	Failed POST 15; CMOS shutdown byte test.
1	0	Failed POST 16; DMA channel 0 test.
1	1	Failed POST 17; DMA channel 1 test.
1	2	Failed POST 18; DMA page register test.
1	5	Failed POST 21; First 64K memory test.
1	6	Failed POST 22; Setup interrupt vector table.
1	7	Failed POST 23; Video initialisation.
1	8	Failed POST 24; Video memory test.

MYLEX/EUROSOFT

Beep	Meaning
1	Always present.
2	Video Adapter
3	Keyboard controller.
4	Keyboard.
5	8259 PIC 1
6	8259 PIC 2
7	DMA page register
8	RAM Refresh
9	RAM data test
10	RAM parity
11	8237 DMA controller 1
12	CMOS RAM
13	8237 DMA controller 2
14	CMOS battery
15	CMOS RAM checksum
16	BIOS ROM checksum

PACKARD BELL

See "Phoenix" on page -170.

PHOENIX

Refer to "POST Codes" on page 233.

QUADTEL

Beeps	Meaning
1	POST OK
2	Configuration Error; CMOS has changed.
1 long, 2 short	Video or adapter RAM
1 long, 3 short	Faulty expansion card.

TANDON

Slimline 286, 386SX and 486; 486 EISA

Beeps	Meaning
L-S-L-S	8254 counter timer.
S-L-S	RAM Refresh
L-L-L	System RAM
S-S-S	BIOS ROM Checksum
L-L	Distinct lack of video adapter
L-L-L-L	Video Adapter Failure

14 Error Messages/ Codes

AMI

Message	Fault	Action
CH-2 Timer Error	Non fatal. Could be a peripheral.	
INTR #1 Error	Interrupt Channel 1 has failed POST	Check exp cards for IRQs 0-7.
INTR #2 Error	As above, but for Interrupt Channel 2	Check exp cards for IRQs 8-15.
CMOS Battery State Low		Replace battery.
CMOS Checksum Failure	A checksum is generated when CMOS values are saved for error checking purposes on subsequent startups. This will appear if the checksum is different	Run Setup again.
CMOS Memory Size Mismatch	You've added memory, or some of what you've got has stopped working	Run Setup.
CMOS System Options Not Set	CMOS values are either corrupt or non-existent	Run Setup.
CMOS Display Type Mismatch	The display in the CMOS does not match what is actually found by the POST	Run Setup.
CMOS Memory Size Mismatch	The memory in the BIOS does not match that actually found on the motherboard	Run Setup again.
Display Switch Not Proper	Some motherboards have a switch or jumper setting which is changed if a monochrome or colour monitor is fitted	Reset the switch.
Keyboard is locked ... Unlock it		Unlock keyboard.
Keyboard Error	There is a timing problem with the keyboard	Check keyboard BIOS compatible, or set to "Not Installed", to skip keyboard test.
K/B Interface Error	Error with the keyboard connector.	
FDD Controller Failure	The BIOS cannot communicate with the floppy drive controller	It may just be disabled, or the cable may be loose.
HDD Controller Failure	As above, but for hard disks.	

C: Drive Error	There is no response from hard disk drive C:	Hard disk type may be set incorrectly, not formatted, or not properly connected.
D: Drive Error	As above.	
C: Drive Failure	As above but more serious.	
D: Drive Failure	As above.	
CMOS Time & Date Not Set		Run the Setup program.
Cache Memory Bad, Do Not Enable Cache!	Speaks for itself	You may need new cache memory. Try reseating first.
8042 Gate-A20 Error	The gate-A20 portion of the keyboard controller has failed	Replace the keyboard chip (8042).
Address Line Short!	There is an error in the memory address decoding circuitry	Try rebooting, it might go away!
DMA #1 Error	There is an error in the first DMA channel on the motherboard	Could be a peripheral device.
DMA #2 Error	There is an error in the second DMA channel on the motherboard	Could be a peripheral device.
DMA Error	There is an error within the DMA controller on the motherboard.	
No ROM Basic	There is nothing to boot from; may be no bootable sector on the boot up disk (A or C). The original IBM PC ran Basic from a ROM at this point (it was in a ROM next to the BIOS), but modern machines don't have it, hence this message	Check you haven't disabled booting from the A: drive, or that you've got A:, C: as the boot sequence. You might not have an active partition.
Diskette Boot Failure	The diskette in drive A: is corrupt.	
Invalid Boot Diskette	As above, but the disk is readable.	
On Board Parity Error	There is a parity error with memory on the motherboard at address XXXX (hex). On board means the memory is not on an expansion card.	Possibly correctable with software from motherboard manufacturer
Off Board Parity Error	There is a parity error with memory installed in an expansion slot at address XXXX (hex)	Possibly correctable with software from the motherboard manufacturer. You could try reseating your SIMMs.
Parity Error ????	A parity error with memory somewhere in the system, but God knows where. Possibly correctable with software from the motherboard manufacturer.	
Memory Parity Error at XXXX	Memory failed. If determined, it is displayed as XXXX. If not, as ????.	
I/O Card Parity Error at XXXX	An expansion card failed. If the address can be determined, it is displayed as XXXX, otherwise ????.	
DMA Bus Time-out	A device has driven the bus signal for more than 7.8 microseconds.	
Memory mismatch, run Setup		Try disabling Memory Relocation.

EISA CMOS Checksum Failure	The checksum for EISA CMOS is bad, or the battery.	
EISA CMOS inoperational	Read/Write error in ext CMOS RAM	The battery may be bad.
Expansion Board not ready at Slot X,Y, Z.	AMI BIOS cannot find the expansion board in whatever slot is indicated	Make sure the board is in the correct slot and is correctly seated.
Fail-Safe Timer NMI Inoperational	Devices that depend on the fail-safe NMI timer are not operating correctly.	
ID information mismatch for Slot X,Y, Z	The ID of the EISA Expansion Board in whatever slot is indicated does not match the ID in EISA CMOS RAM.	
Invalid Configuration Information for Slot X,Y, Z	The configuration information for EISA Expansion Board X,Y or Z is not correct. The board cannot be configured	Run the ECU.
Software Port NMI Inoperational	The software port NMI is not working.	
BUS Timeout NMI at Slot n	There was a bus timeout NMI at whatever slot is indicated.	
(E)nable (D)isable Expansion Board?		Type E to enable the expansion board that had an NMI, or D to disable it.
Expansion Board disabled at Slot n	The expansion board at whatever slot is indicated has been disabled.	
Expansion Board NMI at Slot n.	An expansion board NMI was generated from whatever slot is indicated.	
Fail-Safe Timer NMI	A fail-safe timer NMI has been generated.	
Software Port NMI	A software port NMI has been generated.	

APRICOT

Code	Meaning
02	Drive not ready (disk removed during boot)
04	CRC error (corrupt disk data)
06	Seek error (possible unformatted or corrupt disk)
07	Bad media (corrupt disk media block)
08	Sector not found (unformatted or corrupt diskette)
11	Bad read (corrupt data field on disk)
12	Disk failure (disk hardware or media fault)
20	PROM checksum error (corrupt boot PROM)
21	Sound generator failure (suspect sound chip)
22	Serial I/O failure (Z80 SIO fails r/w test)
23	Video chip failure (CRTC fails r/w test)
24	Video pointer RAM failure (system RAM failed)
25	System RAM failure (system RAM failure)
26	Parallel port failure (port driver problem)
27	Interrupt controller failure (8259A PIC failed r/w test)

28	Floppy disk controller failure (FCD failed r/w test)
29	Counter timer failure (CTC failed r/w test)
30	Serial channel failure (Ch A of Z80 SIO failed test)
31	Keyboard failure (initialisation test failed)
32	Timer accuracy failure (CTC accuracy check against timing loop failed)
33	Timer/PIC interaction failure (CTC/PIC timing interaction test failed)
34	IO processor failure (8089 IOP failed init/memory move test)
99	Non system disk

AST

See *AMI*.

AWARD

v4.5x

Code	Meaning
6	Cache/controller.
10	More than 1 IDE interface.
40	IDE floppy controller.
80	IDE controller.

XT 8086/88 v3.0

Code	Meaning
201	Memory test failed.
301	Keyboard error
601	Diskette power on diagnostic test failed.
1801	I/O expansion unit failed power on diagnostic.
Parity Check 1	Parity error in system board memory. Fatal.
Parity Check 2	Parity error in expansion unit memory. Fatal.

286/386 v 3.03

Msg	Meaning
Refresh Timing Error	The refresh clock is not operating as expected.
Keyboard Error/No Keyboard	Either a keyboard problem, or the keyboard is not attached.
Equipment Configuration Error	The system configuration determined by POST is different from what was defined using SETUP.
Memory Size Error	The amount of memory found by POST is different than the amount defined using SETUP.
Real Time Clock Error	The real time clock is not operating as expected.
Error initialising Hard Drive	Reset of fixed disk failed.
Error Initialising HD Controller	Fixed disk controller fails internal diagnostic.
Floppy Disk Cntrlr Error Or No Cntrlr Present	The floppy disk controller is failing self test, or it is not present.
CMOS RAM Error	The CMOS is invalid. This can be caused by the battery not operating correctly. SETUP must be run.
Press A key To Reboot	A call has been made to ROM BASIC; not in the Award BIOS.

Memory Addressing Error At XXXX	Memory errors. Values are as close as possible.
Disk Boot Failure, Insert System Disk And Press Enter	The system is unable to load the system from the boot disk.
Parity Error In Segment XXXX	This fatal error occurs during POST memory test.
Memory Verify Error	POST error. AA is # of MBytes AA:SSSS:FFFF boundary; SSSS=segment FFFF=offset.
IO Parity Error—System Halted	These occur after POST has finished.

ISA/EISA v4.5

Message	Meaning
CMOS BATTERY HAS FAILED	CMOS battery is no longer functional. It should be replaced.
CMOS CHECKSUM ERROR	Checksum of CMOS is incorrect. This can indicate that CMOS has become corrupt. This error may have been caused by a weak battery. Check the battery and replace if necessary.
DISK BOOT FAILURE, INSERT SYSTEM DISK AND PRESS ENTER	No boot device was found. Either a boot drive was not detected or the drive has no proper system files. Insert a system disk into Drive A: and press Enter. If you assumed the system would boot from the hard drive make sure the controller is inserted correctly and all cables are properly attached. Also be sure the disk is formatted as a boot device. Then reboot the system.
DISKETTE DRIVES OR TYPES MISMATCH ERROR—RUN SETUP	Type of diskette drive installed in the system is different from the CMOS definition. Run Setup to reconfigure the drive type correctly.
DISPLAY SWITCH IS SET INCORRECTLY	Display switch on the motherboard can be set to either monochrome or colour. This indicates the switch is set to a different setting than indicated in Setup. Determine which setting is correct, and then either turn off the system and change the jumper, or enter Setup and change the VIDEO selection.
DISPLAY TYPE HAS CHANGED SINCE LAST BOOT	Since last powering off the system, the display adapter has been changed. Reconfigure the system.
EISA Configuration Checksum Error	Run the EISA Configuration Utility. The EISA non-volatile RAM checksum is incorrect or cannot correctly read the EISA slot. Either the EISA non-volatile memory has become corrupt or the slot has been configured incorrectly. Also make sure the card is installed firmly in the slot. When this error appears, the system will boot in ISA mode, which allows you to run the EISA Configuration Utility.
EISA Configuration Is Not Complete	Run the EISA Configuration Utility. The slot configuration information stored in the EISA non-volatile memory is incomplete. When this error appears, the system will boot in ISA mode, which allows you to run the EISA Configuration Utility.
ERROR ENCOUNTERED INITIALIZING HARD DRIVE	Hard drive cannot be initialized. Be sure the adapter is installed correctly and all cables are correctly and firmly attached. Also make sure the correct hard drive type is selected in Setup.
ERROR INITIALIZING HARD DISK CONTROLLER	Cannot initialize controller. Make sure the cord is correctly installed. Be sure the correct hard drive type is selected in Setup. Also check to see if any jumper needs to be set correctly on the hard drive.
FLOPPY DISK CNTRLR ERROR OR NO CNTRLR PRESENT	Cannot find or initialize the floppy drive controller. make sure the controller is installed correctly and firmly. If there are no floppy drives installed, be sure the Diskette Drive selection in Setup is set to NONE.

Invalid EISA Configuration	Run the EISA Configuration Utility. The non-volatile memory containing EISA configuration information was programmed incorrectly or has become corrupt. Re-run EISA configuration utility to correctly program the memory. When this error appears, the system will boot in ISA mode, which allows you to run the EISA Configuration Utility.
KEYBOARD ERROR OR NO KEYBOARD PRESENT	Cannot initialize the keyboard. Make sure the keyboard is attached correctly and no keys are being pressed during the boot. If you are purposely configuring the system without a keyboard, set the error halt condition in Setup to HALT ON ALL, BUT KEYBOARD. This will cause the BIOS to ignore the missing keyboard and continue the boot.
Memory Address Error at ...	Indicates a memory address error at a specific location. You can use this location along with the memory map for your system to find and replace the bad memory chips.
Memory parity Error at ...	Indicates a memory parity error at a specific location. You can use this location along with the memory map for your system to find and replace the bad memory chips.
MEMORY SIZE HAS CHANGED SINCE LAST BOOT	Memory has been added or removed since the last boot. In EISA mode use Configuration Utility to reconfigure the memory configuration. In ISA mode enter Setup and enter the new memory size in the memory fields.
Memory Verify Error at ...	Indicates an error verifying a value already written to memory. Use the location along with your system's memory map to locate the bad chip.
OFFENDING ADDRESS NOT FOUND	This message is used in conjunction with the I/O CHANNEL CHECK and RAM PARITY ERROR messages when the segment that has caused the problem cannot be isolated.
OFFENDING SEGMENT:	This message is used in conjunction with the I/O CHANNEL CHECK and RAM PARITY ERROR messages when the segment that has caused the problem has been isolated.
PRESS A KEY TO REBOOT	This will be displayed at the bottom screen when an error occurs that requires you to reboot. Press any key and the system will reboot.
PRESS F1 TO DISABLE NMI, F2 TO REBOOT	When BIOS detects a Non-maskable Interrupt condition during boot, this will allow you to disable the NMI and continue to boot, or you can reboot the system with the NMI enabled.
RAM PARITY ERROR—CHECKING FOR SEGMENT ...	Indicates a parity error in Random Access Memory.
Should Be Empty But EISA Board Found	When this error appears, the system will boot in ISA mode, which allows you to run the EISA Configuration Utility. A valid board ID was found in a slot that was configured as having no board ID. When this error appears, the system will boot in ISA mode, which allows you to run the EISA Configuration Utility.
Should Have EISA Board But Not Found	Run EISA Configuration utility. The board installed is not responding to the ID request, or no board ID has been found in the slot. The system will boot in ISA mode, so you can run the EISA Configuration Utility.

Slot Not Empty	A slot designated as empty by the Configuration Utility actually contains a board. When this error appears, the system will boot in ISA mode, which allows you to run the EISA Configuration Utility.
SYSTEM HALTED, (CTRL-ALT-DEL) TO REBOOT ...	Present boot attempt has been aborted and system must be rebooted. Press and hold down the CTRL and ALT keys and press DEL.
Wrong Board In Slot	Run EISA Configuration Utility. The board ID does not match the ID stored in the EISA non-volatile memory. When this error appears, the system will boot in ISA mode, which allows you to run the EISA Configuration Utility.

COMPAQ

101—Processor

Code	Meaning
101—01	CPU test failed
101—02	32 Bit CPU test failed
101—91	Multiplication test failed
101—92	Multiplication test failed
101—93	Multiplication test failed
101—94	Multiplication test failed
102—01	Numeric coprocessor initial status word incorrect
102—02	Numeric coprocessor initial control word incorrect
102—03	Numeric coprocessor tag word not all ones
102—04	Numeric coprocessor tag word not all zeros
102—05	Numeric coprocessor exchange command failed
102—06	Numeric coprocessor masked exception incorrectly handled
102—07	Numeric coprocessor unmasked exception incorrectly handled
102—08	Numeric coprocessor wrong mask bit set in Status register
102—09	Numeric coprocessor unable to store real number
102—10	Numeric coprocessor real number calculation test failed
102—11	Numeric coprocessor speed test failed
102—12	Numeric coprocessor pattern test failed
102—15	Numeric coprocessor is inoperative or socket is unoccupied
102—16	Weitek coprocessor not responding
102—17	Weitek coprocessor failed register transfer test
102—18	Weitek coprocessor failed arithmetic operations test
102—19	Weitek coprocessor failed data conversion test
102—20	Weitek coprocessor failed interrupt test
102—21	Weitek coprocessor failed speed test
103—01	DMA page registers test failed
103—02	DMA byte controller test failed
103—03	DMA word controller test failed
104—01	Interrupt controller master test failed
104—02	Interrupt controller slave test failed
104—03	Interrupt controller software RTC is inoperative
105—01	Port 61 bit not at zero
105—02	Port 61 bit not at zero
105—03	Port 61 bit not at zero

105—04	Port 61 bit not at zero
105—05	Port 61 bit not at zero
105—06	Port 61 bit not at one
105—07	Port 61 bit not at one
105—08	Port 61 bit not at one
105—09	Port 61 bit not at one
105—10	Port 61 I/O test failed
105—11	Port 61 bit not at zero
105—12	Port 61 bit not at zero
105—13	No interrupt generated by fail-safe timer
105—14	NMI not triggered by fail-safe timer
106—01	Keyboard controller self-test failed
107—01	CMOS RAM test failed
108—02	CMOS interrupt test failed
108—03	CMOS interrupt test, CMOS not properly initialized
109—01	CMOS clock load data test failed
109—02	CMOS clock rollover test failed
109—03	CMOS clock test, CMOS not properly initialized
110—01	Programmable timer load data test failed
110—02	Programmable timer dynamic test failed
110—03	Program timer 2 load data test failed
111—01	Refresh detect test failed
112—01	Speed test Slow mode out of range
112—02	Speed test Mixed mode out of range
112—03	Speed test Fast mode out of range
112—04	Speed test unable to enter Slow mode
112—05	Speed test unable to enter Mixed mode
112—06	Speed test unable to enter Fast mode
112—07	Speed test system error
112—08	Unable to enter Auto mode in speed test
112—09	Unable to enter High mode in speed test
112—10	Speed test High mode out of range
112—11	Speed test Auto mode out of range
112—12	Speed test Variable Speed mode inoperative
113—01	Protected mode test failed
114—01	Speaker test failed
116—xx	Way 0 read/write test failed
199—00	Installed devices test failed

200—Memory

Code	Meaning
200—04	Real memory size changed
200—05	Extended memory size changed
200—06	Invalid memory configuration
200—07	Extended memory size changed
200—08	CLIM memory size changed
201—01	Memory machine ID test failed
202—01	Memory system ROM checksum failed

202—02	Failed RAM/ROM map test
202—03	Failed RAM/ROM protect test
203—01	Memory read/write test failed
203—02	Error while saving block under test in read/write test
203—03	Error while restoring block under test in read/write test
204—01	Memory address test failed
204—02	Error while saving block under test in address test
204—03	Error while restoring block under test in address test
204—04	A20 address test failed
204—05	Page hit address test failed
205—01	Walking I/O test failed
205—02	Error while saving block under test in walking I/O test
205—03	Error while restoring block under test in walking I/O test
206—xx	Increment pattern test failed
210—01	Memory increment pattern test
210—02	Error while saving memory in increment pattern test
210—03	Error while restoring memory in increment pattern test
211—01	Memory random pattern test
211—02	Error while saving memory in random memory pattern test
211—03	Error while restoring memory in random memory pattern test

301—Keyboard

Code	Meaning
301—01	Keyboard short test, 8042 self-test failed
301—02	Keyboard short test, interface test failed
301—03	Keyboard short test, echo test failed
301—04	Keyboard short test, keyboard reset failed
301—05	Keyboard short test, keyboard reset failed
302—01	Keyboard long test, failed
303—01	Keyboard LED test, 8042 self-test failed
303—02	Keyboard LED test, reset test failed
303—03	Keyboard LED test, reset failed
303—04	Keyboard LED test, LED command test failed
303—05	Keyboard LED test, LED command test failed
303—06	Keyboard LED test, LED command test failed
303—07	Keyboard LED test, LED command test failed
303—08	Keyboard LED test, command byte restore test failed
303—09	Keyboard LED test, LEDs failed to light
304—01	Keyboard repeat key test failed
304—02	Unable to enter mode 3
304—03	Incorrect scan code from keyboard
304—04	No Make code observed
304—05	Cannot disable repeat key feature
304—06	Unable to return to Normal mode

401—Printer

Code	Meaning
401—01	Printer failed or not connected
402—01	Printer Data register failed
402—02	Printer Control register failed
402—03	Printer Data register and Control register failed
402—04	Printer loopback test failed
402—05	Printer loopback test and Data register failed
402—06	Printer loopback test and Control register failed
402—07	Loopback test; Data register and Control register failed
402—08	Printer interrupt test failed
402—09	Printer interrupt test and Data register failed
402—10	Printer interrupt test and Control register failed
402—11	Printer interrupt; Data register and Control register failed
402—12	Printer interrupt test and loopback test failed
402—13	Interrupt test; loopback test and Data register failed
402—14	Interrupt test; loopback test and Control register failed
402—15	Interrupt test; loopback test Data/Control registers failed
402—16	Unexpected interrupt received
403—01	Printer pattern test failed
498—00	Printer failed or not connected

501—Video

Code	Meaning
501—01	Video controller test failed
502—01	Video memory test failed
503—01	Video attribute test failed
504—01	Video character set test failed
505—01	Video 80 x 25 mode 9 x 14 character cell test failed
506—01	Video 80 x 25 mode 8 x 8 character cell test failed
507—01	Video 40 x 25 mode test failed
508—01	Video 320 x 200 mode colour set 0 test failed
509—01	Video 320 x 200 mode colour set 1 test failed
510—01	Video 640 x 200 mode test failed
511—01	Video screen memory page test failed
512—01	Video grey scale test failed
514—01	Video white screen test failed
516—01	Video noise pattern test failed

600—Diskette Drive

Code	Meaning
600—xx	Diskette drive ID test
600—05	Failed to reset controller
600—20	Failed to get drive type
601—xx	Diskette drive format
601—05	Failed to reset controller
601—09	Failed to format a track

601—23	Failed to set drive type in ID media
602—xx	Diskette read test
602—01	Exceeded maximum soft error limit
602—02	Exceeded maximum hard error limit
602—03	Previously exceeded maximum soft error limit
602—04	Previously exceeded maximum hard error limit
602—05	Failed to reset controller
602—06	Fatal error while reading
603—xx	Diskette drive read/write compare test
603—01	Exceeded maximum soft error limit
603—02	Exceeded maximum hard error limit
603—03	Previously exceeded maximum soft error limit
603—04	Previously exceeded maximum hard error limit
603—05	Failed to reset controller
603—06	Fatal error while reading
603—07	Fatal error while writing
603—08	Failed compare of read/write buffers
604—xx	Diskette drive random seek test
604—01	Exceeded maximum soft error limit
604—02	Exceeded maximum hard error limit
604—03	Previously exceeded maximum soft error limit
604—04	Previously exceeded maximum hard error limit
604—05	Failed to reset controller
604—06	Fatal error while reading
605—xx	Diskette drive ID media test
605—20	Failed to get drive type
605—24	Failed to read diskette media
605—25	Failed to verify diskette media
606—xx	Diskette drive speed test
606—26	Failed to read media in speed test
606—27	Failed speed limits
607—xx	Diskette wrap test
607—10	Failed sector wrap test
608—xx	Diskette drive write-protect test
608—28	Failed write-protect test
609—xx	Diskette drive reset controller test
609—05	Failed to reset controller
610—xx	Diskette drive change line test
610—21	Failed to get change line status
610—22	Failed to clear change line status
694—00	Pin 34 not cut on 360 KB Diskette drive
697—00	Diskette type error
6xx—01	Exceeded maximum soft error limit
6xx—02	Exceeded maximum hard error limit
6xx—03	Previously exceeded maximum soft error limit
6xx—04	Previously exceeded maximum hard error limit
6xx—05	Failed to reset controller
6xx—06	Fatal error while reading

6xx—07	Fatal error while writing
6xx—08	Failed compare of read/write buffers
6xx—09	Failed to format a track
6xx—10	Failed sector wrap test
6xx—20	Failed to get drive type
6xx—22	Failed to clear change line status
6xx—23	Failed to set drive type in ID media
6xx—24	Failed to read diskette media
6xx—25	Failed to verify diskette media
6xx—26	Failed to read media in speed test
6xx—27	Failed speed limits
6xx—28	Failed write-protect test
698—00	Diskette drive speed not within limits
699—00	Drive/media ID error—rerun SETUP

1101—Serial Interface

Code	Meaning
1101—01	Serial port test; UART DLAB bit failure
1101—02	Serial port test; line input or UART fault
1101—03	Serial port test; address line fault
1101—04	Serial port test; data line fault
1101—05	Serial port test; UART control signal failure
1101—06	Serial port test; UART THRE bit failure
1101—07	Serial port test; UART DATA READY bit failure
1101—08	Serial port test; UART TX/RX buffer failure
1101—09	Serial port test; INTERRUPT circuit failure
1101—10	Serial port test; COM1 set to invalid interrupt
1101—11	Serial port test; COM2 set to invalid interrupt
1101—12	Serial port test; DRIVER/RECEIVER control signal failure
1101—13	Serial port test; UART control signal interrupt failure
1101—14	Serial port test; DRIVER/RECEIVER data failure
1109—01	Clock register initialization failure
1109—02	Clock register rollover failure
1109—03	Clock reset failure
1109—04	Input line or clock failure
1109—05	Address line fault
1109—06	Data line fault
1150—xx	Comm port SETUP error (run SETUP)

1201—Modem

Code	Meaning
1201—xx	Modem internal loopback test
1201—01	UART DLAB bit failure
1201—02	Line input or UART failure
1201—03	Address line fault
1201—04	Data line fault
1201—05	UART control signal failure
1201—06	UART THRE bit failure

1201—07	UART DATA READY bit failure
1201—08	UART TX/RX buffer failure
1201—09	Interrupt circuit failure
1201—10	COM1 set to invalid interrupt
1201—11	COM2 set to invalid interrupt
1201—12	DRIVER/RECEIVER control signal failure
1201—13	UART control signal interrupt failure
1201—14	DRIVER/RECEIVER data failure
1201—15	Modem detection failure
1201—16	Modem ROM and checksum failure
1201—17	Tone detection failure
1202—xx	Modem internal test
1202—01	Modem timeout waiting for SYNC (local loopback mode)
1202—02	Modem timeout waiting for response (local loopback mode)
1202—03	Modem exceeded data block retry limit (local loopback mode)
1202—11	Timeout waiting for SYNC (analogue loopback originate mode)
1202—12	Timeout waiting for modem response (analogue loopback originate mode)
1202—13	Exceeded data block retry limit (analogue loopback originate mode)
1202—21	Timeout waiting for SYNC (analogue loopback answer mode)
1202—22	Timeout waiting for modem response (analogue loopback answer mode)
1202—23	Exceeded data block retry limit (analogue loopback answer mode)
1203—xx	Modem external termination test
1203—01	Modem external TIP/RING failure
1203—02	Modem external DATA TIP/RING failure
1203—03	Modem line termination failure
1204—xx	Modem auto originate test
1204—01	Modem timeout waiting for SYNC
1204—02	Modem timeout waiting for response
1204—03	Modem exceeded data block retry limit
1204—04	RCV exceeded carrier lost limit
1204—05	XMIT exceeded carrier lost limit
1204—06	Timeout waiting for dial tone
1204—07	Dial number string too long
1204—08	Modem timeout waiting for remote response
1204—09	Modem exceeded maximum redial limit
1204—10	Line quality prevented remote connection
1204—11	Modem timeout waiting for remote connection
1205—xx	Modem auto answer test
1205—01	Modem timeout waiting for SYNC
1205—02	Modem timeout waiting for response
1205—03	Modem exceeded data block retry limit
1205—04	RCV exceeded carrier lost limit
1205—05	XMIT exceeded carrier lost limit
1205—06	Timeout waiting for dial tone
1205—07	Dial number string too long
1205—08	Modem timeout waiting for remote response
1205—09	Modem exceeded maximum redial limit
1205—10	Line quality prevented remote connection

1205—11	Modem timeout waiting for remote connection
1206—xx	Dial multifrequency tone test
1206—17	Tone detection failure
1210—xx	Modem direct connect test
1210—01	Modem timeout waiting for SYNC
1210—02	Modem timeout waiting for response
1210—03	Modem exceeded data block retry limit
1210—04	RCV exceeded carrier lost limit
1210—05	XMIT exceeded carrier lost limit
1210—06	Timeout waiting for dial tone
1210—07	Dial number string too long
1210—08	Modem timeout waiting for remote response
1210—09	Modem exceeded maximum redial limit
1210—10	Line quality prevented remote connection
1210—11	Modem timeout waiting for remote connection

1700—Hard Drive

Code	Meaning
1700—xx	Hard Drive ID test
1700—05	Failed to reset controller
1700—09	Failed to format a track
1700—41	Failed to ID hard (drive not ready)
1700—42	Failed to recalibrate drive
1700—45	Failed to get drive parameters from ROM
1700—46	Invalid drive parameters found in ROM
1700—66	Failed to initialize drive parameter
1700—69	Failed to read drive size from controller
1700—70	Failed translate mode
1700—71	Failed non-translate mode
1701—xx	Hard drive format
1701—05	Failed to reset controller
1701—09	Failed to format a cylinder
1701—42	Failed to recalibrate drive
1701—58	Failed to write sector buffer
1701—59	Failed to read sector buffer
1701—66	Failed to initialize drive parameter
1702—xx	Hard drive read test
1702—01	Exceeded maximum soft error limit
1702—02	Exceeded maximum hard error limit
1702—03	Previously exceeded maximum soft error limit
1702—04	Previously exceeded maximum hard error limit
1702—05	Failed to reset controller
1702—06	Fatal error while reading
1702—40	Failed cylinder 0
1702—65	Exceeded maximum bad sectors per track
1702—68	Failed to read long
1702—70	Failed translate mode
1702—71	Failed non-translate mode

1702—72	Bad track limit exceeded
1702—73	Previously exceeded bad track limit
1703—xx	Hard drive read/write compare test
1703—01	Exceeded maximum soft error limit
1703—02	Exceeded maximum hard error limit
1703—03	Previously exceeded maximum soft error limit
1703—04	Previously exceeded maximum hard error limit
1703—05	Failed to reset controller
1703—06	Fatal error while reading
1703—07	Fatal error while writing
1703—08	Failed compare of read/write buffers
1703—40	Cylinder 0 error
1703—55	Cylinder 1 error
1703—63	Failed soft error rate
1703—65	Exceeded maximum bad sectors per track
1703—67	Failed to write long
1703—68	Failed to read long
1703—70	Failed translate mode
1703—71	Failed non-translate mode
1703—72	Bad track limit exceeded
1703—73	Previously exceeded bad track limit
1704—xx	Hard drive random seek test
1704—01	Exceeded maximum soft error limit
1704—02	Exceeded maximum hard error limit
1704—03	Previously exceeded maximum soft error limit
1704—04	Previously exceeded maximum hard error limit
1704—05	Failed to reset controller
1704—06	Fatal error while reading
1704—40	Cylinder 0 error
1704—55	Cylinder 1 error
1704—65	Exceeded maximum bad sectors per track
1704—70	Failed translate mode
1704—71	Failed non-translate mode
1704—72	Bad track limit exceeded
1704—73	Previously exceeded bad track limit
1705—xx	Hard drive controller test
1705—05	Failed to reset controller
1705—44	Failed controller diagnostics
1705—56	Failed controller RAM diagnostics
1705—57	Failed controller to drive diagnostics
1706—xx	Hard drive ready test
1706—41	Drive not ready
1707—xx	Hard drive recalibrate test
1707—42	Failed to recalibrate drive
1708—xx	Hard drive format bad track test
1708—02	Exceeded maximum hard error limit
1708—05	Failed to reset controller
1708—09	Format bad track failed

Error Messages/ Codes

185

1708—42	Recalibrate drive failed
1708—58	Failed to write sector buffer
1708—59	Failed to read sector buffer
1709—xx	Hard drive reset controller test
1709—05	Failed to reset controller
1710—xx	Hard drive park head test
1710—45	Failed to get drive parameters from ROM
1710—47	Failed to park heads
1714—xx	Hard drive file write test
1714—01	Exceeded maximum soft error limit
1714—02	Exceeded maximum hard error limit
1714—03	Previously exceeded maximum soft error limit
1714—04	Previously exceeded maximum hard error limit
1714—05	Failed to reset controller
1714—06	Fatal error while reading
1714—07	Fatal error while writing
1714—08	Failed compare of read/write buffers
1714—10	Failed diskette sector wrap during read
1714—48	Failed to move disk table to RAM
1714—49	Failed to read diskette media in file write test
1714—50	Failed file I/O write test
1714—51	Failed file I/O read test
1714—52	Failed file I/O compare test
1714—55	Failed cylinder 1
1714—65	Exceeded maximum bad sectors per track
1714—70	Failed translate mode
1714—71	Failed non-translate mode
1714—72	Bad track limit exceeded
1714—73	Previously exceeded bad track limit
1715—xx	Hard drive head select test
1715—45	Failed to get drive parameters from ROM
1715—53	Failed drive head register test
1715—54	Failed digital input register test
1716—xx	Hard drive conditional format test
1716—01	Exceeded maximum soft error limit
1716—02	Exceeded maximum hard error limit
1716—05	Failed to reset controller
1716—06	Fatal error while reading
1716—07	Fatal error while writing
1716—08	Failed compare of read/write buffers
1716—40	Cylinder 0 error
1716—42	Failed to recalibrate
1716—55	Cylinder 1 error
1716—58	Failed to write sector buffer
1716—59	Failed to read sector buffer
1716—60	Failed to compare sector buffer
1716—65	Exceeded maximum bad sectors per track
1716—66	Failed to initialize drive

1716—70	Failed translate mode
1716—71	Failed non-translate mode
1716—72	Bad track limit exceeded
1716—73	Previously exceeded bad track limit
1717—xx	Hard drive ECC test
1717—01	Exceeded maximum soft error limit
1717—02	Exceeded maximum hard error limit
1717—03	Previously exceeded maximum soft error limit
1717—04	Previously exceeded maximum hard error limit
1717—05	Reset controller failed
1717—06	Fatal error while reading (BIOS statusor0 x 20)
1717—07	Fatal error while writing
1717—08	Compare data failed
1717—40	Cylinder 0 failed
1717—55	Cylinder 1 failed
1717—61	Failed uncorrectable error
1717—62	Failed correctable error
1717—65	Exceeded maximum bad sectors per track
1717—67	Failed to write long
1717—68	Failed to read long
1717—70	Failed translate mode
1717—71	Failed non-translate mode
1717—73	Previously exceeded bad track limit
1719—xx	Hard drive power mode test failed
1799—00	Invalid hard disk drive type
17xx—01	Exceeded maximum soft error limit
17xx—02	Exceeded maximum hard error limit
17xx—03	Previously exceeded maximum soft error limit
17xx—04	Previously exceeded maximum hard error limit
17xx—05	Failed to reset controller
17xx—06	Fatal error while reading
17xx—07	Fatal error while writing
17xx—08	Failed compare of read/write/compare
17xx—09	Failed to format a track
17xx—10	Failed sector wrap test
17xx—19	Controller failed to deallocate bad sectors
17xx—40	Failed cylinder 0
17xx—41	Drive not ready
17xx—42	Recalibrate failed
17xx—43	Failed to format bad track
17xx—44	Failed controller diagnostics
17xx—45	Failed to get drive parameters from ROM
17xx—46	Invalid drive parameters found in ROM
17xx—47	Failed to park heads
17xx—48	Failed to move hard drive table to RAM
17xx—49	Failed to read media in file write test
17xx—50	Failed file I/O write test
17xx—51	Failed file I/O read test

187

17xx—52	Failed file I/O compare test
17xx—53	Failed drive/head register test
17xx—54	Failed digital input register test
17xx—55	Failed cylinder 1
17xx—56	Hard drive controller RAM diagnostics failed
17xx—57	Hard drive controller to drive test failed
17xx—58	Failed to write sector buffer
17xx—59	Failed to read sector buffer
17xx—60	Failed uncorrectable ECC error
17xx—62	Failed correctable ECC error
17xx—63	Failed soft error rate
17xx—65	Exceeded maximum bad sectors per track
17xx—66	Failed initial drive parameter
17xx—67	Failed to write long
17xx—68	Failed to read long
17xx—69	Failed to read drive size from controller
17xx—70	Failed translate mode
17xx—71	Failed non-translate mode
17xx—72	Bad track limit exceeded
17xx—73	Previously exceeded bad track limit

1900—Tape Drive

Code	Meaning
1900—xx	Tape ID failed
1900—01	Hard drive not installed
1900—02	Cartridge not installed
1900—26	Cannot identify hard drive
1900—27	Hard drive incompatible with controller
1900—36	Hard drive not installed in correct position
1901—xx	Tape Servo Write
1901—01	Drive not installed
1901—02	Cartridge not installed
1901—03	Tape motion error
1901—04	Drive busy error
1901—05	Track seek error
1901—06	Tape write-protected error
1901—07	Tape already Servo written
1901—08	Unable to Servo Write
1901—11	Drive recalibration error
1901—21	Servo pulses on second time, but not first
1901—22	Never got to EOT after Servo check
1901—25	Unable to erase cartridge
1901—27	Drive not compatible with controller
1901—91	Power lost during test, replace cartridge, or bulk erase it
1902—xx	Tape format
1902—01	Drive not installed
1902—02	Cartridge not installed
1902—03	Tape motion error

1902—04	Drive busy error
1902—05	Track seek error
1902—06	Tape write-protected error
1902—09	Unable to format
1902—10	Format mode error
1902—11	Drive recalibration error
1902—12	Tape not Servo Written
1902—13	Tape not formatted
1902—21	Got servo pulses second time, but not first
1902—22	Never got to EOT after servo check
1902—27	Drive not compatible with controller
1902—28	Format gap error
1903—xx	Tape drive sensor test
1903—01	Drive not installed
1903—23	Change line unset
1903—27	Drive not compatible with controller
1904—xx	Tape BOT/EOT test
1904—01	Drive not installed
1904—02	Cartridge not installed
1904—03	Tape motion error
1904—04	Drive busy error
1904—05	Track seek error
1904—15	Sensor error flag
1904—27	Drive not compatible with controller
1904—30	Exception bit not set
1904—31	Unexpected drive status
1904—32	Device fault
1904—33	Illegal command
1904—34	No data detected
1904—35	Power-on reset occurred
1905—xx	Tape read test
1905—01	Drive not installed
1905—02	Cartridge not installed
1905—03	Tape motion error
1905—04	Drive busy error
1905—05	Track seek error
1905—14	Drive timeout error
1905—16	Block locate (block ID) error
1905—17	Soft error limit exceeded
1905—18	Hard error limit exceeded
1905—19	Write error (probable ID error)
1905—27	Drive not compatible with controller
1905—30	Exception bit not set
1905—31	Unexpected drive status
1905—32	Device fault
1905—33	Illegal command
1905—34	No data detected
1905—35	Power-on reset occurred

1906—xx	Tape read/write compare test failed
1906—01	Drive not installed
1906—02	Cartridge not installed
1906—03	Tape motion error
1906—04	Drive busy error
1906—05	Track seek error
1906—06	Tape write-protected error
1906—14	Drive timeout error
1906—16	Block locate (block ID) error
1906—17	Soft error limit exceeded
1906—18	Hard error limit exceeded
1906—19	Write error (probable ID error)
1906—20	NEC fatal error
1906—27	Drive not compatible with controller
1906—30	Exception bit not set
1906—31	Unexpected drive status
1906—32	Device fault
1906—33	Illegal command
1906—34	No data detected
1906—35	Power-on reset occurred
1907—xx	Tape write-protected test
1907—24	Failed write-protected test
1907—30	Exception bit not set
1907—31	Unexpected drive status
1907—32	Device fault
1907—33	Illegal command
1907—34	No data detected
1907—35	Power-on reset occurred
19xx—01	Drive not installed
19xx—02	Cartridge not installed
19xx—03	Tape motion error
19xx—04	Drive busy error
19xx—05	Track seek error
19xx—06	Tape write-protected error
19xx—07	Tape already Servo Written
19xx—08	Unable to Servo Write
19xx—09	Unable to format
19xx—10	Format mode error
19xx—11	Drive recalibration error
19xx—12	Tape not Servo Written
19xx—13	Tape not formatted
19xx—14	Drive timeout error
19xx—15	Sensor error flag
19xx—16	Block locate (block ID) error
19xx—17	Soft error limit exceeded
19xx—18	Hard error limit exceeded
19xx—19	Write (probably ID) error
19xx—20	NEC fatal error

19xx—21	Got servo pulses second time but not first
19xx—22	Never got to EOT after servo check
19xx—23	Change line unset
19xx—24	Write-protect error
19xx—25	Unable to erase cartridge
19xx—26	Cannot identify drive
19xx—27	Drive not compatible with controller
19xx—28	Format gap error
19xx—36	Failed to set FLEX format mode
19xx—37	Failed to reset FLEX format mode
19xx—38	Data mismatched on directory track
19xx—39	Data mismatched on track 0
19xx—40	Failed self-test
19xx—91	Power lost during test

2402—Video

Code	Meaning
2402—01	Video memory test failed
2403—01	Video attribute test failed
2404—01	Video character set test failed
2405—01	Video 80 x 25 mode 9 x 14 character cell test failed
2406—01	Video 80 x 25 mode 8 x 8 character cell test failed
2407—01	Video 40 x 25 mode test failed
2408—01	Video 320 x 200 mode colour set 0 test failed
2409—01	Video 320 x 200 mode colour set 1 test failed
2410—01	Video 640 x 200 mode test failed
2411—01	Video screen memory page test failed
2412—01	Video grey scale test failed
2414—01	Video white screen test failed
2416—01	Video noise pattern test failed
2417—01	Lightpen Text mode test failed, no response
2417—02	Lightpen Text mode test failed, invalid response
2417—03	Lightpen medium resolution mode test failed, no response
2417—04	Lightpen medium resolution mode failed, invalid response
2418—01	ECG memory test failed
2418—02	ECG shadow RAM test failed
2419—01	ECG ROM checksum test failed
2420—01	ECG attribute test failed
2421—01	ECG 640 x 200 Graphics mode test failed
2422—01	ECG 640 x 350 16-colour set test failed
2423—01	ECG 640 x 350 64-colour set test failed
2424—01	ECG monochrome Text mode test failed
2425—01	ECG monochrome Graphics mode test failed
2431—01	640 x 480 Graphics test failure
2432—01	320 x 200 Graphics (256-colour mode) test failure
2448—01	Advanced VGA Controller test failed
2451—01	132-column Advanced VGA test failed
2456—01	Advanced VGA 256-colour test failed

3206—Audio

Code	Meaning
3206—xx	Audio System internal error

5234—Advanced Graphics 1024 Board

Code	Meaning
5234—01	Failed AGC controller test
5235—01	Failed AGC memory test, AGC board
5235—02	Failed AGC memory test, expansion board
5235—03	Failed AGC memory test, dualport memory
5235—04	Failed AGC memory test, program memory
5236—01	Failed AGC 640 x 480 Graphics test, 16 colours
5237—01	Failed AGC 640 x 480 Graphics test, 256 colours
5238—01	Failed AGC 1024 x 768 Graphics test, 16 colours
5239—01	Failed AGC 1024 x 768 Graphics test, 256 colours
5240—xx	Failed shared memory arbitration test

6000—Network Interface

Code	Meaning
6000—xx	Pointing device interface
6014—xx	Ethernet Configuration test failed
6016—xx	Ethernet reset test failed
6028—xx	Ethernet internal loopback test failed
6029—xx	Ethernet external loopback test failed
6054—xx	Token Ring Configuration test failed
6056—xx	Token Ring reset test failed
6068—xx	Token Ring internal loopback test failed
6069—xx	Token Ring external loopback test failed
6089—xx	Token Ring open

XXXX—SCSI Interface

Code	Meaning
XXXX—02	Drive not installed
XXXX—03	Media not installed
XXXX—05	Seek failure
XXXX—06	Drive timed out
XXXX—07	Drive busy
XXXX—08	Drive already reserved
XXXX—09	Reserved
XXXX—10	Reserved
XXXX—11	Media soft error
XXXX—12	Drive not ready
XXXX—13	Media error
XXXX—14	Drive hardware error
XXXX—15	Illegal drive command
XXXX—16	Media was changed
XXXX—17	Tape write protected

XXXX—18	No data detected
XXXX—21	Drive command aborted
65XX—24	Media hard error
66XX—24	Media hard error
67XX—24	Media hard error
XXXX—25	Reserved
XXXX—30	Controller timed out
XXXX—31	Unrecoverable error
XXXX—32	Controller/drive not connected
XXXX—33	Illegal controller command
XXXX—34	Invalid SCSI bus phase
XXXX—35	Invalid SCSI bus phase
XXXX—36	Invalid SCSI bus phase
XXXX—39	Error status from drive
XXXX—40	Drive timed out
XXXX—41	SCSI bus stayed busy
XXXX—42	ACK/REQ lines bad
XXXX—43	ACK did not deassert
XXXX—44	Parity error
XXXX—50	Data pins bad
XXXX—51	Data line 7 bad
XXXX—52	MSG, C/D, or I/O lines bad
XXXX—53	BSY never went busy
XXXX—54	BSY stayed busy
XXXX—60	Controller CONFIG-1 register fault
XXXX—61	Controller CONFIG-2 register fault
XXXX—65	Media not unloaded
XXXX—90	Fan failure
XXXX—91	Over temperature condition
XXXX—92	Side panel not installed
XXXX—99	AutoLoader reported tape not loaded properly

8601—Pointing Device

Code	Meaning
8601—xx	Pointing device interface
8601—01	Mouse ID fails
8601—02	Left button is inoperative
8601—03	Left button is stuck closed
8601—04	Right button is inoperative
8601—05	Right button is stuck closed
8601—06	Left block not selected
8601—07	Right block not selected
8601—08	Timeout occurred
8601—09	Mouse loopback test failed
8601—10	Pointing device is inoperative

Error Messages/
Codes

Compaq Expanded Memory Manager (CEMM)

Code	Meaning
00	LGDT instruction
01	LIDT instruction
02	LMSW instruction
03	LL2 instruction
04	LL3 instruction
05	MOV CRx instruction
06	MOV DRx instruction
07	MOV TRx instruction

CEMM Exception Errors

Code	Meaning
00	Divide
01	Debug exception
02	NMI or parity
03	INT 0 (Arithmetic Overflow)
04	INT 3
05	Array bounds check
06	Invalid opcode
07	Coprocessor device not available
08	Double fault
09	Coprocessor segment overrun
10	Invalid TSS
11	Segment not present
12	Stack fault
13	General protection fault
14	Page fault
16	Coprocessor
32	Attempt to write to protected area
33	Reserved
34	Invalid software interrupt

These are in the *XX000B YYZZ* format:

XX represents which bank of 18 chips

B determines which byte the defective chip is in (0=low byte, 1=high byte).

YY or ZZ identifies which bit or individual chip is bad. See below for XX/YY references.

For example, 040001 0010 specifies chip U24.

For Version 2 (Assy No. 000361) and Version 3 (Assy No. 000555) System Boards, use the formula defined above (XX000B YYZZ). If XX = 08 or 09, replace the system board. Does not apply to Version 1 (Assy No. 000094) system boards.

64K Chip	XX = 06, 07	XX = 04, 05	XX = 02, 03	XX = 00, 01
256K Chips	XX = 2027	XX = 181F	XX = 1017	XX = 0007
Bank 4	Bank 3	Bank 2	Bank 1	
Data Bit	B = 0B = 1	B = 0B = 1	B = 0B = 1	B = 0B = 1
YY or ZZ	LowHigh	LowHigh	LowHigh	LowHigh
80	U27U40	U52U66	U82U93	U107 U124
40	U28U41	U53U67	U83U94	U108 U125
20	U29U42	U54U68	U84U95	U109 U126
10	U30U43	U55U69	U85U96	U110 U127
08	U31U44	U56U70	U86U97	U111 U128
04	U32U45	U57U71	U87U98	U112 U129
02	U33U46	U58U72	U88U99	U113 U130
01	U34U47	U59U73	U89U100	U114 U131
00	U35U48	U60U74	U90U101	U115 U132

GENERAL

Message	Meaning
Invalid ROM Parameter Table	Probably from NetWare, on Phoenix 286/386 BIOSes and AMI 286 BIOSes when the user definable parameters are not compatible.
WARNING: Cannot disable Gate A20	Gate A20 is an alternate method of controlling memory above 1Meg, which needs to be actively controlled by HIMEM.SYS. Unset from BIOS.

HP VECTRA

Code	Meaning
000f	Microprocessor error
001x	BIOS ROM error
008x	Video ROM error
009x-bx	Option ROM error while testing address range c800-dfff
00cx-dx	Option ROM error while testing address range e000-efff
011x	RTC error while testing the CMOS register
0120	RTC error
0130	RTC/System configuration error
0240	CMOS memory/system configuration error
0241	CMOS memory error
0250	Invalid configuration
0280	CMOS memory error
02c0-c1	EEPROM error
02d0	Serial # not present
030x-3x	Keyboard/Mouse controller error
034x-5x	Keyboard test failure
03e0-4	Keyboard/Mouse controller error
03e5-b	Mouse test failure
03ec	Keyboard/Mouse controller error

195

0401	Protected Mode failure
050x	Serial Port error
0506	Datacomm conflict
0510-20	Serial Port error
0543-5	Parallel Port error
0546	Datacomm conflict
06xx	Keyboard key stuck
07xx	Processor speed error
0800	Boot ROM conflict
0801	Boot ROM not found
081x	Integrated Ethernet Interface errors
0900	Fan error
110x-01	Timer error
20xa	Memory mismatch
21xx/22xx	DMA error
30xx	HP-HIL error
4xxx	RAM error
5xxx	As above
61xx	Memory address line error
62xx	RAM parity error/memory controller error
630x	RAM test error
6400	As above
6500	BIOS ROM shadow error
6510	Video BIOS shadowing error/system ROM error
6520	Option ROM shadowing error
65a0-f0	Shadow error probably caused by system board memory
66xx	Shadow error probably caused by memory on accessory board
7xxx	Interrupt error
8003	Bad drive configuration
8004	CMOS Drive/System Configuration error
8005-6	Bad drive configuration
8007	CMOS Drive/System Configuration error
8048-a	Hard disk drive identity error
8050	Hard disk drive controller conflict
84xx	Bad boot sector
8x0d	Controller Busy/Controller Error
8x0e	Hard disk error
8x0f	Hard disk drive mismatch
8x10	Controller Busy/Controller Error
8x11	Hard disk drive control error
8x12	Controller Busy/Controller Error
8x13	Hard disk drive control error
8x20-1	Controller Busy/Controller Error
8x28	Hard disk drive splitting error
8x30	Hard disk drive control error
8x38	Controller Busy/Controller Error
8x39-b	Hard disk drive control error
8x3c	Controller Busy/Controller Error

8x40	As above
8x41-4	Hard disk drive control error
8x45	Controller Busy/Controller Error
8x49	Hard disk drive control error
8x4b	As above
9xxx	Flexible disk drive error
9x0a	Flexible disk drive conflict
9x10	As above
A00x	Numeric coprocessor error
B300	Cache controller error
B320	Memory cache module error
Cxxx	Extended RAM error (for HP-HIL PCs)
Exxx	Bus memory error

IBM AT

10X - System Board/Setup/90-95 proc board

Code	Meaning
000	SCSI Adapter not enabled
02X	SCSI Adapter
08X	SCSI terminator
101	System Board or Interrupt failure.
102	ROM Checksum or timer error, 90/95 proc board
102	Timer failure (AT)
103	ROM Checksum Error (PC)
103	Timer interrupt failure (AT)
104	Protected mode failure (AT)
105	Last 8042 command not accepted.
106	Converting logic test
107	Interrupt failure or Hot NMI test.
108	Timer bus test.
109	Direct memory access test error.
110	Planar parity error, memory, system board
111	I/O perity error, memory adapter or memory
112	Watchdog timeout, any adapter, system board
113	DMA arbitration tiimeout, any adapter.
114	Ext ROM error, any adapter
115	80386 protected mode failure/BIOS checksum
116	80386 16/32 bit test failed/planar/read/write
118	System board memory, riser, cache
119	2.88 Mb drive installed but not supported
120	90-95 processor self-test failure
121	Unexpected hardware interrupts occurred.
129	Internal (L2) cache test
131	Cassette wrap test failed (bad system board)
132	DMA extended registers
133	DMA verify logic
134	DMA arbitration logic
151	Real Time Clock Failure (or CMOS error on 5170)

197

152	CMOS Date and Time error (5170)
160	Planar ID not recognised
161	System Options Error (Battery failure) CMOS chip power
162	System options error (Run Setup) CMOS Checksum error
163	Time and date not set (Run Setup).
164	Memory size error (Run Setup) CMOS does not match sys.
165	System options not set – reconfigure
166	Adapter busy; any adapter, comm cartridge
167	Clock not updating
169	Set configuration/features
170	90-95 ASCII setup error, PCC user error
171	I/O card failure, battery
172	90-95 NVRAM rolling bit error
173	PCC only, diskette in use when suspended
174	Set configuration/features
175	Security error; system board. Primary secure data, Riser card
176	Chassis intrusion detector not cleared.
177	Security error; system board, Administrator password
178	Security error; system board, Riser card
179	Run Diags for more info; More Utilites, error log
181	Any adapter, run auto config
182	Privileged access password needed; reset pw jump
183	Enter priv access rather than PW on password
184	Thinkpad 700 system board password corrupt
185	Thinkpad 700 system board password corrupt
186	Security error; system board, Riser Card
187	Set system ID from ref disk
188	Thinkpad 700 system board password corrupt
189	3 password attempts
190	System Board. Chassis intrusion detector cleared.
191	82385 cache test failed, system board
192	N51 Lid switch, Thinkpad 700 run diags
193	System board, memory, riser(90/95), proc bd
194	System board, memory, riser(90/95), proc bd
199	User indicated configuration not correct.

2XX - Memory

Code	Meaning
201	Memory test failed.
202	Memory address error (line error 00..15)
203	Memory address error (line error 16..23)
204	Relocated memory (run diags again)
205	CMOS error
207	ROM failure
210	Processor board or memory riser
211	Base 64K on I/O channel failed
215	Base memory or daughter card
216	Base memory or daughter card

221	This is a COINS error code. ROM-RAM parity
225	Wrong speed SIMM
229	L2 cache test
231	Expanded memory option error
241	Unsupported SIMM
251	SIMM location changed
262	Base or Extended memory error

3XX - Keyboard

Code	Meaning
301	Keyboard software reset failure or stuck key failure
302	User indicated error or PCAT system unit keylock is locked.
303	Keyboard or system unit error.
304	Keyboard or system unit error; CMOS does not match system.
305	Keyboard 5v error, external keypad
306	System board, aux input device
307	System board, aux input device
308	Numeric keyboard, system board
365	Replace Keyboard
366	Replace Interface Cable
367	Replace Enhancement Card or Cable

4XX - Monochrome/Printer Adapter

Code	Meaning
401	Monochrome memory test or horizontal sync frequency test
408	User indicated display attributes failure.
416	User indicated character set failure.
424	User indicated 80X25 mode failure.
432	Parallel port test failed (monochrome adapter).

5XX – CGA or Video Adapter

Code	Meaning
501	Colour memory test failed
508	User indicated display attribute failure.
516	User indicated character set failure.
524	User indicated 80X25 mode failure.
532	User indicated 40X25 mode failure.
540	User indicated 320X200 graphics mode failure.
548	User indicated 640X200 graphics mode failure.
556	Light pen test failed.
564	User indicated screen paging test failure.

6XX - Diskette Drive and Adapter

Code	Meaning
601	Diskette power on diagnostics test failed.
602	Diskette test failed; boot record is not valid.
603	Diskette size failure
604	Wrong diskette drive type
605	POST cannot unlock diskette drive
606	Diskette verify function failed.
607	Write protected diskette.
608	Bad command diskette status returned.
610	Diskette initialization failed.
611	Timeout diskette status returned (could not read dskt)
612	Bad NEC diskette status returned (BIOS dskt routines)
613	Bad DMA diskette status returned (overrun failure)
614	DMA boundary software problem.
621	Bad seek.....Diskette status returned.
622	Bad CRC....diskette status returned. Reformat scratch diskette, retry.
623	Record not found....diskette status returned. Reformat diskette, retry.
624	Bad address mark....diskette status returned. Reformat scratch diskette and retry.
625	Bad NEC seek.....diskette status returned.
626	Diskette data compare error. Reformat scratch diskette, retry before accepting.
627	Diskette line change error
628	Diskette removed (invalid media)
630	Index stuck hi/lo A drive
631	Index stuck hi/lo A drive
632	Track 0 stuck off/on A drive
633	Track 0 stuck off/on A drive
640	Index stuck hi/lo B drive
641	Index stuck hi/lo B drive
642	Track 0 stuck off/on B drive
643	Track 0 stuck off/on B drive
650	Drive speed error
651	Format, verify failure
652	Format, verify failure
653	Read, write
654	Read, write
655	Controller failure
656	Drive failure
662	Wrong drive type installed, drive, cable
663	Wrong media type
657	Write protect stuck
658	Change line stuck
659	Write protect stuck
660	Change line stuck
670	System board, drive, cable
675	System board, drive, cable

7XX - Maths Coprocessor

Code	Meaning
701	CoPro Failure; replace Coprocessor

9XX - Parallel Printer Adapter

Code	Meaning
901	Parallel printer adapter test failed.
914	Conflict between 2 parallel printer adapters.

10XX - Parallel Printer Adapter

Code	Meaning
1001	Parallel printer adapter test failed.
1014	Conflict between 2 parallel printer adapters.

11XX - Async Adapter

Code	Meaning
1101	Asynchronous or 16550 failure. Make sure adapter not set for "current loop".
1102	Card selected feedback error
1103	Port 102h fails register check
1106	Serial option cannot be put to sleep
1107	Serial device cable, system board
1108	Async IRQ3/4 error
1109	Async IRQ3/4 error
1110	Modem Status Register not clear/16550 register test failure
1111	Ring Indicate failure/Internal or external 16550 wrap failed
1112	Trailing Edge Ring indicate failure/ Ring Indicate failure/Internal or external 16550 wrap failed
1113	Receive and Delta Receive line signal detect failure/16550 transmit or receive error
1114	16550 transmit or receive error
1115	Delta Receive line signal detect failure. 16550 receive data not match transmit
1116	Line Control Register (all bits cannot be set). 16550 interrupt.
1117	Line Control Register (all bits cannot be reset). 16550 failed baud rate
1118	Transmit holding and/or shift register stuck on. 16550 interrupt driven wrap
1119	Data Ready stuck on. 16550 FIFO
1120	Interrupt Enable Register (all bits cannot be set)
1121	Interrupt Enable Register (all bits cannot be reset)
1122	Interrupt pending stuck on
1123	Interrupt ID register stuck on
1124	Modem Control Register (all bits cannot be set)
1125	Modem Control Register (all bits cannot be reset)
1126	Modem Status Register (all bits cannot be set)
1127	Modem Status Register (all bits cannot be reset)
1128	Interrupt ID Failure
1129	Cannot force overrun error
1130	No Modem Status Interrupt
1131	Invalid Interrupt status pending
1132	No data ready
1133	No data available Interrupt

1134	No Transmit Holding Interrupt
1135	No Interrupts
1136	No Receive Line Status Interrupt
1137	No Receive data available
1138	Transmit Holding Register not empty
1139	No Modem Status Interrupt
1140	Transmit Holding Register not empty
1141	No Interrupts
1142	NO IRQ4 Interrupt
1143	No IRQ3 Interrupt
1144	No Data Transferred
1145	Max Baud rate failed
1146	Min Baud rate failed
1148	Timeout Error
1149	Invalid Data Returned
1150	Modem Status Register error
1151	No DSR to Delta DSR
1152	No Data Set Ready
1153	No Delta
1154	Modem Status Register not clear
1155	No CTS and Delta CTS
1156	No Clear to Send
1157	No delta CTS

12XX - Alternate Async Adapter

As for 11XX.

13XX - Game Controller

Code	Meaning
1301	Game control adapter test failed.
1302	Joystick test failed.

14XX - Graphics Printer

Code	Meaning
1401	Printer failure
1402	Printer not ready
1403	No paper, interrupt failure
1404	System board timeout
1405	Parallel adapter failure
1406	Presence test failed

15XX - SDLC Adapter

Code	Meaning
1501	Adapter test failed.
1510	8255 port B failure.
1511	8255 port A failure.
1512	8255 port C failure.

1513	8253 timer 1 did not reach terminal count.
1514	8253 timer 1 stuck on.
1515	8253 timer 0 did not reach terminal count.
1516	8253 timer 0 stuck on.
1517	8253 timer 2 did not reach terminal count.
1518	8253 timer 2 stuck on.
1519	8273 port B error
1520	8273 port A error.
1521	8273 command ADAPTER Read timeout.
1522	Interrupt level 4 failure.
1523	Ring Indicate stuck on.
1524	Receive clock stuck on.
1525	Transmit clock stuck on.
1526	Test indicate stuck on.
1527	Ring indicate not on.
1528	Receive clock not on.
1529	Transmit clock not on.
1530	Test indicate not on.
1531	data set ready not on.
1532	Carrier detect not on.
1533	Clear to send not on.
1534	Data set ready stuck on.
1536	Clear to send stuck on.
1537	Level 3 interrupt failure.
1538	Receive interrupt results error.
1539	Wrap data miscompare.
1540	DMA channel 1 error.
1541	DMA channel 1 error.
1542	Error in 8273 error checking or status reporting.
1547	Stray interrupt level 4.
1548	Stray interrupt level 3.
1549	Interrupt presentation sequence timeout.

16XX - Display Station Emulation

Code	Meaning
1604	Adapter error
1608	Adapter error
1624	Adapter error.
1634	Adapter error.
1644	Adapter error.
1652	Adapter error.
1654	Adapter error.
1658	Adapter error.
1664	Adapter error.

1662	Interrupt Level switches set incorrectly or DSEA Adapter error.
1668	Interrupt Level switches set incorrectly or DSEA Adapter error.
1674	Station address error or DSEA Adapter error.
1684	Feature not installed or Device address switches set incorrectly.
1688	Feature not installed or Device address switches set incorrectly.

17XX - Fixed Disk Drive and Adapter (ST 506)

Code	Meaning
1701	PC Fixed disk POST error (drive not ready)
1701	PCAT Hardfile adapter test failed
1702	PC Fixed disk adapter error.
1702	PCAT Timeout error
1703	PC Fixed disk drive error.
1703	PCAT Seek Failure
1704	PC Fixed disk adapter or drive error.
1704	PCAT Controller Failure
1705	No Record Found
1706	Write Fault Error
1707	Track "0" Error
1708	Head Select Error
1709	Bad ECC.
1710	Read Buffer Overrun. drive not ready
1711	Bad Address Mark. Drive not ready
1712	Bad Address Mark. Load Adv. Diags. from cold boot (5170 only)
1713	Data Compare Error. DMA boundary
1714	Drive Not Ready. POST error
1715	Track 0 error (wrong drive?)
1716	Diag track (CE) bad
1717	Surface read errors
1726	Data compare error
1730	Replace Adapter
1731	Replace Adapter
1732	Replace Adapter
1735	Bad command
1750	Drive verify/read/write error
1751	Drive verify/read/write error
1752	Drive verify/read/write error
1753	Random read test error
1754	Seek test error
1755	ST506 controller
1756	ECC test error
1757	Head select test error
1780	Fixed disk 0 failure (fatal no IPL Capability). Timeout
1781	Fixed disk 1 failure (fatal drive "0" may still be OK). Timeout
1782	Fixed disk controller failure (fatal no IPL from hardfile)
1790	Fixed disk 0 error (non fatal...f1 can attempt IPL from drive) check for improper cabling.
1791	Fixed disk 1 error (non fatal...f1 can attempt IPL from drive)

18XX - Expansion Unit Errors

Code	Meanings
1800	PCI adapter requested a hardware interrupt not available.
1801	I/O expansion unit POST error. PCI adapter requested memory resources not available.
1802	System board PCI adapter requested I/O address not available.
1803	PCI adapter requested memory address not available.
1804	PCI adapter requested memory address not available
1805	PCI adapter ROM error.
1810	Enable/Disable failure.
1811	Extender card warp test failed (disabled).
1812	High order address lines failure (disabled).
1813	Wait state failure (disabled). If 3278/79 adapter or /370 adapter installed check for down level Extender Adapter (ECA011).
1814	Enable/Disable could not be set on.
1815	Wait state failure (disabled).
1816	Extender card warp test failed (enabled).
1817	High order address lines failure (enabled).
1818	Disable not functioning.
1819	Wait request switch not set correctly.
1820	Receiver card wrap test failure.
1821	Receiver high order address lines failure.
1850	PnP adapter requested a hardware interrupt not available.
1851	PnP adapter requested memory resources not available.
1852	PnP adapter requested I/O address not available.
1853	PnP adapter requested memory address not available.
1854	PnP adapter requested memory address not available.
1855	PnP adapter ROM error.
1856	PnP adapter requested DMA address not available
1962	Startup sequence error.

20XX - Binary Synchronous Communications Adapter

Code	Meaning
2001	POST failed.
2010	8255 port A failure.
2011	8255 port B failure.
2012	8255 port C failure.
2013	8253 timer 1 did not reach terminal count.
2014	8253 timer 1 stuck on.
2016	8253 timer 2 did not reach terminal count or timer 2 stuck on.
2017	8251 Data set ready failed to come on.
2018	8251 Clear to send not sensed.
2019	8251 Data set ready stuck on.
2020	8251 error
2021	8251 hardware reset failed.
2022	8251 software reset failed.
2023	8251 software "error reset" failed.
2024	8251 transmit ready did not come on.
2025	8251 receive ready did not come on.

2026	8251 could not force "overrun" error status.
2027	Interrupt failure—no timer interrupt.
2028	Interrupt failure....transmit, replace card or planar.
2029	Interrupt failure....transmit, replace card.
2030	Interrupt failure....receive, replace card or planar.
2031	Interrupt failure....receive, replace card.
2033	Ring indicate stuck on.
2034	Receive clock stuck on.
2035	Transmit clock stuck on.
2036	Test indicate stuck on.
2037	Ring indicate stuck on.
2038	Receive clock not on.
2039	Transmit clock not on.
2040	Test indicate not on.
2041	Data set ready not on.
2042	Carrier detect not on.
2043	Clear to send not on.
2044	Data set ready stuck on.
2045	Carrier detect stuck on.
2046	Clear to send stuck on.
2047	Unexpected transmit interrupt.
2048	Unexpected receive interrupt.
2049	Transmit data did not equal receive data.
2050	8251 detected overrun error.
2051	Lost data set ready during data wrap.
2052	Receive timeout during data wrap.

21XX - Alternate Binary Synchronous Communications Adapter

As for 20XX.

22XX - Cluster Adapter Errors

Code	Meaning
2201	Cluster Adapter Failure
2221	Replace Cluster Adapter

23XX - Plasma Monitor Adapter

24XX - EGA Adapter

Code	Meaning
2401	Enhanced Graphics Adapter Failure
2402	Diagnostic video error planar 8512
2409	Display
2410	System board
2462	Video configuration error.

26XX - PC/370

27XX - PC/3277

28XX - 3278/79 Emulation Adapter

Code	Meaning
2801	Adapter failure (coax not attached). If 3270PC, check Keyboard/Timer ROM (ECA040)
2854	Diagnostic Incompatibility
2859	Possible bad BSC Card

29XX - Colour Printer

Code	Meaning
2901	COLOUR PRINTER Colour Graphics printer tests failed

30XX - LAN Network

Code	Meaning
3001	Adapter Failure Replace Primary LAN Adapter
3002	ROM Failure....Replace Primary LAN Adapter
3003	ID Failure....Replace Primary LAN Adapter
3004	RAM Failure....Replace Primary LAN Adapter
3005	Host Interrupt Failure....Replace Primary LAN Adapter
3006	NEG 12V DC Failure....Replace Primary LAN Adapter
3007	Digital Wrap Failure....Replace Primary LAN Adapter
3008	Host Interrupt Failure....Replace Primary LAN Adapter
3009	Sync Failure....Replace Primary LAN Adapter
3010	Time Out Failure....Replace Primary LAN Adapter
3011	Time Out Failure....Replace Primary LAN Adapter
3012	Adapter Failure....Replace Primary LAN Adapter
3013	Digital Failure....Replace Primary LAN Adapter
3014	Digital Failure....Replace Primary LAN Network Adapter
3015	Analogue Failure (RF) (adapter not hooked to translator)
3016	Analogue failure
3020	ROM BIOS Failure
3041	Continuous RF Signal Detected. Hot carrier (not this card)
3042	Continuous RF Signal Sent.. Hot carrier (this card)

31XX - Alternate LAN Network

As for 30XX.

32XX - 3270 PC Display Adapter

35XX - Enhanced Display Station Adapter

Code	Meaning
3504	Adapter connected to twinax during off line tests
3508	Workstation address conflict, Incorrect Diags or Adapter
3588	Feature not installed or Device addr. switches set
3588	incorrectly or Adapter error.

36XX - GPIB Adapter

Code	Meaning
3601	Base Address incorrect
3602	Write to SPMR failed
3603	Write to ADR failed or addressing problems
3610	Adapter cannot be programmed to listen
3611	Adapter cannot be programmed to talk
3612	Adapter cannot take control with IFC
3613	Adapter cannot go to standby
3614	Adapter cannot take control asynchronously
3615	Adapter cannot take control synchronously
3616	Adapter cannot pass control
3617	Adapter cannot be addressed to listen
3618	Adapter cannot be unaddressed to listen
3619	Adapter cannot be addressed to talk
3620	Adapter cannot be unaddressed to talk
3621	Adapter unaddressable to listen with extended addressing
3622	Adapter unaddressable to listen with extended addressing
3623	Adapter unaddressable to listen with extended addressing
3624	Adapter unaddressable to listen with extended addressing
3625	Adapter cannot write to self
3626	Adapter cannot generate handshake error
3627	Adapter cannot detect DCL message
3628	Adapter cannot detect SDC message
3629	Adapter cannot detect END with EOI
3630	Adapter cannot detect EOI with EOI
3631	Adapter cannot detect END with 8 bit EOS
3632	Adapter cannot detect END with 7 bit EOS
3633	Adapter cannot detect GET
3634	Mode 3 addressing not functioning
3635	Adapter cannot recognize undefined command
3636	Adapter cannot detect REM
3637	Adapter cannot clear REM or LOK
3638	Adapter cannot detect SRQ
3639	Adapter cannot conduct serial poll
3640	Adapter cannot conduct parallel poll
3650	Adapter cannot DMA to 7210
3651	Data error on DMA to 7210
3652	Adapter cannot DMA form 7210
3653	Data error on DMA from 7210
3658	Unevoked interrupt received
3659	Adapter cannot interrupt of ADSC
3660	Adapter cannot interrupt on ADSC
3661	Adapter cannot interrupt on CO
3662	Adapter cannot interrupt on DO
3663	Adapter cannot interrupt on DI
3664	Adapter cannot interrupt on ERR
3665	Adapter cannot interrupt on DEC

3666	Adapter cannot interrupt on END
3667	Adapter cannot interrupt on DET
3668	Adapter cannot interrupt on APT
3669	Adapter cannot interrupt on CPT
3670	Adapter cannot interrupt on REMC
3671	Adapter cannot interrupt on LOKC
3672	Adapter cannot interrupt on SRQI
3673	Adapter cannot interrupt terminal count on DMA to 7210
3674	Adapter cannot interrupt terminal count on DMA from 7210
3675	Spurious DMA terminal count interrupt
3697	Illegal DMA configuration setting detected
3698	Illegal interrupt level configuration setting detected

38XX - Data Acquisition Adapter

Code	Meaning
3801	Adapter test failed
3810	Timer read test failed
3811	Timer interrupt test failed
3812	Delay, BI14 test failed
3813	Rate, BI13 test failed
3814	BO14, ISIRQ test failed
3815	BOO, Counting test failed
3816	Countout, BISTB test failed
3817	BOO, BOCTS test failed
3818	BO1, BIO test failed
3819	BO2, BI1 test failed
3820	BO3, BI2 test failed
3821	BO4, BI3 test failed
3822	BO5, BI4 test failed
3823	BO6, BI5 test failed
3824	BO7, BI6 test failed
3825	BO8, BI7 test failed
3826	BO9, BI8 test failed
3827	BO10, BI9 test failed
3828	BO11, BI10 test failed
3829	BO12, BI11 test failed
3830	BO13, BI12 test failed
3831	BO15, AICE test failed
3832	BOSTB, BOGATE test failed
3833	BICTS, BIHOLD test failed
3834	AICO, BI15 test failed
3835	Counter interrupt test failed
3836	Counter read test failed
3837	AO0 Ranges test failed
3838	AO1 Ranges test failed
3839	AI0 Values test failed

3840	AI1 Values test failed
3841	AI2 Values test failed
3842	AI3 Values test failed
3843	Analog input interrupt test failed
3844	AI23 Address or Value test failed

39XX - Professional Graphics Adapter

Code	Meaning
3901	Adapter Tests failed
3902	Rom1 self test failure
3903	Rom2 self test failure
3904	Ram self test failure
3905	Coldstart failure cycle power
3906	Data error in communications RAM
3907	Address error in communications RAM
3918	Bad data detected while read/write to 6845 'like' registers
3909	Bad data in lower EOH bytes read/writing 6845 'like' registers
3910	PGC display bank output latches
3911	Basic clock failure
3912	Command control error
3913	VSYNC scanner
3914	HSYNC scanner
3915	Intech failure
3916	LUT address error
3917	LUT red RAM chip error
3918	LUT green RAM chip error
3919	LUT blue RAM chip error
3920	LUT data latch error
3921	Horizontal display failure
3922	Vertical display failure
3923	Light pen
3924	Unexpected error
3925	Emulator addressing error
3926	Emulator data latch
3927	Emulator RAM base for error codes 27—30
3931	Emulator H/V display problem
3932	Emulator cursor position
3933	Emulator attribute display problem
3934	Emulator cursor display
3935	Fundamental emulation RAM problem
3936	Emulation character set problem
3937	Emulation graphics display
3938	Emulator character display problem
3939	Emulator bank select error
3940	Display RAM U2
3941	Display RAM U4
3942	Display RAM U6
3943	Display RAM U8

3944	Display RAM U10
3945	Display RAM U1
3946	Display RAM U3
3947	Display RAM U5
3948	Display RAM U7
3949	Display RAM U9
3950	Display RAM U12
3951	Display RAM U14
3952	Display RAM U16
3953	Display RAM U18
3954	Display RAM U20
3955	Display RAM U11
3956	Display RAM U13
3957	Display RAM U15
3958	Display RAM U17
3959	Display RAM U19
3960	Display RAM U22
3961	Display RAM U24
3962	Display RAM U26
3963	Display RAM U28
3964	Display RAM U30
3965	Display RAM U21
3966	Display RAM U23
3967	Display RAM U25
3968	Display RAM U27
3969	Display RAM U29
3970	Display RAM U32
3971	Display RAM U34
3972	Display RAM U36
3973	Display RAM U38
3974	Display RAM U40
3975	Display RAM U31
3976	Display RAM U33
3977	Display RAM U35
3978	Display RAM U37
3979	Display RAM U39
3980	PGC RAM timing failure
3981	PGC R/W latch
3982	S/R bus output latches
3983	Addressing error (vertical column of memory..U2 at top)
3984	Addressing error (vertical column of memory..U4 at top)
3985	Addressing error (vertical column of memory..U6 at top)
3986	Addressing error (vertical column of memory..U8 at top)
3987	Addressing error (vertical column of memory..U10 at top)

3988	Base for error codes 8891 (hbank data latch errors)
3992	RAS/CAS PGC failure
3993	Multiple write modes/nibble mask errors
3994	Row nibble failure (display RAM)
3995	PGC addressing failure

44XX - 3270/G/GX Display

45XX - IEEE-488 Adapter

46XX - Mulitport Adapter

5001-5017 - Thinkpad, L40, N51 System Board

5018 - Thinkpad, L40, N51 LCD Assembly

5019,22,23 - Thinkpad, L40, N51 System Board or LCD Assembly

5030,31 - Thinkpad, L40, N51 External display or system board

5032,33,37 - Thinkpad, L40, N51 External display

5038 – Thinkpad, L40, N51 External CRT

5041 - Thinkpad, N51 External display, system board, I/O panel

5051,62 - Thinkpad, N51 System Board, LCD components

56XX - Financial Adapter

Code	Meaning
5601	Personal System 2 keyboard is not attached.
5602	Keyboard self test failed. Use a keyboard
5603	Invalid configuration of keyboards detected.
5604	No port has keyboard attached to financial input conn.
5605	Keyboard self test failed.
5606	Selected 4700 keyboard not attached to system.
5607	Invalid key code from keyboard on PIN Keypad (diagnostic selection invalid).
5608	4700 keyboard not operating correctly
5609	Invalid system for the keyboard program.
5610	No PIN Keypad attached (diagnostic selection error)
5611	Key code received other than expected by DIAG PROG. PIN keypad failed.
5612	Encrypting PIN Keypad detected data of an incorrect length
5614	No PIN Keypad attached to Financial Input Conn.
5615	Key on 4700 Kybd used to cancel PIN entries has incorrect code. Pin Pad Failed Self Test.
5616	The Pin Keypad is not attached to the pointing device connector
5617	Pin Keypad failed self test
5618	Pin Keypad has a communication error
5619	System invalid for PIN keypad driver
5621	Magnetic Stripe device error
5622	Magnetic Stripe reader/encoder error Wrong Diagnostic Diskette Level.
5623	No Magnetic Stripe device connected to the Financial Input Conn.
5624	The key on the 4700 Kybd that is used to cancel PIN entries has an incorrect code.
5625	No Magnetic Stripe device connected
5626	Data read and data encoded by mag stripe device do not match
5627	Magnetic stripe unit self test failed

5629	System invalid for the magnetic stripe unit driver
5630	STATUS = F1 system attempted unsuccessful IPL from diskette.
5631	STATUS REMOTE START attempt to establish connection with 4700 controller has begun.
5632	Diagnostics failed to load from diskette drive
5633	STATUS REMOTE IPL. Initial loading of a program from the 4700 controller is in progress.
5634	remote ipl error between 4700 pc and controller
5641	Financial Input adapter failed
5651	Financial Output adapter failed
5652	Output failure of printer or adapter
5653	The customization data for the printer missing
5654	Loop cable for the printer not connected
5655	PRINTER REDIRECT error in the order of config.sys
5661	Financial Security adapter failed
5662	Data Encryption tried during normal operation without the Financial Security adapter installed
5663	No "Master Key" is present in the Financial Security adapter
5690	4700PC banking features not those expected

62XX - Store Loop Adapter

64XX – Ethernet terminator or cable

69XX - SYS 36/PC Driver Card

Code	Meaning
6907	System/36PC expansion cable left attached to PC while running 36 Driver Card diagnostics

71XX - Voice Communications Adapter

73XX - 3.5" Adapter

74XX - PS/2 Display Adapter

75XX – XGA Display

76XX - Personal Page Printer

Code	Meaning
7601	Adapter failure
7602	Adapter failure
7603	Failure
7604	Cable problem

78XX - High Speed Adapter

79XX - 3117 Scanner

Code	Meaning
7901	Adapter failure
7902	Lamp problem
7902	Device Card problem
7903	Device Card problem

82XX - 4055 Info Window

Code	Meaning
8200	INFO WINDOW INVALID error. Contact your support structure.
8201	INFO WINDOW NORMAL POWER ON. No action necessary
8202	INFO WINDOW TIMER RESET (TIMEOUT) System controller
8203	INFO WINDOW 8031 CHIP System controller board
8204	INFO WINDOW RAM System controller board
8205	INFO WINDOW ROM CRC ROM System controller board
8206	INFO WINDOW RAM CRC System controller board
8207	INFO WINDOW NVRAM CRC. Could be setting display power switch off during an update.
8208	INFO WINDOW NVRAM BATTERY NVRAM battery System controller board
8209	INFO WINDOW NVRAM FAILURE System controller board
8210	INFO WINDOW NVRAM DATA INVALID
8211	INFO WINDOW ANALOG-TO-DIGITAL System controller board
8212	INFO WINDOW GRAPHIC SYNC FAILURE Sync card System controller board
8213	INFO WINDOW TIME OF DAY Clock Set time and Date
8214	INFO WINDOW SPEECH LOGIC FAILURE Audio card System controller board Power supply
8215	INFO WINDOW INTERNAL RS 232C WRAP System controller
8216	INFO WINDOW EXTERNAL RS 232C WRAP Run test with the wrap plug on display to identify failure. System controller board
8217	INFO WINDOW HIGH RESOLUTION SYNCS If the test screen was distorted: IBM EGA card IBM EGA jumper card If the test screen was readable: Sync card System controller board
8218	INFO WINDOW LOW FREQUENCY SYNCS If the test screen was distorted: IBM EGA card IBM EGA jumper card. If the test screen was readable: Sync card System controller board
8219	INFO WINDOW EGA RGB SIGNALS TEST IBM EGA card IBM EGA jumper card Sync card System controller board
8220	INFO WINDOW RGB INSERT COMPARE Sync card
8221	INFO WINDOW MISSING HI/LOW BEEPS Audio card System controller board

8222	**INFO WINDOW RT CHANNEL AUDIO**
	Audio card
	System controller board
8223	**INFO WINDOW LT CHANNEL AUDIO**
	Audio card
	System controller board
8224	**INFO WINDOW NO SYNCS VIDEO #1**
	Sync card
	Decoder card
	System controller board
8225	**INFO WINDOW NO SYNCS VIDEO #2**
	Sync card
	Decoder card
	System controller board
8226	**INFO WINDOW 16/64 COLOUR MODE**
	Switching card
	System controller board
8227	**INFO WINDOW LEFT/RIGHT SHIFT**
	Deflection board
	System controller board
	Switching card
8228	**INFO WINDOW AUX MONITOR ON/OFF**
	Decoder card
	System controller board
8229	**INFO WINDOW INTERLACE ON/OFF**
	Sync card
	Deflection board
8230	**INFO WINDOW VIDEO INPUT SELECT**
	Decoder card
	System controller board
8231	**INFO WINDOW RGB ONLY MODE**
	Sync card
8232	**INFO WINDOW COMPOSITE ONLY MODE**
	Sync card
	System controller board
	Switching card
	Decoder card
8233	**INFO WINDOW OVERLAY**
	Switching card
	Deflection board
	Sync card
8234	**INFO WINDOW RGB/VIDEO**
	Sync card
8235	**INFO WINDOW SYSTEM TIMER TEST**
	System controller card
8236	**INFO WINDOW INTERNAL PROGRAM**
	Verify system diskette and ROM levels are compatible.
	System controller board

8237	INFO WINDOW CANNOT CALIBRATE
	System controller board
	Touch screen
	Power supply
8238	INFO WINDOW CONTROL PROGRAM
	Contact your support structure. Possible system controller board
8239	INFO WINDOW CONTROL PROGRAM
	Contact your support structure. Possible system controller board
8240	INFO WINDOW CPU NOT LISTENING
	IBM GPIB card
	System controller board
8241	INFO WINDOW GPIB SEND/RECV COUNT
	Contact your support structure.
8242	INFO WINDOW RS-232C INTERFACE
	Run the wrap test with the wrap plug on the System controller board
8243	INFO WINDOW TOUCH SCREEN
	System controller board
8244	INFO WINDOW FAILURE OF VDP-1
	Problem in VDP-1 cable
8245	INFO WINDOW FAILURE OF VDP-2
	Problem in VDP-2 cable
8246	INFO WINDOW A1/A2 DETECTION
	Sync card/System controller board
8247	INFO WINDOW HIGH RESOLUTION SYNCS
	Sync card
8248	INFO WINDOW TV FREQUENCY SYNCS
	Sync card
8249	INFO WINDOW GPIB (BUS)
	System controller board
8250	INFO WINDOW CRC errors DETECTED
	IEEE 488 cable
	IBM GPIB card
	System controller board
8251	INFO WINDOW CRC errors DETECTED
	IEEE 488 cable
	IBM PC GPIB card
	System controller board
8252	INFO WINDOW GPIB TIME OUT
	IBM PC GPIB card
	System controller board
	IEEE 488 cable
	Power supply
	Videodisc player problem
8253	INFO WINDOW GPIB TIME OUT
	IBM PC GPIB card
	System controller board
	IEEE 488 cable
	Power supply
	Videodisc player problem
8254	INFO WINDOW GPIB SEQUENCE
	Contact your support structure.

8255	INFO WINDOW INT PROGRAM error Contact your support structure. System controller board
8256	INFO WINDOW TIME OUT System controller board Sync card IEEE 488 cable IBM PC GPIB card
8257	INFO WINDOW RETRIES OF CRC errors System controller board IEEE 488 cable IBM PC GPIB card
8258	INFO WINDOW error IN GPIB COMMS System controller board IEEE 488 cable IBM PC GPIB card
8259	INFO WINDOW GPIB CONTROLLER error IBM PC GPIB card IEEE 488 cable System controller board
8260	INFO WINDOW INSERT CONTROL LOGIC Sync card System controller board
8261	INFO WINDOW WRONG RGB COLOUR Video output board Switching card Sync card System controller board CRT and yoke assembly
8262	INFO WINDOW PLAYER RESPONSE Verify that videodisc is on and contains a videodisc Go to the IBM Infowindow Guide to Operations and test the videodisc player interface.
8263	INFO WINDOW ADDITIONAL EQUIPMENT Audio problem: Replace audio card Dual frequency monitor failure: Replace switching card Colour composite monitor failure: Replace decoder card
8264	INFO WINDOW RGB OUTPUT SIGNALS Sync card
8265	INFO WINDOW EGA CLOCK error IBM EGA jumper card IBM EGA card
8266	IBM EGA JUMPER INTERRUPT error IBM EGA card switch settings IBM EGA jumper card IBM EGA card
8267	INFO WINDOW EGA GRAPHICS SYNC IBM PC graphic sync cable IBM EGA jumper card Sync card IBM EGA card

8268	SYNC PRESENT WITHOUT CABLE IBM EGA card
8269	NO AUDIO VIDEODISC 1/L INPUT Audio card
8270	NO AUDIO VIDEODISC 2/R INPUT Audio card
8271	INFO WINDOW IBM EGA CARD MAP 0222: Failure isolation for the IBM EGA card. Perform IBM EGA card failure isolation
8272	INFO WINDOW EGA MEMORY FAILURE Replace IBM EGA card
8273	INFO WINDOW EGA GRAPHICS MEMORY MAP 0225: Failure isolation for memory modules. Perform memory module failure isolation
8274	RESERVED Contact your support structure and report this error code.
8275	RESERVED Contact your support structure and report this error code.
8276	DISKETTE CANNOT SUPPORT See IBM Infowindow DISPLAY ROM LEVEL compatibility levels
8277	RESERVED Contact your support structure and report this error code
8278	INFO WINDOW HI RES DISPLAY Switching card Sync card MAP 0222: Failure isolation for the IBM EGA card. Perform IBM EGA card failure isolation.
8279	INFO WINDOW TIME OF DAY CLOCK System controller board
8280	IBM PC DOS error OCCURRED Follow directions on screen. Contact your support structure and report this error code.

84XX - Speech Adapter errors

85XX - Expanded Memory Adapter errors

86XX – Mouse System Board

Code	Meaning
8601	Mouse defective
8602	User indicated error
8603	System board failure
8604	System board or mouse failure
8611	Thinkpad 700 Keyboard (pointing stick)
8612	Thinkpad 700 Keyboard control card
8613	Thinkpad 700 system board

89XX – IBM Music Card

91XX - 3363 Optical Disk Drive

Code	Meaning
9101	POST error—Drive #1 failed—Reseat Cables and Adapter
9102	Drive #1 failed—Reinsert Cartridge, Reseat Adapter
9103	Drive #1 failed—Reseat Cables and Adapter
9104	Drive #2 failed—Reseat Cables and Adapter

9105	Drive #2 failed—Reinsert cartridge. Reseat Cables and Adapter
9106	Drive #2 failed—Reseat Cables and Adapter
9107	Adapter hung on BUSY—Reseat Cables and Adapter
9110	DIAGS error—Data not recorded—Check Adapter, Drive, Cable
9111	Data not readable—Check Adapter, Drive, Cable
9112	Sector demarked—Check Adapter, Drive, Cable
9113	Controller Error—Check Adapter, Drive, Cable, switches on Adapter DS302 (8088 vs 80286)
9114	Sector Read/Write Error—Check Drive, Adapter, or Cable
9115	Scramble Buffer Error—Check Drive, Adapter, Cable
9116	Data Buffer Error—Check Drive, Adapter, Cable
9117	Drive RAM/ROM Error—Check Drive, Adapter, Cable
9118	Invalid Command—Check Drive, Adapter, Cable
9119	Track Jump Error—Check Drive, Adapter, Cable
9120	Laser Error—Check Drive, Adapter or Cable
9121	Focus Error—Check Cartridge, Drive, Adapter or Cable
9122	Motor Sync Error—Cartridge upside down, Check Drive, Adapter, Cable
9123	Write Fault—Check Drive, Adapter or Cable
9124	General Drive Error—Check Drive, Adapter, Cable
9125	Sense Command Failed—Check Drive, Adapter, Cable
9126	Invalid Command—Check Drive, Adapter, Cable
9127	Sense Command Failed—Check Drive, Adapter, Cable
9128	Disk Not Initialized—Check Drive, Adapter, Cable
9129	Disk ID Did Not Match—Check Drive, Adapter, Cable
9130	Read-Only Disk Installed—Check Disk, Drive
9131	No Disk Present—Check Disk, Drive, Adapter, Cable
9132	Illegal Disk Detected—Check Disk, Adapter, Drive, Cable
9133	No Disk Change Detected—Check Drive, Adapter, Cable
9134	Read-Only Disk Detected—Check Drive, Adapter, Cable
9135	Illegal Disk Detected—Check Drive, Adapter, Cable
9136	Sense Command Failed—Check Adapter, Drive, Cable
9138	No Disk Change Detected—Retry test again. Check Drive, Adapter, Cable
9141	No Disk Change Detected—Retry tests. Check Drive, Adapter, Cable
9144	WRITE-PROTECT Window Not Opened—Retry tests. Check Drive, Adapter, Cable
9145	No Disk Change Detected—Retry tests. Check Drive, Adapter, Cable
9146	WRITE-PROTECT Window Not Closed—Retry tests. Check Drive, Adapter, Cable
9148	Adapter Card—Check Adapter, Drive or Cable
9150	Seek Command Failed—Check Drive, Adapter, cable
9151	Not At Track Zero—Check Drive, Adapter, Cable
9152	Track Address Error—Check Drive, Adapter, cable
9153	Not At Track 17099—Check Drive, Adapter, Cable
9154	Track Address Error—Check Drive, Adapter, Cable
9155	Track Address 17K Not Found—Check Drive, Adapter, Cable
9156	Seek Time Too Long—Check Drive, Adapter, Cable
9157	Sense Command Failed—Check Drive, Adapter, Cable
9158	No Data Read Error Found—Check Drive, Adapter, Cable
9159	No Null Sector Found—Check Drive, Adapter, Cable
9160	Sense Command Failed—Check Drive, Adapter, Cable
9161	Write Command Failed—Check Drive, Adapter, Cable

9162	Data Compare Error—Check Drive, Adapter, Cable
9163	Read Verify Error—Check Drive, Adapter, Cable
9164	Demark Verify Failed—Check Drive, Adapter, Cable
9165	Demark Bit Not Set—Check Drive, Adapter, Cable
9166	Seek 1/3 Timing Error—Check Drive, Adapter, Cable
9167	Seek 2/3 Timing Error—Check Drive, Adapter, Cable
9168	Seek 3/3 Timing Error—Check Drive, Adapter, Cable
9170	Seek Error Set—Check Drive
9171	Controller RAM/ROM Error—Check Drive, Adapter, Cable
9172	Demark Function Error—Check Drive, Adapter
9173	Detected Error Set—Check Drive, Adapter, Cable
9174	Modulator/Demodulator Error—Check Drive, Adapter, Cable
9175	Invalid Command—Check Adapter, Drive, Cable
9176	Illegal Disk Error—Check Adapter, Drive, Cable
9177	Both drives set to same address or wrong address
9178	ID Mismatch—Check Drive, Adapter or Cable
9179	Sector Not Found—Check Drive, Adapter, Cable
9181	Sense Command Failed—Check Drive, Adapter, Check Cable
9182	Read Command Error—Check Drive, Adapter, Cable
9185	Diagnostic Track Error—Check Drive, Adapter, Cable
9186	Diagnostic Demark Error—Check Drive, Adapter, Cable
9187	No Demark Bit Set—Check Drive, Adapter, Cable
9198	Invalid Command—Re-IPL CPU with ON/OFF switch

96XXXY – SCSI Adapter

100XX – Multiprotocol Adapter

101XX – 300/1200 internal modem/fax

104XX – ESDI drive

Code	Meaning
10400	Unknown failure; replace drive, controller then system board
10436	Thinkpad, N51, system board, fixed disk, cable
10450	Read/write/verify failure; replace drive
10451	Read/write/verify failure; replace drive
10452	Seek test failure, replace drive
10453	Wrong drive type detected
10454	Controller failure (sector buffer test)
10455	Controller failure
10456	Controller failure
10458	Hard disk (integrated controller)
10459	Drive diagnostic command failure
10460	Unknown failure; replace drive then controller, system board
10461	Drive format error
10462	Controller seek error
10464	Primary map not readable
10465	ECC error bit 8,9
10466	ECC error bit 8,9
10467	Drive, soft/hard seek error

10468	Drive, soft/hard seek error
10469	Drive, soft error count exceeded
10470	Controller wrap error
10471	Controller wrap error
10472	Controller wrap error
10473	Corrupt data; low level format HD
10474	Unknown, refer to 10460
10475	Unknown, refer to 10460
10476	Unknown, refer to 10460
10477	Unknown, refer to 10460
10478	Unknown, refer to 10460
10479	Unknown, refer to 10460
10480	ESDI HD, cable, controller or system board. Switches 2,3,5 ON with 70/115 drive
10481	ESDI wrap mode interface error
10482	Drive sel/transfer acknowledgement bad
10483	Controller head select XX selected bad
10484	Controller head select XX selected bad
10485	Controller head select XX selected bad
10486	Controller head select XX selected bad
10487	Controller head select XX selected bad
10490	Drive 0,1 read failure
10499	Controller failure

107XX – External 360/1.2Mb drive

109XX – Action Media Adapter

Code	Meaning
10917	Audio wrap or apeaker problem
10919	Video cable bad/not connected
1094X	Capture option bad

112XX – SCSI Adapter

119XX – 3119 Adapter

121XX – 3/12/2400 Internal Modem

Code	Meaning
12101	ISDN adapter error
121110	Defective ISDN connector
121120	ISDN wrap connector or adapter

129XX – L2 processor board

Code	Meaning
12901	Processor card or system board
12902	Processor card or system board
12903	Processor card or system board
12917	Processor card (90/95). Verify jumper at 1-2 (20 MHz)
12930	90/95 only. J4 not on correct pins

130XX – Thinkpad Indicator Assy

137XX – Thinkpad 700, N51

Any serial component

141XX – Real Time Interface

148XX – P75 Display Card

149XX – Plasma Display Adapter

Code	Meaning
14932	External diaplay (P75)
14952	Plasma display assembly (P75)

152XX – XGA Adapter

Video memory module, system board

161XX – Fax Concentrator Adapter

164XX – Internal Streaming Adapter

165XX – 6157 Tape Adapter

166XX – Primary Token Ring Adapter

167XX - Token Ring Adapter

184XX – Enhanced 80386 Memory Adapter

Code	Meaning
18441	Unsupported memory module
18451	Reconfigure – module changed

194XX – 2-8 80286 Memory Adapter

200XX – Image Adapter

208XX – Any SCSI Device

210XXXY – SCSI Device

211XXxx – Sequential Access (SCSI 2.3Gb Tape)

212XX – SCSI printer

213XX – SCSI processor

214XX – WORM Drive

215XXxx – SCSI CD-ROM

216XX – Scanner

217XX – 128Mb Optical R/W Drive

218XX – Changer

219XX – SCSI Communications Device

Parity errors

Code	Meaning
Parity Check 1 Error	Memory on System Board
Parity Check 2 Error	Memory on Memory Expansion Card

ROM errors

Code	Meaning
F0000-ROM error	Replace System Board
F1000-ROM error	Replace System Board
F2000-ROM error	Replace System Board
F3000-ROM error	Replace System Board
F4000-ROM error	Replace System Board
F5000-ROM error	Replace System Board
F6000-ROM error	Replace System Board
F7000-ROM error	Replace System Board
F8000-ROM error	Replace System Board
F9000-ROM error	Replace System Board
FA000-ROM error	Replace System Board
FB000-ROM error	Replace System Board
FC000-ROM error	Replace System Board
FD000-ROM error	Replace System Board
FE000-ROM error	Replace System Board
C0000-ROM error	Replace keyboard timer card
CA000-ROM error	Replace Keyboard timer card
C8000-ROM error	Replace Fixed Disk Adapter
C8000-ROM error	Replace System Board
CC000-ROM error	Replace System Board
D0000-ROM error	Replace Cluster Adapter
D8000-ROM error	Replace Store Loop Adapter

OLIVETTI M24 MEMORY ERRORS

Code	Meaning
XXX	Last bank tested
CC	RAM configuration number 01 128K on m'bd 02 256K on m'bd 03 384K (256+128 exp) 04 512K (256+256 exp) 05 640K (256+384 exp) 06 640K (512 on bank 0 + 128K on bank 1)
Y	128K bank failure number (000=segment, ZZZZ=Offset) 1 Bank 0 on m'bd 2 Bank 1 on m'bd 3 Bank 1 on expansion 4 Bank 1 on expansion 5 Bank 2 on expansion
WWWW	Data Written (good byte)
RRRR	Data Read (bad byte)

PHOENIX

Message	Fault	Action
Diskette Drive x Error	Drive x is present, but fails the POST tests.	Check cabling and Setup.
Diskette drive reset failed		Check adapter.
Diskette read failure-strike F1 to retry boot	The diskette is either not formatted or defective.	Replace with bootable diskette and retry.
Display adapter failed—using alternate.	Colour/mono switch is set wrong, or primary video adapter failed.	Check switch or adapter.
Errors found; incorrect configuration information. Memory size miscompare.	The size of base or extended memory does not agree with the CMOS contents.	Run Setup.
Extended RAM failed at offset:nnnn	Extended memory not working or configured properly.	Try restoring original values, or contact your dealer.
Failing Bits:nnnn	Hex number nnnn is a map of the bits at the RAM address (System, Extended or Shadow Memory) which failed the memory test. Each 1 represents a failed bit.	Contact your dealer on this one.
Fixed Disk configuration error.	Specified configuration is not supported.	
Fixed Disk drive failure.		Reboot, or replace fixed disk.
Fixed Disk read failure—strike F1 to retry boot.		Reboot, or replace fixed disk.
Gate A20 function not operating.	The 8042 is not accepting commands.	Check system board.
Keyboard error nn	nn represents the scan code for a stuck key.	
Keyboard clock line failure.	Either keyboard or cable is defective.	Check connections.

Keyboard data line failure.	Keyboard controller firmware has failed.	
Memory failure at xxxx, read xxxx expecting xxxx.	Memory chip circuitry has failed.	Turn PC off, then on again. Otherwise, contact dealer.
No boot device available—press F1 to retry boot.	Either diskette drive A:, the diskette or fixed disk is defective.	
No boot sector on fixed disk—press F1 to retry boot.	Drive C: is not formatted or otherwise bootable.	
No timer tick interrupt.	Timer chip has failed.	Turn PC off, then on again. Otherwise, contact dealer.
Option ROM checksum failure.	An expansion card contains a defective ROM.	Reboot, or replace card.
Parity Check 1	Parity error in the system bus.	
Parity Check 2	Parity error found in the I/O bus.	
Pointer device failure.	Mouse failed.	Reboot, check mouse and cable.
Real Time Clock Error	RTC failed BIOS test.	May require board repair.
Shadow RAM failed at offset:nnnn	Shadow RAM failed at offset nnnn of the 64K block at which the error was detected.	
Shutdown failure.	Keyboard controller or associated logic has failed.	Check keyboard controller.
System Cache Error—Cache disabled	RAM cache failed the BIOS test, and has been disabled.	Contact your dealer.
System RAM failed at offset:nnnn	Shadow RAM failed at offset nnnn of the 64K block at which the error was detected.	
System Timer Error		Requires repair of motherboard.
Timer 2 failure	Timer chip failed	Turn PC off, then on again. Otherwise, contact dealer.
Timer or interrupt controller bad.	Either timer chip or interrupt controller is defective.	Check timer chip on system board.
Timer interrupt did not occur.	Either timer chip or interrupt controller is defective.	Check timer chip on system board.
Unexpected interrupt in prot mode	Hardware interrupt or NMI occurred.	Check timer chip or int controller.

SIRIUS

Code	Meaning
11	Noise encountered on sync line
12	Bad header block ID
13	Checksum error in header
14	Header GCR error
15	Wrong track
16	Wrong sector
17	Bad job code
21	Bad data block ID (Invalid data on diskette)
22	Checksum error in data (Invalid data on diskette)
23	GCR error (Invalid data on diskette)

24	Sync time out (Invalid data on diskette)
31	Bad data block ID (Defective drive or diskette)
32	Verify error (Defective drive or diskette)
33	Checksum error (Defective drive or diskette)
34	GCR error (Defective drive or diskette)
41	No sync found—bad or missing diskette (Format program)
42	Bad header ID (Format program)
43	Wrong track (Format program)
44	Wrong sector (Format program)
45	Bad header checksum (Format program)
46	Gap error (Format program)
47	GCR error (Format program)
48	No data sync (Format program)
49	Bad data ID (Format program)
4A	Data verify error (Format program)
4B	Data checksum (Format program)
4C	Gap 2 error (Format program)
4D	GCR error (Format program)
F1	Cannot address second side of diskette
F2	Step error—cannot find track
F3	Data not written due to disk change
F4	Cannot write to disk until logged
F5	Wrong diskette type
F6	Cannot start disk operation
F7	Illegal track number
F8	Illegal drive number
F9	Illegal disk operation
FA	Door open
FB	Drive motor not up to speed
FC	Write-protected diskette
FD	Bad track on diskette
FE	Cannot complete disk operation
FF	Bad or unformatted diskette

15 Known BIOS Problems

Intel says that the DX/4 overdrive should not be used with BIOSes pre June '94. Microsoft say that 1987 is the cutoff date for running Windows successfully. ROM Autoscan appeared after Oct 27 1982. Award BIOS 4.5G prior to Nov 1995 can only accept dates between 1994-1999.

AMI BIOSes dated 7-25-94 and later and support drive translation, as do some versions of Award 4.0G, which implies various versions of the same BIOS! Revision 1.41a is the latest I have seen, but if yours is earlier than 12/13/1994, the address translation table is faulty, so for drives with more than 1024 cylinders, you must use *LBA* rather than *Large*. MR have supported it since early 1990.

GENERAL

ALR

Possible Seagate hard drive problems.

AMI

Pre 4-9-90 versions have compatibility problems with IDE and SCSI drives. According to AMI, this is because IDE drives don't stick to IDE standards, so they changed some of the read routines at this point (plus some other bits they won't talk about).

Pre 12-15-89 versions have problems with IDE and ESDI.

1987 version causes a reboot when accessing floppies with File Manager.

Pre 25/09/88 version did not fully support the 82072 floppy controller, and have trouble with MFM, RLL, ESDI and SCSI drives with OS/2.

1989 version causes intermittent hangs and crashes.

1991 version has some serial port problems.

Pre 09-25-88 versions have compatibility problems with SCSI/RLL/MFM drives. Keyboard BIOS must be revision F.

Keyboard revision should be **K8** with AMI designed motherboards.

With Netware 3.1, the user defined drive feature does not work because the parameters are kept in ROM address space and the pointers INT 41H (C:) and INT 46H (D:) are set accordingly; INT 41H points to F7FA:003D (if C: is present). INT 46H points to F7FA:004D (if D: is present). Novell doesn't work with these, but with them set as INT 41H- F000: 7FDD (basically same as F7FA:003D); INT 46H F000: 7FED (basically same as F7FA:004D). A program called **usernov.com** sets the pointers properly.

Versions 2.12, 2.15, 2.2 of Netware will not accept a pointer to a drive parameter table below C800:0000. With drive type 47, data is copied into low DOS memory. If BIOS Shadow is enabled, the data will be copied back into Shadow (which is in the F000:0000 segment). To use type 47, ROM BIOS Shadow must be enabled.

Not all chip sets and motherboards have this option (BIOS date should also be 4/9/90 or later). If Shadow is not available, the only other option is to have a custom drive table burned for the BIOS; *Upgrades Etc.* or *Washburn & Co.*

AST

Premium/286 has many problems.

Manhattan P/V may issue false thermal and voltage sensor warning after upgrading to 1.08.

AWARD

Early versions have compatibility problems with IDE and SCSI drives. The 2nd decimal number refers to **OEM revisions**, so 3.12 is not necessarily better than 3.11.

Versions **prior to 3.05** have floppy read errors.

With **3.03**, switch to low speed occurs during floppy accesses to ensure greater reliability of data transfer, which Windows may not like. Disable speed switching (NSS) or floppy speed switching (NFS).

BIOS Nos. **4.50, 4.50G, 4.50PG &4.51PG** when operating **Windows '95**; maybe only certain versions of the 4.50 BIOS have this bug.

COMPAQ

If an LTE 5000 is left on between 1159 and 1201 on certain dates, the date may change to the year 2019 or later. A fix for the flash BIOS can be downloaded from **www.compaq.com**, SoftPaq 2451, which upgrades the BIOS to version 5.20a.

DTK

No IDE support prior to version 35.

Windows Enhanced Mode might not run with version 35.

CMOS setup utilities must be disabled with version 36.

IBM

PS/2 35sx and 40sx, ValuePoint I, and some ValuePoint Si models—incorrectly handle more than 1024 cylinders by making drives with more appear to have relatively few cylinders.

MicroFirmware

Early versions of BIOS upgrade P4HS00 (for the Packard Bell PB400 motherboard) do not properly handle the amounts of RAM cached by the external cache with certain configurations. Fixed in the P4HS00 upgrade.

BIOS upgrades based on 4.03 code do not natively support drives larger than 2 Gb, because not enough bits in CMOS are used for the cylinder number.

Peak/DM

Minimum safe version is 1.30. With 1.1, you may get UAEs or Internal Stack Overflow errors while Windows 3.0 is running in enhanced mode.

Phoenix

Minimum safe version is 1989; 11/05/92 for OS/2.

3.06	No user-definable drive types, no support for 1.44 Mb floppies.
3.07	No user-definable drive types, support for 1.44 Mb floppies.
3.10	No user-definable drive types; minimum for 286 and Windows.
3.10D	User-definable drives 48-49.
1.00 ABIOS	Incorporates RLL geometries.

Quadtel

Minimum safe version is 3.05.

Tandon

Keyboard failures with old versions.

Toshiba

Must have version >4.2 for T3100/20.

Must have version >1.7 T3100e.

Wyse

You have to force 101-key keyboard selection in Setup.

Zenith

Must have >2.4D for Turbosport 386.

WINDOWS 95

The BIOS is normally only used for Plug and Play and Power Management, once '95 is running. If the system runs in safe mode, a BIOS problem is unlikely.

AWARD

These issues were introduced by OEMs and are the result of motherboard manufacturers' modifications. Problems include:

Can't turn off BIOS virus protection

Run **setup /ir**, create an emergency disk. Boot up on the emergency disk, run **sys c:**, remove the emergency disk, and reboot. You should now be booting Win95 off of the hard disk.

Motherboards affected have the following serial nos: 2A5L7F09 214X2002 2C403AB1 2A5L7F09 2C419S23

IDE Address Conflict with floppy disk controller

No news yet.

Motherboards affected: 2A59CB09 2A5UNMZE

Plug and Play functionality misreported

Run **setup /P i**, which will turn off plug and play. To turn it back on after the BIOS has been upgraded, run **setup /P j**.

Motherboards affected: 2A5L7F09 2A5197000 2A51CJ3A 2A5L7F0HC 2A59CF54C

System Registry writing

Try above.

Power Management

Lockups with APM turned on, etc. Turn off power management at BIOS setup.

System Instability with Intel Triton motherboards. Try setting all PIO IDE settings to Mode 2 (default is Auto).

Before ringing your motherboard manufacturer, try the following:

> Boot Dos/Windows 3.1.
>
> Run **scandisk /f**. *Fix any problems before proceeding.*
>
> Rename **config.sys** and **autoexec.bat**.
>
> Copy your Windows '95 CDROM to a subdirectory on the hard disk.
>
> Reboot with DOS only.
>
> Run **setup** from the hard disk. *Do not overwrite the old Windows directory*; you will have to reinstall all of your applications.
>
> Reboot under Windows 95.

If Windows '95 works, and all the devices under the device manager in the system icon are correct, and don't have yellow or red circles, you have finished. *Do not reload 16 bit legacy drivers unless Windows '95 did not recognize the device*. If so, the driver may not work and cause system instability.

If Windows '95 incorrectly identifies a device and is unstable or not working, you must replace the hardware. *Do not load the legacy driver.*

If you still have problems, reboot and use the F8 key to create a **bootlog.txt** file.

Neptune Chipset

There is an incompatibility problem between Intel's Neptune chipset and the Plug and Play system, which gives erratic operation and random shutdowns on early 90 MHz Pentium Micron Power Station systems.

16 POST Codes

During the POST on AT-compatibles and above, special signals are sent to I/O port 80H at the beginning of each test (XT-class machines don't issue POST codes, although some with compatible BIOSes do). Some computers may use a different port, such as 84 for the Compaq, or 378 (LPT1) for Olivettis. IBM PS/2s use 90, whilst some EISA machines send them to 300H as well. Those at 50h are chipset or custom platform specific.

POST Diagnostic cards, such as the **POSTmortem** from Xetal Systems (see "Useful Numbers" on page 405) can display these POST codes, so you can check your PC's progress as it starts and hopefully diagnose errors when the POST stops, though a failure at any given location does not necessarily mean that part has the problem; it's meant to be a guidepost for further troubleshooting. In this chapter, some general instructions are given for a typical POST diagnostic card, which were provided by Xetal Systems, together with some of the more obscure POST codes. Having obtained a POST code, identify the manufacturer of the chipset on the motherboard, then refer to the tables that follow.

The POST checks at three levels, *Early, Late* and *System Initialization*. Early POST failures are generally fatal and will produce a beep code, because the video will not be active; in fact, the last diagnostic during Early POST is usually on the video, so that Late failures can actually be seen. System Initialization involves loading configuration from the CMOS, and failures will generate a text message. Consistent failures at that point indicate a bad battery backup.

SHUTDOWN OR RESET COMMANDS

The Reset command stops the current operation and begins fetching instructions from the BIOS, as if the power has just been switched on. The Shutdown command, on the other hand, just forces the CPU to leave protected mode for real mode, so the system behaves differently after each one. Before issuing the shutdown command, the BIOS sets a value into the *shutdown byte* in the CMOS, which is checked after a reset, so the BIOS can branch to the relevant code and continue where it left off.

One of the problems with shutdown handling is that the POST must do some handling before anything else, immediately after power-on or system reset. The path between the CPU and the BIOS ROM, as well as basic control signals, has to be working before the POST gets to its first diagnostic test (usually the CPU register test), so some of the circuitry that the CPU test is supposed to check will be checked by the shutdown handling instead, and you will get no POST indication if a critical failure occurs.

MANUFACTURING LOOP JUMPER

The phrase *Check for Manufacturing Jumper* in the tables refers to one on the motherboard that makes the POST run in a continuous loop, so you can burn in a system, or use repetitive cycling to monitor a failing area with an oscilloscope or logic analyzer. It usually forces a reset, so the POST has to start from the beginning every time. Compaq used the shorted jumper to make the POST to jump to another ROM at E000 just after power-on, which could have diagnostic code in it. IBM and NCR used a germanium or silicon diode to short together the keyboard connector pins 1 (cathode, bar) and 2 (5-pin DIN) or 1 (anode, arrow) and 5 (6-pin mini-DIN), so the POST checks the keyboard controller to see if the jumper is there.

WHAT IS A POST DIAGNOSTIC CARD?

NOTE: Under no circumstances shall the publisher, author any manufacturer of POST diagnostic cards, or their agents be held liable in any way for damages, including lost profits, lost savings, or other incidental or consequential damages arising out of the use of, or inability to use, any product designed to make POST diagnostic codes visible on your system.

A POST diagnostic card (or POST card) is an operating system independent expansion card designed to be used with any x86-based computer with an ISA/EISA expansion bus (although the cards are usually 8-bit, XT class machines do not generally issue POST codes). There may be conversion products for purely Micro Channel and PCI systems, depending on the manufacturer. Some POST cards also use LEDs to provide information on the status of the power supply and other devices.

WHO WOULD USE A POST CARD?

POST cards can be used by:

Systems Integrators and **Technicians** in the field, plant, office or service centre, diagnosing faults in non-booting systems to determine components to exchange.

Computer Manufacturers, to display POST codes of system boards or partial systems set to loopback/manufacturing test mode during burn in.

Computer Hobbyists and End Users, to determine if their hardware is faulty or just set up wrong. Faulty components can be identified before being sent out for service, saving hours of trial and error module swapping at service centre repair rates (less than one hour of labour or one module saved would often have the card pay for itself). Many hobbyists report very high success rates with non-booting or unrepairable systems obtained for next to nothing at flea-markets or surplus stores.

The faults most of them found did not even involve soldering, just:

o wrong switch settings or setup information

o bent and shorted component leads or bus-connector pins

o bad RAM chip(s)

o faulty 8042 Keyboard chip (quite often socketed)

o defective BIOS ROM

INSTALLATION

NOTE: CAUTION CMOS!!! STATIC ELECTRICITY WARNING!

Your system's circuit boards and the POST card may contain CMOS based logic devices or chips which can be DAMAGED through careless handling. Though most CMOS devices these days are protected by internal diodes and resistors against *ElectroStatic Discharge* (ESD) the following precautions should be taken:

BEFORE touching, installing or removing any circuit board or CMOS logic chip, ground yourself by touching any bare metal that is connected to earth and **NOT** to a live electrical outlet. Touching the computer case only really works if the PC is actually plugged into a grounded electrical outlet, but this may be illegal in some countries, and in some others the switch may as well not be there at all!

Handle the CMOS device by its ends so static will be conducted away by the supply pins.

Use a special static free/conductive insertion tool which shorts together all the package pins during insertion.

Never keep CMOS devices in white polystyrene foam.

Leave the CMOS devices in their anti-static packaging until they are required.

Touch the circuit ground and the anti-static packaging together before removing devices.

Use a grounded soldering iron.

NOTE: **CAUTION:** There are two types of anti-static bags/packaging. The first is treated with a conductive coating, normally carbon based and black/dark grey in colour. Then there are coatings which are not conductive but inhibit the plastic from generating electrostatic charges, normally being pink, light green or light blue. When storing circuit boards that have batteries on them, use the latter type of bag so as not to damage/discharge the battery. Otherwise remove battery or open-circuit it.

OBTAINING INFORMATION ABOUT YOUR COMPUTER

At least the BIOS ROM's manufacturer and firmware revision number should be known, so you can check the codes in the following pages (see the front of the book for BIOS IDs). The manufacturing port or POST address port should also be known.

REQUIRED TOOLS

To access the memory chips and circuit boards in most computer cases you should have a selection of the following tools:

Phillips –type screw driver(s)	Tweezers
Slotted screw driver	IC inserter
Torx driver	IC extractor
Needle nose pliers	

POST Codes

To perform repair work on circuit boards, try also the items listed below.

NOTE: **WARNING!** These tools would only be of use to qualified engineers and computer technicians. As a typical end/business user of a POST card, please DO NOT attempt any system board repair. Such activities would void your warranty and may cause accidental damage to your computer. The potential savings would be minuscule with respect to the repair cost and wasted time. Please consult your dealer/repair centre or manufacturer.

POST card

Low end multimeter for resistance and voltage measurement (AC and DC)

Plastic Leadless Chip Carrier (PLCC) Removal Tool

Pin Grid Array (PGA) removal tool

Grounded soldering iron (NOT a soldering gun - the current in the tip will fry most solid state components)

Vacuum hand pump solder pull (Antistatic tip preferred)

Resin core solder, 63% Tin and 37% Lead. The solder wire diameter to be approximately 0.025" to 0.031" (0.040" diameter solder will do).

NOTE: DO NOT use acid core flux based solder, as it leaves a corrosive and conductive residue. Do NOT use water soluble flux based solder unless you plan to wash the board well, since the residue is both conductive and a mild corrosive.

OPENING THE COMPUTER CASE

Turn OFF the computer's main AC power and unplug the AC power cable. Disconnect all cables to the peripherals. Remove the case in accordance with the manufacturer's service manual/instructions. The most common desk-top case has a lid that slides off backwards and is held in place by four or six screws at the rear. Be careful not to confuse these screws with the four that look the same but normally hold the power supply in place.

CARD CONFIGURATION

The less expensive cards only support I/O address 80h. Others have selectable port addresses. Ensure your card is set properly for your motherboard.

INSTALLING THE CARD

Locate any empty 16 Bit or 8 Bit expansion slot. The 8 Bit portion of the connector is the one closest to rear of the computer (where the "L" shaped blanking covers or add-on card mounting brackets are located). For our purposes, the front is where in most cases the floppy drives are located. Since most POST cards do not have a mounting bracket (the first thing any technician removes from diagnostics and test boards to save time), they can easily be inserted the wrong way, especially if small.

NOTE: **CAUTION!** Please NOTE the ARROW with the marking "REAR OF COMPUTER: DO NOT REVERSE THE BOARD!" on any POST card you might have.

Insert the card into the 8-bit part of any 8- or 16-bit expansion slot so that the above mentioned ARROW points to the REAR of the computer system/board. Also note the components should be facing the same way as the components on any other board in your system's bus (the exception may be some old network boards, and PCI cards, which have their components on the opposite side to ISA ones).

NOTE: CAUTION! Some 386, 486 and Pentium based systems have 32 Bit bus extensions or some special additional high speed expansion slots towards the front of the computer, or may use riser or slot extender cards that are electrically different. Even if it sort of fits, DO NOT insert your card into any of these, as the consequences may prove to be disastrous and expensive!

TESTING THE POST CARD

If uncertain whether your computer support s a POST card, or yours may have become damaged, there is an easy way to test it with some programs that come with DOS, such as **gwbasic.exe** or **basic.com**, not forgetting **debug.com**.

Using GWBASIC/BASIC:

Insert your card into a working computer system and execute the following little program:

```
10 PRINT "Enter a value between 0 and 255 ":;INPUT X
20 H$ = HEX$(X)
30 PRINT X "Decimal is " H$ " Hexadecimal as shown on POST card"
40 FOR L=1 TO 500
50 OUT 128,X
60 OUT 132,X
70 OUT 640,X
80 OUT 644,X
90 NEXT L
100 PRINT
110 GOTO 10
RUN

Enter a value between 0 and 255 ? 165
165 Decimal is A5 Hexadecimal as shown on the POST card.
Enter a value between 0 and 255 ?
```

To break out of this endless loop press **Ctrl-C** or **Ctrl-Break**.

Note: Regarding the OUT statement,
128 Decimal is 80 Hexadecimal
132 Decimal is 84 Hexadecimal

which are the 2 most common addresses. The FOR-NEXT loop is just a timing loop re-sending the codes to all 4 ports 500 times because on some (XT) system boards Bus/DMA activity will overwrite the value as soon as it has been written to the card and it will flash only once. This way it will flash 500 times or more depending on the value you may choose for this loop. In-between the 500 port writes other activity may occur on the Bus (depending on System board design) which the POST card will display if it is within the set POST port range. So some other segments on the 7 segment display may flicker.

237

POST Codes

Using DEBUG:

If jumper selectable, set the port address jumper to 80 and insert the card into a working computer. Execute **debug**. At the "-" prompt type the sequence below followed by **Enter**:

    -o 280 b6

where:

> o is letter "O" as in Oscar.

> 280 (Two Eight Zero) in Hexadecimal is the POST Port Address.

> b6 in hexadecimal is the data which will display on the card and show you the difference between a "b" and a "6" on a seven segment display.

> The above debug command is not case sensitive, but here it is shown in lower case to emphasize the differences in points a) and c).

To exit **debug** press **q** and then **Enter**.

You can repeat the above with different data and different POST address ports. Since DEBUG writes the data only once it may only display as a short flash on system boards as described in the note for the above BASIC program.

OPERATION AND TECHNICAL INFORMATION

After the power has been turned on and the CPU's Reset input is past the reset state, the system starts to execute the program stored in the system's Firmware/BIOS ROM chips. First the system executes the program in the system board's BIOS then it goes to the programs stored in the expansion board's BIOS ROMs. Upon execution of the program in the system board BIOS, the POST is performed first before the system boots. The POST routines initialize the system's circuitry and test it (clear registers and memory locations and set them to their default values).

Rephrased more technically: after a system reset or power-up the BIOS ROM's program located at the top of the highest paragraph in the system's memory map (8086/8088 at F000:FFF0 or 80286 and up at FFFFF:0000) executes a long jump to F000:E05B which is the start of the POST sequence.

THE POST DISPLAY

POST codes are normally just 1-byte or 8-bit codes, so 256 possible ones can be sent. They are customarily displayed in hexadecimal format allowing values between 00 and FF hex. Most cards have two 7-segment displays at the top of the board which display the hexadecimal POST code.

Please note that B and D have to be displayed in lower case on a 7-segment display.

Hexadecimal Display and Conversion

Dec	HEX	Display	Binary
0	0	0	0000
1	1	1	0001
2	2	2	0010
3	3	3	0011

4	4	4	0100
5	5	5	0101
6	6	6	0110
7	7	7	0111
8	8	8	1000
9	9	9	1001
10	A	A	1010
11	B	b	1011
12	C	C	1100
13	D	d	1101
14	E	E	1110
15	F	F	1111

In order not to confuse the 6 and the lower case B, the 6 has a serif/bar at the top.

POWER SUPPLY STATUS LEDS AND VOLTAGE MEASUREMENT POINTS

Some POST cards have four DC power indicator LEDs which show the presence of DC power on all the system board's/expansion bus' voltage supply rails. There may also be test points for a VOM which may not have fusing or a current limiting circuit, so take care when performing measurements. A fifth reference Ground test point should be there as well.

TROUBLESHOOTING/DIAGNOSTIC STRATEGY

Though the following strategy is not the most complete, it is an outline of a system repair procedure using the information a POST card provides.

System will not boot, power supply fan not running, Power LEDs do not light
Check if the power supply receives AC and is switched on. The presence of AC can be tested with a multimeter at the power supply's monitor outlet. If you see 115/230 VAC at this point and the power supply is plugged correctly into the system/motherboard, some peripheral board or disk drive may trigger the overload/short-circuit protection. Unplug all drives and peripheral cards except the POST card with the power off and try again. If the LEDs light and fan is running, reinstall peripherals one at a time until the defective one(s) is/(are) found. Check the system board and peripherals for burnt components or capacitors since they may short circuit when they fail. If this is not it, replace the power supply.

NOTE: Switching power supplies require some minimum load at the DC output to work correctly, so with no load, or a load below the minimum, the power supply would shut down or provide DC power at voltages out of specification respectively.

System will not boot, power supply fan is running, one or more Power LEDs do not light, are dim and/or flicker
Check if the system's power supply outputs the correct voltages by using a volt/multimeter in DCV mode between the test-points described earlier. Also check the ripple voltage on the power supply by setting your multimeter to ACV and measure

239

between ground and the test-point for the voltage rail in question. On the -5V and +5V lines the ripple should be not more than 0.25V AC and on the -12V and +12V lines you should see less than 0.5V AC. If one or more voltages or the ripple are out of range, replace the power supply.

System will not boot or show POST codes (except for "00" or "FF") but Power LEDs do light solid and the DC voltages and ripple are within specification

Press the hardware reset button (if there is one) repeatedly, otherwise switch the system on and off a few times. If the system boots and you see POST codes, the "Power Good/Reset" circuit of either the power supply or the motherboard is defective. Determine where the reset originates and replace either the power supply or motherboard. Some systems receive their reset from the power supply after its DC output is stable and some others have a reset circuit which allows enough time for most power supplies to stabilize. Note that the reset/power good from a PC/XT supply is not of sufficient duration to reset most AT/286 and upsystem/motherboards which do not have their own on-board reset circuit.

If that is not it, remove with power off all peripherals from the system board except the POST card and try again. If the system boots and POST codes appear, one or more peripheral boards may have been "shorting" the bus and thus hanging the system. Reinstall them one at a time until the culprit is found.

The next thing to try would be the ROM chips, exchanging them against another set, ensuring that High and Low chips are in the correct sockets, if required. Check the ROM jumpers on the system/motherboard are set correctly (for ROM chip size and memory map location). Also check the clock lines on the bus with a logic probe to see if the clocks are working and check all bus connectors on the motherboard for bent under and shorted pins.

Check if any components are cracked or their pins are shorted together due to mechanical abuse when peripheral boards were inserted.

Is the POST card set for the correct POST port address and does the system/motherboard BIOS generate POST codes? Check with your manufacturer's manuals.

System will not boot but shows POST codes other than "00" or "FF", Power LEDs do light solid and the DC voltages and ripple are within specification.

Look up the POST code for the BIOS of the system/motherboard tested in the listings below or in the manufacturer's manual. The code displayed in a boot sequence does point to the part of the circuitry which is defective and hanging the system. Check the part of the circuit in question again for mechanical abuse and/or shorts, wrong jumper settings. If the chip of the circuit flagged as defective is socketed, replace it. If your system has an Award AT BIOS, for example, and the code displayed is "02" it could be a defective keyboard controller.

ACER

Based on Award BIOS 3.03, but not exactly the same.

Code	Meaning
04	Start
08	Shutdown
0C	Test BIOS ROM checksum
10	Test CMOS RAM shutdown byte
14	Test DMA controller
18	Initialise system timer
1C	Test memory refresh
1E	Determine memory type
20	Test 128K memory
24	Test 8042 keyboard controller
28	Test CPU descriptor instruction
2C	Set up and test 8259 interrupt controller
30	Set up memory interrupts
34	Set up BIOS interrupt vectors and routines
38	Test CMOS RAM
3C	Determine memory size
XX	Shut down 8 (system halt C0h + checkpoint)
40	Shutdown 1
44	Initialise Video BIOS ROM
45	Set up and test RAM BIOS
46	Test cache memory and controller
48	Test memory
4C	Shutdown 3
50	Shutdown 2
54	Shutdown 7
55	Shutdown 6
5C	Test keyboard and auxiliary I/O
60	Set up BIOS interrupt routines
64	Test real time clock
68	Test diskette
6C	Test hard disk
70	Test parallel port
74	Test serial port
78	Set time of day
7C	Scan for and invoke option ROMs
80	Determine presence of math coprocessor
84	initialize keyboard
88	Initialise svstem 1
8C	Initialize system 2
90	Invoke INT 19 to boot operating system
94	Shutdown 5
98	Shutdown A
9C	Shutdown B

ALR

See *Phoenix*.

AMBRA

See *Phoenix*.

AMI

Not all tests are performed by all AMI BIOSes. Those below refer to the 2 Feb 91 BIOS.

POST Procedures

Procedure	Explanation
NMI Disable	NMI interrupt line to the CPU is disabled by setting bit 7 I/O port 70h (CMOS).
Power On Delay	Once the keyboard controller gets power, it sets the hard and soft reset bits. Check the keyboard controller or clock generator.
Initialise Chipsets	Check the BIOS, CLOCK or chipsets.
Reset Determination	The BIOS reads the bits in the keyboard controller to see if a hard or soft reset is required (a soft reset will not test memory above 64K). Failure could be the BIOS or keyboard controller.
ROM BIOS Checksum	The BIOS performs a checksum on itself and adds a preset factory value that should make it equal 00. Failure is due to the BIOS chips.
Keyboard Test	A command is sent to the 8042 (keyboard controller) which performs a test and sets a buffer space for commands. After the buffer is defined the BIOS sends a command byte, writes data to the buffer, checks the high order bits (Pin 23) of the internal keyboard controller and issues a No Operation (NOP) command.
CMOS	Shutdown byte in CMOS RAM offset 0F is tested, the BIOS checksum calculated and diagnostic byte (0E) updated before the CMOS RAM area is initialised and updated for date and time. Check RTC/CMOS chip or battery.
8237/8259 Disable	The DMA and Interrupt Controller are disabled before the POST proceeds any further. Check the 8237 or 8259 chips.
Video Disable	The video controller is disabled and Port B initialised. Check the video adapter if you get problems here.
Chipset Init/Memory Detect	Memory addressed in 64K blocks; failure would be in the chipset. If all memory is not seen, failure could be in a chip in the block after the last one seen.
PIT test	The timing functions of the 8254 interrupt timer are tested. The PIT or RTC chips normally cause problems here.
Memory Refresh	PIT's ability to refresh memory tested (if an XT, DMA controller #1 handles this). Failure is normally the PIT (8254) in ATs or the 8237 (DMA #1) in XTs.
Address Lines	Test the address lines to the first 64K of RAM. An address line failure.
Base 64K	Data patterns are written to the first 64K, unless there is a bad RAM chip in which case you will get a failure.
Chipset Initialisation	The PIT, PIC and DMA controllers are enabled.
Set Interrupt Table	Interrupt vector table used by PIC is installed in low memory, the first 2K.
8042 check	The BIOS reads the buffer area of the keyboard controller I/O port 60. Failure here is normally the keyboard controller.
Video Tests	The type of video adapter is checked for then a series of tests is performed on the adapter and monitor.

BIOS Data Area	The vector table is checked for proper operation and video memory verified before protected mode tests are entered into. This is done so that any errors found are displayed on the monitor.
Protected Mode Tests	Perform reads and writes to all memory below 1 Mb. Failures at this point indicate a bad RAM chip, the 8042 chip or a data line.
DMA Chips	The DMA registers are tested using a data pattern.
Final Initialisation	These differ with each version. Typically, the floppy and hard drives are tested and initialised, and a check made for serial and parallel devices. The information gathered is then compared against the contents of the CMOS, and you will see the results of any failures on the monitor.
Boot	The BIOS hands over control to the Int 19 bootloader; this is where you would see error messages such as non-system disk.

AMI BIOS 2.2x

Code	Meaning
00	Flag test
03	Register test
06	System hardware initialisation
09	BIOS ROM checksum
0C	Page register test
0F	8254 timer test
12	Memory refresh initialisation
15	8237 DMA controller test
18	8237 DMA initialisation
1B	8259 interrupt controller initialisation
1E	8259 interrupt controller test
21	Memory refresh test
24	Base 64K address test
27	Base 64K memory test
2A	8742 keyboard self test
2D	MC 146818 CMOS test
30	Start first protected mode test
33	Memory sizing test
36	First protected mode test
39	First protected mode test failed
3C	CPU speed calculation
3F	Read 8742 hardware switches
42	Initialise interrupt vector area
45	Verify CMOS configuration
48	Test and initialise video system
4B	Unexpected interrupt test
4E	Start second protected mode test
51	Verify LDT instruction
54	Verify TR instruction
57	Verify LSL instruction
5A	Verify LAR instruction
5D	Verify VERR instruction
60	Address line 20 test
63	Unexpected exception test

243

66	Start third protected mode test
69	Address line test
6C	System memory test
6F	Shadow memory test
72	Extended memory test
75	Verify memory configuration
78	Display configuration error messages
7B	Copy system BIOS to shadow memory
7E	8254 clock test
81	MC 146818 real time clock test
84	Keyboard test
87	Determine keyboard type
8A	Stuck key test
8D	Initialise hardware interrupt vector
90	Math coprocessor test
93	Determine COM ports available
96	Determine LPT ports available
99	Initialise BIOS data area
9C	Fixed/Floppy controller test
9F	Floppy disk test
A2	Fixed disk test
A5	External ROM scan
A8	System key lock test
AE	F1 error message test
AF	System boot initialisation
B1	Interrupt 19 boot loader

AMI Old BIOS (AMI Plus BIOS); 08/15/88—04/08/90

Code	Meaning
01	NMI disabled & 286 reg. test about to start
02	286 register test over
03	ROM checksum OK
04	8259 initialization OK
05	CMOS pending interrupt disabled
06	Video disabled & system timer counting OK
07	CH-2 of 8253 test OK
08	CH-2 delta count test OK
09	CH-1 delta count test OK
0A	CH-0 delta count test OK
0B	Parity status cleared
0C	Refresh & system timer OK
0D	Refresh link toggling OK
0E	Refresh period ON/OFF 50% OK
10	Confirmed refresh ON & about to start 64K memory
11	Address line test OK
12	64K base memory test OK
13	Interrupt vectors initialized
14	8042 keyboard controller test OK

15	CMOS read/write test OK
16	CMOS checksum/battery check OK
17	Monochrome mode set OK
18	Colour mode set OK
19	About to look for optional video ROM
1A	Optional video ROM control OK
1B	Display memory read/write test OK
1C	Display memory read/write test for alt display OK
1D	Video retrace check OK
1E	Global equipment byte set for video OK
1F	Mode set call for Mono/Colour OK
20	Video test OK
21	Video display OK
22	Power on message display OK
30	Virtual mode memory test about to begin
31	Virtual mode memory test started
32	Processor in virtual mode
33	Memory address line test in progress
34	Memory address line test in progress
35	Memory below 1MB calculated
36	Memory size computation OK
37	Memory test in progress
38	Memory initialization over below 1MB
39	Memory initialization over above 1MB
3A	Display memory size
3B	About to start below 1MB memory test
3C	Memory test below 1MB OK
3D	Memory test above 1MB OK
3E	About to go to real mode (shutdown)
3F	Shutdown successful and entered in real mode
40	About to disable gate A-20 address line
41	Gate A-20 line disabled successfully
42	About to start DMA controller test
4E	Address line test OK
4F	Processor in real mode after shutdown
50	DMA page register test OK
51	DMA unit-1 base register test about to start
52	DMA unit-1 channel OK; about to begin CH-2
53	DMA CH-2 base register test OK
54	About to test f/f latch for unit-1
55	f/f latch test both unit OK
56	DMA unit 1 & 2 programmed OK
57	8259 initialization over
58	8259 mask register check OK
59	Master 8259 mask register OK; about to start slave
5A	About to check timer and keyboard interrupt level
5B	Timer interrupt OK
5C	About to test keyboard interrupt

5D	ERROR! timer/keyboard interrupt not in proper level
5E	8259 interrupt controller error
5F	8259 interrupt controller test OK
70	Start of keyboard test
71	Keyboard BAT test OK
72	Keyboard test OK
73	Keyboard global data initialization OK
74	Floppy setup about to start
75	Floppy setup OK
76	Hard disk setup about to start
77	Hard disk setup OK
79	About to initialize timer data area
7A	Verify CMOS battery power
7B	CMOS battery verification done
7D	About to analyze diagnostic test results for memory
7E	CMOS memory size update OK
7F	About to check optional ROM C000:0
80	Keyboard sensed to enable setup
81	Optional ROM control OK
82	Printer global data initialization OK
83	RS-232 global data initialization OK
84	80287 check/test OK
85	About to display soft error message
86	About to give control to system ROM E000:0
87	System ROM E000:0 check over
00	Control given to Int-19; boot loader

AMI BIOS 04/09/90-02/01/91

Code	Meaning
01	NMI disabled and 286 register test about to start.
02	286 register test passed.
03	ROM BIOS checksum (32K at F800:0) passed.
04	Keyboard controller test with and without mouse passed.
05	Chipset initialization over; DMA and Interrupt controller disabled.
06	Video disabled and system timer test begin.
07	CH-2 of 8254 initialization half way.
08	CH-2 of timer initialization over.
09	CH-1 of timer initialization over.
0A	CH-0 of timer initialization over.
0B	Refresh started.
0C	System timer started.
0D	Refresh link toggling passed.
10	Refresh on and about to start 64K base memory test.
11	Address line test passed.
12	64K base memory test passed.
15	Interrupt vectors initialized.
17	Monochrome mode set.
18	Colour mode set.

19	About to look for optional video ROM at C000 and give control to ROM if present.
1A	Return from optional video ROM.
1B	Shadow RAM enable/disable completed.
1C	Display memory read/write test for main display type as set in the CMOS setup program over.
1D	Display memory read/write test for alternate display type complete if main display memory read/write test returns error.
1E	Global equipment byte set for proper display type.
1F	Video mode set call for mono/colour begins.
20	Video mode set completed.
21	ROM type 27256 verified.
23	Power on message displayed.
30	Virtual mode memory test about to begin.
31	Virtual mode memory test started.
32	Processor executing in virtual mode.
33	Memory address line test in progress.
34	Memory address line test in progress.
35	Memory below 1MB calculated.
36	Memory above 1MB calculated.
37	Memory test about to start.
38	Memory below 1MB initialized.
39	Memory above 1MB initialized.
3A	Memory size display initiated. Will be updated when BIOS goes through memory test.
3B	About to start below 1MB memory test.
3C	Memory test below 1MB completed; about to start above 1MB test.
3D	Memory test above 1MB completed.
3E	About to go to real mode (shutdown).
3F	Shutdown successful and processor in real mode.
40	Cache memory on and about to disable A20 address line.
41	A20 address line disable successful.
42	486 internal cache turned on.
43	About to start DMA controller test.
50	DMA page register test complete.
51	DMA unit-1 base register test about to start.
52	DMA unit-1 base register test complete.
53	DMA unit-2 base register test complete.
54	About to check F/F latch for unit-1 and unit-2.
55	F/F latch for both units checked.
56	DMA unit 1 and 2 programming over; about to initialize 8259 interrupt controller.
57	8259 initialization over.
70	About to start keyboard test.
71	Keyboard controller BAT test over.
72	Keyboard interface test over; mouse interface test started.
73	Global data initialization for keyboard/mouse over.
74	Display 'SETUP' prompt and about to start floppy setup.
75	Floppy setup over.
76	Hard disk setup about to start.
77	Hard disk setup over.
79	About to initialize timer data area.

7A	Timer data initialized and about to verify CMOS battery power.
7B	CMOS battery verification over.
7D	About to analyze POST results.
7E	CMOS memory size updated.
7F	Look for <DEL> key and get into CMOS setup if found.
80	About to give control to optional ROM in segment C800 to DE00.
81	Optional ROM control over.
82	Check for printer ports and put the addresses in global data area.
83	Check for RS232 ports and put the addresses in global data area.
84	Coprocessor detection over.
85	About to display soft error messages.
86	About to give control to system ROM at segment E000.
00	System ROM control at E000 over now give control to Int 19h boot loader.

AMI New BIOS; 02/02/91—12/12/91

Code	Meaning
01	Processor register test about to start and NMI to be disabled.
02	NMI is Disabled. Power on delay starting.
03	Power on delay complete. Any initialization before keyboard BAT is in progress.
04	Init before keyboard BAT complete. Reading keyboard SYS bit to check soft reset/ power-on.
05	Soft reset/ power-on determined. Going to enable ROM. i. e. disable shadow RAM/Cache.
06	ROM enabled. Calculating ROM BIOS checksum, waiting for KB controller input buffer to be free.
07	ROM BIOS Checksum passed. KB controller I/B free. Going to issue BAT comd to kboard controller.
08	BAT command to keyboard controller issued. Going to verify BAT command.
09	Keyboard controller BAT result verified. Keyboard command byte to be written next.
0A	Keyboard command byte code issued. Going to write command byte data.
0B	Keyboard controller command byte written. Going to issue Pin-23 & 24 blocking/unblocking command
0C	Pin 23 & 24 of keyboard controller is blocked/unblocked. NOP command of keyboard controller to be issued next.
0D	NOP command processing done. CMOS shutdown register test to be done next.
0E	CMOS shutdown register R/W test passed. Going to calculate CMOS checksum, update DIAG byte.
0F	CMOS checksum calculation is done DIAG byte written. CMOS init. to begin (If INIT CMOS IN EVERY BOOT is set).
10	CMOS initialization done (if any). CMOS status register about to init for Date and Time.
11	CMOS Status register initialised. Going to disable DMA and Interrupt controllers.
12	DMA Controller #1 & #2, interrupt controller #1 & #2 disabled. About to disable Video display and init port-B.
13	Video display disabled and port-B initialized. Chipset init/auto mem detection about to begin.
14	Chipset initialization/auto memory detection over. 8254 timer test about to start.
15	CH-2 timer test halfway. 8254 CH-2 timer test to be complete.
16	Ch-2 timer test over. 8254 CH-1 timer test to be complete.
17	CH-1 timer test over. 8254 CH-0 timer test to be complete.
18	CH-0 timer test over. About to start memory refresh.
19	Memory Refresh started. Memory Refresh test to be done next.
1A	Memory Refresh line is toggling. Going to check 15 microsecond ON/OFF time.

1B	Memory Refresh period 30 microsec test complete. Base 64K memory test about to start.
20	Base 64k memory test started. Address line test to be done next.
21	Address line test passed. Going to do toggle parity.
22	Toggle parity over. Going for sequential data R/W test.
23	Base 64k sequential data R/W test passed. Setup before Interrupt vector init about to start.
24	Setup before vector initialization complete. Interrupt vector initialization about to begin.
25	Interrupt vector initialization done. Going to read I/O port of 8042 for turbo switch (if any).
26	I/O port of 8042 is read. Going to initialize global data for turbo switch.
27	Global data initialization is over. Any initialization after interrupt vector to be done next.
28	Initialization after interrupt vector is complete. Going for monochrome mode setting.
29	Monochrome mode setting is done. Going for Colour mode setting.
2A	Colour mode setting is done. About to go for toggle parity before optional ROM test.
2B	Toggle parity over. About to give control for any setup before optional video ROM check.
2C	Processing before video ROM control is done. About to look for optional video ROM and give control.
2D	Optional video ROM control done. About to give control to do any processing after video ROM returns control.
2E	Return from processing after the video ROM control. If EGA/VGA not found then do display memory R/W test.
2F	EGA/VGA not found. Display memory R/W test about to begin.
30	Display mem R/W test passed. About to look for retrace checking.
31	Display mem R/W test/ retrace check failed. About to do alternate Display memory R/W test.
32	Alternate Display memory R/W test passed. About to look for alternate display retrace checking.
33	Video display checking over. Verification of display with switch setting and card to begin.
34	Verification of display adapter done. Display mode to be set next.
35	Display mode set complete. BIOS ROM data area about to be checked.
36	BIOS ROM data area check over. Going to set cursor for power on message.
37	Cursor setting for power on message id complete. Going to display the power on message.
38	Power on message display complete. Going to read new cursor position.
39	New cursor position read and saved. Going to display the reference string.
3A	Reference string display is over. Going to display the Hit <Esc> message.
3B	Hit <Esc> message displayed. Virtual mode memory test about to start.
40	Preparation for virtual mode test started. Going to verify from video memory.
41	Returned after verifying from display memory. Going to prepare the descriptor tables.
42	Descriptor tables prepared. Going to enter in virtual mode for memory test.
43	Entered in the virtual mode. Going to enable interrupts for diagnostics mode.
44	Interrupts enabled (if diagnostics switch is on). Going to initialize data to check memory wrap around at 0:0.
45	Data initialized. Going to check for memory wrap around at 0:0and finding the total system memory size.
46	Memory wrap around test done. Memory size calculation over. About to go for writing patterns to test memory.
47	Pattern to be tested written in extended memory. Going to write patterns in base 640k.
48	Patterns written in base memory. Going to find out amount of memory below 1Mb.
49	Amount of memory below 1Mb found and verified. Going to find out amount of memory above 1M memory.
4A	Amount of memory above 1Mb found and verified. Going for BIOS ROM data area check.
4B	BIOS ROM data area check over. Going to check <Esc> and clear mem below 1Mb for soft reset.
4C	Memory below 1M cleared. (SOFT RESET). Going to clear memory above 1M.

4D	Memory above 1M cleared.(SOFT RESET). Going to save the memory size.
4E	Memory test started. (NO SOFT RESET).About to display the first 64k memory test.
4F	Memory size display started.This will be updated during memory test. Going for sequential and random memory test.
50	Memory test below 1Mb complete. Going to adjust memory size for relocation/ shadow.
51	Memory size adjusted due to relocation/shadow. Memory test above 1Mb to follow.
52	Memory test above 1Mb complete. Going to prepare to go back to real mode.
53	CPU registers are saved including memory size. Going to enter in real mode.
54	Shutdown successful. CPU in real mode. Going to restore registers saved during preparation for shutdown.
55	Registers restored. Going to disable gate A20 address line.
56	A20 address line disable successful. BIOS ROM data area about to be checked.
57	BIOS ROM data area check halfway. BIOS ROM data area check to be complete.
58	BIOS ROM data area check over. Going to clear Hit <Esc>message.
59	Hit <Esc> message cleared.WAIT. . . message displayed.About to start DMA and interrupt controller test.
60	DMA page register test passed.About to verify from display memory.
61	Display memory verification over.About to go for DMA #1 base register test.
62	DMA #1 base register test passed.About to go for DMA #2 base register test.
63	DMA #2 base register test passed.About to go for BIOS ROM data area check.
64	BIOS ROM data area check halfway. BIOS ROM data area check to be complete.
65	BIOS ROM data area check over.About to program DMA unit 1 and 2.
66	DMA unit 1 and 2 programming over.About to initialize 8259 interrupt controller
67	8259 initialization over.About to start keyboard test.
80	Keyboard test started. Clearing output buffer, checking for stuck key.About to issue keyboard reset
81	Keyboard reset error/stuck key found.About to issue keyboard controller i/f test command.
82	Keyboard controller interface test over.About to write command byte and init circular buffer.
83	Command byte written Global data init done.About to check for lock-key.
84	Lock-key checking over.About to check for memory size mismatch with CMOS.
85	Memory size check done.About to display soft error; check for password or bypass setup.
86	Password checked.About to do programming before setup.
87	Programming before setup complete. Going to CMOS setup program.
88	Returned from CMOS setup and screen cleared.About to do programming after setup.
89	Programming after setup complete. Going to display power on screen message.
8A	First screen message displayed.About to display WAIT. . . message.
8B	WAIT. . . message displayed.About to do Main and Video BIOS shadow.
8C	Main/Video BIOS shadow successful. Setup options programming after CMOS setup about to start.
8D	Setup options are programmed, mouse check and init to be done next
8E	Mouse check and initialisation complete. Going for hard disk floppy reset.
8F	Floppy check returns that floppy is to be initialized. Floppy setup to follow.
90	Floppy setup is over.Test for hard disk presence to be done.
91	Hard disk presence test over. Hard disk setup to follow.
92	Hard disk setup complete.About to go for BIOS ROM data area check.
93	BIOS ROM data area check halfway. BIOS ROM data area check to be complete.
94	BIOS ROM data area check over. Going to set base and extended memory size.
95	Memory size adjusted due to mouse support hdisk type 47. Going to verify from display memory.

96	Returned after verifying from display memory. Going to do any init before C800 optional ROM control.
97	Any init before C800 optional ROM control is over. Optional ROM check and control next.
98	Optional ROM control is done. About to give control to do any required processing after optional ROM returns control.
99	Any initialization required after optional ROM test over. Going to setup timer data area and printer base address.
9A	Return after setting timer and printer base address. Going to set the RS-232 base address.
9B	Returned after RS-232 base address. Going to do any initialization before Copro test.
9C	Required initialization before coprocessor is over. Going to initialize the coprocessor next.
9D	Coprocessor initialized. Going to do any initialization after Coprocessor test.
9E	Initialization after co-pro test complete. Going to check extd keyboard; ID and num-lock.
9F	Extd keyboard check done ID flag set. num-lock on/off. Keyboard ID command to be issued.
A0	Keyboard ID command issued. Keyboard ID flag to be reset.
A1	Keyboard ID flag reset. Cache memory test to follow.
A2	Cache memory test over. Going to display any soft errors.
A3	Soft error display complete. Going to set the keyboard typematic rate.
A4	Keyboard typematic rate set. Going to program memory wait states.
A5	Memory wait states programming over. Screen to be cleared next.
A6	Screen cleared. Going to enable parity and NMI.
A7	NMI and parity enabled. Going to do any initialization required before giving control to optional ROM at E000.
A8	Initialization before E000 ROM control over. E000 ROM to get control next.
A9	Returned from E000 ROM control. Going to do any initialization required after E000 optional ROM control.
AA	Initialization after E000 optional ROM control is over. Going to display system configuration.
00	System configuration is displayed. Going to give control to INT 19h boot loader.

AMI New BIOS; 06/06/92-08/08/93

Code	Meaning
01	Processor register test about to start and NMI to be disabled.
02	NMI is Disabled. Power on delay starting.
03	Power on delay complete. Any initialization before keyboard BAT is in progress next.
04	Any init before keyboard BAT is complete. Reading keyboard SYS bit, to check soft reset/power on.
05	Soft reset/ power-on determined. Going to enable ROM; i.e. disable shadow RAM/Cache if any.
06	ROM is enabled. Calculating ROM BIOS checksum and waiting for 8042 keyboard controller input buffer to be free.
07	ROM BIOS checksum passed; KB controller input buffer free. Going to issue BAT command to the keyboard controller.
08	BAT command to keyboard controller is issued. Going to verify the BAT command.
09	Keyboard controller BAT result verified. Keyboard command byte to be written next.
0A	Keyboard command byte code is issued. Going to write command byte data.
0B	Keyboard controller command byte is written. Going to issue Pin-23 & 24 blocking/unblocking command.
0C	Pin-23 & 24 of keyboard controller is blocked/ unblocked. NOP command of keyboard controller to be issued next.
0D	NOP command processing is done. CMOS shutdown register test to be done next.

0E	CMOS shutdown register R/W test passed. Going to calculate CMOS checksum and update DIAG byte.
0F	CMOS checksum calculation is done; DIAG byte written. CMOS init to begin (If "INIT CMOS IN EVERY BOOT" is set).
10	CMOS initialization done (if any). CMOS status register about to init for Date and Time.
11	CMOS Status register initialised. Going to disable DMA and Interrupt controllers.
12	DMA controller #1 & #2, interrupt controller #1 & #2 disabled. About to disable Video display and init port-B.
13	Disable Video display and initialise port B. Chipset init/auto memory detection about to begin.
14	Chipset initialization/auto memory detection over. 8254 timer test about to start.
15	CH-2 timer test halfway. 8254 CH-2 timer test to be complete.
16	Ch-2 timer test over. 8254 CH-1 timer test to be complete.
17	CH-1 timer test over. 8254 CH-0 timer test to be complete.
18	CH-0 timer test over. About to start memory refresh.
19	Memory Refresh started. Memory Refresh test to be done next.
1A	Memory Refresh line is toggling. Going to check 15 microsecond ON/OFF time.
1B	Memory Refresh period 30 microsecond test complete. Base 64K memory test about to start.
20	Base 64k memory test started. Address line test to be done next.
21	Address line test passed. Going to do toggle parity.
22	Toggle parity over. Going for sequential data R/W test.
23	Base 64k sequential data R/W test passed. Any setup before Interrupt vector init about to start.
24	Setup required before vector initialization complete. Interrupt vector initialization about to begin.
25	Interrupt vector initialization done. Going to read I/O port of 8042 for turbo switch (if any).
26	I/O port of 8042 is read. Going to initialize global data for turbo switch.
27	Global data initialization is over. Any initialization after interrupt vector to be done next.
28	Initialization after interrupt vector is complete. Going for monochrome mode setting.
29	Monochrome mode setting is done. Going for Colour mode setting.
2A	Colour mode setting is done. About to go for toggle parity before optional ROM test.
2B	Toggle parity over. About to give control for any setup required before optional video ROM check.
2C	Processing before video ROM control is done. About to look for optional video ROM and give control.
2D	Optional video ROM control done. About to give control for processing after video ROM returns control.
2E	Return from processing after video ROM control. If EGA/VGA not found do display memory R/W test.
2F	EGA/VGA not found. Display memory R/W test about to begin.
30	Display memory R/W test passed. About to look for the retrace checking.
31	Display memory R/W test or retrace checking failed. About to do alternate Display memory R/W test.
32	Alternate Display memory R/W test passed. About to look for the alternate display retrace checking.
33	Video display checking over. Verification of display type with switch setting and actual card to begin.
34	Verification of display adapter done. Display mode to be set next.
35	Display mode set complete. BIOS ROM data area about to be checked.
36	BIOS ROM data area check over. Going to set cursor for power on message.
37	Cursor setting for power on message complete. Going to display power on message.
38	Power on message display complete. Going to read new cursor position.

39	New cursor position read and saved. Going to display the reference string.
3A	Reference string display over. Going to display the Hit <ESC> message.
3B	Hit <ESC> message displayed. Virtual mode memory test about to start.
40	Preparation for virtual mode test started. Going to verify from video memory.
41	Returned after verifying from display memory. Going to prepare descriptor tables.
42	Descriptor tables prepared. Going to enter in virtual mode for memory test.
43	Entered in virtual mode. Going to enable interrupts for diagnostics mode.
44	Interrupts enabled (if diags switch on). Going to initialize data to check mem wrap around at 0:0.
45	Data initialized. Going to check for memory wrap around at 0:0 and finding total memory size.
46	Mem wrap around test done. Size calculation over. About to go for writing patterns to test memory.
47	Pattern to be tested written in extended memory. Going to write patterns in base 640k memory.
48	Patterns written in base memory. Going to find out amount of memory below 1M b.
49	Amount of memory below 1Mb found and verified. Going to find amount of memory above 1Mb.
4A	Amount of memory above 1Mb found and verified. Going for BIOS ROM data area check.
4B	BIOS ROM data area check over. Going to check <ESC> and clear mem below 1 Mb for soft reset.
4C	Memory below 1Mb cleared. (SOFT RESET). Going to clear memory above 1 Mb.
4D	Memory above 1Mb cleared. (SOFT RESET). Going to save memory size.
4E	Memory test started. (NO SOFT RESET). About to display first 64K memory test.
4F	Memory size display started. This will be updated during memory test. Going for sequential and random memory test.
50	Memory test below 1Mb complete. Going to adjust memory size for relocation/shadow.
51	Memory size adjusted due to relocation/shadow. Memory test above 1Mb to follow.
52	Memory test above 1Mb complete. Preparing to go back to real mode.
53	CPU registers saved including memory size. Going to enter real mode.
54	Shutdown successful; CPU in real mode. Going to restore registers saved during prep for shutdown.
55	Registers restored. Going to disable gate A20 address line.
56	A20 address line disable successful. BIOS ROM data area about to be checked.
57	BIOS ROM data area check halfway. BIOS ROM data area check to be complete.
58	BIOS ROM data area check over. Going to clear Hit <ESC> message.
59	Hit <ESC> message cleared. <WAIT...> message displayed. About to start DMA and PIC test.
60	DMA page register test passed. About to verify from display memory.
61	Display memory verification over. About to go for DMA #1 base register test.
62	DMA #1 base register test passed. About to go for DMA #2 base register test.
63	DMA #2 base register test passed. About to go for BIOS ROM data area check.
64	BIOS ROM data area check halfway. BIOS ROM data area check to be complete.
65	BIOS ROM data area check over. About to program DMA unit 1 and 2.
66	DMA unit 1 and 2 programming over. About to initialize 8259 interrupt controller.
67	8259 initialization over. About to start keyboard test.
80	Keyboard test started. Clearing output buffer, checking for stuck key. About to issue keyboard reset.
81	Keyboard reset error/stuck key found. About to issue keyboard controller interface command.
82	Keyboard controller interface test over. About to write command byte and init circular buffer.
83	Command byte written, Global data init done. About to check for lock-key.
84	Lock-key checking over. About to check for memory size mismatch with CMOS.
85	Memory size check done. About to display soft error and check for password or bypass setup.
86	Password checked. About to do programming before setup.

87	Programming before setup complete. Going to CMOS setup program.
88	Returned from CMOS setup program, screen is cleared. About to do programming after setup.
89	Programming after setup complete. Going to display power on screen message.
8A	First screen message displayed. About to display <WAIT...> message.
8B	<WAIT...> message displayed. About to do Main and Video BIOS shadow.
8C	Main/Video BIOS shadow successful. Setup options programming after CMOS setup about to start.
8D	Setup options programmed; mouse check and initialisation to be done next.
8E	Mouse check and initialisation complete. Going for hard disk and floppy reset.
8F	Floppy check returns that floppy is to be initialized. Floppy setup to follow.
90	Floppy setup is over. Test for hard disk presence to be done.
91	Hard disk presence test over. Hard disk setup to follow.
92	Hard disk setup complete. About to go for BIOS ROM data area check.
93	BIOS ROM data area check halfway. BIOS ROM data area check to be complete.
94	BIOS ROM data area check over. Going to set base and extended memory size.
95	Mem size adjusted due to mouse support, hard disk type 47. Going to verify from display memory.
96	Returned after verifying from display memory. Going to do any init before C800 optional ROM control
97	Any init before C800 optional ROM control is over. Optional ROM check and control will be done next.
98	Optional ROM control is done. About to give control to do any required processing after optional ROM returns control.
99	Any init required after optional ROM test over. Going to setup timer data area and printer base address.
9A	Return after setting timer and printer base address. Going to set the RS-232 base address.
9B	Returned after RS-232 base address. Going to do any initialization before coprocessor test
9C	Required initialization before co-processor over. Going to initialize the coprocessor next.
9D	Coprocessor initialized. Going to do any initialization after coprocessor test.
9E	Initialization after coprocessor test complete. Going to check extd keyboard keyboard ID and num lock.
9F	Extd keyboard check is done, ID flag set. num lock on/off. Keyboard ID command to be issued.
A0	Keyboard ID command issued. Keyboard ID flag to be reset.
A1	Keyboard ID flag reset. Cache memory test to follow.
A2	Cache memory test over. Going to display soft errors.
A3	Soft error display complete. Going to set keyboard typematic rate.
A4	Keyboard typematic rate set. Going to program memory wait states.
A5	Memory wait states programming over. Screen to be cleared next.
A6	Screen cleared. Going to enable parity and NMI.
A7	NMI and parity enabled. Going to do any init before giving control to optional ROM at E000.
A8	Initialization before E000 ROM control over. E000 ROM to get control next.
A9	Returned from E000 ROM control. Going to do any initialisation after E000 optional ROM control.
AA	Initialization after E000 optional ROM control is over. Going to display the system configuration.
00	System configuration is displayed. Going to give control to INT 19h boot loader.

AMI WinBIOS; 12/15/93 Onwards

Code	Meaning
01	Processor register test about to start; disable NMI next.
02	NMI is Disabled. Power on delay starting.
03	Power on delay complete (to check soft reset/power-on).
05	Soft reset/power-on determined, going to enable ROM (i.e. disable shadow RAM cache, if any).
06	ROM is enabled. Calculating ROM BIOS checksum.
07	ROM BIOS checksum passed. CMOS shutdown register test to be done next.
08	CMOS shutdown register test done. CMOS checksum calculation next.
09	CMOS checksum calculation done; CMOS diag byte written; CMOS initialisation to begin.
0A	CMOS initialization done (if any). CMOS status register about to init for Date and Time.
0B	CMOS status register init done. Any initialization before keyboard BAT to be done next.
0C	KB controller I/B free. Going to issue the BAT command to keyboard controller.
0D	BAT command to keyboard controller is issued. Going to verify the BAT command.
0E	Keyboard controller BAT result verified. Any initialization after KB controller BAT next.
0F	Initialisation after KB controller BAT done. Keyboard command byte to be written next.
10	Keyboard controller command byte is written. Going to issue Pin-23 & 24 blocking/unblocking command.
11	Keyboard controller Pin-23 & 24 blocked/unblocked; check press of <INS> key during power-on .
12	Checking for pressing of <INS> key during power-on done. Going to disable DMA/Interrupt controllers.
13	DMA controller #1 and #2 and Interrupt controller #1 and #2 disabled; video display disabled and port B initialised; chipset init/auto memory detection next.
14	Chipset init/auto memory detection over. To uncompress the POST code if compressed BIOS.
15	POST code is uncompressed. 8254 timer test about to start.
19	8254 timer test over. About to start memory refresh test.
1A	Memory Refresh line is toggling. Going to check 15 micro second ON/OFF time.
20	Memory Refresh 30 microsecond test complete. Base 64K memory/address line test about to start.
21	Address line test passed. Going to do toggle parity.
22	Toggle parity over. Going for sequential data R/W test on base 64k memory.
23	Base 64k sequential data R/W test passed. Going to set BIOS stack and do any setup before Interrupt
24	Setup required before vector initialization complete. Interrupt vector initialization about to begin.
25	Interrupt vector initialization done. Going to read Input port of 9042 for turbo switch (if any) and clear password if POST diag switch is ON next.
26	Input port of 8042 is read. Going to initialize global data for turbo switch.
27	Global data initialization for turbo switch is over. Any initialization before setting video mode to be done next.
28	Initialization before setting video mode is complete. Going for mono mode and colour mode setting.
2A	Monochrome and colour mode setting is done. About to go for toggle parity before optional ROM test.
2B	Toggle parity over. About to give control for any setup required before optional video ROM check next.
2C	Processing before video ROM control is done. About to look for optional video ROM and give control.
2D	Optional video ROM control is done. About to give control to do any processing after video RON returns control.

255

2E	Return from processing after video ROM control. If EGA/VGA not found do display memory R/W test.
2F	EGA/VGA not found. Display memory R/W test about to begin.
30	Display memory R/W test passed. About to look for the retrace checking.
31	Display mem R/W test or retrace checking failed. About to do alternate Display memory R/W test.
32	Alternate Display memory R/W test passed. About to look for the alternate display retrace checking.
34	Video display checking over. Display mode to be set next.
37	Display mode set. Going to display the power on message.
39	New cursor position read and saved. Going to display the Hit <DEL> message.
3B	Hit <DEL> message displayed. Virtual mode memory test about to start.
40	Going to prepare the descriptor tables.
42	Descriptor tables prepared. Going to enter in virtual mode for memory test.
43	Entered in virtual mode. Going to enable interrupts for diagnostics mode.
44	Interrupts enabled (if diags switch is on). Going to initialize data to check memory wrap around at 0:0.
45	Data initialized. Going to check for memory wrap around at 0:0 and find total system memory size.
46	Memory wrap around test done. Memory size calculation over. About to go for writing patterns to test memory.
47	Pattern to be tested written in extended memory. Going to write patterns in base 640k memory.
48	Patterns written in base memory. Going to find amount of memory below 1Mb.
49	Amount of memory below 1Mb found and verified. Going to find out amount of memory above 1Mb memory.
4B	Amount of memory above 1Mb found and verified. Check for soft reset and going to clear memory below 1Mb for soft reset next (if power on go to POST # 4Eh).
4C	Memory below 1Mb cleared.(SOFT RESET)
4D	Memory above 1Mb cleared.(SOFT RESET); save memory size next (go to POST # 52h).
4E	Memory test started. (NOT SOFT RESET); display first 64K memory size next.
4F	Memory size display started. This will be updated during memory test; sequential and random memory test next.
50	Memory testing/initialisation below 1Mb complete. Going to adjust displayed memory size for relocation/ shadow.
51	Memory size display adjusted due to relocation/ shadow. Memory test above 1Mb to follow.
52	Memory testing/initialisation above 1Mb complete. Going to save memory size information.
53	Memory size information is saved. CPU registers are saved. Going to enter real mode.
54	Shutdown successful, CPU in real mode, disable gate A20 line next.
57	A20 address line disable successful. Going to adjust memory size depending on relocation/shadow.
58	Memory size adjusted for relocation/shadow. Going to clear Hit <DEL> message.
59	Hit <DEL> message cleared. <WAIT...> message displayed. About to start DMA and interrupt controller test.
60	DMA page register test passed. About to go for DMA #1 base register test.
62	DMA #1 base register test passed. About to go for DMA #2 base register test.
65	DMA #2 base register test passed. About to program DMA unit 1 and 2.
66	DMA unit 1 and 2 programming over. About to initialize 8259 interrupt controller.
67	8259 initialization over. About to start keyboard test.
F4	Extended NMI sources enabling is in progress (EISA).

80	Keyboard test. Clear output buffer; check for stuck key; issue reset keyboard command next.
81	Keyboard reset error/stuck key found. About to issue keyboard controller interface test command.
82	Keyboard controller interface test over. About to write command byte and init circular buffer.
83	Command byte written; global data init done; check for lock-key next.
84	Lock-key checking over. About to check for memory size mismatch with CMOS.
85	Memory size check done. About to display soft error and check for password or bypass setup.
86	Password checked. About to do programming before setup.
87	Programming before setup complete. Uncompress SETUP code and execute CMOS setup.
88	Returned from CMOS setup and screen is cleared. About to do programming after setup.
89	Programming after setup complete. Going to display power on screen message.
8B	First screen msg displayed. <WAIT...> message displayed. About to do Main/Video BIOS shadow.
8C	Main and Video BIOS shadow successful. Setup options programming after CMOS setup about to start.
8D	Setup options are programmed; mouse check and init next.
8E	Mouse check and initialisation complete. Going for hard disk controller reset.
8F	Hard disk controller reset done. Floppy setup to be done next.
91	Floppy setup complete. Hard disk setup to be done next.
94	Hard disk setup complete. Going to set base and extended memory size.
96	Memory size adjusted due to mouse support, hard disk type 47; any init before C800, optional ROM control next.
97	Init before C800 optional ROM control is over. Optional ROM check and control next.
98	Optional ROM control done. About to give control for any required processing after optional ROM returns control next.
99	Any initialization required after optional ROM test over. Going to setup timer data area and printer base address.
9A	Return after setting timer and printer base address. Going to set the RS-232 base address.
9B	Returned after RS-232 base address. Going to do any initialization before coprocessor test.
9C	Required initialization before co-processor is over. Going to initialize the coprocessor next.
9D	Coprocessor initialized. Going to do any initialization after coprocessor test.
9E	Init after coprocessor test complete. Going to check extd keyboard; keyboard ID and NumLock.
9F	Extd keyboard check is done; ID flag set; NumLock on/off, issue keyboard ID command next.
A0	Keyboard ID command issued. Keyboard ID flag to be reset.
A1	Keyboard ID flag reset. Cache memory test to follow.
A2	Cache memory test over. Going to display any soft errors.
A3	Soft error display complete. Going to set the keyboard typematic rate.
A4	Keyboard typematic rate set. Going to program memory wait states.
A5	Memory wait states programming over. Going to clear the screen and enable parity/NMI.
A7	NMI and parity enabled. Going to do any initialization required before giving control to optional ROM at E000 next.
A8	Initialization before E000 ROM control over. E000 ROM to get control next.
A9	Returned from E000 ROM control. Going to do init required.
AA	Init after E000 optional ROM control is over. Going to display the system configuration.
B0	System configuration is displayed. Going to uncompress SETUP code for hot-key setup.
B1	Uncompressing of SETUP code is complete. Going to copy any code to specific area.
00	Copying of code to specific area done. Going to give control to INT 19h boot loader.

EISA

Code	Meaning
F0	Initialisation of I/O cards in slots is in progress (EISA).
F1	Extended NMI sources enabling is in progress (EISA).
F2	Extended NMI test is in progress (EISA).
F3	Display any slot initialisation messages.
F4	Extended NMI sources enabling in progress.

ARCHE TECHNOLOGIES

Legacy BIOS

Derives from AMI (9 April 90), using port 80; certain codes come up if a copy is made without AMI's copyright notice. The major differences are at the end.

Code	Explanation
01	Disable NMI and test CPU registers
02	Verify ROM BIOS checksum (32K at F800:0)
03	Initial keyboard controller and CMOS RAM communication
04	Disable DMA and interrupt controllers; test CMOS RAM interrupt
05	Reset Video
06	Test 8254 timer
07	Test delta count for timer channel 2 (speaker)
08	Test delta count for timer channel 1 (memory refresh)
09	Test delta count for timer channel 0 (system timer)
0A	Test parity circuit and turn on refresh
0B	Enable parity check circuit and test system timer
0C	Test refresh trace link toggle
0D	Test refresh timing synchronization of high and low period
10	Disable cache and shadow BIOS; test 64K base memory address lines
11	Test base 64K memory for random addresses and data read/write
12	Initialize interrupt vectors in lower 1K of RAM
14	Test CMOS RAM shutdown register read/write; disable DMA and interrupt controllers
15	Test CMOS RAM battery and checksum, and different options such as diagnostic byte
16	Test floppy information in CMOS RAM; initialize monochrome video
17	Initialise colour video
18	Clear parity status if any
19	Test for EGA/VGA video ROM BIOS at C000:0 and pass control to it if there
1A	Returned from video ROM. Clear parity status if any; update system parameters for any video ROM found; test display memory read/write
1B	Primary video adapter: check vertical and horizontal retrace; write/read test video memory
1C	Secondary video adapter: check vertical and horizontal retrace; write/read test video memory
1D	Compare and verify CMOS RAM video type with switches and actual video adapter; set equipment byte if correct
1E	Call BIOS to set mono/colour video mode according to CMOS RAM
20	Display CMOS RAM write/read errors and halt if any
21	Set cursor to next line and call INT 10 to display
22	Display Power on "386 BIOS" message and check CPU speed is 25 or 33 MHz
23	Read new cursor position and call INT 10 to display
24	Skip 2 rows of text and display (C)AMI at bottom of screen

25	Refresh is off, so call shadow RAM test
F0	Failure inside shadow RAM test
30	Verify (C)AMI... and overwrite with blanks before entering protected mode
31	Enter protected mode and enable timer interrupt (IRQ0). Errors indicate gate A20 circuit failed
32	Size memory above 1Mb
33	Size memory below 640K
34	Test memory above 1Mb
35	Test memory below 1Mb
36	Unknown AMI function
37	Clear memory below 1Mb
38	Clear memory above 1Mb
39	Set CMOS shutdown byte to 3 and go back to real mode
3A	Test sequential and random data write/read of base 64K RAM
3B	Test RAM below 1Mb and display area being tested
3C	Test RAM above 1Mb and display area being tested
3D	RAM test OK
3E	Shutdown for return to real mode
3F	Back in real mode; restore all variables
40	Disable gate A20 since now in real mode
41	Check for (C)AMI in ROM
42	Display (C)AMI message
43	Clear <Esc> message; test cache
4E	Process shutdown 1; go back to real mode
4F	Restore interrupt vectors and global data in BIOS RAM area
50	Test 8237 DMA controller and verify (c)AMI in ROM
51	Initialize DMA controller
52	Test various patterns to DMA controller
53	Verify (C)AMI in ROM
54	Test DMA control flip-flop
55	Initialize and enable DMA controllers 1 and 2
56	Initialize 8259 interrupt controllers—clear write request and mask registers
57	Test 8259 controllers and setup interrupt mask registers
61	Check DDNIL status bit and display message if clear
70	Perform keyboard BAT (Basic Assurance Test)
71	Program keyboard to AT type
72	Disable keyboard and initialize keyboard circular buffer
73	Display "DEL" message for setup prompt and initialize floppy controller/drive
74	Attempt to access floppy drive
75	If CMOS RAM is good, check and initialize hard disk type identified in CMOS RAM
76	Attempt to access hard disk and set up hard disk
77	Shuffle any internal error codes
78	Verify (C)AMI is in ROM
79	Check CMOS RAM battery and checksum; clear parity status
7A	Compare size of base/extended memory to CMOS RAM info
7B	Unknown AMI function
7C	Display (C)AMI
7D	Set/reset AT compatible memory expansion bit
7E	Verify (C)AMI is in ROM

POST Codes

7F	Clear <DEL> message from screen and check if DEL pressed
80	Find option ROM in C800 to DE00 and pass control to any found
81	Return from adapter ROM; initialize timer and data area
82	Setup parallel and serial port base info in global data area
83	Test for presence of 80387 numeric coprocessor and initialize
84	Check lock key for keyboard
85	Display soft error messages if CMOS RAM data error was detected such as battery or checksum
86	Test for option ROM in E000:0 and pass control to any found
A0	Error in 256 Kbit or 1Mbit RAM chip in lower 640K memory
A1	Base 64K random address/data pattern test (only in 386APR and Presto 386SX BIOS)
A9	Initialize on-board VGA (Presto 386SX)
B0	Error in 256 Kbit RAM chip in lower 640K memory
B1	Base 64K random address/data pattern test (only in Presto 386SX BIOS)
E0	Returned to real mode; initialise base 64K RAM (Presto)
E1	initialize base 640K RAM (Presto)
EF	Configuration memory error in Presto -can't find memory
F0	Test shadow RAM from 0:4000 RAM area
00	Call INT 19 boot loader

AST

See also *Phoenix* or *Award*. AST introduced an enhanced BIOS in 1992 with 3 beeps before all early POST failure messages, for Field Replaceable Unit identification. Otherwise, the most significant (left) digit of the POST code indicates the number of Iong beeps, and the least significant (right) digit indicates the short beeps. 17 therefore means 1 long beep and 7 short. Doesn't work after 20.

Early POST Codes

These are usually fatal and accompanied by a beep code:

Code	Meaning
1	System Board
2	SIMM Memory; System Board
3	SIMM Memory; System Board
4	SIMM Memory; System Board
5	Processor; System Board
6	Keyboard Controller; System Board
7	Processor; System Board
8	Video Adapter; Video RAM; System Board
9	BIOS; System Board
10	System Board
11	External cache; System Board

Code	Meaning
00	Reserved
	Beep and Halt if Error occurs
01	Test CPU registers and functionality
02	Test empty 8042 keyboard controller buffer
03	Test 8042 keyboard controller reset
04	Verify keyboard ID and low-level keyboard communication

05	Read keyboard input port (WS386SX16 only)
06	Initialise system board support chipset
09	Test BIOS ROM checksum; flush external cache
0D	Test 8254 timer registers (13 short beeps)
0E	Test ASIC registers (CLEM only, 14 short beeps)
0F	Test CMOS RAM shutdown byte (15 short beeps)
10	Test DMA controller 0 registers
11	Test DMA controller 1 registers
12	Test DMA page registers (see code 17)
13	see code 17
14	Test memory refresh toggle (see code 17)
15	Test base 64K memory
16	Set interrupt vectors in base memory
17	Initialize video; if EGA/VGA, issue code 12-13 if error, but only use this POST code beep pattern
12	EGA/VGA vertical retrace failed (different from normal beep)
13	EGA/VGA RAM test failed (different than normal beep tone)
14	EGA/VGA CRT registers failed (different than normal beep)
18	Test display memory
	Don't beep and don't halt if error occurs
20	EISA bus board power up (EISA Systems only)
30	Test interrupt controller #1 mask register
31	Test interrupt controller #2 mask register
32	Test interrupt controllers for stuck interrupt
33	Test for stuck NMI (P386 25/33, P486, CLEM and EISA)
34	Test for stuck DDNIL status bit (CLEM only)
40	Test CMOS RAM backup battery
41	Calculate and verify CMOS RAM checksum
42	Setup CMOS RAM options (except WS386SX16)
50	Test protected mode
51	Test protected mode exceptions
60	Calculate RAM size
61	Test RAM
62	Test shadow RAM (WS386SX16, P386 25/33, P486, CLEM, EISA), or test cache (P386/16)
63	Test cache (P38625/33, P486, CLEM, EISA), or copy system BIOS to shadow RAM (P386C, P386/16, WS386SX16)
64	Copy system BIOS to shadow RAM (P386 25/33, P486, CLEM, EISA), or copy video BIOS to shadow RAM (P38616, SW386SX16)
65	Copy video BIOS to shadow RAM (P386 25/33, P486, CLEM, EISA), or test cache (WS386SX16)
66	Test 8254 timer channel 2 (P386 25/33, P486, EISA)
67	Initialize memory (Eagle only)

AT&T

Either Phoenix or Olivetti BIOS. See Olivetti M24 for early 6300 series motherboards., and Phoenix for later ones with Intel motherboards. After 1991 see NCR.

AWARD

The general procedures below are valid for greater than XT v3.0 and AT v3.02-4.2. The sequence may vary slightly between versions.

Award Test Sequence—up to v4.2

Procedure	Meaning
CPU	BIOS sets verifies and resets the error flags in the CPU (i.e. carry; sign; zero; stack overflow). Failure here is normally due to the CPU or system clock.
POST Determination	BIOS determines whether motherboard is set for normal operation or a continuous loop of POST (for testing). If the POST test is cycled 1-5 times over and over either the jumper for this function is set to burn-in or the circuitry involved has failed.
Keyboard Controller	BIOS tests the internal operations of the keyboard controller chip (8042). Failure here is normally due to the keyboard chip.
Burn In Status	1-5 will repeat if the motherboard is set to burn in (you will see the reset light on all the time). If you haven't set the board for burn-in mode, there is a short in the circuitry.
Initialise Chipset	BIOS clears all DMA registers and CMOS status bytes 0E & 0F. BIOS then initialises 8254 (timer). Failure of this test is probably due to the timer chip.
CPU	A bit-pattern is used to verify the functioning of the CPU registers. Failure here is normally down to the CPU or clock chip.
RTC	BIOS verifies that that the real time clock is updating CMOS at normal intervals. Failure is normally the CMOS/RTC or the battery.
ROM BIOS Checksum	BIOS performs a checksum of itself against a predetermined value that will equal 00. Failure is down to the ROM BIOS.
Initialise Video	BIOS tests and initialises the video controller. Failure is normally the video controller (6845) or an improper setting of the motherboard or CMOS.
PIT	BIOS tests the functionality of channels 0 1 2 in sequence. Failure is normally the PIT chip (8254/53).
CMOS Status	Walking-bit pattern tests CMOS shutdown status byte 0F. Failure normally in CMOS.
Extended CMOS	BIOS checks for any extended information of the chipset and stores it in the extended RAM area. Failure is normally due to invalid information and can be corrected by setting CMOS defaults. Further failure indicates either the chipset or the CMOS RAM.
DMA	Channels 0 and 1 are tested together with the page registers of the DMA controller chip(s)—8237. Failure is normally due to the DMA chips.
Keyboard	The 8042 keyboard controller is tested for functionality and for proper interfacing functions. Failure is normally due to the 8042 chip.
Refresh	Memory refresh is tested; the standard refresh period is 120-140 ns. Failure is normally the PIT chip in ATs or the DMA chip in XTs.
Memory	The first 64K of memory is tested with walking-bit patterns. Failure is normally due to the first bank of RAM or a data line.
Interrupt Vectors	The BIOS interrupt vector table is loaded to the first bank of RAM. Failure here is not likely since memory in this area has been tested. If a failure does occur suspect the BIOS or the PIC.
Video ROM	Video ROM is initialised which performs an internal diagnostic before returning control to the System BIOS. Failure is normally the video adapter or the BIOS.
Video Memory	This is tested with a bit-pattern. This is bypassed if there is a ROM on the video adapter. Failure is normally down to the memory on the adapter.
PIC	The functionality of the interrupt controller chip(s) is tested (8259). Failure is normally down to the 8259 chips but may be the clock.

CMOS Battery	BIOS verifies that CMOS byte 0D is set which indicates the CMOS battery power. Suspect the battery first and the CMOS second.
CMOS Checksum	A checksum is performed on the CMOS. Failure is either incorrect setup or CMOS chip or battery. If the test is passed the information is used to configure the system.
Determine System Memory	Memory up to 640K is addressed in 64K blocks. Failure is normally due to an address line or DMA chip. If all of the memory is not found there is a bad RAM chip or address line in the 64K block above the amount found.
Memory Test	Tests are performed on any memory found and there will normally be a message with the hex address of any failing bit displayed at the end of boot.
PIC	Further testing is done on the 8259 chips.
CPU protected mode	Processor is placed into protected mode and back into real mode; the 8042 is used for this. In case of failure suspect the 8042; CPU; CMOS; or BIOS in that order.
Determine Extended Memory	Memory above 1 Mb is addressed in 64K blocks. The entire block will be inactive if there is a bad RAM chip on a block.
Test Extended Memory	Extended memory is tested with a series of patterns. Failure is normally down to a RAM chip, and the hex address of the failed bit should be displayed.
Unexpected Exceptions	BIOS checks for unexpected exceptions in protected mode. Failure is likely to be a TSR or intermittent RAM failure.
Shadow/Cache	Shadow RAM and cache is activated; failure may be due to the cache controller or chips. Check the CMOS first for invalid information.
8242 Detection	BIOS checks for an Intel 8242 keyboard controller and initialises it if found. Failure may be due to an improper jumper setting or the 8242.
Initialise Keyboard	Failure could be the keyboard or the controller.
Initialise Floppy	All those set in the CMOS. Failure could be incorrect CMOS setup or floppy controller or the drive.
Detect Serial Ports	BIOS searches for and initialises up to four serial ports at 3F8/2F8/3E8 and 2E8. Detection failure is normally due to an incorrect jumper setting somewhere or an adapter failure.
Detect Parallel Ports	BIOS searches for and initialises up to four parallel ports at 378/3BC and 278. Detection failure is normally due to an incorrect jumper setting somewhere or an adapter failure.
Initialise Hard Drive	BIOS initialises any hard drive set in CMOS. Failure could be due to invalid CMOS setup, hard drive or controller.
Detect NPU Coprocessor	Initialisation of any NPU Coprocessor found. Failure is due to either an invalid CMOS setup or the NPU is failing.
Initialise Adapter ROM	Any adapter ROMs between C800 and EFFF are initialised. The ROM will do an internal test before giving back control to the System ROM. Failure is normally due to the adapter ROM or the attached hardware.
Initialise External Cache	Any cache external to the 486 is enabled. Failure would indicate invalid CMOS setup, cache controller or chips.
NMI Unexpected Exceptions	A final check for unexpected exceptions before giving control to the Int 19 boot loader. Failure is normally due to a memory parity error or an adapter.
Boot Errors	Failure when the BIOS attempts to boot off the default drive set in CMOS is normally due to an invalid CMOS drive setup or as given by an error message. If the system hangs there is an error in the Master Boot Record or the Volume Boot Record.

Award Test Sequence—after v4.2 (386/486)

Procedure	Meaning
CPU	BIOS sets verifies and resets the error flags in the CPU then performs a register test by writing and reading bit patterns. Failure is normally due to the CPU or clock chip.
Initialise Support Chips	Video is disabled as is parity/DMA and NMI. Then the PIT/PIC and DMA chips are initialised. Failure is normally down to the PIT or DMA chips.
Init Keyboard	Keyboard and Controller are initialised.
ROM BIOS Test	A checksum is performed by the ROM BIOS on the data within itself and is compared to a preset value of 00. Failure is normally due to the ROM BIOS.
CMOS Test	A test of the CMOS chip which should also detect a bad battery. Failure is due to either the CMOS chip or the battery.
Memory Test	First 356K of memory tested with any routines in the chipsets. Failure normally due to defective memory.
Cache Initialisation	Any cache external to the chipset is activated. Failure is normally due to the cache controller or chips.
Initialise Vector Table	Interrupt vectors are initialised and the interrupt table is installed into low memory. Failure is normally down to the BIOS or low memory.
CMOS RAM	CMOS RAM checksum tested, BIOS defaults loaded if invalid. Check CMOS RAM.
Keyboard Init	Keyboard initialised and Num Lock set On. Check the keyboard or controller.
Video Test	Video adapter tested and initialised.
Video Memory	Tested on Mono and CGA adapters. Check the adapter card.
DMA Test	DMA controllers and page registers are tested. Check the DMA chips.
PIC Tests	8259 PIC chips are tested.
EISA Mode Test	A checksum is performed on the extended data area of CMOS where EISA information is stored. If passed the EISA adapter is initialised.
Enable Slots	Slots 0-15 for EISA adapters are enabled if the above test is passed.
Memory Size	Memory addresses above 265K written to in 64K blocks and addresses found are initialised. If a bit is bad, entire block containing it and those above will not be seen
Memory Test	Read/Write tests performed to memory over 256K; failure due to bad bit in RAM.
EISA Memory	Memory tests on any adapters initialised previously. Check the memory chips.
Mouse Initialisation	Checks for a mouse and installs the appropriate interrupt vectors if one is found. Check the mouse adapter if you get a problem.
Cache Init	The cache controller is initialised if present.
Shadow RAM Setup	Any Shadow RAM present according to the CMOS Setup is enabled.
Floppy Test	Test and initialise floppy controller and drive.
Hard Drive Test	Test and initialise hard disk controller and drive. You may have an improper setup or a bad controller or hard drive.
Serial/Parallel	Any serial/parallel ports found at the proper locations are initialised.
Maths Copro	Initialised if found. Check the CMOS Setup or the chip.
Boot Speed	Set the default speed at which the computer boots.
POST Loop	Reboot occurs if the loop pin is set; for manufacturing purposes.
Security	Ask for password if one has been installed. If not check the CMOS data or the chip.

Write CMOS	The BIOS is waiting to write the CMOS values from Setup to CMOS RAM. Failure is normally due to an invalid CMOS configuration.
Pre-Boot	BIOS is waiting to write the CMOS values from Setup to CMOS RAM.
Adapter ROM Initialise	Adapter ROMs between C800 and EFFF are initialised. The ROM will do an internal test before giving back control to the System ROM. Failure is normally due to the adapter ROM or the attached hardware.
Set Up Time	Set CMOS time to the value located at 40h of the BIOS data area.
Boot System	Control is given to the Int 19 boot loader.

3.0x

Uses IBM beep patterns. Version 3.xx sends codes 1-24 to port 80 and 300 and the system hangs up. Afterwards, codes are sent to the POST port and screen without hanging up.

Code	Meaning
01	CPU test 1: verify CPU status bits
02	Powerup check—Wait for chips to come up; initialize motherboard and chipset (if present) with defaults. Read 8042 status and fail if its input buffer contains data but output buffer does not.
03	Clear 8042 Keyboard interface—send self-test command AA, fail if status not 2 output buffer full.
04	Reset 8042 Keyboard controller—fail if no data input (status not equal 1) within a million tries, or if input data is not 55 in response to POST 03.
05	Get 8042 manufacturing status—read video type and POST type bits from 8042 discrete input port; test for POST type = manufacturing test or normal; fail if no response from 8042.
06	Initialize on-board chips—disable colour & mono video, parity, and 8237 DMA; reset 80x87 math chip, initialize 8255 timer 1, clear DMA chip and page registers and CMOS RAM shutdown byte; initialize motherboard chipset if present.
07	CPU test 2: read/write/verify registers except SS, SP, BP with FF and 00 data
08	Initialize CMOS RAM/RTC chip—update timer cycle normally; disable PIE, AIE, UIE and square wave. Set BCD date and 24-hour mode.
09	Checksum 32K of BIOS ROM; fail if not 0
0A	Initialize video interface—read video type from 8042 discrete input port. Fail if can't read it. Initialize 6845 controller register at either colour or mono adapter port to 80 columns, 25 rows, 8/14 scan lines per row, cursor lines at 6/11 (first) & 7/12 (last), offset to 0.
0B	Test 8254 timer channel 0- this test is skipped; already initialized for mode 3.
0C	Test 8254 timer channel 1—this test is skipped; already initialized for mode 0.
0D	Test 8254 timer channel 2—write/read/verify FF, then 00 to timer registers; initialize with 500h for normal operation.
0E	Test CMOS RAM shutdown byte (3.03: CMOS date and timer—this test is skipped and its functions performed
0F	Test extended CMOS RAM if present (3.03: test CMOS shutdown byte—write/read/verify a walk-to-left I pattern at CMOS RAM address 8F)
10	Test 8237 DMA controller ch 0—write/read/verify pattern AA, 55, FF and 00.
11	Test 8237 DMA controller ch 1—write/read/verify pattern AA, 55, FF and 00.
12	Test 8237 DMA controller page registers—write/read/verify pattern AA, 55, FF and 00: use port addresses to check out address circuitry to select page registers. At this point, POST enables user reboot.
13	Test 8741 keyboard controller interface—read 8042 status, verify buffers are empty, send AA self-test command, verify 55 response, send 8741 write command to 8042, wait for 8042 acknowledgement, send 44 data for 8741 (keyboard enabled, system flag, AT interface), wait for ack, send keyboard disable command, wait for ack. Fail if no ack or improper responses.
14	Test memory refresh toggle circuits—fail if not toggling high and low.

POST Codes

265

15	Test first 64K of base system memory—disable parity checking, zero all of memory, 64K at a time, to clear parity errors, enable parity checking, write/read/verify 00, 5A, FF and A5 at each address.
16	Set up interrupt vector tables in low memory.
17	Set up video I/O operations—read 8042 (motherboard switch or jumper) to find whether colour or mono adapter installed; validate by writing a pattern to mono memory B0000 and select mono I/O port if OK or colour if not, and initialize it via setting up the hardware byte and issuing INT 10. Then search for special video adapter BIOS ROM at C0000 (EGA/VGA), and call it to initialize if found. Fail if no 8042 response.
18, 1 beep	Test MDA/CGA video memory unless EGA/VGA adapter is found—disable video, detect mono video RAM at B0000 or colour at B8000, write/read/verify test it with pattern A5A5, fill it with normal attribute, enable the video card. No error halt unless enabled by CMOS. Beep once to let user know first phase of testing is complete. From now on, POST will display test and error messages on the screen.
19	Test 8259 PIC mask bits, channel 1—write/read/verify 00 to mask register.
1A	Test 8259 PIC mask bits, channel 2—write/read/verify 00 to mask register.
1B	Test CMOS RAM battery level—poll CMOS RTC/RAM chip for battery level status. Display error if level is low, but do not halt.
1C	Test CMOS RAM checksum—check CMOS RAM battery level again, calculate checksum of normal and extended CMOS RAM. Halt if low battery or checksum not 0; otherwise reinitialize motherboard chipset if necessary.
1D	Set system memory size parameters from CMOS RAM data, Cannot fail.
1E	Size base memory 64K at a time, and save in CMOS RAM. Cannot fail, but saves diagnostic byte in CMOS RAM if different from size in CMOS.
1F	Test base memory found from 64K to 640K—write/read/verify FFAA and 5500 patterns by byte. Display shows failing address and data.
20	Test stuck bits in 8259 PICs
21	Test for stuck NMI bits (parity /IO check)
22	Test 8259 PIC interrupt functionality—set up counter timer 0 to count down and issue an interrupt on IRQ8. Fail if interrupt does not occur.
23	Test protected mode, A20 gate. and (386 only) virtual 86 & 8086 page mode.
24	Size extended memory above 1Mb; save size into CMOS RAM. Cannot fail, but saves diagnostic byte in CMOS RAM if different from size in CMOS.
25	Test all base and extended memory found (except the first 64K) up to 16 Mb. Disable parity check but monitor for parity errors. Write/read/verify AA55 then 55AA pattern 64K at a time. On 386 systems use virtual 8086 mode paging system. Displays actual and expected data and failing address.
26	Test protected mode exceptions—creates the circumstances to cause exceptions and verifies they happen; out-of-bounds instruction, invalid opcode, invalid TSS (JMP, CALL, IRET, INT), segment not present on segment register instruction, generate memory reference fault by writing to a read-only segment.
27	Initialise shadow RAM and move system BIOS and/or video BIOS into it if enabled by CMOS RAM setup. Also (386 only) initialise the cache controller if present in system. This is not implemented in some versions of 3.03
28	Detect and initialise Intel 8242/8248 chip (not implemented in 3.03)
29	Reserved
2A	Initialise keyboard
2B	Detect and initialise floppy drive
2C	Detect and initialise serial ports
2D	Detect and initialise parallel ports
2E	Detect and initialise hard drive

2F	Detect and initialise math coprocessor
30	Reserved
31	Detect and initialise adapter ROMs
BD	Initialize Orvonton cache controller if present
CA	Initialize 386 Micronics cache if present
CC	Shutdown NMI handler
EE	Test for unexpected processor exception
FF	INT 19 boot

3.00—3.03 8/26/87

Code	Meaning
01	Processor test part 1; Processor status verification. Tests following CPU status flags: set/clear carry zero sign and overflow (fatal). Output: infinite loop if failed; continue test if OK. Registers: AX/BP.
02	Determine type of POST test. Manufacturing (e.g. 01-05 in loop) or normal (boot when POST finished). Fails if keyboard interface buffer filled with data. Output: infinite loop if failed; continue test if OK. Registers: AX/BX/BP.
03	Clear 8042 keyboard interface. Send verify TEST_KBRD command (AAh). Output: infinite loop if failed; continue test if OK. Registers: AX/BX/BP.
04	Reset 8042 keyboard controller. Verify AAh return from 03. Infinite loop if test fails.
05	Get 8042 keyboard controller manufacturing status. Read input port via keyboard controller to determine manufacturing or normal mode operation. Reset system if manufacturing status from 02. Output: infinite loop if failed; continue test if OK. Registers: AX/BX/BP.
06	Init chips on board LSI chips. Disable colour/mono video; parity and DMA (8237A). Reset coprocessor; initialise (8254) timer 1; clear DMA page registers and CMOS shutdown byte.
07	Processor test #2. read/write verify SS/SP/BP registers with FFh and 00h data pattern.
08	Initialize CMOS chip
09	EPROM checksum for 32 Kbytes
0A	Initialize video interface
0B	Test 8254 channel 0
0C	Test 8254 channel 1
0D	Test 8254 channel 2
0E	Test CMOS date and timer
0F	Test CMOS shutdown byte
10	Test DMA channel 0
11	Test DMA channel 1
12	Test DMA page registers
13	Test 8741 keyboard controller
14	Test memory refresh toggle circuits
15	Test 1st 64k bytes of system memory
16	Setup interrupt vector table
17	Setup video I/O operations
18	Test video memory
19	Test 8259 channel 1 mask bits
1A	Test 8259 channel 2 mask bits
1B	Test CMOS battery level
1C	Test CMOS checksum
1D	Setup configuration byte from CMOS
1E	Sizing system memory & compare w/CMOS

1F	Test found system memory
20	Test stuck 8259'S interrupt bits
21	Test stuck NMI (parity/IO chk) bits
22	Test 8259 interrupt functionality
23	Test protected mode and A20 gate
24	Sizing extended memory above 1MB
25	Test found system/extended memory
26	Test exceptions in protected mode
27	Reserved

286 N3.03 Extensions

Code	Meaning
2A	POST_KEYBOARD present during reset keyboard before boot has no relationship to POST 19.
2B	POST_FLOPPY present during init of floppy controller and drive(s)
2C	POST_COMM present during init of serial cards.
2D	POST_PRN present during init of parallel cards
2E	POST_DISK present during init of hard disk controller and drive(s)
2F	POST_MATH present during init of math coprocessor. Result remains after DOS boot; left on the port 80 display
30	POST_EXCEPTION present during protected mode access or when processor exceptions occur. A failure indicates that protected mode return was not possible
CC	POST_NMI present when selecting the F2 system halt option

XT 8088/86 BIOS v3.1

Code	Meaning
01	Processor test 1; processor status verification
02	Determine type of POST test. Failed if keyboard interface buffer filled with data.
06	Init 8259 PIC and 8237 DMA controller chips. Disable colour and mono video, parity circuits and DMA chips. Reset math coprocessor. Initialise 8253 Timer channel 1. Clear DMA chip and page registers.
07	Processor test #2. Write, read and verify all registers except SS, SP and BP with data patterns 00 and FF.
09	EPROM checksum for 32 Kbytes
0A	Initialize video controller 6845 registers as follows: 25 lines x 80 columns, first cursor scan line at 6/11 and last at 7/12, reset display offset to 0.
15	Test 1st 64K of system memory
16	Setup interrupt vector table in 1st 64K
17	Setup video I/O operations
18	Test video memory
19	Test 8259 channel 1 mask bits
1A	Test 8259 channel 2 mask bits
1D	Setup configuration byte from CMOS
1E	Sizing system memory & compare w/CMOS
1F	Test found system memory
20	Test stuck 8259's interrupt bits
21	Test stuck NMI (parity/IO chk) bits
22	Test 8259 interrupt functionality
2A	Initialise keyboard

2B	Initialise floppy controller and drive
2C	Initialise COM ports
2D	Initialised LPT ports
2F	Initialise maths coprocessor
31	Initialise option ROMs
FF	Int 19 Boot attempt

Modular (386) BIOS v3.1

Also for PC/XT v3.0+ and AT v3.02+. Tests do not necessarily execute in numerical order.

Code	Meaning
01	Processor test part 1. Processor status verification. Tests the following processor-status flags: set/clear carry; zero; sign and overflow (fatal). BIOS sets each flag; verifies they are set and turns each flag off verifying its state. Failure of a flag means a fatal error. Output: infinite loop if failed; continue test if OK. Registers: AX/BP.
02	Determine POST type; whether normal (boot when POST finished) or manufacturing (run 01-05 in loop) which is often set by a jumper on some motherboards. Fails if keyboard interface buffer filled with data. Output: infinite loop if failed; continue test if OK. Registers: AX/BX/BP.
03	Clear 8042 keyboard interface. Send verify TEST_KBRD command (AAh). Output: infinite loop if failed; continue test if OK. Registers: AX/BX/BP.
04	Reset 8042 keyboard controller. Verify AAh return from 03. Infinite loop if test fails. Registers: AX/BX/BP.
05	Get 8042 keyboard controller manufacturing status; read input port via keyboard controller to determine manufacturing or normal mode operation. Reset system if manufacturing; i.e. if 02 found the status to be Manufacturing triggers a reset and 01-05 are repeated continuously. Output: infinite loop if failed; continue test if OK. Registers: AX/BX/BP.
06	Initialise chips on board LSI chips. Disables colour and mono video/parity circuits/DMA (8237) chips; resets maths coprocessor; initialises timer 1 (8255); clears DMA chip and all page registers and the CMOS shutdown byte.
07	Processor Test 2. Reads writes and verifies all CPU registers except SS/SP/BP with data pattern FF and 00.
08	Initialises CMOS timer/RTC and updates timer cycle; normally CMOS (8254) timer; (8237A) DMA; (8259) interrupt and EPROM.
09	EPROM Checksum; test fails if not equal to 0. Also checksums sign-on message.
0A	Initialise Video Interface; specifically register 6845 to 80 characters per row and 25 rows per screen and 8/14 scan lines per row for mono/colour; first scan line of cursor 6/11; last scan line of cursor 7/12; reset display offset to 0.
0B	Test Timer (8254) Channel 0. See also below.
0C	Test Timer (8254) Channel 1.
0D	Test Timer (8254) Channel 2.
0E	Test CMOS Shutdown Byte using a walking-bit algorithm.
0F	Test Extended CMOS. On motherboards supporting extended CMOS configuration such as C & T the BIOS tables of CMOS information configure the chipset which has an extended storage facility enabling you to keep the configuration with the power off. A checksum is used for verification.
10	Test DMA Channel 0. This and the next two tests initialise the DMA chip and test it with an AA/55/FF/00 pattern. Port addresses are used to check the address circuit to DMA page circuit registers.
11	DMA Channel 1
12	DMA Page Registers
13	Test keyboard controller interface.

14	Test memory refresh toggle circuits.
15	First 64K of system memory which is used by the BIOS; an extensive parity test.
16	Interrupt Vector Table. Sets up and loads interrupt vector tables in memory for the 8259 PIC.
17	Video I/O operations. Initialises the video; EGA and VGA ROMs are used if present.
18	Video memory test for CGA and mono cards (EGA and VGA have their own procedures).
19	Test 8259 mask bits—Channel 1.Interrupt lines turned alternately off and on. Failure is fatal.
1A	8259 Mask Bits—Channel 2
1B	CMOS battery level; verifies battery status bit set to 1. 0 could indicate bad battery at CMOS.
1C	Tests the CMOS checksum data at 2E and 2Fh and extended CMOS checksum if present.
1D	Configuration of the system from CMOS values if the checksum is good.
1E	System memory size is determined by writing to addresses from 0-640K continuing till there is no response. The size is then compared to the CMOS and a flag set if they do not compare. An error message will then be displayed.
1F	Tests memory from the top of 64K to the top of memory found by writing patterns FFAA and 5500 and reading them back byte by byte for verification
20	Stuck 8259 Interrupt Bits.
21	Stuck NMI bits (parity or I/O channel check).
22	8259 function.
23	Verifies protected mode; 8086 virtual and page mode.
24	As for 1E but for extended memory from 1-16Mb on 286/386SX systems and 64 Mb on 386s and above. The value found is compared to the CMOS settings.
25	Tests extended memory found above using virtual 8086 paging mode and writing an FFFF/AA55/0000 pattern.
26	Protected Mode Exceptions; tests other aspects of protected mode operations.
27	Tests cache control (386/486) or Shadow RAM. Systems with CGA and MDA indicate that video shadow RAM is enabled even though there is no BIOS ROM to shadow.
28	Set up cache controller or 8242 keyboard controller. Optional Intel 8242/8248 keyboard controller detection and support.
29	Reserved.
2A	Initialise keyboard and controller.
2B	Initialise floppy drive(s) and controller.
2C	Detect and initialise serial ports.
2D	Detect and initialise parallel ports.
2E	Initialise hard drive and controller.
2F	Detect and initialise maths coprocessor.
30	Reserved.
31	Detect and initialise option ROMs. Initialises any between C800-EFFF.
3B	Initialise secondary cache with OPTi chipset (486 only).
CC	NMI Handler Shutdown. Detects untrapped NMIs during boot.
EE	Unexpected Processor Exception.
FF	Boot Attempt; if POST is complete and all components are initialised with no errors.

ISA/EISA BIOS v4.0

EISA BIOS

Code	Meanings
1	CPU flags
2	CPU registers
3	Initialise DMA
4	Memory refresh
5	Keyboard initialisation
06	ROM checksum
07	CMOS
08	256K memory
09	Cache
0A	Set interrupt table
0B	CMOS checksum
0C	Keyboard initialisation
0D	Video adapter
0E	Video memory
0F	DMA channel 0
10	DMA channel 1
11	DMA page register
14	Timer chip
15	PIC controller 1
16	PIC controller 2
17	PIC stuck bits
18	PIC maskable IRQs
19	NMI bit check
1F	CMOS XRAM
20	Slot 0
21	Slot 1
22	Slot 2

EISA BIOS

Code	Meanings
1	CPU flags
2	CPU registers
3	Initialise DMA
4	Memory refresh
5	Keyboard initialisation
06	ROM checksum
07	CMOS
08	256K memory
09	Cache
0A	Set interrupt table
0B	CMOS checksum
0C	Keyboard initialisation
0D	Video adapter
0E	Video memory

POST Codes

271

0F	DMA channel 0
10	DMA channel 1
11	DMA page register
14	Timer chip
15	PIC controller 1
16	PIC controller 2
17	PIC stuck bits
18	PIC maskable IRQs
19	NMI bit check
1F	CMOS XRAM
20	Slot 0
21	Slot 1
22	Slot 2

Late Award BIOS (4.5x-non PnP)

Code	Meanings
23	Slot 3
24	Slot 4
25	Slot 5
26	Slot 6
27	Slot 7
28	Slot 8
29	Slot 9
2A	Slot 10
2B	Slot 11
2C	Slot 12
2D	Slot 13
2E	Slot 14
2F	Slot 15
30	Memory size 256K
31	Memory test over 256K
32	EISA memory
3C	CMOS setup on
3D	Mouse
3E	Cache RAM
3F	Shadow RAM
40	N/A
41	Floppy drive
42	Hard drive
43	RS232/parallel
45	NPU
47	Speed
4E	Manufacturing loop
4F	Security
50	CMOS update
51	Enable NMI
52	Adapter ROMs
53	Set time

63	Boot
B0	NMI in protected
B1	Disable NMI
BF	Chipset program
C0	Cache on/off
C1	Memory size
C2	Base 256K test
C3	DRAM page select
C4	Video switch
C5	Shadow RAM
C6	Cache program
C8	Speed switch
C9	Shadow RAM
CA	OEM chipset
FF	Boot

Code	Meaning
C0	Turn Off Chipset Cache; OEM specific cache control
01	Processor Test 1; Processor Status (1Flags) Verification. Tests carry/zero/sign/overflow processor status flags.
02	Processor Test 2; Read/Write/Verify all CPU registers except SS/SP and BP with data pattern FF and 00.
03	Initialise Chips; Disable NMI/PIE/UEL/SQWV; video; parity checking; DMA; reset maths coprocessor. Clear all page registers and CMOS shutdown byte. Initialise timer 0 1 and 2 including set EISA timer to a known state. Initialise DMA controllers 0 and 1; interrupt controllers 0 and 1 and EISA extended registers.
04	Test Memory Refresh Toggle
05	Blank video; initialise keyboard
06	Reserved
07	Test CMOS Interface and battery status. Detects bad battery. BE and Chipset Default Initialisation. Program chipset registers with power-on BIOS defaults.
C1	Memory Presence Test; OEM specific test to size on-board memory
C5	Early Shadow; OEM specific—enable for fast boot
C6	Cache Presence Test; External cache size detection
08	Setup Low Memory; Early chipset initialisation. Memory presence test. OEM chipset routines. Clear low 64K of memory. Test first 64K memory
09	Early Cache Initialisation. Cyrix CPU Initialisation. Cache Initialisation
0A	Setup Interrupt Vector Table; Initialise first 120 interrupt vectors with SPURIOUS_INT_HDLR and initialise INT 00-FF according to INT_TBL.
0B	Test CMOS RAM Checksum if bad or Insert key depressed; load defaults.
0C	Initialise keyboard; Set NUM LOCK status.
0D	Initialise video interface; Detect CPU Clock. Read CMOS location 14h to find out type of video. Detect and initialise video adapter.
0E	Test Video Memory. Write signon message to screen. Set up Shadow RAM and enable according to Setup.
0F	Test DMA Controller 0. BIOS Checksum Test. keyboard detect and initialisation.
10	Test DMA Controller 1
11	Test DMA Page Registers
12-13	Reserved

14	Test Timer Counter 2. Test 8254 Timer 0 Counter 2
15	Test 8259-1 Mask Bits. Alternately turns on and off interrupt lines.
16	Test 8259-2 Mask Bits. Alternately turns on and off interrupt lines.
17	Test Stuck 8259 interrupt bits. Turn off interrupts then verify no interrupt mask register is on.
18	Test 8259 Interrupt Functionality. Force an interrupt and verify that it occurred.
19	Test Stuck NMI Bits (Parity/I/O check). Verify NMI can be cleared.
1A	Display CPU Clock
1B-1E	Reserved
1F	Set EISA Mode. If EISA NVR checksum is good execute EISA initialisation. If not execute ISA tests and clear EISA mode flag. Test EISA configuration memory integrity (checksum and communication interface).
20	Enable Slot 0. Motherboard
21-2F	Enable Slots 1-15
30	Size Base and Extended Memory. From 256-640K and that above 1 Mb.
31	Test Base and Extended Memory. Various patterns are used on that described above. This will be skipped in EISA mode and can be skipped in ISA mode with Esc.
32	Test EISA Extended Memory. If EISA Mode flag is set then test EISA memory found in slots initialisation. This will be skipped in ISA mode and can be skipped in EISA mode with Esc.
33-3B	Reserved
3C	Setup Enabled
3D	Initialise and Install Mouse
3E	Setup Cache Controller
3F	Reserved
BF	Chipset Initialisation. Program registers with Setup values.
40	Display virus protect enable or disable.
41	Initialise floppy drive(s) and controller
42	Initialise hard drive(s) and controller
43	Detect and initialise Serial/Parallel Ports and game port.
44	Reserved
45	Detect and Initialise Maths Coprocessor
46	Reserved
47	Reserved
48-4D	Reserved
4E	Manufacturing POST Loop or Display Messages. Reboot if manufacturing POST Loop Pin is set. Otherwise display any messages (i.e. non-fatal errors detected during POST) and enter Setup.
4F	Security Check. Ask password (optional)
50	Write CMOS. Write all CMOS values back to RAM and clear screen.
51	Pre-boot Enable. Enable Parity Checker; NMI and cache before boot.
52	Initialise Option ROMs. Between C800-EFFF. When FSCAN option is enabled will initialise between C800-F7FF
53	Initialise Time Value In 40h BIOS area.
60	Setup Virus Protect. According to Setup
61	Set Boot Speed
62	Setup NumLock. According to Setup

63	Boot attempt. Set Low Stack. Boot via INT 19
B0	Spurious. If interrupt occurs in protected mode
B1	Unclaimed NMI. If unmasked NMI occurs display "Press F1 to disable NMI; F2 reboot"
E1-EF	Setup Pages. E1=Page 1; E2=Page 2 etc
FF	Boot

Late Award BIOS (4-5x PnP)

Code	Meaning
C0	1. Turn off OEM specific cache, shadow 2. Initialize standard devices with default values: DMA controller (8237) Programmable Interrupt Controller (8259) Programmable Interval Timer (8254) RTC chip
C1	Auto detection of onboard DRAM & Cache
C3	1. Test the first 256K DRAM 2. Expand the compressed codes into temporary DRAM area including the compressed system BIOS & Option ROMs
C5	Copy the BIOS from ROM into E000FFFF shadow RAM so that POST will go faster
01-02	Reserved
03	Initialize EISA registers (EISA BIOS only)
04	Reserved
05	1. Keyboard Controller Self Test 2. Enable Keyboard Interface
06	Reserved
07	Verifies CMOS's basic R/W functionality
BE	Program defaults values into chipset according to the MODBINable Chipset Default Table
09	1. Program configuration register of Cyrix CPU according to the MODBINable Cyrix Register Table 2. OEM specific cache initialization
0A	1. Initialize the first 32 interrupt vectors with corresponding interrupt handlers Initialize INT No from 33120 with Dummy (Spurious) interrupt handler 2. Issue CPUID instruction to identify CPU type 3. Early Power Management initialization (OEM specific)
0B	1. Verify the RTC time is valid or not 2. Detect bad battery 3. Read CMOS data into BIOS stack area 4. PnP initializations including (PnP BIOS only) Assign CSN to PnP ISA card Create resource map from ESCD 5. Assign IO & Memory for PCI devices (PCI BIOS only)
0C	Initialization of the BIOS data area (40:040:FF)
0D	1. Program some of the chipset's value according to setup. (Early setup value program) 2. Measure CPU speed for display & decide the system clock speed 3. Video initialization including Monochrome, CGA, EGA/VGA If no display device found, the speaker will beep.

0E	1.Initialize the APIC (MultiProcessor BIOS only) 2.Test video RAM (If Monochrome display device found) 3.Show message including: Award logo Copyright string BIOS date code & Part No OEM specific sign on messages Energy Star logo (Green BIOS only) CPU brand, type & speed
0F	DMA channel 0 test
10	DMA channel 1 test
11	DMA page registers test
12-13	Reserved
14	Test 8254 timer 0 counter 2
15	Test 8259 interrupt mask bits for channel 1
16	Test 8259 interrupt mask bits for channel 2
17	Reserved
19	Test 8259 functionality
1A-1D	Reserved
1E	If EISA NVM checksum is good, execute EISA initialization (EISA BIOS only)
1F-29	Reserved
30	Get base memory & extended memory size
31	1.Test base memory from 256K to 640K 2.Test extended memory from 1M to the top of memory
32	1.Display the Award Plug & Play BIOS extension message(PnP BIOS only) 2.Program all onboard super I/O chips(if any) including COM ports, LPT ports, FDD port according to setup value
33-3B	Reserved
3C	Set flag to allow users to enter CMOS setup utility
3D	1.Initialise keyboard 2.Install PS2 mouse
3E	Try to turn on level 2 cache Note: Some chipset may need to turn on the L2 cache in this stage. But usually, the cache is turn on later in Post 61h
3F-40	Reserved
BF	1.Program the rest of the chipset's value according to setup (later setup value program) 2.If auto configuration is enabled, programmed the chipset with predefined values in the MODBINable AutoTable
41	Initialize floppy disk drive controller
42	Initialize hard drive controller
43	If it is a PnP BIOS, initialize serial & parallel ports
44	Reserved
45	Initialize math coprocessor
46-4D	Reserved
4E	If there is any error detected (such as video, KB....), show all the error messages on the screen & wait for user to press <F1> key
4F	1.If password is needed, ask for password 2.Clear the Energy Star logo (Green BIOS only)
50	Write all the CMOS values currently in the BIOS stack are back into the CMOS
51	Reserved

52	1.Initialize all ISA ROMs 2.Later PCI initializations(PCI BIOS only) assign IRQ to PCI devices initialize all PCI ROMs 3.PnP initializations (PnP BIOS only) assign IO, Memory, IRQ & DMA to PnP ISA devices initialize all PnP ISA ROMs 4.Program shadow RAM according to setup settings 5.Program parity according to setup setting 6.Power Management initialization Enable/Disable global PM APM interface initialization
53	1.If it is not a PnP BIOS, initialize serial & parallel ports 2.Initialize time value in BIOS data area by translate the RTC time value into a timer tick value
54-5F	Reserved
60	Setup virus protection (boot sector protection) functionality according to setup setting
61	1.Try to turn on level 2 cache (if L2 cache already turned on in post 3D, this part will be skipped) 2.Set the boot up speed according to setup setting 3.Last chance for chipset initialization 4.Last chance for Power Management initialization (Green BIOS only) 5.Show the system configuration table
62	1.Setup daylight saving according to setup values 2.Program the NUM lock, typematic rate & typematic speed according to setup setting
63	1.If there is any changes in the hardware configuration, update the ESCD information (PnP BIOS only) 2.Clear memory that have been used 3.Boot system via INT 19h
FF	Boot

Unexpected Errors

Code	Meaning
B0	If interrupt occurs in protected mode
B1	Unclaimed NMI occurs

v3.3

Code	Meaning
1-5	Keyboard controller
06	On board LSI
07	CPU
8-0E	CMOS; 8254; 8237; 8259; EPROM
0F	Extended CMOS
10-14	Refresh
15	First 64K RAM
16	Interrupt vector tables
17	Video initialisation
18	Video memory
19-1A	Interrupt line mask
1B	Battery good
1C	CMOS checksum

1D	CMOS chip
1E	Memory size
1F	Memory verifier
20-23	CPU support chips
24	Extended memory size
25	Extended memory size
26	Protected mode
27-28	Shadow RAM
29	Reserved
2A	Initialise keyboard
2B	Floppy drive initialisation
2C	Serial port initialisation
2D	Parallel port initialisation
2E	Hard disk initialisation
2F	Maths coprocessor
30	Reserved
31	Optional ROMs
FF	Boot

CHIPS AND TECHNOLOGIES

Some are sent to the display in decimal as well as port 80 in hex. Micro Channel BIOSes use ports 680 and 3BC.

POST Procedures

Procedure	Meaning
Power On Tests	CPU synchronises with clock. Check the CPU or clock.
System ROM Check	The BIOS runs a checksum on itself. Check the BIOS chips.
DMA Controller Fail	DMA Controllers are initialised and tested. Check the DMA chips.
System Timer Failed	Channels 0/1/2 are tested in sequence. Check the PIT chips.
Base 64K Memory Testing	Walking-bit test performed on 1st 64K of RAM which is critical for the BIOS vector area to be initialised. Check for bad RAM chips or a data or address line.
Interrupt Contr Failed	Test the 8259 chip.
CPU Still In Protected Mode	Attempts are made to read the configuration of the system through the 8042 keyboard controller.
Refresh Not Occurring	Memory refresh is tested; standard refresh is 120-140 ns. Check the PIT chip.
Keyboard Controller Not Responding	Tests are run on the keyboard controller. Check the 8042 chip.
Could Not Enter Protected Mode	BIOS attempts to enter protected mode to test extended memory. Check the 8042 chip or the A20 address line.
Initialise Timer	Attempts are made to initialise the PIT.
Init DMA Controller	Attempts are made to initialise the DMA Controller.
Entering/Exiting Protected Mode	The transition is handled by the keyboard controller and the A20 line. Check the 8042 or the A20.
Relocate Shadow RAM	BIOS attempts to shadow itself into extended memory. Check for memory problems.
Test For EMS	Check the EMS adapter or an improper CMOS/Jumper setting.
Test Video Capabilities	Normally includes a memory test on the adapter memory up to 256K.
Test Memory	Extensive testing of Base, Extended, Expanded memory. Check for defective memory modules; 8042 chip; A20 line or an improper CMOS/Jumper setting.

Check System Options	The hardware in the system is compared with the values stored in CMOS. The PIT/PIC/8042/RTC and other system board chips are tested again.
Peripheral Check/Test	Checks are made for peripherals at standard I/O ports including serial and parallel ports keyboards and maths coprocessors. You should see an error message on screen at this point.
Floppy Test	Floppy devices set in CMOS are checked and initialised. If a bootable floppy is found the fixed disks are tested and the BIOS will boot to the floppy disk. Check for defective controllers or an improper CMOS Setup.
Fixed Disk Test	Checks for fixed disks in CMOS. If no bootable floppy in the A: drive the BIOS loads the first sector off the first fixed disk and jumps to the area of memory where the sector was loaded. You may just see a flashing cursor or an error message from the potential operating system. Check for improper CMOS setup/defective controller/fixed disk or corruption of bootloader software on the fixed disk.
Advanced Options	These include mouse/cache etc. You should see an error message on the screen at this point, except that a defective cache may hang the system; in most cases, the cache will be disabled by the BIOS.

NEAT, PEAK/DM, OC8291, ELEAT BIOS

Hex	Dec	Code
00h	00	Error in POS register.
01h	01	Flag register failed.
02h	02	CPU register failed.
03h	03	System ROM did not checksum
04h	04	DMA controller failed
05h	05	System timer failed
06h	06	Base 64K RAM failed address test: not installed, misconfigured, or bad addressing
07h	07	Base 64K RAM failed data test
08h	08	Interrupt controller failed
09h	09	Hot (unexpected) interrupt occurred
0Ah	10	System timer does not interrupt
0Bh	11	CPU still in protected mode
0Ch	12	DMA page registers failed
0Dh	13	Refresh not occurring
0Eh	14	Keyboard controller not responding
0Fh	15	Could not enter protected mode
10h	16	GDT or IDT failed
11h	17	LDT register failed
12h	18	Task register failed
13h	19	LSL instruction failed
14h	20	LAR instruction failed
15h	21	VERR/VERW failed
16h	22	Keyboard controller gate A20 failed
17h	23	Exception failed/unexpected exception
18h	24	Shutdown during memory test
19h	25	Last used error code
1Ah	26	Copyright checksum error
1Bh	27	Shutdown during memory sizing

POST Codes

1Ch	28	CHIPSet initialization
50h	80	Initialize hardware
51h	81	Initialize timer
52h	82	Initialize DMA controller
53h	83	Initialize interrupt controller
54h	84	Initialize CHIPSet
55h	85	Setup EMS configuration
56h	86	Entering protected mode for first time
57h	87	Size memory chips
58h	88	Configure memory chip interleave
59h	89	Exiting protected mode for first time
5Ah	90	Determine system board memory size
5Bh	91	Relocate shadow RAM
5Ch	92	Configure EMS
5Dh	93	Set up wait state configuration
5Eh	94	Re-test 64K RAM
5Fh	95	Test shadow RAM
60h	96	Test CMOS RAM
61h	97	Test video
62h	98	Test and initialize DDNIL bits
63h	99	Test protected mode interrupt
64h	100	Test address line A20
65h	101	Test memory address lines
66h	102	Test memory
67h	103	Test extended memory
68h	104	Test timer interrupt
69h	105	Test real time clock (RTC)
6Ah	106	Test keyboard
6Bh	107	Test 80x87 math chip
6Ch	108	Test RS232 serial ports
6Dh	109	Test parallel ports
6Eh	110	Test dual card
6Fh	111	Test floppy drive controller
70h	112	Test hard drive controller
71h	113	Test keylock
72h	114	Test pointing device
90h	144	Setup RAM
91h	145	Calculate CPU speed
92h	146	Check configuration
93h	147	Initialize BIOS
94h	148	POST Bootstrap
95h	149	Reset ICs
96h	150	PEAK: System board POS. NEAT/OC8291 ELEAT: Test/initialise cache RAM and controller.
97h	151	VGA Power on Diagnostics and setup
98h	152	Adapter POS
99h	153	Re-initialize DDNIL bits
A0h	160	Exception 0

A1h	161	Exception 1
A2h	162	Exception 2
A3h	163	Exception 3
A4h	164	Exception 4
A5h	165	Exception 5
A6h	166	Exception 6
A7h	167	Exception 7
A8h	168	Exception 8
A9h	169	Exception 9
AAh	170	Exception A
ABh	171	Exception B
ACh	172	Exception C
ADh	173	Exception D
C0h	224	System board memory failure
C1h	225	I/O Channel Check activated
C2h	226	Watchdog timer timeout
C3h	227	Bus timer timeout

COMPAQ

Port 84 codes indicate errors while port 85 codes show the category:

00	System BIOS
01	Error after boot

Video POST

General

Code	Meaning
00	Initialise flags
01	Read manufacturing jumper
02	8042 Received Read command
03	No response from 8042
04	Look for ROM at E000
05	Look for ROM at C800
06	Normal CMOS reset code
08	Initialise 8259
09	Reset code in CMOS byte
0A	Vector Via 40:67 reset function
0B	Vector Via 40:67 with E01 function
0C	Boot reset function
0D	Test #2 8254 Counter 0
0E	Test #2 8254 Counter 2
0F	Warm Boot

Overall Power Up Sequence

Code	Meaning
10	PPI disabled
11	Initialise (blast) VDU controller
12	Clear Screen; turn on video
13	Test time 0
14	Disable RTC interrupts
15	Check battery power
16	Battery has lost power
17	Clear CMOS diags
18	Test base memory (first 128K)
19	Initialise base memory
1A	Initialise VDU adapters
1B	The system ROM
1C	CMOS checksum
1D	DMA controller/page registers
1E	Test keyboard controller
1F	Test 286 protected mode
20	Test real and extended memory
21	Initialise time-of-day
22	Initialise 287 coprocessor
23	Test the keyboard and 8042
24	Reset A20
25	Test diskette subsystem
26	Test fixed disk subsystem
27	Initialise parallel printer
28	Perform search for optional ROMs
29	Test valid system configuration
2A	Clear screen
2B	Check for invalid time and date
2C	Optional ROM search
2D	Test timer 2
2F	Write to diagnostic byte

Base RAM Initialization

Code	Meaning
30	Clear first 128K bytes of RAM
31	Load interrupt vectors 70-77
32	Load interrupt vectors 00-1F
33	Initialise MEMSIZE and RESETWD
34	Verify CMOS checksum
35	CMOS checksum not valid
36	Check battery power
37	Check for game adapters
38	Check for serial ports
39	Check for parallel printer ports
3A	Initialise port and comm timeouts
3B	Flush keyboard buffer

Base RAM Test

Code	Meaning
40	Save RESETWD value
41	Check RAM refresh
42	Start write of 128K RAM test
43	Rest parity checks
44	Start verify of 128K RAM test
45	Check for parity errors
46	No RAM errors
47	RAM error detected

VDU Initialization and Test

Code	Meaning
50	Check for dual frequency in CMOS
51	Check CMOS VDU configuration
52	Start VDU ROM search
53	Vector to VDU option ROMs
54	Initialise first display adapter
55	Initialise second display adapter
56	No display adapters installed
57	Initialise primary VDU mode
58	Start of VDU test (each adapter)
59	Check existence of adapter
5A	Check VDU registers
5B	Start screen memory test
5C	End test of adapter
5D	Error detected on an adapter
5E	Test the next adapter
5F	All adapters successfully tested

Memory Test

Code	Meaning
60	Start of memory tests
61	Enter protected mode
62	Start memory sizing
63	Get CMOS size
64	Start test of real memory
65	Start test of extended memory
66	Save size memory (base
67	128K option installed CMOS bit
68	Prepare to return to Real Mode
69	Back in Real Mode—successful
6A	Protected mode error during test
6B	Display error message
6C	End of memory test
6D	Initialise KB OK string
6E	Determine size to test

283

6F	Start MEMTEST
70	Display XXXXXKB OK
71	Test each RAM segment
72	High order address test
73	Exit MEMTEST
74	Parity error on bus

80286 Protected Mode

Code	Meaning
75	Start protected mode test
76	Prepare to enter protected mode
77	Test software exceptions
78	Prepare to return to Real Mode
79	Back in Real Mode—successful
7A	Back in Real Mode—error occurred
7B	Exit protected test
7C	High order address test failure
7D	Entered cache controller test
7E	Programming memory cache
7F	Copy system ROM to high RAM

8042 and Keyboard

Code	Meaning
80	Start of 8042 test
81	Do 8042 self test
82	Check result received
83	Error result
84	OK 8042
86	Start test
87	Got acknowledge
88	Got result
89	Test for stuck keys
8A	Key seems to be stuck
8B	Test keyboard interface
8C	Got result
8D	End of Test

System Board Test

Code	Meaning
90	Start of CMOS test
92	CMOS seems to be OK
92	Error on CMOS read/write test
93	Start of DMA controller test
94	Page registers seem OK
95	DMA controller is OK
96	8237 initialisation is complete
97	Start of NCA RAM test

Diskette Test

Code	Meaning
A0	Start of diskette tests
A1	FDC reset active (3F2h bit 2)
A2	FDC reset inactive (3F2h bit 2)
A3	FDC motor on
A4	FDC timeout error
A5	FDC failed reset
A6	FDC passed reset
A8	Start to determine drive type
A9	Seek operation initiated
AA	Waiting for FDC seek status
AF	Diskette tests completed
B0	Start of fixed disk drive tests
B1	Combo board not found—exit
B2	Combo controller failed—exit
B3	Testing drive 1
B4	Testing drive 2
B5	Drive error (error condition)
B6	Drive failed (failed to respond)
B7	No fixed drives—exit
B8	Fixed drive tests complete
B9	Attempt to boot diskette
BA	Attempt to boot fixed drive
BB	Boot attempt failed FD/HD
BC	Boot record read, jump to boot record
BD	Drive error, retry booting
BE	Weitek coprocessor test (386, 386/xxe, 386&486/33L, P486c)

EISA TESTS

Deskpro/M, /LT, /33L, P486

Code	Meaning
C0	EISA non-volatile memory checksum
C1	EISA DDF map initialization
C2	EISA IRQ initialization
C3	EISA DMA initialization
C4	EISA slot initialization
C5	EISA display configuration error messages
C6	EISA PZ initialization begun
C7	EISA PZ initialization done
C8	System manager board self-test

LT, SLT, LTE

Code	Meaning
C0	Disable NMI
C1	Turn off hard disk subsystem
C2	Turn off video subsystem
C3	Turn off floppy disk subsystem
C4	Turn off hard disk/modem subsystems
C5	Go to standby
C6	Update BIOS time of day
C7	Turn on hard disk/modem subsystems
C8	Turn on floppy disk subsystem
C9	Turn on video subsystem
CB	Flush keyboard input buffer
CC	Re-enable MNI

Standard POST Functions

Code	Meanings
D0	Entry to clear memory routine
D1	Ready to go to protected mode
D2	Ready to clear extended memory
D3	Ready to reset back to real mode
D4	Back in real mode, ready to clear
D5	Clear base memory, CLIM register init failure (SLT/286)
D7	Scan and clear DDNIL bits
D9	Orvonton 4-way cache detect
DD	Built-in self-test failed

Option ROM Replacement

Code	Meaning
E0	Ready to replace E000 ROM
E1	Completed E000 ROM replacement
E2	Ready to replace EGA ROM
E3	Completed EGA ROM replacement
E8	Looking for serial external boot ID str (Deskpro 2/386N, 386s/20)
E9	Receiving for serial external boot sector (2/386N, 386s/20)
EA	Looking for parallel external boot ID str (2/386N, 386s/20)
EB	Receiving parallel external boot sector (2/386N, 386s/2O)
EC	Boot record read, jump to boot record (2/386N, 386s/20)

Port 85=05 (Video POST)

Code	Meaning
00	Entry into video option ROM
01	Alternate adapter tests
02	Vertical sync tests
03	Horizontal sync tests
04	Static tests
05	Bus tests
06	Configuration tests
07	Alternate ROM tests
08	Colour gun off tests
09	Colour gun on tests
0A	Video memory tests
0B	Board present tests
10	Illegal configuration error
20	No vertical sync present
21	Vertical sync out of range
30	No horizontal sync present
40	Colour register failure
50	Slot type conflict error
51	Video memory conflict error
52	ROM conflict error
60	Red DAC stuck low error
61	Green DAC stuck low error
62	Blue DAC stuck low error
63	DAC stuck high error
64	Red DAC fault error
65	Green DAC fault error
66	Blue DAC fault error
70	Bad alternate ROM version
80	Colour gun stuck ON base code
90	Colour gun stuck OFF base code
A0	Video memory failure base code
F0	Equipment failure base code
00	Video POST over (also send 00 to 85)

After the POST, the BIOS boots the operating system. If it detects a run-time error, it sends category code 01 to port 85, and the error code to port 84 in the same way it sends POST codes before booting. These are the run-time codes

Code	Meaning
10	Entered dummy end-of-interrupt routine
11	Entered "int 2" module (parity error)
12	Emulating "lock" instruction

13	Emulating "loadall' instruction
14	Illegal opcode instruction encountered
15	Entered "dum iret" module
16	Entered "irg9" module
17	Entered "287err" module

286 DeskPro

Code	Meaning
01	CPU
02	Coprocessor
03	DMA
04	Interrupt Controller
05	Port 61
06	Keyboard Controller
07	CMOS
08	CMOS
09	CMOS
10	Programmable Timer
11	Refresh Detect Test
12	Speed Test
14	Speaker Test
21	Memory Read/Write
24	Memory Address
25	Walking I/O
31	Keyboard Short Test
32	Keyboard Long Test
33	Keyboard LED Test
35	Security Lock Test
41	Printer Failed
42	Printer Date
43	Printer Pattern Test
48	Printer Failed
51	VDU Controller Test
52	VDU Controller Test
53	VDU Attribute Test
54	VDU Character Set Test
55	VDU 80x25 Mode
56	VDU 80x25 Mode
57	VDU 40x25 Mode
60	Diskette Drive ID Test
61	Format
62	Read Test
63	Write/Read Compare Test
64	Random Seek

65	ID Media Test
66	Speed Test
67	Wrap Test
68	Write Protect Test
69	Reset Controller Test

386 DeskPro

Code	Meaning
01	I/O ROM Error
02	System Memory Board Failure
12	System Option Error
13	Time and Date not set
14	Memory Size Error
21	Memory Error
23	Memory Address Error
25	Memory Error
26	Keyboard Error
33	Keyboard Controller Error
34	Keyboard or System Unit Error
41	Printer Error
42	Mono Adapter Failure
51	Display Adapter Failure
61	Diskette Controller Error
62	Diskette Boot Recorder Error
65	Diskette Drive Error
67	Ext FDC Failed—Go To Internal F
6A	Floppy Port Address Conflict
6B	Floppy Port Address Conflict
72	Coprocessor Detection

486 DeskPro

Code	Meaning
01	CPU Test Failed
02	Coprocessor or Weitek Error
03	DMA Page Registers
04	Interrupt Controller Master
05	Port 61 Error
06	Keyboard Controller Self Test
07	CMOS RAM Test Failed
08	CMOS Interrupt Test Failed
09	CMOS Clock Load Data Test
10	Programmable Timer
11	Refresh Detect Test Failed
12	Speed Test Slow Mode out of range
13	Protected Mode Test Failed
14	Speaker Test Failed
16	Cache Memory Configuration
19	Installed Devices Test

POST Codes

21	Memory Machine ID Test Failed
22	Memory System ROM Checksum
23	Memory Write/Read Test Failed
24	Memory Address Test Failed
25	Walking I/O Test Failed
26	Increment Pattern Test Failed
31	Keyboard Short Test, 8042
32	Keyboard Long Test Failed
33	Keyboard LED Test, 8042
34	Keyboard Typematic Test Failed
41	Printer Failed or Not Connected
42	Printer Data Register Failed
43	Printer Pattern Test
48	Printer Not Connected
51	Video Controller Test Failed
52	Video Memory Test Failed
53	Video Attribute Test Failed
54	Video Character Set Test Failed
55	Video 80x25 Mode
56	Video 80x25 Mode
57	Video 40x25 Mode Test Failed
58	Video 320x200 Mode Colour Set 1
59	Video 320x200 Mode Colour Set 1
60	Diskette ID Drive Types Test
61	Diskette Format Failed
62	Diskette Read Test Failed
63	Diskette Write
65	Diskette ID Media Failed
66	Diskette Speed Test Failed
67	Diskette Wrap Test Failed
68	Diskette Write Protect Test
69	Diskette Reset Controller Test
82	Video Memory Test Failed
84	Video Adapter Test Failed

DELL

OEM version of Phoenix, sent to Port 80. Also uses Smartvu display on front of machine.

Code	Beeps	SmartVu	Meaning
01	1-1-2	Regs xREG xCPU(2)	CPU register test in progress
02	1-1-3	CMOS xCMS	CMOS write/read test failed
03	1-1-4	BIOS xROM	ROM BIOS checksum bad
04	1-2-1	Timr xTMR	Programmable interval timer failed
05	1-2-2	DMA xDMA	DMA initialization failed
06	1-2-3	Dpge xDPG	DMA page register write/read bad
08	1-3-1	Rfsh xRFH	RAM refresh verification failed
09	1-3-2	Ramp RAM?	First 64K RAM test in progress
0A	1-3-3	xRAM	First 64K RAM chip or data line bad, multi-bit
0B	1-3-4	xRAM	First 64K RAM odd/even logic bad

0C	1-4-1	xRAM	Address line bad first 64K RAM
0D	1-4-2	64K? x64K	Parity error detected in first 64K RAM
10	2-1-1		Bit 0 first 64K RAM bad
11	2-1-2		Bit 1 first 64K RAM bad
12	2-1-3		Bit 2 first 64K RAM bad
13	2-1-4		Bit 3 first 64K RAM bad
14	2-2-1		Bit 4 first 64K RAM bad
15	2-2-2		Bit 5 first 64K RAM bad
16	2-2-3		Bit 6 first 64K RAM bad
17	2-2-4		Bit 7 first 64K RAM bad
18	2-3-1		Bit 8 first 64K RAM bad
19	2-3-2		Bit 9 first 64K RAM bad
1A	2-3-3		Bit 10 first 64K RAM bad
1B	2-3-4		Bit 11 first 64K RAM bad
1C	2-4-I		Bit 12 first 64K RAM bad
1D	2-4-2		Bit 13 first 64K RAM bad
1E	2-4-3		Bit 14 first 64K RAM bad
1F	2-4-4		Bit 15 first 64K RAM bad
20	3-1-1	SDMA xDMS	Slave DMA register bad
21	3-1-2	MDMA xDMM	Master DMA register bad
22	3-1-3	PICO xICO	Master interrupt mask register bad
23	3-1-4	PIC1 xIC1	Slave interrupt mask register bad
25	3-2-2	Intv	Interrupt vector loading in progress
27	3-2-4	Kybd xKYB	Keyboard controller test failed
28	3-3-1	CmCk	CMOS RAM power bad; calculating checksum
29	3-3-2	Cnfg	CMOS configuration validation in progress
2B	3-3-4		Video memory test failed
2C	3-4-1	CRTI	Video initialization failed
2D	3-4-2		Video retrace failure
2E	3-4-3	CRT?	Search for video ROM in progress
30	none		Screen operable, running with video ROM
31	none		Monochrome monitor operable
32	none		Colour monitor (40 column) operable
33	none		Colour monitor (80 column) operable

Only if Manufacturing Jumper is on POST

Code	Beeps	Smartvu	Meaning
34	4-2-1	Tick	Timer tick interrupt test in progress or bad
35	4-2-2	Shut	Shutdown test in progress or bad
36	4-2-3	A20	Gate A20 bad
37	4-2-4		Unexpected interrupt in protected mode

POST Codes

38	4-3-1	Emem	RAM test in progress or high address line bad > FFFF
3A	4-3-3	Tmr2	Interval timer channel 2 test or bad
3B	4-3-4	Time	Time-of-Day clock test or bad
3C	4-4-1	Asyn	Serial port test or bad
3D	4-4-2	Prnt	Parallel port test or bad
3E	4-4-3		Math coprocessor test or bad
3F	4-4-4	XCsh	Cache test failure

DTK

Evolved from ERSO (Taiwan).

Post Procedures—Symphony 486 BIOS POST Codes

Procedure	Meaning
Initialise Interrupt Controller	Check the PIC chips.
Initialise Video Card	
Initialise DMA Controller	
Initialise Page Register	Check the 74612 chips.
Test Keyboard Controller	Internal operations of the keyboard controller are tested (8042).
Initialise DMA Contr/Timer	All DMA registers and CMOS status bytes 0E/0F are cleared. The BIOS then initialises the 8254 chip. Check the DMS or PIT chips.
DRAM Refresh Testing	
Base 64K Memory Testing	A walking-bit test of the first 64K of RAM address which is critical for the BIOS vector area to be initialised. Check for bad RAM chips or a data or address line.
Set System Stack	An area of memory is set aside by BIOS as a stack. Check bad DMA/memory.
Read System Configuration via 8042	e.g. the keyboard controller. Check for incorrect setup or bad keyboard controller or CMOS chip.
Test Keyboard Clock and Data Line	The keyboard's ability to handle the A20 line is tested as well as its internal clock. Check the keyboard controller or a bad address line.
Determine Video Type	
Check RS232/Printer	Test serial/parallel ports. Check I/O cards.
FDC Check	Test floppy controller. Check the drive as well.
Count Shadow RAM	Run a series of memory tests on the system. Check for bad memory chips address lines or data lines.
Display Total Mem/Return to Real Mode	Total memory detected is displayed and the machine is returned to real mode. Check the keyboard controller or A20 line.
Back to Real Mode	Transition is attempted through the A20 line and the keyboard controller.
Check HDC	The hard drive controller is tested.
Check FDD	Attempts are made to initialise the floppy drives.
Turn off Gate A20 and Test CoProcessor	Attempts are made to transition back to real mode by disabling the A20 line then the coprocessor is tested if present. Check the keyboard controller coprocessor or improper setup in CMOS.
Set Time and Date	Time and date will be read from the RTC.

Code	Meaning
01	Power on start
03	Initialise interrupt controller—8259
05	Initialise video card—MCA and CGA
0D	Initialise DMA controller—8237
0E	Initialise page register—74612
12	Test keyboard controller—8042
16	Initialise DMA controller and timer
22	DRAM refresh testing
25	Base 64K memory testing
30	Set system stack
33	Read system configuration through 8042
37	Test keyboard clock and data line
40	Determine video type
44	Testing MGA and CGA if existing
48	Video 80 x 25 mode initialisation
4D	Display DTK BIOS title
4F	Check RS232 and printer
50	FDC check
55	Count shadow RAM
58	Display total memory and return to real mode
5A	Back to real mode
60	Check HDC
62	Check FDD
65	Check HDC
67	Initialise FDC and HDC
6A	Turn off gate A20 and test coprocessor
70	Set time and date according to RTC
77	Boot

EUROSOFT

See *Mylex/Eurosoft*.

FARADAY A-TEASE

Owned by Western Digital.

Code	Meaning
01	CPU test failed
02	BIOS ROM checksum test
03	Shutdown
04	DMA page register test
05	8254 timer test
06	Start refresh
07	8042 keyboard controller test
08	Test lower 128K RAM
09	Setup video
0A	Test 128K-640K

0B	Test DMA controller #1
0C	Test DMA controller #2
0D	Test interrupt controller #1
0E	Test interrupt controller #2
0F	Test control port
10	Test parity
11	Test CMOS RAM
12	Test for manufacturing mode
13	Set up interrupt vectors
14	Test keyboard
15	Configure parallel port
16	Configure serial ports
17	Configure lower 640K RAM
18	Configure RAM above 1 Mb
19	Configure keyboard
1A	Configure floppy drive
1B	Configure hard drive
1C	Configure game card
1D	Configure 80287 math chip
1E	Check CMOS real time clock
1F	Generate and verify CMOS RAM checksum
21	Initialize PROM drivers
22	Test parallel port loopback
23	Test serial port loopback
24	Test CMOS real time clock
25	Test shutdown
26	Test memory over 1mb; output codes for errors 80-FF
80	Divide overflow
81	Single step
82	NMI
83	Breakpoint
84	Int 0 detect
85	Bound error
86	Invalid opcode
87	Processor extension not available
88	Double exception
89	Processor extended segment error
8A	Invalid task state segment
8B	Segment not present
8C	Stack segment not present
8D	General protection error
8E	General protection error
8F	General protection error
90	Processor extension error
91-FF	Spurious interrupts (except F3 and F0)
F3	CPU virtual (protected mode) test error
F0	Virtual block move error

HEADSTART

See *Philips*.

HP

Derived from Phoenix, all POST information is sent to the screen.

Vectra

A failure during POST will emit four beeps, and a 4-digit hex code to the monitor. Failures that occur before EGA/VGA monitors are initialized will not be displayed, so use a mono instead. BIOSes prior to March 1989 initialized the video before getting on with the POST.

POST Procedures

Code	Meaning
CPU	Registers in CPU tested with data patterns; error flags are set, verified and reset.
ROM BIOS Checksum	Checksums are performed on High and low BIOS Chips.
PIC Test	Test Timer Channels 0-2 then the memory refresh signal. Initialise timer if tests are passed. Check the 8254 chip.
64K Test	Walking-bit and address collision tests are performed on the first 64K of memory. Check for a bad memory chip or address line.
Cache Controller	Test the CPU cache controller and memory.
Video Adapter	Initialise the video adapter. If EGA/VGA is present wait for adapter to finish internal diagnostics. check the adapter or for improper setup.
DMA Test	Bit-patterns written to all DMA controller registers (inc page registers) and verifies the patterns written. If the tests pass the registers are reset and the controller initialised.
PIC Test	Test mask register of master and slave interrupt controllers. Generate interrupt and monitor CPU to test success. Failure is normally down to the PIC but the interrupt test uses the BIOS clock (interrupt) and the RTC so check those.
Keyboard Controller	Perform several tests on the 8042 keyboard controller then send a series of interrupt request commands via the 8259 PIC.
HP-HIL Test	Test HP-HIL (Hardware Interrupt Level) controller with data patterns and verify it.
CMOS Test	Perform a checksum on the standard and extended CMOS RAM areas; perform a register test and check Byte 0D to determine power status. Check the CMOS extended CMOS RAM or battery respectively.
Manufacturing Test	Search for diagnostic tool used in manufacturing and run predetermined tests if found. Otherwise continue POST.
Base Memory Test	Test RAM between 64-640K with several pattern tests; the bit failure and bank can be determined by the displayed hex code.
Ext Memory Test	Test extended memory found. Bank and failing bit displayed by the hex code.
RTC Test	Test the RTC portion of the CMOS chip.
Keyboard Controller	Test keyboard controller; initialise k/b if no errors.

POST Codes

Floppy Disk	Test and initialise floppy controllers and drives found; check specific errors with the displayed hex code. Check for correct setup or defective CMOS chip or battery.
Maths Copro	Test NPU registers and interrupt request functions.
CPU Clock Test	Test interface between CPU and system at different speeds. Check for incorrect clock setting for system peripherals or a bad CPU or clock generator chip.
Serial/Parallel Test	Test and initialise serial/parallel ports. Failure here will not halt the POST. The Vectra RS BIOS does not test the parallel port.
Boot	Initialise the BIOS vector table; standard and extended CMOS data areas and any adapter ROMs present. Then call Int 19 and give control to the boot loader. Failures past this point are usually down to the hard drive or corrupt OS code.

POST Codes

Code	Meaning
01	LED test
02	Processor test
03	System (BIOS) ROM test
04	RAM refresh timer test
05	Interrupt RAM test
06	Shadow the System ROM BIOS
07	CMOS RAM test
08	Internal cache memory test
09	Initialize the Video Card
10	Test external cache
11	Shadow option ROMs
12	Memory Subsystem test
13	Initialize EISA/ISA hardware
14	8042 self-test
15	Timer 0/Timer 2 test
16	DMA Subsystem test
17	Interrupt controller test
18	RAM address line independence test
19	Size extended memory
20	Real-Mode memory test (first 640K)
21	Shadow RAM test
22	Protect Mode RAM test (extended RAM)
23	Real Time clock test
24	Keyboard test
25	Mouse test
26	Hard disk test
27	LAN test
28	Flexible disk controller subsystem test
29	Internal numeric coprocessor test
30	Weitek coprocessor test
31	Clock speed switching test
32	Serial Port test
33	Parallel Port test

IBM

Tests are performed by PC/XT/AT and PS/2 machines. There will be POST Codes (below), beep codes and screen displays if possible, but the XT does not give POST codes. ATs emit codes to 80h, while PS/2 models 25 and 30 emit to 90h, and 35 and above to 680. The BIOS will test main system components first, then non-critical ones. If there is an error, the BIOS will look for a reference diskette in drive A: so diagnostics can be performed.

IBM POST I/O Ports

Architecture	Typical Computer	Port
PC	PC	none
ISA	XT	60
	AT	80
	PS/2 25,30	90, 190
MCA	PS/2 50 up	680, 3BC
EISA	none	none

POST Procedures

Procedure	Meaning
CPU	Perform register test on the CPU by writing data patterns to the registers and reading the results of the write.
ROM BIOS Checksum	The value of the bits inside the BIOS chip(s) is added to a preset value that should create a total of 00.
CMOS RAM	RAM within the CMOS chip is tested by writing data patterns to the area and verifying that the data was stored correctly.
DMA	Test DMA chips by forcing control inputs to the CPU to an active state and verifying that the proper reactions occur.
8042/8742 Keyboard Controller	Test including Gate A20 and the reset command. The buffer space is prepared and data is sent to the determined area via the keyboard controller to see if commands are received and executed correctly.
Base 64K System RAM.	Perform a walking-bit test of the first 64K of RAM so the BIOS vector area can be initialised. Check for bad RAM chips or a data/address line.
8259A PIC	Determine if commands to interrupt CPU processes are carried out correctly. Check the PIC/PIT/RTC/CMOS or Clock chip(s).
8254 PIT	Check that proper setup and hold times are given to the PIC for interrupts of the CPU processes. Check the PIT or Clock chip.
82385 Cache Controller	This is normally responsible for cache and shadow memory.
CMOS RAM Configuration Data	Check information in CMOS RAM before further testing so any failures after this could also be down to the CMOS chip.
CRT controllers	Test any video adapters listed in the CMOS.
RAM above 64K	Perform a walking-bit test on memory above 64K listed in the CMOS.
Keyboard	Test interface to the keyboard including scan code stuck keys etc.

Pointing Device (mouse etc)	Test and initialise vector for any pointing devices found. Failure to see a device may be down to the device itself but there may be a problem with the CMOS or 8042/8742.
Diskette Drive A:	Test and initialise the A: drive.
Serial Interface Circuitry	Test any RS232 devices found at the proper I/O address.
Diskette Controllers	If an A: drive has been found further testing is performed before proceeding to the bootloader. This test includes reading the first sector of any diskette in the drive to see if a valid boot code is there.
Fixed Disk Controllers	Test and initialise any hard drives set in the CMOS including reading the first sector of the hard drive to see if a valid boot code exists.

XT (Port 60)

The PC uses an irregular way of sending codes to ports 10 and 11, which makes it impractical to monitor them on a POST card. The XT, on the other hand, uses three methods; before initializing the display, it issues a few codes to port 60 (the 8255 controller for the keyboard) for critical system board errors. It beeps to indicate successful or unsuccessful POST, and displays error messages.

After initializing the display, it writes error codes to memory address 15, which are sent to the screen to make up part of other error messages.

Code	Meaning
00 or FF	CPU register test failed
01	BIOS ROM (ROS) checksum failed
02	Timer I failed
03	8237 DMA register write/read failed or unexpected timer 1 request for DMA ch 1
04	After enabling port 213 expansion box, base 32K memory write/read of AA, 55, FF, 01 and 00 test failed; POST output alternates between POST code and failing bit pattern.
	Size memory, initialize the 8259 PIC, setup BIOS interrupt vectors in RAM, read the configuration switches, poll the manufacturing jumper. If installed, load the manufacturing test via the keyboard port and run it. If not, initialize the rest of the system.

Code	Meaning
00	Main board damaged
01	80286 test in real mode; verify read/write registers, flags and conditional jumps.
02	ROM checksum test—test 32K ROMs; POST BASIC and BIOS.
03	Test CMOS shutdown byte—rolling bit pattern and verified at shutdown address.
04	8254 timer 1; all bits on; set timer count; check all bits on.
05	8254 timer 1; all bits off; set timer count; check all bits off.
06	8237 DMA 0 initialisation channel register test. Disable DMA controller; r/w current address to all channels
07	8237 DMA 1 initialisation channel register test. Disable DMA controller; r/w current address to all channels
08	DMA page register test—r/w all page registers. Check 74LS612.
09	Storage refresh test—verify refresh occurring. 8042 i/face test I/O issue self test; check 55H received
0A	Keyboard controller test 1; Soft reset

0B	Keyboard controller test 2; Reset 8042
0C	Keyboard controller test 3; Test switch settings
0D	Keyboard controller test 4: Write byte 0 of 8042 mem; issue comd to 8042, await response.
0E	Base 64K r/w memory test—r/w data patterns AAh, 55h.
0F	Get I/P buffer switch setting. Also Base 64K r/w memory test #2—r/w data patterns AAh, 55h.
10	Roll error code to MFG Port
11	Initialise display row count. Verify 286 LGDT.SGDT LIDT/SIDT instruction
12	Protected mode register test failure
13	Initialise 8259
14	Setup interrupt vector to temp interrupt
15	Establish BIOS interrupt call subroutine vectors. Verify CMOS checksum/battery OK
16	Set data segment or Check CMOS battery condition.
17	Set defective battery flag or CMOS checksum error.
18	Ensure CMOS dividers set or enable protected mode.
19	Set return address byte in CMOS.
1A	Set temporary stack or protected mode test. Determine memory size; verify parity.
1B	Segment address 01-0000 (second 64K memory test)
1C	Set or reset; check 512—640 memory installed
1E	Set (expanded?) memory size determined in CMOS; or determine memory size above 1024K.
1F	Test address lines 19-23
20	Fatal addressing error; Shutdown.
21	Return 1 from shutdown. Initialise and start CRT controller (6845); test video r/w; test video enable; select alpha mode; w/r patterns; or check CMOS config data.
22	Enable video signal and set mode; CRT interface test; verify video enable and horizontal sync. Video card initialisation failure or invalid switch setting.
23	Check for advanced video card; Video card initialisation failure or invalid switch setting.
24	8259 PIC test -r/w interrupt mask register with 1s and 0s; mask device interrupts off.
25	Check for hot interrupts; test interrupt mask registers.
26	Display 101 error; Check for unexpected interrupts.
27	Check the converting logic (106 error)
28	Check hot NMI interrupts (error 107)
29	Test data bus to timer 2 (error 108). 8253 timer register failure.
2A	8253 Timer speed failure (error 102)
2B	Too fast; or 8253 Timer interrupt initialisation.
2C	Too slow; or Timer 0 interrupt failure (error 103)
2D	Check 8042 (k/b controller) for last command excepted (error 105)
2F	Check for warm boot
30	Set shutdown return 2; Protected mode r/w memory test step 1.
31	Enable protected mode; Protected mode r/w memory test step 2.
32	Address lines 0-15
33	Next block of 64K; Protected mode r/w memory test step 3.
34	Restore checkpoint; Protected mode r/w memory test step 4.
35	Keyboard test; Check for manufacturing burn in test.
36	Check <AA> scan code; keyboard clock error.
38	Error—check 8042 working; also 37 and 39

3A	Initialise 8042; keyboard locked
3B	Check for ROM in 2K blocks
3C	Check for floppy diskette drive
3D	Initialise floppy for drive type
3E	Initialise hard drive
3F	Initialise printer; non-fatal error; press F1 to continue.

Additional Protected Mode Tests

Code	Meaning
40	Enable hardware interrupt if 80287; initialisation
41	System code @ segment code E000.0
42	Exit to system code
43	Go to boot loader diskette attachment test
44	Boot from fixed disk
45	Unable to boot; go to BASIC
81	Build descriptor table
82	Switch to virtual mode
90-B6	EXEC_00 to EXEC_31 & SYS_32 to SYS_38 tests; memory test; boot loader.
DD	Transmit error code to MFG_PORT
F0	Set data segment
F1	Interrupt test (programming interrupt 32)
F2	Exception interrupt test
F3	Verify 286 LDT/SDT and LTR/STR instructions.
F4	Verify 286 bound instruction
F5	Verify push and pop all instruction; stack/register test.
F6	Verify access rights function correctly.
F7	Verify Adjust RPL field of selector instructions (ARPL) functions
F8	Verify LAR function
F9	Verify LSL i(Load Segment Limits) instruction
FA	Low meg chip select test

Code	Meaning
00	CPU test; FFAA0055 pattern
01	32 bit CPU register test; setup system timer
02	System ROM checksum
03	Test system enable/system port 94 enable/check
04	Test system POS register; port 102 enable/check
05	Test adapter setup port; POS port 96 enable/check
06	Test RTC/CMOS shutdown byte; Byte 0F CMOS (NMI disable)
07	Test extended CMOS location; ports 74-76 test
08	Test DMA & page register 8 channels; ports 2
09	Initialise DMA command & mode registers
0A	Test refresh (port 61)
0B	Test keyboard controller buffers (8042—port 61
0C	Keyboard controller self test (8042—port 60)
0D	Keyboard controller test continuation (8042)

0E	Keyboard self test error indicated (port 64)
0F	Setup system memory configuration
10	Test first 512K RAM in real mode
11	Half system if memory test error
12	Verify LGDT/SGDR LIDT/SIDT (keyboard commands)
13	Initialise PIC #1 (Master)
14	Initialise PIC #2 (Slave)
15	Initialise A20 interrupt vectors
16	Setup extended vector table
17	Check power RTC/CMOS power good signal (byte 0D)
18	Check RTC/CMOS checksum
19	RTC/CMOS lost power (0D 80h)
1A	Skip memory test in protected mode if warm reset
1B	Prepare for shutdown; protected mode initialisation
1C	Setup stack pointer point to the end of first 64K
1D	Decide low memory size in protected mode; Size base memory
1E	Save memory size detected
1F	Setup system memory split address
20	Check for extended memory beyond 64 Mb
21	Test memory address bus lines
22	Clear parity error and channel check; Disable NMI
23	Initialise interrupt 00; system timer
24	Determine CMOS validity
25	Write keyboard controller (8042) command byte
40	Check valid CMOS and video
41	Display error code 160. Check CMOS, AC ripple.
42	Test PIC #1 & PIC #2 registers; Master/Slave test
43	Test PIC #1 & PIC #2 registers with another pattern
44	Check for interrupt with interrupt masked; check for NMI when disabled.
45	Test NMI
46	NMI error detected
47	Test system timer 0
48	Check stuck speaker clock; speaker bitstuck test
49	Test timer 0 count
4A	Test timer 2 output
4B	Check if timer interrupt occurred
4C	Test timer 0 for count too fast or slow
4D	Verify timer 0 interrupt
4E	Check 8042 ready for command; buffer free
4F	Check for soft reset
50	Prepare for shutdown/protected mode
51	Start protected mode test
52	Test memory in 64K increments
53	Check if memory test done
54	Shutdown system and return to real mode
55	Test for manufacture or regular test; test for loop. Check jumper.
56	Disable keyboard
57	Check for keyboard self test

58	Keyboard test passed; check for errors
59	Test keyboard interface
5A	Initialise mouse
5B	Disable mouse
5C	Initialise interrupt vectors
5D	Initialise interrupt vectors
5E	Initialise interrupt vectors
5F	BIOS data area
60	Determine diskette rate
61	Reset floppy controller/drive
62	Floppy drive test
63	Turn floppy motor off
64	Serial port setup
65	Enable/test RTC interrupt
66	Configure floppy drives
67	Configure hard drive
68	Enable system CPU arbitration; wait states
69	Scan for optional ROMs
6A	Verify serial and parallel ports
6B	Setup equipment byte
6C	Setup configuration errors reported
6D	Set keyboard typematic rate
6E	Reset page register; boot up system (Int 19 bootloader)
70	Reset disk
71	Read bootcode for E6/E9
72	Control to bootcode
73	Bootcode/ROM Basic

LANDMARK

BIOS came with POST card and replaced that in motherboard being tested; same as BIOSYS
BIOS. Beeps as for IBM AT. Codes sent to ports 280 and 80.

XT Jumpstart

Code	Meaning
01	Jump to reset area in ROM BIOS
02	Initialize DMA page register
03	Initialize DMA refresh register
04	Clear all RAM
05	Perform RAM test on 1st 64k
06	Clear 1st 64k
07	Initialize BIOS stack to 0:FC0
08	Set the equipment flag based on switches
09	Initialize default interrupt vectors
0A	Initialize 8255 if it exists and enable parity
0B	Initialize 8259 and enable interrupts
0C	Setup adapters and peripherals
0D	Setup video
0E	Initialize video
0F	Initialize equipment

10	Initialize memory configuration in RAM (currently = 64K)
11	Setup timer function
12	Initialize timer function
13	Setup time of day function
14	Initialize time of day function
15	Setup and init print screen function
16	Setup and init cassette function
17	Setup and init bootstrap function
18	Setup and init keyboard function
19	Enable speaker
1A	Setup timer 0 for the real time clock
1B	Enable RTC
1C	Setup timer 2 for the beeper
1D	Size memory: write 55AA/AA55 to 1st/last word in segment
1E	Read 1st and last word of segment
1F	Compare 1st and last words
20	Report determined memory size to screen
21	Perform checksum on ROM BIOS
22	If cold boot perform complete RAM testing
23	Move system stack to bottom of memory and save pointer at 40:0E
24	Reset parity after RAM sizing
25	Enable timer and keyboard interrupts
26	Setup the serial and parallel ports
27	Setup the game port
28	Setup the floppy disk controller
29	Scan for optional ROM in 2K chunk from C8000 to start of BIOS
2A	Boot System

AT Jumpstart

03	1 short beep when first awake
04	Initialize bell tone
05	Enable CMOS RAM
06	Reset video controller
07	Disable I/O parity
08	Start memory refresh
09	Clear reset flag in RAM
0A	Test DMA page registers
10	Use CMOS to determine if soft reset
11	Perform ROM checksum
12	Test timer A
13	Test DMA channel A
14	Test DMA channel B
15	Test refresh
16	Flush 8042 input buffer
17	Reset 8042
18	Get keyboard switch
19	Initialise keyboard

POST Codes

1A	Clear any existing parity
1B	Enable on-board parity
1C	Test base 64K memory
1D	Test base 64k parity
1E	Initialize POST stack
20	Put keyboard # in RAM
65	Set video speed
21	Test protected mode registers
22	Initialize 8259 interrupts
23	Zero all 256 interrupts
24	Initialize interrupts 0-1fh
25	Perform DRAM checksum
26	Adjust configuration based on hardware found
27	Check manufacturing switch (may exit POST)
28	Initialize video controller
2A	Test video memory
2B	Test video sync
2C	Look for external video
2D	Change video configuration if external video
2E	Unused
2F	Initialize video controller
30	Change video interrupt
31	Print any POST messages
32	Size memory by testing it
33	Adjust memory configuration
33	Verify CMOS RAM size
34	Enable I/O parity
35	Test 8259
36	Bytes swap test
37	Test NMI
38	Timer test
39	Initialize timer A
3A	Protected mode memory test
3B	Test keyboard
3C	Test keyboard interrupt
3D	Enable A20
3E	Reset hard disk controller
3F	Setup floppy controller
40	Test floppies
41	Setup keyboard (NumLock)
42	Enable timer interrupt
43	Check for dual floppy/hard disk controller
44	Find floppy drive A type
45	Find floppy drive B type
46	Reset hard disk
47	Enable slave DMA
63	Set video interrupt vector
48	Call any external ROMs

49	Initialize printer
4A	Initialize serial
4B	Initialize 80287
4C	Read CMOS RAM status
4D	Check CMOS configuration against hardware found
70	Check CMOS configuration against memory found
4E	Initialize timer ticks
4F	Enable IRQ9
50	Enable on-board parity
51	Call add-on card ROM
52	Enable keyboard interrupt
53	Reset printer
60	Check for any errors
61	One short beep
62	Print sign-on message
64	Perform boot

MAGNAVOX

See *Philips.*

MR BIOS

The last code emitted is the one that failed. There may also be a message on screen. Beep codes are in a binary format and are preceded by a high and low tone (described elsewhere). Check also *Nasty Noises* for more codes.

POST Procedures

Procedure	
Reset	See if a warm boot (Ctrl+Alt+Del) or a cold boot (Reset) is needed.
Chipset Initialisation	Reset the support chips (8259) DMAs and timers to defaults before proceeding.
Disable Chips	Disable NMI/DMA and Video (6845) to get accurate results later. Failure here is normally a NMI generated by one of the disabled chips.
ROM BIOS Checksum	Perform checksum test, add a preset value stored in BIOS to create value of 00.
DMA Test	Perform a test of the page registers in the DMA controller.
Keyboard Controller Test	Send a command to the 8042 keyboard controller to perform a selftest. The keyboard controller will return a buffer and error buffer address.
Chipset Initialisation	Initialise the DMA (8237)/PIC (8259)/PIT (8254) and RTC chips.
DMA Test	Test the registers of the master 16-bit and slave 8-bit DMA controllers by writing bit patterns and reading the results.
Cache/Shadow Disable	Disable cache and shadow RAM before processing with POST.
Refresh	Test interval in which PIT (8254) chip sends a refresh signal to the DMA chips.
Base 64K Memory	Test the first 64K of system memory with a walking-bit pattern.
PIC Test	Test the mask registers of the master and slave interrupt controllers by setting the mask-bit in the registers and generating an interrupt to see if the interrupt is trapped. Then test the additional registers in the PICs with a walking-bit pattern.

PIT Test	Test the interrupt timer channels 0-2 and initialise if no failures occur.
RTC	Perform read/write test of RTC portion of CMOS and initialise if no failures occur.
Video	Test and initialise the video adapter, which will perform an internal diagnostic and sign on before returning an OK status.
CMOS Checksum	Perform a checksum on the system RAM.
Keybd Initialisation	Initialise the keyboard and read the buffer address for errors.

OEM Specific

Procedure	
Base Memory Test	Test memory addresses between 64-640K with a walking-bit pattern. There may be a hex display of the failing it.
Keyboard 2nd Init	Tries again if the first failed.
Protected Mode Test	Test the ability of the keyboard controller address line 20 to respond to commands that switch the CPU in and out of protected mode.
Extended Memory Test	Test addresses above 1 Mb in 64K blocks and perform pattern tests.
OEM Memory	Normally test the cache controller and shadow RAM.
RTC Time Test	Test the write active line of the RTC/CMOS chip. Check bad CMOS/battery
Serial Port	Generate an interrupt of the CPU through I/O ports reserved for RS232 devices. Failure to see a device could be the device itself or more than one set to the same port. Checks are only made for two devices.
Parallel	Check for parallel devices. Failure to see a device could be the device itself or more than one using the same port. Checks are only made for three.
NPU Test	Perform a register test on the NPU then initialise if passed.
Floppy Test	Test floppy controller and drive.
Fixed Disk	Test fixed disk controller and drive and compare the results against the CMOS setting. This is skipped if no drive is installed.
CMOS Update	Update information in CMOS RAM based on the previous results.

Non-Fatal Errors

Procedure	Meaning
Lock Check	Check if a system lock-byte is set and wait for user response if an error is generated. Check the panel lock or circuitry.
NumLock/Pwd/Setup	Set NumLock on (if set) and ask for password (if set) and display setup message.
Typematic Rate	Set the typematic rate.
Floppy Disk	Perform any further initialisation needed.
Hard Disk	Perform any further initialisation needed.
Video Mode	Set primary video mode and display any errors found during initialisation routines.
Shadow/Cache Enable	

Adapter ROM	Initialise adapters with a ROM signature of 55AA. Self tests will be performed by the equipment concerned before handing back control to the POST.
Video Monitor Mode	Set the video mode based on the information in the CMOS and update the time variables from the RTC.
Parity/NMI Enable	Enable NMI by setting bit 7 of CMOS address 41 and enable parity. There should be no failures during this.
Set Stack	Set the last significant byte of the stack pointer and install the shadow RAM at E000 if set by CMOS.
Acknowledge	Acknowledge errors and set primary video mode before calling Int 19 boot loader. Errors reported will await a keyboard response before proceeding. Errors beyond this point are normally software related.

POST Codes (inc 3.4x)

Code	Meaning
00	Cold-Boot commences (Not seen with warm-boot). Output EDX register to I/O ports 85h, 86h, 8Dh, 8Eh for later use
01	HOOK 00 OEM specific typically resets chipset to default. Initialize any Custom KBD controller, disable CPU cache, cold initialize onboard I/O chipset, size & test RAM, size cache
02	Disable critical I/O: 6845s CRT; 8237s DMA; 7675 floppy and parity latches (monitor, DMA, FDC, I/O ports, Speaker, NMI).
03	BIOS checksum test
04	DMA Page register test (Ports 81-8F)
05	8042 (Keyboard Controller) Self test. Enable A20 Gate.
06	Init ISA I/O: Game Port: 8237 master/slave; 8254 ch2/1; RTC Reg3 F/A; 8259 master/slave
07	HOOK 01. OEM specific; typically disables cache/shadow/ or memory refresh circuit test, or warm initialize custom KBD controller, warm initialize onboard I/O chipset.
08 (09?)	Refresh toggle test (PORTB)
09 (08?)	Pattern test master/slave 8237s; eight 16-bit regs each
0A	Base 64K memory test—check beep code.
0B	Pattern test master/slave 8259 mask regs
0C	8259/IRQ tests purge powerup ints—check beep code. Test 8259 Slave, test 8259 slave's interrupt range, initialize interrupt vectors 00-77h, init KBD buffer variables.
0D	8254 channel-0 test and initialization
0E	8254 channel-2 toggle test speaker circuitry
0F	RTC tests/inits: Init REG-B; write/readback NVRAM. PIE test
10	Video Initialization; display cold boot sign-on message or possible error messages.
11	CMOS Checksum test
12	Sign-on msg. Accept KB BAT; perform 1st try KB unit; cold boot delay
13	HOOK 02. OEM specific; select 8MHz bus
14	Size/Test base memory (low 64K already done)
15	Perform 2nd try KB init if necessary
16	HOOK 03. OEM specific. Size/Test cache
17	Test A20 gate off; then on; stuck in asserted state.
18	Size/Test extended memory
19	HOOK 04 and Size/Test system memory ("special" OEM memory)
1A	Test RTC Update-In-Progress and validate time; RTC settings invalid.
1B	Serial port determination off-board/on-board
1C	Parallel port determination off-board/on-board
1D	Copro determination/initialization

1E	Floppy controller test/determination CMOS validation
1F	Fixed Disk controller test/determination CMOS validation
20	Rigorous CMOS parameter validation display other config changes
21	Front-Panel lock check; wait for user to acknowledge errors
22	Set NumLock; Password-Security Trap; despatch to setup utility
23	HOOK 05. OEM specific. Final determination of onboard Serial/Parallel ports.
24	Set typematic rate
25	Floppy subsystem initialization
26	Fixed subsystem initialization
27	ACK errors; set primary adapter video mode
28	HOOK 06. OEM specific; typically enables shadow, cache, turbo. Cyrix WB-CPU support, Green PC: purge 8259 slave, relieve any trapped IRRs before enabling PwrMgmt, set 8042 pins, Ctrl-Alt-Del possible now, Enable CPU Features.
29	Disable A20-gate; set low stack, install C800, E000 ROMs.
2A	ACK errors; set video mode, set DOS time variables from RTC.
2B	Enable parity checking and NMI
2C	Set low stack, Install E000 ROM
2D	ACK errors, set primary video mode.
2E	HOOK 07. OEM specific. Log-in EMS (if built-in). Fast A20: Fix A20.
2F	Purge 8259 slave; relieve any trapped IRRs before enabling Green-PC. Pass control to INT 19.
32	Test CPU Burst
33	Reserved
34	Determine 8042, Set 8042 Warm-Boot flag STS.2
35	Test HMA Wrap, Verify A20 enabled via F000:10 HMA
36	Reserved
37	Validate CPU: CPU Step NZ, CPUID Check. Disable CPU features
38	Set 8042 pins (Hi-Speed, Cache-off)
39	PCI Bus: Load PCI; Processor Vector init'd, BIOS Vector init'd, OEM Vector init'd
3A	Scan PCI Bus
3B	Initialize PCI Bus with intermediate defaults
3C	Initialize PCI OEM with intermediate defaults, OEM bridge
3D	PCI Bus or PLUGnPLAY: Initialize AT Slotmap from AT-Bus CDE usage
3E	Find phantom CDE ROM PCI-cards
3F	PCI Bus: final Fast-Back-to-Back state
40	OEM POST Initialization, Hook Audio
41	Allocate I/O on PCI-Bus, logs-in PCI-IDE
42	Hook PCI-ATA chips
43	Allocate IRQs on the PCI Bus
44	Allocate/enable PCI Memory/ROM space
45	Determine PS/2 Mouse
46	Map IRQs to PCI Bus per user CMOS, Enable ATA IRQs.
47	PCI-ROM install, note user CMOS
48	If Setup conditions: execute setup utility

49	Test F000 Shadow integrity, Transfer EPROM to Shadow-RAM
4A	Hook VL ATA Chip
4B	Identify and spin-up all drives
4C	Detect Secondary IRQ, if VL/AT-Bus IDE exists but its IRQ not known yet, then autodetect it
4D	Detect/log 32-bit I/O ATA devices
4E	ATAPI drive M/S bitmap to Shadow-RAM, Set INT13 Vector
4F	Finalize Shadow-RAM variables
50	Chain INT 13
51	Load PnP, Processor Vector init'd, BIOS Vector init'd, OEM Vector init'd
52	Scan PLUGnPLAY, update PnP Device Count
53	Supplement IRQ usage—AT IRQs
54	Conditionally assign everything PnP wants
58	Perform OEM Custom boot sequence just prior to INT 19 boot
59	Return from OEM custom boot sequence. Pass control to 1NT 19 boot
5A	Display MR BIOS logo
88	Dead motherboard and/or CPU and/or BIOS ROM.
FF	BIOS POST Finished.

Msg	Low-High	Problem
03	LH-LLL	ROM-BIOS Checksum Failure
04	LH-HLL	DMA Page Register Failure
05	LH-LHL	Keyboard Controller Selftest Failure
08	LH-HHL	Memory Refresh Circuitry Failure
09	LH-LLH	Master (16 bit) DMA Controller Failure
09	LH-HLH	Slave (8 bit) DMA Controller Failure
0A	LH-LLLL	Base 64K Pattern Test Failure
0A	LH-HLLL	Base 64K Parity Circuitry Failure
0A	LH-LHLL	Base 64K Parity Error
0A	LH-HHLL	Base 64K Data Bus Failure
0A	LH-LLHL	Base 64K Address Bus Failure
0A	LH-HLHL	Base 64K Block Access Read Failure
0A	LH-LHHL	Base 64K Block Access Read/Write Failure
0B	LH-HHHL	Master 8259 (Port 21) Failure
0B	LH-LLLH	Slave 8259 (Port A1) Failure
0C	LH-HLLH	Master 8259 (Port 20) Interrupt Address Error
0C	LH-LHLH	Slave 8259 (Port A0) Interrupt Address Error
0C	LH-HHLH	8259 (Port 20/A0) Interrupt Address Error
0C	LH-LLHH	Master 8259 (Port 20) Stuck Interrupt Error
0C	LH-HLHH	Slave 8259 (Port A0) Stuck Interrupt Error
0C	LH-LHHH	System Timer 8254 CH0 / IRQ0 Interrupt Failure
0D	LH-HHHH	8254 Channel 0 (System Timer) Failure
0E	LH-LLLLH	8254 Channel 2 (Speaker) Failure
0E	LH-HLLLH	8254 OUT2 (Speaker Detect) Failure
0F	LH-LHLLH	CMOS RAM Read/Write Test Failure

0F	LH-HHLLH	RTC Periodic Interrupt / IRQ8 Failure
10	LH-LLHLH	Video ROM Checksum Failure at Address XXXX Mono Card Memory Error at Address XXXX Mono Card Memory Address Line Error at XXXX CGA Card Memory Error at Address XXXX CGA Card Address Line Error at Address XXXX
11	(None)	Real Time Clock (RTC) Battery is Discharged
11	(None)	Battery Backed Memory (CMOS) is Corrupt
12	LH-HLHLH	Keyboard Controller Failure
14/18/19	LH-LHHLH	Memory Parity Error
14/18/19	LH-HHHLH	I/O Channel Error
14		
18		
19	(None)	RAM Pattern Test Failed at XXXX Parity Circuit Failure in Bank XXXX Data Bus Test Failed: Address XXXX Address Line Test Failed at XXXX Block Access Read Failure at Address XXXX Block Access Read/Write Failure: Address XXXX Banks Decode to Same Location: XXXX and YYYY
15	(None)	Keyboard Error—Stuck Key Keyboard Failure or no Keyboard Present
17	LH-LLLHH	A20 Test Failure Due to 8042 Timeout
17	LH-HLLHH	A20 Gate Stuck in Disabled State (A20=0)
17	(None)	A20 Gate Stuck in Asserted State (A20 Follows CPU)
1A	LH-LHLHH	Real Time Clock (RTC) is Not Updating
1A	(None)	Real Time Clock (RTC) Settings are Invalid
1E	(None)	Diskette CMOS Configuration is Invalid Diskette Controller Failure Diskette Drive A: Failure Diskette Drive B: Failure
1F	(None)	Fixed Disk CMOS Configuration is Invalid Fixed Disk C: (80) Failure Fixed Disk D: (81) Failure Please Wait for Fixed Disk to Spin Up
20	(None)	Fixed Disk Configuration Change Diskette Configuration Change Serial Port Configuration Change Parallel Port Configuration Change Video Configuration Change Memory Configuration Change Numeric Coprocessor Configuration Change
21	(None)	System Key is in Locked Position—Turn Key to Unlocked Position
29	(None)	Adapter ROM Checksum Failure at Address XXXX

MYLEX/EUROSOFT

Msg	Low-High	Problem
03	LH-LLL	ROM-BIOS Checksum Failure
04	LH-HLL	DMA Page Register Failure
05	LH-LHL	Keyboard Controller Selftest Failure
08	LH-HHL	Memory Refresh Circuitry Failure
09	LH-LLH	Master (16 bit) DMA Controller Failure
09	LH-HLH	Slave (8 bit) DMA Controller Failure
0A	LH-LLLL	Base 64K Pattern Test Failure
0A	LH-HLLL	Base 64K Parity Circuitry Failure
0A	LH-LHLL	Base 64K Parity Error
0A	LH-HHLL	Base 64K Data Bus Failure
0A	LH-LLHL	Base 64K Address Bus Failure
0A	LH-HLHL	Base 64K Block Access Read Failure
0A	LH-LHHL	Base 64K Block Access Read/Write Failure
0B	LH-HHHL	Master 8259 (Port 21) Failure
0B	LH-LLLH	Slave 8259 (Port A1) Failure
0C	LH-HLLH	Master 8259 (Port 20) Interrupt Address Error
0C	LH-LHLH	Slave 8259 (Port A0) Interrupt Address Error
0C	LH-HHLH	8259 (Port 20/A0) Interrupt Address Error
0C	LH-LLHH	Master 8259 (Port 20) Stuck Interrupt Error
0C	LH-HLHH	Slave 8259 (Port A0) Stuck Interrupt Error
0C	LH-LHHH	System Timer 8254 CH0 / IRQ0 Interrupt Failure
0D	LH-HHHH	8254 Channel 0 (System Timer) Failure
0E	LH-LLLLH	8254 Channel 2 (Speaker) Failure
0E	LH-HLLLH	8254 OUT2 (Speaker Detect) Failure
0F	LH-LHLLH	CMOS RAM Read/Write Test Failure
0F	LH-HHLLH	RTC Periodic Interrupt / IRQ8 Failure
10	LH-LLHLH	Video ROM Checksum Failure at Address XXXX Mono Card Memory Error at Address XXXX Mono Card Memory Address Line Error at XXXX CGA Card Memory Error at Address XXXX CGA Card Address Line Error at Address XXXX
11	(None)	Real Time Clock (RTC) Battery is Discharged
11	(None)	Battery Backed Memory (CMOS) is Corrupt
12	LH-HLHLH	Keyboard Controller Failure
14/18/19	LH-LHHLH	Memory Parity Error
14/18/19	LH-HHHLH	I/O Channel Error
14		
18		
19	(None)	RAM Pattern Test Failed at XXXX Parity Circuit Failure in Bank XXXX Data Bus Test Failed: Address XXXX Address Line Test Failed at XXXX Block Access Read Failure at Address XXXX Block Access Read/Write Failure: Address XXXX Banks Decode to Same Location: XXXX and YYYY

POST Codes

15	(None)	Keyboard Error—Stuck Key
		Keyboard Failure or no Keyboard Present
17	LH-LLLHH	A20 Test Failure Due to 8042 Timeout
17	LH-HLLHH	A20 Gate Stuck in Disabled State (A20=0)
17	(None)	A20 Gate Stuck in Asserted State (A20 Follows CPU)
1A	LH-LHLHH	Real Time Clock (RTC) is Not Updating
1A	(None)	Real Time Clock (RTC) Settings are Invalid
1E	(None)	Diskette CMOS Configuration is Invalid
		Diskette Controller Failure
		Diskette Drive A: Failure
		Diskette Drive B: Failure
1F	(None)	Fixed Disk CMOS Configuration is Invalid
		Fixed Disk C: (80) Failure
		Fixed Disk D: (81) Failure
		Please Wait for Fixed Disk to Spin Up
20	(None)	Fixed Disk Configuration Change
		Diskette Configuration Change
		Serial Port Configuration Change
		Parallel Port Configuration Change
		Video Configuration Change
		Memory Configuration Change
		Numeric Coprocessor Configuration Change
21	(None)	System Key is in Locked Position—Turn Key to Unlocked Position
29	(None)	Adapter ROM Checksum Failure at Address XXXX

Derived from Eurosoft BIOS.

4.71

Pass	Fail	Meaning
03	04	DMA page registers test
05	06	Keyboard reply test
07	08	Keyboard self-test
09	0A	8042 keyboard controller able to read links
0B		RATMOD/DIAG link
0C	0D	Keyboard acceptance of 60H
0E	0F	Keyboard acceptance of parameter
10	11	Read keyboard command byte
12	13	Keyboard command byte came back
14	15	RAM refresh toggle test
16	17	RAM bit test
18	19	RAM parity test
1A	1B	CMOS RAM test
1C	1D	CMOS RAM battery test
1E	1F	CMOS RAM checksum test
	20	CMOS RAM battery fault bit set
21	22	Master DMA controller test
21	23	Slave DMA controller 2 test
24		Protected mode entered safely
25		RAM test completed

26	27	BIOS ROM checksum test
28		Protected mode exit
29	2A	Keyboard power-up reply received test
2B	2C	Keyboard disable command acceptance test
	2D	Video display presence check
	2E	POST Errors were reported
	2F	About to halt
30		Protected mode entered safely (2)
31		RAM test complete
33		Master interrupt controller test
34	35	Slave interrupt controller test
36	37	Chipset initialization
38	39	System BIOS shadowed
3A	3B	Video BIOS shadowed

EISA/ISA

Code	Meaning
1	Always present—indicates start of beep coding
2	Video adapter bad or not detected
3	Keyboard controller error
4	Keyboard error
5	8259 Programmable Interrupt Controller (PIC) 1 error
6	8259 PIC 2 error
7	DMA page register failure
8	RAM refresh error
9	RAM data test failed
10	RAM parity error occurred
11	8237 DMA controller 1 failed
12	CMOS RAM failure
13	8237 DMA controller 2 failed
14	CMOS RAM battery failure
15	CMOS RAM checksum error
16	BIOS ROM checksum error

Code	Meaning
01	Processor test
02	DMA Page Register
03	8042 keyboard controller
04	BIOS ROM Checksum error
05	Send keyboard command test bad
06	CMOS RAM Test
07	RAM Refresh Test
08	1st 64K memory test
09	8237 DMA controller test
0A	Initialise DMA controller
0B	Interrupt Test

313

0C	Determine RAM size
0D	Initialise video
0E	EGA/VGA ROM checksum test failed
10	Search for monochrome card
11	Search for colour card
12	Word splitter and byte shifter test failed
13	Keyboard Test
14	RAM Test failed
15	Timer test error
16	Initialise output port of keyboard controller
17	Keyboard interrupt test
18	Initialise keyboard
19	RTC clock test failure
1A	Maths copro test failure
1B	Reset hard/floppy controller
1C	Initialise floppy drive
1D	Initialise hard drive
1E	Initialise ROMs in C000-DFFF
1F	Initialise serial and parallel ports
20	Initialise time of day in RTC
21	Initialise ROMs in E000-EFFF
22	Look for boot device
23	Boot from floppy disk
24	Boot from hard disk
25	Gate A20 enable/disable failure
26	Parity error occurred
30	DDNIL bit scan failure
FF	Fatal error occurred and system halted

NCR

Purchased in 1991 by AT&T. 3 main types of motherboards: OEM from AMI, AT and Micro channel clones. See AMI pre-0490 for PC386, and below for others. All NCR-designed systems send POST codes to LPT1, but see table.

Architecture	Typical PC	BIOS	POST Code Port
XT	PC6	NCR	378 or 3BC (LPT 1)
AT (ISA)	3728, 3204, PC 916	NCR	80 and 378 or 3BC (LPT 1)
	PC386	AMI Pre-0490	80
Micro Channel	3421	Phoenix	680 and 3BC

PC6

Code	Meanings
AA	8088 CPU failure
B1	2764 EPROM checksum failure
B2	8237 DMA controller failure

B3	8253 timer failure
B4	RAM failure. Halts if error in first 64K, otherwise displays MEMORY ERROR.
B5	8259 interrupt controller failure. Displays INTERRUPT FAILURE
B6	RAM parity error. Displays ERROR IN BASE MEMORY or ERROR ON EXPANSION CARD.
BB	All tests passed

3302/3304/3728/PC916SX

Code	Meaning
01	Test CPU registers
02	Test system I/O port—write and read port 61 to confirm it will handle RAM refresh.
03	Test ROM BIOS checksum
04	Test DMA page registers
05	Test timer channel 1 (refresh)
06	Test timer channel 2 (speaker)
07	Test RAM refresh logic. Also verifies timer is working.
08	Test base 64K RAM
09	Test 8/16 bit bus conversion
0A	Test interrupt controller 1
0B	Test interrupt controller 2
0C	Test I/O controller
0D	Test CMOS RAM read/write
0E	Test for battery power low or interrupted since last test
0F	Test CMOS RAM checksum
10	Test CPU protected mode
11	Test video configuration in CMOS RAM or display switch
12	Test primary video controller
13	Test secondary video controller
20	Display results of tests to this point
21	Test DMA controller 1
22	Test DMA controller 2
23	Test Timer channel 0 (system timer tick)
24	Initialize interrupt controllers
25	Test interrupts
26	Test interrupts
30	Check base 640K memory size
31	Check extended memory size
32	Test higher 8 address lines
33	Test base memory
34	Test extended memory
40	Test keyboard—enable/disable
41	Test keyboard—reset
42	Test keyboard—clock low
43	Test keyboard—for interrupt, enable keyboard, init pointers, write out subcommand
44	Test 8086 address overrun compatibility (gate A20)
50	Set up hardware interrupt vectors
51	Enable interrupt from timer channel 0
52	Security ROM
60	Test floppy disk controller and drive

POST Codes

315

61	Test hard disk controller
62	Initialize floppy drives
63	Initialize hard drives
70	Test real time clock
71	Set time of day in real time clock
72	Check parallel interfaces
73	Check serial interfaces
74	Check for and execute adapter option ROMs
75	Check if math coprocessor is installed and enable interrupt
76	Enable keyboard and real time clock interrupts
F0	System not configured correctly, or hardware defect
F1	Scan for and execute motherboard option ROMs
F2	INT 19 to boot operating system—No POST errors.

PC916 5/6

*halt on error if loop jumper installed in keyboard connector

Code	Meaning
01	Test CPU registers, reset video cards, display diagnostic messages
02	Verify port 61, disable non-maskable interrupt, start speaker timer channel 2
03	Test ROM BIOS checksum
04	Test DMA page registers
05	Test timer channel 1 (refresh)
06	Test timer channel 2 (speaker)
07	Test refresh logic by reading port 61 bit 4 every 15 microseconds
08	Test base 64K RAM
09	Test 8/16-bit bus converting logic, initialize both interrupt controllers
0A	Test interrupt mask register A
0B	Test interrupt mask register B, write temporary interrupt vector table for INT 00-77
0C	Test 8042/8742 keyboard controller
0D	Test CMOS RAM shutdown byte
0E*	Test CMOS RAM battery power low or interrupted since last test
0F*	Test CMOS RAM checksum; initialize periodic rate
10	Test CPU protected mode
11	Test video configuration in CMOS RAM or display switch, look for advanced video card ROM in segment C000, initialize interrupt vectors.
12	Initialize and test primary video controller
13	Primary video error, test secondary video controller
14	Test disabling Speed stretch enable/disable port 69 bit 0=1
15	Start refresh timer 1 counter 1, disable speed switch timer 2, counter 2
16	Enable then disable speed stretch enable/disable port 69 bit 0
17	Clear write protect bit
18	Write/verify global/local/interrupt descriptor table registers; copy ROM BIOS to shadow RAM F000
19	Verify RAM to ROM BIOS copy OK; reinitialize restart vector, check and execute for burn-in ROM D000. Disable real time clock in CMOS status reg B, reset and initialize video cards.
IA	Command 8042 to execute self-test and verify result
1B	Test 64K Shadow RAM in segment F000
20	Display results of tests to this point

21	Test DMA controller 1
22	Test DMA controller 2 and initialize all 8 channels
23	Test timer 1 counter 0 840 ns clock timer for IRQ0 (INT8)
24	Initialize both interrupt controllers
25	Check for unexpected (hot) interrupts
26	Wait for interrupt
27*	Test timer 2 counter 0 for NMI (INT02), failsafe
28*	Test timer 2 counter 1 (INT72-74)
30	Check base 640K memory size
31	Check extended memory size (max 256M RAM on 5.2, 6 BIOS)
32	Test higher 8 address lines for mirror addresses (5.x BIOS)
33*	Test base memory
34*	Test extended memory (up to 256M)
35*	Test RAM in E000 (v6 BIOS—also test keyboard shutdown command FE—shutdown path 0B)
40	Test keyboard—enable/disable
41	Test keyboard—reset command FF (halt on error if loop jumper not installed)
42	Test keyboard—clock low (halt on err if loop jumper not installed)
43	Test keyboard—check for interrupt, enable keyboard, initialize buffer pointers, verify keyboard unlocked, disable external interrupts mask A=F, turn on write protect for RAM E000-FFFF, write out subcommand (halt on error if loop jumper not installed).
44	Test address overrun compatibility (turn off gate A20, 8042 P2 bit 1 = 0)
45	v6 BIOS—Init mouse, en IRQ1 (INT09)keyboard (15 IRQs, 1 disabled), disp "Press F1 for Setup".
50	Set up hardware interrupt vectors 0-15, 70-77
51	Enable IRQ0 interval interrupt 08 from timer channel 0; enable external interrupts (STI)
60	Test for floppy/hard disk controller and drive
61	Test cylinder register for disk controller
62	Initialize floppy drives
63	Initialize hard drives
70*	Test real time clock
71	Set interval timer RAM counts
72	Configure and test parallel interfaces
73	Configure and test serial interfaces
74	Check for and execute adapter option ROMs C8000-DFFFF
75*	Test math coprocessor if installed, and enable interrupt
76	Enable keyboard and real time clock IRQ8 (INT 70) interrupts; enable slave interrupt controller 2 via PIC 1 mask bit 2=0.
F0	Display logged errors. Halt if locked; loop if loop jumper installed
F1	Test system code at segment E000 (v5.x BIOS only); v6 BIOS—copy video ROM BIOS (if present) to shadow RAM if system ROM is absent and switch pack switch 1 is on
F2	INT 19 to boot operating system—No POST errors
F3	Go to setup if F1 key pressed. v6 BIOS: execute floppy diagnostic if Ctrl-D pressed, enable failsafe NMI port 61 bit 2=0, enable parity error port 61 bit 3=0, enable NMI.
F4	v5.x BIOS only—Display speed setting
F4	v6 BIOS—Display speed setting Auto, high, fixed
F5	v5.x BIOS only—initialize counter 2 for speed requested
F6	v5.x BIOS only—Test base memory (long test in 5.2 BIOS)
F6	v6 BIOS only—Test base memory (long test) if F2 pressed
F7	v5.x BIOS only—Test extended memory (long test in 5.2 BIOS)
F7	v6 BIOS only—Long test extended memory if F2 pressed

317

OLIVETTI

For EISA and PS/2, the code is issued after the test has passed, so a stuck code indicates the next test failed. Codes are sent to printer ports 3BC (the mono adapter's parallel port), 278, or 378; they will not be printed because no strobe data is sent. AT&Ts using the Olivetti motherboard and BIOS (e.g. the AT&T 6300) do the same.

1076/AT&T 6312/WGS 80286

The first checkpoint, 40, resets and initializes a test monitoring device on the parallel port. When an error occurs, the most recent checkpoint code sent to port 378 is exclusive-ored with 3F to complement the lower 6 bits, and then sent to 378, so if the refresh test fails (45), the POST card will show 7B because the most recent code sent before the failure was 44.

If an error occurs, the POST tries to run through a sequence of activities that display a message on the monitor, showing "*tttt* Error: xx", where *tttt* is the name of the failing routine, and *xx* is a suberror number. If the error is fatal, the display will show "Unrecoverable power-up error", wait for you to press F1, and return to the failing test. If video has failed, the POST will output beep codes.

Pass	Fail	Meaning
40		Dummy check—reset black box
41	7F	80286 CPU flags and register test
42	7E	Check and verify shutdown code—read keyboard status from port 64. if shutdown bit is set, read the shutdown byte from CMOS RAM (and clear the location there), check it for an illegal shutdown condition, initialize the 8259s unless shutdown is 9 or A, and jump to the correct routine to handle the shutdown: 0= warm boot (go to next test), 1= return to advanced protected mode test, 2= return to memory test above 1 Mb, 3=return to protected mode test 2, 4=INT19, 5=send EOI to 8259 and return to user routine, 9=int15 block move, and A=return to user routine.
43	7D	Checksum test the BIOS ROMs—verify contents add up to 0.
44	7C	Test the 8253 timer—check all 3 timers for not counting, counting too slowly, or counting too fast. Suberror display is the bad timer number 0, 1, or 2.
45	7B	Start memory refresh and verify it occurs every 15.1 microseconds. Init the manufacturing test byte in RAM.
46	7A	Command the 8041 keyboard controller to do a self-test. Suberror display is 1 if error return, 2 if self-test times out.
47	79	Test the first 8K of RAM in 4 passes: 1) write into each word a data value corresponding to the address; 2) invert all bits written; 3) write an odd parity pattern; 4) write zeros. Only pass 4 is done on a warm boot. Beep once when this test passes. Install dummy interrupt vectors, set up the stack and other memory areas. display power-on banner on screen.
48	78	Test 80286 in protected mode 1—pattern test all IDT and GDT registers, verify LIDT, SIDT, LGDT, and SGDT instructions.
49	77	Test CMOS RAM shutdown byte with a pattern, then clear it.
4A	76	Test 80286 in protected mode 2—put CPU into protected mode, check it's there, then return to real mode
4B	75	Test RAM from 8K to 640K (cold boot only)—display progress for each 128K block; write, read, and compare the address and inverted address into each word.
4C	74	Test all RAM above IM—same as below 1 Mb test. Also verify CPU runs properly in protected mode.

4D	73	Test for NMI—installs NMI vector in interrupt table and small service routine. Disables I/O and memory parity errors, then checks for hot NMI.
4E	72	Test for RAM parity—turn NMI parity checking back on, and run a pattern test on the parity checking circuit, monitoring for a parity error.
50	71	Test 8259 interrupt controller 1—pattern test the mask register, install interrupt vectors for IRQs, mask them all off. look for hot interrupt coming through mask, set timer 0 to issue an interrupt, unmask it, count down, and expect the interrupt. Suberror display is I=no in, 2=timer doesn't count, 3=int occurred when masked, 4=bad mask register.
51	6F	Test 8259 interrupt controller 2—same as # 1, but no timer test is done. Suberror display is 5=int occurs wen masked, 6=bad mask register. When the test passes, install the interrupt service routine pointer in the vector table, mask off all interrupts. and display PASS message.
52	6E	Test DMA page register—marching bit test on all page registers.
53	6D	Test 8237 DMA controller 1—pattern test all read/write registers. Initialize each channel into the correct mode for BIOS. Suberror 1 display if failure.
54	6C	Test 8237 DMA controller 2—pattern test all read/write registers. Initialize each channel into the correct mode for BIOS. Suberror 3 display if failure.
55	6B	Test PIC port—write/read pattern test speaker port 61.
56	6A	Test keyboard controller—reset the keyboard and initiate self-test Suberror display is I=bad keyboard self-test completion code. 2=stuck key. 3=no keyboard interrupt Otherwise, display pass message, and set up keyboard id flags and buffer in BIOS RAM area.
57	69	Test CMOS clock/calendar chip—verify accurate time keeping and display pass message.
59	68	Test 80286 advanced protected mode—tests LDT, SDT, LTR, STR, VERR, VERW, LAR, SLR, ARPL instructions; forces exception ints 13 and 5. Suberror display is 3=instruction error, 4=no exception or protection violation. Otherwise display protected mode pass message.
5A	66	Test CMOS RAM battery and display message if low.
5B	65	Test CMOS RAM non-destructively—copy contents to base memory, write/read pattern test CMOS RAM, restore contents. Suberror 2 if failure.
5C	64	Verify CMOS RAM checksum.
5D	63	Test parallel port by writing AA to 3BC, 278 and 378, and set config info in BIOS RAM area.
5E	62	Test serial port configuration—read 3FA and 3FA and assume a UART is present if values not FF. Set up port addresses and timeout values in BIOS RAM area.
5F	61	Test configuration of memory below 640K—compare memory size stored in CMOS RAM with result of earlier test. Display message to run setup if different.
60	60	Test configuration of memory above 1M—compare memory size stored in CMOS RAM with result of earlier test. Display message to run setup if different.
61	5F	Test configuration of 80287 math coprocessor chip -verify math chip same as in CMOS RAM info. Display pass or run setup message.
62	5E	Test configuration of game port at 201 and set equipment bit in BIOS RAM data area.

62	5D	Test keylock switch and wait till unlocked.
63	5D	Test hard drive configuration—initialize controller and drive. Display whether drives are present, and message to run setup if not same as CMOS RAM info.
64	5C	Configure floppy drives A and B—initialize controller and drive. Display whether drives are present, and message to run setup if not same as CMOS RAM info.
66	5B	Test option ROMs—look for signature AA5 each 2K beginning at C8000, run checksum and display error if it occurs. Otherwise pass control to the ROM so it can initialize, and display pass message when done.
		INT 19—boot the system.

M20

Not a true IBM clone, as it had a Zilog Z8001 CPU. Also, a typical POST card will not fit in a slot, so you can only monitor codes from the parallel port. The POST shows a triangle, diamond, or 4 lines on the screen to indicate early POST failure, as shown in the table.

Code	Meaning
	Program video controller using load, output, and jump relative instructions (need video).
Triangle	Test Z8001 CPU registers and instructions; infinite loop if failure.
Triangle	Test RAM module; infinite loop if failure; also send message to printer: E Mc bb ssss wwww. c = RAM configuration # (3 = 1 32K memory card); bb = hex 16K bank # (0,4,5,6,9,A=motherboard; 1,7,B=expansion board 1; 2=expansion board 2; 3,11,12=cxpansion board 3); ssss = what data should be; wwww = what data was (hex).
4 vertical lines	Test CPU call and trap instructions; infinite loop if failure.
Diamond	Initialize screen and printer drivers.
	Program UARTs (serial chips) and 8253 baud rate generator for keyboard at 1200 baud and RS232 at 9600. Now test remaining circuits and send codes to display and printer.
EC0	8255 parallel interface chip test failed
EC1	6845 CRT controller chip test failed
EC2	1797 floppy disk controller chip test failed
EC3	8253 timer chip test failed
EC4	8251 keyboard serial interface chip test failed
EC5	8251 RS232 serial interface chip test failed
EC6	8259 interrupt controller chip test failed
EK0	Keyboard did not respond
EK1	Keyboard responded, but self-test failed
ED1	Disk drive 1 test failed
ED0	Disk drive 0 test failed
E10	Non-vectored interrupt error
E11	Vectored interrupt error

M21/M24 (AT&T 6300)

The M24 went to the US as the AT&T 6300. It had an 8086, so was faster than the PC, albeit difficult to work on.

POST codes are sent to 378 (LPT1). If a fatal error occurs, it performs more initialization of DMA and interrupt controller circuits, tries to display an error message, complements the lower 6 bits of the POST code, sends the result to port 378, and halts the CPU, so numbers will flicker on the POST display with bit 6 on and the lower bits running from 0 upward. The codes start at 40 because a black box was used to monitor POST status at the parallel port. Bit 6 was set true (to a 1) to alert the box that the POST was starting.

Code	Meaning
40	CPU flags and register test failed (fatal)
41	BIOS ROM checksum test failed (fatal)
42	Disable pdma controller command and test 8253 timer channel 1, mode 2, refresh counter (fatal); display sub-error code of 1 if interval is below window, 2 if above, and 3 if timer does not respond.
43	8237 DMA controller test failed (fatal)—master clear the controller, set the mask register, read the control registers, test all 8 read/writeable channel registers. Test registers 0-3 DMA address and count with FFFF then 0000. Set up channel 0 for 64K RAM address refresh. Set up memory-to-I/O transfer, unmask the RAM refresh, and let refresh begin for the first time. Set up the 8253 for proper refresh count. Test for unexpected DMA request (suberror 3), and init DMA channel 1 (not used), 2 (floppy), 3 (display), and init nibble latches. Check for proper DMA transfer into lowest 64K bank of RAM (suberror 4 if parity error).
44	8259 PIC test failed (halt)—initialize stack to lower 64K RAM area just tested, init and disable 8259A, set up interrupt vectors in RAM, set up software then hardware diagnostic interrupt vectors, test software interrupts, then hardware interrupts. Disable interrupts via 8259 mask register, check for hot interrupts, convert hot mask to IRQ number, save any error code, install interrupt vectors, initialize video, and display any error messages (H:#, where # is the hot IRQ#).
45	Install real interrupt vectors, determine system configuration from switches, and initialize video mono and colour. Set video mode 3, clear the screen, and display any passing error messages for CPU, ROM, DMA, or interrupt controller. Size and clear RAM at every 64K bank past the lowest 64K, displaying the tested RAM as test progresses. Display errors in form cc:y000:zzz:wwww:rrrr, where cc is the config number, y the failing segment, z the offset, w the written data and r the read data. Test the MM58174 clock calendar, and display message if fails Test 8253 real time clock count capability, and tone generator. Display any error, and halt if failure.
48	Send beep to display and initialize all basic hardware. Init 8041 keyboard controller, determine parallel port configurations and test their registers, determine serial 8250 and Z8530 configurations, check for game card, set up interrupt controller, set all 4 Z8530 serial controllers to 9600 baud, no parity, 1 stop and 8 data. Set up interrupt vectors, initialize RAM variables, clear the screen, initialize the hard disk controller, test for and initialize option ROMs, verify ROM checksums okay, initialize floppy disk controller, allow user to select alternate Z8000 processor if installed and perform INT 19 cold boot.

EISA 2.01

Port 278, 378, Or 3BC (i.e. printer ports)

Code	Meaning
01	Test CPU flags, registers. Initialize interrupt controller
02	Test memory refresh
03	Test CMOS RTC periodic interrupt
04	Test gate A20 line
05	Test mapping memory SRAM
06	Test first 128K RAM. Stack has now been established
07	Test for console presence and initialize
08	Verify system BIOS ROM checksum
09	Test 8042 keyboard controller Normal burn-in/manufacturing mode established
0A	Test timer ratio

0B	Test CMOS RAM battery
0C	Verify CMOS RAM checksum
0D	Test for unexpected NMI
0E	Test interrupt controller #1
0F	Test interrupt controller #2
10	Test timer 1 counter 0
11	Test system control port B
12	Test system control port A
13	Verify checksum of NVRAM configuration memory
14	Initialize system board
15	Initialize adapter
16	Initialize ESC SCSI adapter
17	Initialize system video
18	Test and copy shadow RAM. Video is initialized—display banner and non-fatal errors
19	Test DMA page registers
1A	Test DMA address registers
1B	Test DMA count registers
1C	Test DMA mask registers
1D	Test DMA stop registers. Initialize DMA controllers
1E	Test IDTR and GDTR
1F	Test CMOS shutdown byte
20	Test real/protected mode
21	Check system memory configuration
22	Size memory
23	Test 640K base memory
24	Verify base memory configuration
25	Test extended memory (above 1 Mb)
26	Verify extended memory configuration
27	Check for contiguous extended memory
28	Test cache memory. Extended BIOS data area created and POST errors logged
29	Test protected mode instructions
2A	Test CMOS RAM
2B	Test real time clock
2C	Check calendar values
2D	Test keyboard/AUX device fuse
2E	Test keyboard
2F	Initialize keyboard typematic rate and delay
30	Test auxiliary device
31	Test 80x87 math coprocessor
32	Test and initialize Weitek math coprocessor
33	Run 1860 CPU basic and advanced diagnostics
34	Test and configure serial ports
35	Test and configure parallel ports
36	Detect game port
37	Test and initialize hard drives
38	Test and initialize floppy drives
39	Scan for and pass control to adapter ROMs
3A	INT 19 boot—load operating system

PS/2 Compatible

Code	Meaning
01	Processor test
02	Shutdown
03	Interrupt controller initialisation
04	Refresh test
05	CMOS periodic interrupt test
06	Timer ratio
07	Test first 64k RAM
08	Test the KBC (8742)
09	NMI test
0A	8254 test
0B	Port 94h test
0C	Port 103h test
0D	Port 102h test
0E	Port 96h test
0F	Port 107h test
10	Blank the screen
11	KB/Aux device fuse check
12	CMOS battery test
13	CMOS RAM checksum test
14	Extended CMOS checksum 0-8K
15	System board and adapter initialisation
16	RAM test and initialisation
17	Protected mode register test
18	CMOS RAM shutdown byte test
19	80286 protected mode test
1A	Video option ROM scan
1B	EPROM checksum test
1C	Interrupt controller #1 test
1D	Interrupt controller #2 test
1E	Interrupt vector initialisation
1F	CMOS RAM test
20	Extended CMOS r/w test
21	CMOS clock test
22	Clock calendar test
23	Dummy checkpoint
24	Watchdog timer test
25	Test RAM from 64K to 640K
26	Configure memory 640K
27	Text expansion memory
28	Initialize extended BIOS data segment and log POST errors
29	Configure memory above 1 Mb
2A	Dummy checkpoint
2B	Test RAM parity
2C	Test DMA page registers
2D	Test DMA controller base/current address registers
2E	Test DMA transfer count register

323

2F	Initialize DMA controller
30	Test PIO 61
31	Test keyboard
32	Initialize keyboard typematic rate and delay
33	Test AUX device
34	Test advanced protected mode
35	Configure parallel ports
36	Configure 8250 serial ports
37	Configure coprocessor
38	Configure game card
39	Configure and initialize hard disk
3A	Floppy disk configuration
3B	Initialize ROM drivers
3C	Display total memory and hard drives
3D	Final initialization, Checkpoints complete
3E	Detect and initialize parallel ports
3F	Initialize hard drive and controller
40	Detect and initialize math coprocessor
41	Reserved
42	Initiate adapter ROM scan
CC	Unexpected processor exception occurred
DD	Save DDNIL status
EE	NMI handler shutdown
FF	INT 19 boot

PACKARD BELL

See *Phoenix.*

PHILIPS/MAGNAVOX/HEADSTART

Philips, Magnavox, and HeadStart use motherboards designed by Philips Home Electronics in Montreal. Most use a Philips-designed BIOS, although at least one of their portables uses one from Award Software. The beep pattern consists of a series of long and short beeps that correspond to the binary representation of the POST code where leading zeroes are omitted; a zero means a short and a one means a long beep. The various Philips platforms do not all execute the same POST tests.

Philips Platform Cross Reference

Platform	CPU	System Model/Name
Avenger	80286	Magnavox MaxStation 286, Magnum GL; Headstart Series 300
P3212	80286	Magnavox MaxStation 480, Headstart System 380
P 3239	80286 80386SX	Magnavox Headstart/Maxstation/Magnum/Professional 1200, 48CD, 1600, 64CD, P160, SR16CD
P 3349	80386SX-20	Magnavox Headstart/Maxstation/Magnum/Professional SX20, 80CD
P3345	80386SX	Magnavox Maxstation 386SX, Magnum SX; Headstart Series 500
P33711	80386DX	Headstart/Maxstation/Magnum/Professional 3300

Code	Beeps 0=sh 1=lg	Meanings (Port 80)
0A	1010	DMA page register write/read bad
10	1 0000	CMOS RAM read/write error (only after hard reset)
11	1 0001	System ROM BIOS checksum error
12	1 0010	Timer A error
13	1 0011	DMA controller A error
14	1 0100	DMA controller B error
15	1 0101	Memory refresh error
16	1 0110	Keyboard controller error
17	1 0111	Keyboard controller error
19	1 1001	Keyboard controller error
1C	1 1100	Base 64K RAM error
1D	1 1101	Base 64K RAM parity error
1F	1 1111	Orvonton LSI sync missing
21	10 0001	PVAM register error
25	10 0101	System options error
2B	10 1011	Video sync error (incorrect switch setting or CMOS RAM—run SETUP)
2C	10 1100	Video BIOS ROM error
2D	10 1101	Monochrome/colour configuration error
2E	10 1110	No video memory
35	11 0101	Interrupt controller error
36	11 0110	Byte swapper error
37	11 0111	NMI error
38	11 1000	Timer interrupt
39	11 1001	LSI timer halted
3A	11 1010	Main memory test error
3B	11 1011	Keyboard error
3C	11 1100	Keyboard interrupt error (only after hard reset)
3D	11 1101	DDNIL scan halted, cache disabled
40	100 0000	Diskette error
48	100 1000	Adapter card error
4c	100 1100	CMOS battery/checksum error (run SETUP)
4D	100 1101	System options error (run Setup)
52	101 0010	Keyboard controller error
6A	110 1010	Failure shadowing BIOS ROM
70	111 0000	Memory size configuration error (run SETUP)

POST Codes

PHOENIX

Created the first clone of IBM's BIOS. On 4.3 and above, the system will attempt to generate a code with four groups of beeps, with 1-4 per group. The micro channel version sends codes to port 680, with an execution sequence of: 01, 03, 41, 02, 42, 05, 06, 08, 04, 09—22, 23, 25, 27, 28, 29, 2E, 2B, 2C, 2D, 30, 31, 32, 61, 62, 34, 35, 3A, 38, 3B.

Architecture	Typical Computer	POST Port
ISA	XT	60
	AT	80
	PS/2 25/30	90
EISA	Intel chipset	80
MCA	PS/2 50 up	68O

POST Procedures

Procedure	Meaning
CPU	Check internal operations e.g. ALE/IRQ status; Request; ALU and Memory Read/Write.
CMOS RAM	Test with walking-bit pattern.
ROM BIOS	Perform checksum on ROM BIOS where all bits are added and compared to a factory-set total.
PIT	Check to ensure interrupt requests are properly executed.
DMA	Check DMA from CPU to memory without BIOS. Also check page registers.
Base 64K	Check first 64K block.
Serial and Parallel	I/O data areas for any devices found are assigned; they are not tested.
PIC	Check that proper interrupt request levels are addressed.
Keyboard Controller	Check 8240 for proper operation, including scan code response and Gate A20 which allows CPU operation in protected mode.
CMOS	Check data within CMOS and compare to BIOS information. Failure of the extended area is often due to wrong data setup. Constant failure after resetting CMOS is either battery CMOS chip or RTC.
Video Controller	Test and initialise controller and ROM on the video adapter.
RTC	Check to ensure proper frequencies are on proper lines for the Video Colour CPU and DMA Frequency. Check RTC/PIT or system crystal.
CPU	Return From Protected Mode. CPU is put into protected mode and returns to the POST at the point indicated by the CMOS ROM data area byte 0F. Failure here is normally due to the CPU/keyboard controller/CMOS chip or an address line.
PIC	Test Counter 2.
NMI	Check the Non-Maskable Interrupt request vector for active status. Failure is normally due to the CMOS but could also be the BIOS IRQ or CPU chips.
Keyboard	Check for NumLock/Caps and Shift Keys.
Mouse	Initialise through the keyboard controller; this is only done if a mouse is present and it is initialised in this way.
RAM above 64K	Test in 64K blocks with a walking-bit pattern and parity enabled.
Fixed/Floppy Controllers	Test for proper response to BIOS calls.
Shadow RAM Areas	Look in CMOS for settings on which adapter or system ROMs are to be shadowed.
Option ROM	Look for ROM signatures of 55AA in extended memory then initialise the ROM and halt testing while internal checks are carried out.

External Cache	Check controller chip for external cache.
CPU Internal Cache	
Hardware Adapters	Initialise and test video/floppy/hard I/O adapters/serial and parallel.
Cassette	Test internal or external cassette drives.
	Errors occurring after this point are normally a corrupt boot record.

2.52 BNP XT

Code	Meaning
01	Test 8253 timer
02	First 64K RAM failed
03	First 1K parity check failed
04	Initialize 8259 interrupt controller
05	Second 1K RAM test (BIOS data area) failed

BIOS Plus or v1.0 POST/Beep Codes

Only for BIOS PLUS or A286/A386/A486 Version 1.xx on an AT-class (80286 or higher) systems. Codes in the 50h range or beyond are chipset or custom platform specific, and will vary from system to system.

Code	Beeps	Meaning
01	none	CPU register test in progress.
02	1-1-3	CMOS write/read failure.
03	1-1-4	ROM BIOS Checksum Failure.
04	1-2-1	Programmable interval timer failure.
05	1-2-2	DMA Initialisation failure.
06	1-2-3	DMA page register write/read failure.
08	1-3-1	RAM refresh verification failure.
09	none	1st 64K RAM test in progress.
0A	1-3-3	1st 64K RAM chip or data line failure multi-bit.
0B	1-3-4	1st RAM odd/even logic failure.
0C	1-4-1	Address line failure 1st 64K RAM.
0D	1-4-2	Parity failure 1st 64K RAM.
10	2-1-1	Bit 0 1st 64K RAM failure.
11	2-1-2	Bit 1 1st 64K RAM failure.
12	2-1-3	Bit 2 1st 64K RAM failure.
13	2-1-4	Bit 3 1st 64K RAM failure.
14	2-2-1	Bit 4 1st 64K RAM failure.
15	2-2-2	Bit 5 1st 64K RAM failure.
16	2-2-3	Bit 6 1st 64K RAM failure.
17	2-2-4	Bit 7 1st 64K RAM failure.
18	2-3-1	Bit 8 1st 64K RAM failure.
19	2-3-2	Bit 9 1st 64K RAM failure.
1A	2-3-3	Bit A(10) 1st 64K RAM failure.
1B	2-3-2	Bit B(11) 1st 64K RAM failure.
1C	2-4-2	Bit C(12) 1st 64K RAM failure.
1D	2-4-2	Bit D(13) 1st 64K RAM failure.
1E	2-4-3	Bit E(14) 1st 64K RAM failure.
1F	2-4-4	Bit F(15) 1st 64K RAM failure.

20	3-1-1	Slave DMA register failure.
21	3-1-2	Master DMA register failure.
22	3-1-3	Master interrupt mask register failure.
23	3-1-4	Slave interrupt mask register failure.
25	none	Interrupt vector loading in progress.
27	3-2-4	8042 keyboard controller test failure.
28	none	CMOS power failure/checksum calculation in progress.
29	none	CMOS configuration validation in progress.
2B	3-3-4	Screen memory test failure.
2C	3-4-1	Screen initialisation failure.
2D	3-4-2	Screen retrace test failure.
2E	none	Search for video ROM in progress.
30	none	Screen believed running with video ROM.
31	none	Mono monitor believed operable.
32	none	Colour monitor (40 col) believed operable.
33	none	Colour monitor (80 col) believed operable.
34	4-2-1	Timer tick interrupt test in progress or failed (non-fatal).
35	4-2-2	Shutdown failure (non-fatal).
36	4-2-3	Gate A20 failure (non-fatal).
37	4-2-4	Unexpected interrupt in protected mode (non-fatal).
38	4-3-1	Mem high address line fail at 01000-0A000 (non-fatal).
39	4-3-2	Mem high addr line fail at 100000-FFFFFF (non-fatal).
3A	4-3-3	Timer chip counter 2 failed (non-fatal).
3B	4-3-4	Time-of-day clock stopped
3C	4-4-1	Serial port test
3D	4-4-2	Parallel port test
3E	4-4-3	Maths coprocessor test
41	low 1-1-2	System board select bad
42	low 1-1-3	Extended CMOS RAM bad

UMC Chipset PCI

Code	Beep	Meaning
02	1-1-1-3	Verify Real Mode
04	1-1-2-1	Get CPU type
06	1-1-2-3	Initialise system hardware
08	1-1-3-1	Initialise chipset registers with initial POST values
09	1-1-3-2	Set in POST flag
0A	1-1-3-3	Initialise CPU registers
0C	1-1-4-1	Initialise cache to initial POST values
0E	1-1-4-3	Initialise I/O
10	1-2-1-1	Initialise power management
11	1-2-1-2	load alternate registers with initial POST values
12	1-2-1-3	Jump to User Patch 0
14	1-2-2-1	Initialise keyboard controller
16	1-2-2-3	BIOS ROM checksum
18	1-2-3-1	8254 timer initialisation
1A	1-2-3-3	8237 DMA controller initialisation
1C	1-2-4-1	Reset PIC

20	1-3-1-1	Test DRAM refresh
22	1-3-1-3	Test 8742 keyboard controller
24	1-3-2-1	Set ES segment register to 4 Gb
26	1-3-2-3	Enable Address Line A20
28	1-3-3-1	Autosize DRAM
2A	1-3-3-3	Clear 512K base RAM
2C	1-3-4-1	Test 512K base address lines
2E	1-3-4-3	Test 512K base memory
30	1-4-1-1	Test base address memory
32	1-4-1-3	Test CPU bus clock frequency
34	1-4-2-1	Test CMOS RAM
35	1-4-2-2	Test chipset register initialise
36	1-4-2-3	Test check resume
37	1-4-2-4	Reinitialise the chipset
38	1-4-3-1	Shadow System BIOS ROM
39	1-4-3-2	Reinitialise the cache
3A	1-4-3-3	Autosize the cache
3C	1-4-4-1	Configure advanced chipset registers
3D	1-4-4-2	Load alternate registers with CMOS values
3E	1-4-4-3	Read hardware configuration from keyboard controller
40	2-1-1-1	Set initial CPU speed
42	2-1-1-3	Initialise interrupt vectors
44	2-1-2-1	Initialise BIOS interrupts
46	2-1-2-3	Check ROM copyright notice
47	2-1-3-1	Initialise manager for PCI option ROMs
48	2-1-2-4	Check video configuration against CMOS
49	2-1-3-2	Initialise PCI bus and devices
4A	2-1-3-3	Initialise all video adapters
4C	2-1-4-1	Shadow video BIOS ROM
4E	2-1-4-3	Display copyright notice
50	2-2-1-1	Display CPU type and speed
52	2-2-1-3	Test keyboard
54	2-2-2-1	Set key click if enabled
56	2-2-2-3	Enable keyboard
58	2-2-3-1	Test for unexpected interrupts
5A	2-2-3-3	Display prompt "Press F2 to Enter Setup"
5C	2-2-4-1	Test RAM between 512 and 640K
5E	2-2-4-3	Test base memory
60	2-3-1-1	Test expanded memory
62	2-3-1-3	Test extended memory address lines
64	2-3-2-1	Jump to User Patch 1
66	2-3-2-3	Configure advanced cache registers
68	2-3-3-1	Enable external and CPU caches
69	2-3-3-2	Set up power management
6A	2-3-3-3	Display external cache size
6C	2-3-4-1	Display shadow message
6E	2-3-4-3	Display non-disposable segments
70	2-4-1-1	Display error messages

72	2-4-1-3	Check for configuration errors
74	2-4-2-1	Test RTC
76	2-4-2-3	Check for keyboard errors
7A	2-4-3-3	Enable keylock
7C	2-4-4-1	Set up hardware interrupt vectors
7E	2-4-4-3	Test coprocessor if present
80	3-1-1-1	Disable onboard I/O ports
82	3-1-1-3	Detect and install external RS232 ports
84	3-1-2-1	Detect and install external parallel ports
86	3-1-2-3	Reinitialise onboard I/O ports
88	3-1-3-1	Initialise BIOS data area
8A	3-1-3-3	Initialise extended BIOS data area
8C	3-1-4-1	Initialise floppy controller
8E	3-1-4-3	Hard disk autotype configuration
90	3-2-1-1	Initialise hard disk controller
91	3-2-1-2	Initialise local bus hard disk controller
92	3-2-1-3	Jump to User Patch 2
94	3-2-2-1	Disable A20 address line
96	3-2-2-3	Clear huge ES segment register
98	3-2-3-1	Search for option ROMs
9A	3-2-3-3	Shadow option ROMs
9C	3-2-4-1	Set up Power Management
9E	3-2-4-3	Enable hardware interrupts
A0	3-3-1-1	Set time of day
A2	3-3-1-3	Check key lock
A4	3-3-2-1	Initialise typematic rate
A8	3-3-3-1	Erase F2 prompt
AA	3-3-3-3	Scan for F2 key stroke
AC	3-3-4-1	Enter Setup
AE	3-3-4-3	Clear in-POST flag
B0	3-4-1-1	Check for errors
B2	3-4-1-3	POST done
B4	3-4-2-1	One beep
B6	3-4-2-3	Check password (optional)
B8	3-4-3-1	Clear global descriptor table
BC	3-4-4-1	Clear parity checkers
BE	3-4-4-3	Clear screen (optional)
BF	3-4-4-4	Check virus and backup reminders
C0	4-1-1-1	Try to boot with INT 19
D0	4-2-1-1	Interrupt handler error
D2	4-2-1-3	Unknown interrupt error
D4	4-2-2-1	Pending interrupt error
D6	4-2-2-3	Initialise option ROM error
D8	4-2-3-1	Shutdown error
DA	4-2-3-3	Extended Block Move
DC	4-2-4-1	Shutdown 10 error

These are for boot block in Flash ROM:

Code		
Flash BIOS Integrity Test		
E2	4-3-1-3	Initialise the chipset
E3	4-3-1-4	Check for Forced Flash
E4	4-3-2-1	
E5	4-3-2-2	Check HW status of ROM
E6	4-3-2-3	BIOS ROM is OK
E7	4-3-2-4	Do a complete RAM test
Flash Recovery		
E8	4-3-3-1	Do OEM initialisation
E9	4-3-3-2	Initialise interrupt controller
EA	4-3-3-3	Read in the bootstrap code
EB	4-3-3-4	Initialise all vectors
EC	4-3-4-1	Boot the flash program
ED	4-3-4-2	Initialise the boot device
EE	4-3-4-3	Boot code was read OK.

PCI

Code	Meaning
02	If the CPU is in protected mode turn on A20 and pulse the reset line; forcing a shutdown 0.
04	On a cold boot save the CPU type information value in the CMOS.
06	Reset DMA controllers. Disable videos. Clear pending interrupts from RTC. Setup port B register.
08	Initialise chipset control registers to power on defaults.
0A	Set a bit in the CMOS that indicates POST; used to determine if the current configuration causes the BIOS to hang. If so default values will be used on next POST.
0C	Initialise I/O module control registers.
0E	External CPU caches are initialised. Cache registers are set to default.
10/12/14	Verify response of 8742.
16	Verify BIOS ROM checksums to zero.
18	Initialise all three of 8254 timers.
1A	Initialise DMA command register. Initialise 8 DMA channels.
1C	Initialise 8259 interrupt controller to :ICW4 needed; Cascade and edge-triggered mode.
20	Test DRAM refresh by polling refresh bit in PORTB.
22	Test 8742 keyboard controller. Send self test command to 8742 and await results. Also read the switch inputs from the 8742 and write the keyboard controller command byte.
24	Set ES segment register to 4 Gb
26	Enable Address Line A20
28	Autosize DRAM
2A	Clear first 64K of RAM
2C	Test RAM address lines
2E	Test first 64K bank of memory consisting of a chip address line test and a RAM test.
30/32	Find true MHz value
34	Clear CMOS diagnostic byte (register E). Check RTC and verify battery has not lost power. Checksum the CMOS and verify it has not been corrupted.
36/38/3A	External cache is autosized and its configuration saved for enabling later in POST.

3C	Configure advanced cache features. Configure external cache's configurable parameters.
3E	Read hardware configuration from keyboard controller
40	Set system power-on speed to the rate determined by the CMOS. If the CMOS is invalid use a conservative speed.
42	Initialise interrupt vectors 0-77h to the BIOS general interrupt handler.
44	Initialise interrupt vectors 0-20h to proper values from the BIOS interrupt table.
46	Check copyright message checksum.
48	Check video configuration.
4A	Initialise both monochrome and colour graphics video adapters.
4C/4E	Display Copyright message.
50	Display CPU type and speed
52	Test for the self-test code if a cold start. When powered the keyboard performs a self-test and sends an AA if successful.
54	Initialise keystroke clicker during POST.
56	Enable keyboard
58	Test for unexpected interrupts. First do an STI for hot interrupts; secondly test NMI for unexpected interrupt. Thirdly enable parity checkers and read from memory checking for unexpected interrupt.
5A	Display prompt "Press F2 to Enter Setup"
5C	Determine and test the amount of memory available. Save the total memory size in the BIOS variable called bdaMemorySize.
5E	Perform address test on base memory. The following address lines are tested based on the memory size.
60	Determine and test the amount of extended memory available. Save the total extended memory size in the CMOS at CMOSExtended.
62	Perform an address line test on A0 to the amount of memory available. This test is dependent on the processor since the test will vary depending on the width of memory (16 or 32 bits). This test will also use A20 as the skew address to prevent corruption of the system memory.
68	External and CPU caches if present are enabled. Non-cacheable regions are configured if necessary.
6A	Display cache size on screen if non-zero.
6C	Display BIOS shadow status.
6E	Display the starting offset of the non-disposable section of the BIOS.
70	Check flags in CMOS and in the BIOS data area to see if any errors have been detected during POST. If so, display error messages on the screen.
72	Check status bits for configuration errors. If so display error messages on the screen.
74	Test RTC if the battery has not lost power. If the RTC is not running or the battery has lost powerset the incorrect time bit in register E of the CMOS.
76	Check status bits for keyboard errors. If so display error messages on the screen.
78	Check for stuck keys on the keyboard. If so display error messages on the screen.
7A	Enable keylock
7C	Set up hardware interrupt vectors
7E	Test coprocessor if present
80-82	Detect and install RS232 ports
84	Detect and install parallel ports
86-88	Initialise timeouts/key buffer/soft reset flag.
8A	Initialise extended BIOS data area and initialise the mouse.

8C	Initialise both floppy disks and display an error message if failure was detected. Both drives are checked so the appropriate diskette types are established in the BIOS data area.
8E	Hard disk autotype configuration
90	If the CMOS RAM is valid and intact and fixed disks are defined call the fixed disk init routine to initialise the fixed disk system and take over the appropriate interrupt vectors.
92-94	Disable A20 address line
96-98-	Scan for ROM BIOS extensions.
9E	Enable hardware interrupts
A0	Set time of day
A2	Set up NumLock indicator. Display a message if key switch is locked.
A4	Initialise typematic rate.
A6	Initialise hard disk autoparking.
A8	Erase F2 prompt.
AA	Scan for F2 key strokes.
AC	Check to see if SETUP should be executed.
AE	Clear ConfigFailedBit and InPostBit in CMOS.
B0	Check for POST errors
B2	Set/clear status bits to reflect POST complete.
B4	One beep.
B6	Check for password before boot.
B8	Clear global descriptor table (GDT).
BA	Initialise the screen saver.
BC	Clear parity error latch.
BE	Clear screen.
C0	Try to boot with INT 19
D0-D2	If an interrupt occurs before interrupt vectors have been initialised this interrupt handler will try to see if the interrupt caused was an 8259 interrupt and which one. If the interrupt is unknown, InterruptFlag will be FF. Otherwise it will contain the IRQ number that occurred
D4	Clear pending timer, kbd interrupts, transfer control to double word address at RomCheck.
D6-D8-DA	Return from extended block move.

Phoenix v3.07

see Quadtel.

ISA/EISA/MCA BIOS POST/Beep Codes (fatal)

Msg	Beeps	Meaning
01	none	CPU register test in progress.
02	1-1-3	CMOS write/read failure.
03	1-1-4	ROM BIOS Checksum Failure.
04	1-2-1	Programmable interval timer failure.
05	1-2-2	DMA Initialisation failure.
06	1-2-3	DMA page register write/read failure.
08	1-3-1	RAM refresh verification failure.
09	none	1st 64K RAM test in progress.
0A	1-3-3	1st 64K RAM chip or data line failure multi-bit.
0B	1-3-4	1st RAM odd/even logic failure.
0C	1-4-1	Address line failure 1st 64K RAM.

POST Codes

0D	1-4-2	Parity failure 1st 64K RAM.
0E	1-4-3	Fail-safe timer failure.
0F	1-4-4	Software NMI port failure.
10	2-1-1	Bit 0 1st 64K RAM failure.
11	2-1-2	Bit 1 1st 64K RAM failure.
12	2-1-3	Bit 2 1st 64K RAM failure.
13	2-1-4	Bit 3 1st 64K RAM failure.
14	2-2-1	Bit 4 1st 64K RAM failure.
15	2-2-2	Bit 5 1st 64K RAM failure.
16	2-2-3	Bit 6 1st 64K RAM failure.
17	2-2-4	Bit 7 1st 64K RAM failure.
18	2-3-1	Bit 8 1st 64K RAM failure.
19	2-3-2	Bit 9 1st 64K RAM failure.
1A	2-3-3	Bit A 1st 64K RAM failure.
1B	2-3-2	Bit B 1st 64K RAM failure.
1C	2-4-2	Bit C 1st 64K RAM failure.
1D	2-4-2	Bit D 1st 64K RAM failure.
1E	2-4-3	Bit E 1st 64K RAM failure.
1F	2-4-4	Bit F 1st 64K RAM failure.
20	3-1-1	Slave DMA register failure.
21	3-1-2	Master DMA register failure.
22	3-1-3	Master interrupt mask register failure.
23	3-1-4	Slave interrupt mask register failure.
25	none	Interrupt vector loading in progress.
27	3-2-4	Keyboard controller test failure.
28	none	CMOS pwr failure; checksum calculation in progress.
29	none	CMOS RAM configuration validation in progress.
2B	3-3-4	Screen memory test failure.
2C	3-4-1	Screen initialisation failure.
2D	3-4-2	Screen retrace test failure.
2E	none	Search for video ROM in progress.
30	none	Screen believed running with video ROM.
31	none	Mono monitor believed operable.
32	none	Colour monitor (40 col) believed operable.
33	none	Colour monitor (80 col) believed operable.

ISA/EISA/MCA BIOS POST/Beep Codes (non-fatal)

Non-fatal if manufacturing jumper is on.

Msg	Beeps	Meaning
34	4-2-1	No time tick.
35	4-2-2	Shutdown test in progress or failure.
36	4-2-3	Gate A20 failure.
37	4-2-4	Unexpected interrupt in protected mode.
38	4-3-1	Memory high address line failure at 01000-0A000. Also RAM test in progress or address failure >FFFH.
39	4-3-2	Memory high address line failure at 100000-FFFFFF.
3A	4-3-3	Interval Timer channel 2 test or failure.
3B	4-3-4	Time-of-day clock test or failure.

3C	4-4-1	Serial port test or failure.
3D	4-4-2	Parallel port test or failure.
3E	4-4-3	Maths coprocessor test
3F		Cache test (Dell)
41	low 1-1-2	System board select bad (Micro Channel only)
42	low 1-1-3	Extended CMOS RAM bad (Micro Channel only)

Phoenix v4.0

Beeps	Code	Meaning
1-1-1-3	02	Verify Real Mode
1-1-2-1	04	Get CPU type
1-1-2-3	06	Initialize system hardware
1-1-3-1	08	Initialize chipset registers with initial POST values
1-1-3-2	09	Set in POST flag
1-1-3-3	0A	Initialize CPU registers
1-1-4-1	0C	Initialize cache to initial POST values
1-1-4-3	0E	Initialize I/O
1-2-1-1	10	Initialize Power Management
1-2-1-2	11	Load alternate registers with initial POST values
1-2-1-3	12	Jump to UserPatch0
1-2-2-1	14	Initialize keyboard controller
1-2-2-3	16	BIOS ROM checksum
1-2-3-1	18	8254 timer initialization
1-2-3-3	1A	8237 DMA controller initialization
1-2-4-1	1C	Reset Programmable Interrupt Controller
1-3-1-1	20	Test DRAM refresh
1-3-1-3	22	Test 8742 Keyboard Controller
1-3-2-1	24	Set ES segment to register to 4 GB
1-3-3-1	28	Autosize DRAM
1-3-3-3	2A	Clear 512K base RAM
1-3-4-1	2C	Test 512 base address lines
1-3-4-3	2E	Test 512K base memory
1-4-1-3	32	Test CPU bus-clock frequency
1-4-2-4	37	Reinitialize the chipset
1-4-3-1	38	Shadow system BIOS ROM
1-4-3-2	39	Reinitialize the cache
1-4-3-3	3A	Autosize cache
1-4-4-1	3C	Configure advanced chipset registers
1-4-4-2	3D	Load alternate registers with CMOS values
2-1-1-1	40	Set Initial CPU speed
2-1-1-3	42	Initialize interrupt vectors
2-1-2-1	44	Initialize BIOS interrupts
2-1-2-3	46	Check ROM copyright notice
2-1-2-4	47	Initialize manager for PCI Options ROMs
2-1-3-1	48	Check video configuration against CMOS
2-1-3-2	49	Initialize PCI bus and devices
2-1-3-3	4A	Initialize all video adapters in system
2-1-4-1	4C	Shadow video BIOS ROM

POST Codes

335

2-1-4-3	4E	Display copyright notice
2-2-1-1	50	Display CPU type and speed
2-2-1-3	52	Test keyboard
2-2-2-1	54	Set key click if enabled
2-2-2-3	56	Enable keyboard
2-2-3-1	58	Test for unexpected interrupts
2-2-3-3	5A	Display prompt "Press F2 to enter SETUP"
2-2-4-1	5C	Test RAM between 512 and 640k
2-3-1-1	60	Test expanded memory
2-3-1-3	62	Test extended memory address lines
2-3-2-1	64	Jump to UserPatch1
2-3-2-3	66	Configure advanced cache registers
2-3-3-1	68	Enable external and CPU caches
2-3-3-3	6A	Display external cache size
2-3-4-1	6C	Display shadow message
2-3-4-3	6E	Display non-disposable segments
2-4-1-1	70	Display error messages
2-4-1-3	72	Check for configuration errors
2-4-2-1	74	Test real-time clock
2-4-2-3	76	Check for keyboard errors
2-4-4-1	7C	Set up hardware interrupts vectors
2-4-4-3	7E	Test coprocessor if present
3-1-1-1	80	Disable onboard I/O ports
3-1-1-3	82	Detect and install external RS232 ports
3-1-2-1	84	Detect and install external parallel ports
3-1-2-3	86	Re-initialize onboard I/O ports
3-1-3-1	88	Initialize BIOS Data Area
3-1-3-3	8A	Initialize Extended BIOS Data Area
3-1-4-1	8C	Initialize floppy controller
3-2-1-1	90	Initialize hard-disk controller
3-2-1-2	91	Initialize local-bus hard-disk controller
3-2-1-3	92	Jump to UserPatch2
3-2-2-1	94	Disable A20 address line
3-2-2-3	96	Clear huge ES segment
3-2-3-1	98	Search for option ROMs
3-2-3-3	9A	Shadow option ROMs
3-2-4-1	9C	Set up Power Management
3-2-4-3	9E	Enable hardware interrupts
3-3-1-1	A0	Set time of day
3-3-1-3	A2	Check key lock
3-3-3-1	A8	Erase F2 prompt
3-3-3-3	AA	Scan for F2 key stroke
3-3-4-1	AC	Enter SETUP
3-3-4-3	AE	Clear in-POST flag
3-4-1-1	B0	Check for errors
3-4-1-3	B2	POST done--prepare to boot operating system
3-4-2-1	B4	One beep
3-4-2-3	B6	Check password (optional)

3-4-3-1	B8	Clear global descriptor table
3-4-4-1	BC	Clear parity checkers
3-4-4-3	BE	Clear screen (optional)
3-4-4-4	BF	Check virus and backup reminders
4-1-1-1	C0	Try to boot with INT 19
4-2-1-1	D0	Interrupt handler error
4-2-1-3	D2	Unknown interrupt error
4-2-2-1	D4	Pending interrupt error
4-2-2-3	D6	Initialize option ROM error
4-2-3-1	D8	Shutdown error
4-2-3-3	DA	Extended Block Move
4-2-4-1	DC	Shutdown 10 error
		Flash BIOS Integrity Test
4-3-1-3	E2	Initialize the chipset
4-3-1-4	E3	Initialize refresh counter
4-3-2-1	E4	Check for Forced Flash
4-3-2-2	E5	Check HW status of ROM
4-3-2-3	E6	BIOS ROM is OK
4-3-2-4	E7	Do a complete RAM test
		Flash recovery
4-3-3-1	E8	Do OEM initialization
4-3-3-2	E9	Initialize interrupt controller
4-3-3-3	EA	Read in bootstrap code
4-3-3-4	EB	Initialize all vectors
4-3-4-1	EC	Boot the Flash program
4-3-4-2	ED	Initialize the boot device
4-3-4-3	EE	Boot code was read OK

Phoenix v4.0

Beeps	Code	Meaning
1-1-1-3	02	Verify Real Mode
1-1-2-1	04	Get CPU type
1-1-2-3	06	Initialize system hardware
1-1-3-1	08	Initialize chipset registers with initial POST values
1-1-3-2	09	Set in POST flag
1-1-3-3	0A	Initialize CPU registers
1-1-4-1	0C	Initialize cache to initial POST values
1-1-4-3	0E	Initialize I/O
1-2-1-1	10	Initialize Power Management
1-2-1-2	11	Load alternate registers with initial POST values
1-2-1-3	12	Jump to UserPatch0
1-2-2-1	14	Initialize keyboard controller
1-2-2-3	16	BIOS ROM checksum
1-2-3-1	18	8254 timer initialization
1-2-3-3	1A	8237 DMA controller initialization
1-2-4-1	1C	Reset Programmable Interrupt Controller
1-3-1-1	20	Test DRAM refresh
1-3-1-3	22	Test 8742 Keyboard Controller

1-3-2-1	24	Set ES segment to register to 4 GB
1-3-3-1	28	Autosize DRAM
1-3-3-3	2A	Clear 512K base RAM
1-3-4-1	2C	Test 512 base address lines
1-3-4-3	2E	Test 512K base memory
1-4-1-3	32	Test CPU bus-clock frequency
1-4-2-4	37	Reinitialize the chipset
1-4-3-1	38	Shadow system BIOS ROM
1-4-3-2	39	Reinitialize the cache
1-4-3-3	3A	Autosize cache
1-4-4-1	3C	Configure advanced chipset registers
1-4-4-2	3D	Load alternate registers with CMOS values
2-1-1-1	40	Set Initial CPU speed
2-1-1-3	42	Initialize interrupt vectors
2-1-2-1	44	Initialize BIOS interrupts
2-1-2-3	46	Check ROM copyright notice
2-1-2-4	47	Initialize manager for PCI Options ROMs
2-1-3-1	48	Check video configuration against CMOS
2-1-3-2	49	Initialize PCI bus and devices
2-1-3-3	4A	Initialize all video adapters in system
2-1-4-1	4C	Shadow video BIOS ROM
2-1-4-3	4E	Display copyright notice
2-2-1-1	50	Display CPU type and speed
2-2-1-3	52	Test keyboard
2-2-2-1	54	Set key click if enabled
2-2-2-3	56	Enable keyboard
2-2-3-1	58	Test for unexpected interrupts
2-2-3-3	5A	Display prompt "Press F2 to enter SETUP"
2-2-4-1	5C	Test RAM between 512 and 640k
2-3-1-1	60	Test expanded memory
2-3-1-3	62	Test extended memory address lines
2-3-2-1	64	Jump to UserPatch1
2-3-2-3	66	Configure advanced cache registers
2-3-3-1	68	Enable external and CPU caches
2-3-3-3	6A	Display external cache size
2-3-4-1	6C	Display shadow message
2-3-4-3	6E	Display non-disposable segments
2-4-1-1	70	Display error messages
2-4-1-3	72	Check for configuration errors
2-4-2-1	74	Test real-time clock
2-4-2-3	76	Check for keyboard errors
2-4-4-1	7C	Set up hardware interrupts vectors
2-4-4-3	7E	Test coprocessor if present
3-1-1-1	80	Disable onboard I/O ports
3-1-1-3	82	Detect and install external RS232 ports
3-1-2-1	84	Detect and install external parallel ports
3-1-2-3	86	Re-initialize onboard I/O ports
3-1-3-1	88	Initialize BIOS Data Area

3-1-3-3	8A	Initialize Extended BIOS Data Area
3-1-4-1	8C	Initialize floppy controller
3-2-1-1	90	Initialize hard-disk controller
3-2-1-2	91	Initialize local-bus hard-disk controller
3-2-1-3	92	Jump to UserPatch2
3-2-2-1	94	Disable A20 address line
3-2-2-3	96	Clear huge ES segment
3-2-3-1	98	Search for option ROMs
3-2-3-3	9A	Shadow option ROMs
3-2-4-1	9C	Set up Power Management
3-2-4-3	9E	Enable hardware interrupts
3-3-1-1	A0	Set time of day
3-3-1-3	A2	Check key lock
3-3-3-1	A8	Erase F2 prompt
3-3-3-3	AA	Scan for F2 key stroke
3-3-4-1	AC	Enter SETUP
3-3-4-3	AE	Clear in-POST flag
3-4-1-1	B0	Check for errors
3-4-1-3	B2	POST done--prepare to boot operating system
3-4-2-1	B4	One beep
3-4-2-3	B6	Check password (optional)
3-4-3-1	B8	Clear global descriptor table
3-4-4-1	BC	Clear parity checkers
3-4-4-3	BE	Clear screen (optional)
3-4-4-4	BF	Check virus and backup reminders
4-1-1-1	C0	Try to boot with INT 19
4-2-1-1	D0	Interrupt handler error
4-2-1-3	D2	Unknown interrupt error
4-2-2-1	D4	Pending interrupt error
4-2-2-3	D6	Initialize option ROM error
4-2-3-1	D8	Shutdown error
4-2-3-3	DA	Extended Block Move
4-2-4-1	DC	Shutdown 10 error
		Flash BIOS Integrity Test
4-3-1-3	E2	Initialize the chipset
4-3-1-4	E3	Initialize refresh counter
4-3-2-1	E4	Check for Forced Flash
4-3-2-2	E5	Check HW status of ROM
4-3-2-3	E6	BIOS ROM is OK
		Flash recovery
4-3-2-4	E7	Do a complete RAM test
4-3-3-1	E8	Do OEM initialization
4-3-3-2	E9	Initialize interrupt controller
4-3-3-3	EA	Read in bootstrap code
4-3-3-4	EB	Initialize all vectors
4-3-4-1	EC	Boot the Flash program
4-3-4-2	ED	Initialize the boot device
4-3-4-3	EE	Boot code was read OK

POST Codes

Quadtel

v3.07 AT BIOS (Phoenix 3.07)

Code	Meaning
02	Flag test
04	Register test
06	System hardware initialisation
08	Initialise chipset registers
0A	BIOS ROM checksum
0C	DMA page register test
0E	8254 timer test
10	8254 timer initialisation
12	8237 DMA controller test
14	8237 DMA initialisation
16	Initialise 8259/reset coprocessor
18	8259 interrupt controller test
1A	Memory refresh test
1C	Base 64K address test
1E	Base 64K memory test
20	Base 64K test (upper 16 bits) for 386 systems
22	8742 keyboard self test
24	MC 146818 CMOS test
26	Start first protected mode test
28	Memory sizing test
2A	Autosize memory chips
2C	Chip interleave enable test
2E	First protected mode test exit
30	Unexpected shutdown
31	DDNIL bit scan failure
32	System board memory size
34	Relocate shadow RAM if configured
36	Configure EMS system
38	Configure wait states
3A	Retest 64K base RAM
3C	CPU speed calculation
3E	Get switches from 8042
40	Configure CPU speed
42	Initialise interrupt vectors
44	Verify video configuration
46	Initialise video system
48	Test unexpected interrupts
4A	Start second protected mode test
4C	Verify LDT instruction
4E	Verify TR instruction
50	Verify LSL instruction
52	Verify LAR instruction
54	Verify VERR instruction
56	Unexpected exception
58	Address line 20 test

5A	Keyboard ready test
5C	Determine AT or XT keyboard
5E	Start third protected mode test
60	Base memory test
62	Base memory address test
64	Shadow memory test
66	Extended memory test
68	Extended address test
6A	Determine memory size
6C	Display error messages
6E	Copy BIOS to shadow memory
70	8254 clock test
72	MC 146818 RTC test
74	Keyboard stuck key test
76	Initialise hardware interrupt vectors
78	Maths coprocessor test
7A	Determine COM ports available
7C	Determine LPT ports available
7E	Initialise BIOS data area
80	Determine floppy/fixed disk controller
82	Floppy disk test
84	Fixed disk test
86	External ROM scan
88	System key lock test
8A	Wait for <F1> key pressed
8C	Final system initialisation
8E	Interrupt 19 boot loader
B0	Unexpected interrupt before or after boot up.

16K XT

Code	Meaning
03	Test flag register
06	Test CPU Register
09	Initialize system hardware
0C	Test BIOS ROM checksum
0F	Initialize 8237 DMA page register
12	Test 8237 address and count registers
15	Initialize 8237 DMA
18	Test 8253 timer
1B	Initialize 8253 timer
1E	Start memory refresh test
21	Test base 64K RAM, Cycling POST display shows POST code, the upper then lower bytes of the failing address, separated by delays
24	Set up common INT temp stack
27	Initialize 8259 interrupt controller
2A	Test interrupt mask register
2D	Test for hot (unexpected) interrupt
30	Test V40 DMA if present

341

31	Test for DDNIL bits present
33	Verify system clock interrupt
36	Test keyboard
39	Set up interrupt table
3C	Read system configuration switches
3F	Test video
42	Determine COM ports available
45	Determine LPT ports available
48	Determine if game port available
4B	Display copyright message
4E	Calculate CPU speed
54	Test system memory
55	Test floppy drive
57	Initialize system before boot
5A	Call Interrupt 19 boot loader

SuperSoft

PC/XT/AT

	XT	AT
11	CPU register or logic error	CPU register or logic
12	ROM POST checksum error	ROMPOST A checksum error
13	8253 timer channel 0 error	ROMPOST B checksum error
14	8253 timer channel 1 error	8254 timer channel 0 error
15	8253 timer channel 2 error	8254 timer channel 1 error
16	8237A DMA controller error	8254 timer channel 2 error
17	8255 parity error detected	8237A DMA controller 1 err
18	16K critical RAM region error	8237A DMA controller 2 err
19	Memory refresh error	DMA page registers error
1A	-	8042 parity error detected
21	8259 Interrupt controller error	16K critical RAM region
22	Unexpected interrupt detected	Memory refresh error
23	Interrupt 0 (timer) error	CPU protected mode error
24	Nonmaskable interrupt error	8259 Interrupt controller 1 err
25	MDA video memory error	8259 Interrupt controller 2 err
26	CGA video memory error	Unexpected interrupt detected
27	EGA/VGA memory error	Interrupt 0 (timer) error
28	8087 math chip error	CMOS real time clock error
29	Keyboard controller error	Nonmaskable interrupt error
2A	-	80x87 math chip error
31	Keyboard scan lines/stuck key	Keyboard controller error
32	Floppy controller error	Stuck key or CMOS RAM err
33	Floppy disk read error	Floppy controller error
34	Memory error at address x	Floppy disk read error
35	Slow refresh, address x	MDA video memory error
36, 37	-	CGA, EGA/VGA RAM error

38	-	BIOS checksum error
41	BIOS checksum error	Memory error at address x
42	BASIC ROM 1 checksum	Slow refresh, address x
43-45	BASIC ROM 2, 3, 4	Display pass count
59	No monitor	No monitor

TANDON

Slimline 286, 386SX and 486; 486 EISA

Type A AT 29 Feb 1988

Code	Meaning
01	Test 80286 CPU flags and registers
02	Test BIOS ROM checksum
03	Test MC146818 CMOS RAM battery (RTC)
04	Test 8254 timer
05	8254 timer test failed
06	Initialize RAM refresh
07	Test first 16K RAM
08	Initialize cold boot interrupt vectors
09	Test 8259 interrupt controller and interrupt vectors
0A	Fill in temporary interrupt vectors
0B	Initialize interrupt vector table 1
0C	Initialize interrupt vector table 2
0D	Initialize fixed disk vector
0E	Interrupt vector test failed
0F	Clear keyboard controller input buffer
10	Keyboard controller input buffer clearing failed
11	Run keyboard controller self-test
12	Initialize equipment check data area
13	Determine presence of and install 80287 math coprocessor
14	Test MC146818 CMOS RAM disk value range
15	Test for and install parallel port
16	Test for and install serial port
17	Invoke INT 19 to boot operating system

Type B AT—1992

Code	Meaning
01	Cold boot started
06	Initialize chipset if any
07	Warm boot entry. About to start 8042 keyboard controller self-test
08	Part of cold boot keyboard initialization passed
09	Keyboard self-test finished. Test ROM BIOS checksum.
0A	Test CMOS RAM battery level
0B	Save CMOS RAM battery condition in CMOS diagnostic/status register
0C	Finished saving CMOS RAM battery condition
0D	Test 8254 PIT. Disable RAM parity, I/O parity, DMA controllers, and speaker; enable timer channel 2.
0E, AA, xx	8245 test failed. xx is the failing channel number.

343

0F	Initialize 8254 timer channels (0 to mode 3 for 55 ms square wave, 1 to mode 2 as rate generator for refresh) and conduct memory refresh test.
10	Refresh test failed
11	Test base 64K RAM and fill with zeros
12	64K RAM test failed. 3 long beeps and halt.
13	RAM test passed
14	Set up stack, disable mappers for systems that support EMS drivers (for warm boot), initialize battery beep flag parameters for notebook, perform read/write test of CMOS RAM, enable error message if failed.
15	CMOS RAM read/write test complete
16	Calculating CPU speed; may set to low if CMOS RAM failed
18	Test and initialize both 8259 interrupt controllers
1A	8259 initialization complete
1B	Install interrupt handler and vector for INT 0F to check for unexpected (spurious) interrupts. Halt if spurious interrupt occurs.
1C	Spurious interrupt did not occur (test pass). Test 8254 timer channel 0, IRQ0, and software INT8 tests.
1D	Error. Timer 0 interrupt did not occur when expected. Halt system.
1E	Both 8259 interrupt controllers passed the tests
20	Set up interrupt vectors 02-1F
21	Set up interrupt vectors 70-77
22	Clear interrupt vectors for 41 and 46 (disk parameter pointers).
23	Read 8042 self-test result, DMA page reg ch 2 (port 81).
24	Test for proper 8042 self-test result (55).
25	Error: Keyboard controller self-test failed, display message and halt.
26	Keyboard controller self-test passed
27	Confirm DMA working; prepare DMA channel 2 for floppy data transfer
28	Reinitialize video (cold boot)
29	Reinitialize video with cursor off (warm boot)
2A	Video parameters are initialized
2B	Enable NMI and I/O channel check, disable 8254 timer channel 2 and speaker
2C	Run RAM test to determine size of RAM
2D	RAM sizing complete
2E	Send reset command to keyboard controller to initiate a keyboard scan cycle
2F	Keyboard has been initialized. Initialize the CMOS RTC
30	CMOS RTC has been initialized. Initialize on-board floppy if any
31	Install the hard disk controller
32	Disk controller has been installed; prepare DMA channel 2 for floppy transfers
33	Perform equipment check and initialize numeric data processor (math chip)
34	Install the serial/parallel ports
35	Test CMOS RAM battery level
36	Check for keypress—Esc=Setup, Spacebar=menu; do speed beeps 2=high, 1=low
37	Enable 8254 timer channel 0 for system tick, enable keyboard and slave interrupt controller 8259 #2
38	Timer tick, keyboard and 8259 #2 have been enabled; enable/disable cache per CMOS RAM
39	Enable keyboard interface and interrupts. Go to built-in Setup program as necessary; shadow ROMs as appropriate.
3A	Setup finished, so clear the screen and display Please Wait message

3B	Test the fixed and floppy drives
3C	Scan for and invoke the adapter ROMs in C800-E000
3D	Turn off Gate A20; restore vectors 3bh-3fh with temporary interrupt service routines.
3E	Gate A20 is turned off
3F	Invoke INT19 to boot operating system.

These accompanied by 5 long beeps:

Code	Meaning
BF	486-based, 386SX/20c or 386SX/25c processor module boards are used in a system where the WD76C10 chipset is not revision F or above.
CF	CPU on a 486-based processor module has failed its internal self-test.
DF	386SX/20c or 386SX/25c processor module board failed correctly to initialize its on-board cache (bad cache RAM. illegal configuration, etc., or unknown module ID).
EF	Extended CMOS RAM within the WD76C10 chipset failed its self-test

486 EISA—10 Oct 1989

Code	Meaning
	Power on or system reset: enable 8042, RTC; disable 82C601 chip serial, parallel, floppy, hard drive, NMI; check 8042 status.
AA, 01, xx	Show 80486 BIST (built-in self-test) result: xx=00 if OK, FF if not.
01	Disable cache, enable ROM, high speed on, turn off caches, disable EISA NMIs, set master and slave IRQs to edge-triggered, disable reset chaining. disable 82C601 chip but set it valid.
05	Initialize address decoder, 640K RAM; set BIOS as cacheable, enable extended memory.
06	Clear Shutdown Flag.
07	8042 and keyboard test: wait till 8042 buffer empty, disable 8042 command, read 8042 output buffer, set response OK to DMA page reg channel 2.
08	Send 8042 NOP command, self-test command; get 8042 self-test result, send to DMA page reg channel 2.
AA, 01, xx	Show 8042 self-test result: xx=55 if OK
09	Test BIOS ROM checksum; 3 short beeps and halt if bad
0A	Read CMOS registers 3 times to clear pending CMOS RTC interrupts, and disable RTC interrupts. Check battery.
0B	Bad CMOS RAM battery.
0C	Send command to port 61 to disable parity and speaker, enable timer; disable DMA.
0D	Test 8254 counter timer: set all 3 counters to mode 3 (square wave), start them and read the counts.
0E	A counter timer is bad (at least one is 0 and not counting).
AA, 01, xx	Show the failing counter address (xx = 40, 41, or 42), then beep long-short-long-short and halt.
0F	Enable and check memory refresh (set timer 1 to mode 2 for 15 microsecond refresh, and turn on DMA to perform it); delay 1 millisecond and check bit 4 of port 61 for 0-to-1 toggle.
10	Memory refresh failed (no toggle); beep short-long-short, and halt.
11	Check and clear the first 64K of RAM in real mode: disable NMI, clear parity latches, fill 64K with 5555 and check it, then AAAA and check it, then 0000.
AA, 06, mmnn, oopp, qqrr	First 64K memory test failed. mmnn=location lsb, msb; oopp= value read lsb, msb; qqrr=value expected lsb, msb.

AA, 01, xx	Test port 61 for parity error (bits 7, 6=1) and display error xx=value read from port 61 if parity error occurred.
12	First 64K memory test failed. Clear parity latches, give 3 long beeps, and halt.
13	First 64K memory test passed.
14	Reset the warm boot flag (40:72) and test CMOS RAM. Turn off caches, shadow the BIOS, set speed high, calculate high speed and initialize GP flag, set speed low and turn off cache if CMOS not good or CMOS speed not high, otherwise turn on cache and set speed high.
16	Check Shutdown Flag 123x.
17	Reset was cold boot. Set 40:e9 bit 7 (disk_status).
18	Prepare 8259 interrupt controllers; send FF to mask register and check it.
19	Interrupt controller initialization failed; initialize video, display the error message, and halt.
1A	Test interrupt controller: set all 256 ints to slipped interrupt vector. If warm boot (40:e9 bit 7), skip to POST 1E.
1B	Set int 0F to spurious interrupt vector, check for spurious interrupts.
1C	Set int 08 (timer 0) to timer 0 int vector, enable timer and int, wait for int from timer.
1D	Timer interrupt did not occur. Initialize video, display error message and halt.
1E	Initialize interrupt vectors.
1F	Initialize interrupt vectors 00-6F to temporary interrupt service routine.
20	Set vectors for interrupt 02-1F.
21	Set interrupt vectors for 70-77, clear vectors 60-67 and 78-FF.
22	Clear interrupt vectors for 41 and 46 (disk parameter pointers).
23	Read 8042 self-test result from DMA page reg ch 2 (port 81).
24	Test for proper 8042 self-test result (55).
25	8042 self-test failed. Get keyboard controller status, initialize video, display error message, and halt.
26	Initialize 8042 keyboard controller, transfer 128K mem. exp. bit from 8042 to CMOS RAM (IBM compatible, but not used), read state of security switch and initialize RAM variable.
27	Check Shutdown Flag = 123x. No= cold boot.
28	If cold boot or CMOS RAM is bad, install video ROM and establish video, initialize equipment flags according to primary video adapter and CMOS RAM content, initialize POST status, initialize video.
29	If not cold boot and CMOS RAM is OK, install Video ROM and establish video for mono/CGA, initialize equipment flags according to primary video adapter and CMOS RAM contents, initialize video warm boot, initialize video.
2A	Check for bad CMOS RAM and queue the message if so; command port 61 to clear parity latches, disable the speaker and disable timer channel 2; enable NMI.
2B	Check Shutdown Flag = 123x. if warm boot, use memory sizes from CMOS RAM.
2C	If cold boot, turn caches off, test memory for appropriate size, and restore cache status.
2D	Turn off "POST Fail" CMOS RAM bit and display any queued error messages; initialize keyboard RAM (40:17-30) + (40:E0-E7).
2E	Initialize 8042 keyboard controller and test keyboard.
2F	Initialize time of day in the real time clock chip.
30	Test for and install floppy controller.
31	Enable C&T 82C601 chip IDE interface, test for and install hard drive.
32	Test 8259 DMA registers with 55 then AA, and initialize them to 0 (ports D2 and D4).
33	Test for and initialize math coprocessor chip
34	Test for and initialize parallel and serial ports, on and off board.

35	Initialize RAM variables for bad CMOS time, date, checksum, and battery condition.
36	Wait for user to press Esc, space. Check keyboard lock, clear the keyboard lock override, beep to indicate speed, display any queued messages. Esc=setup, space=boot menu.
37	Enable system clock tick (IRQ0), keyboard (IRQ1), and slave interrupt controller (IRQ2)
38	Initialize RAM variables for Ctrl-Alt-Esc, Ctrl-Alt-Ins
39	Enter setup if user pressed Ctrl-Alt-Esc. If EISA, revert to ISA if tab key pressed.
3A	Clear screen and update equipment flags according to CMOS contents (may have changed during setup). Shadow any ROMs per setup. Enable/disable cache per CMOS RAM.
3B	Initialize floppy and fixed disk drives.
3C	Set POST Fail bit in CMOS RAM, then scan for and invoke adapter option ROMs.
3D	Clear the Shutdown Flag to 0, turn off gate A20 to enable memory wrap in real mode.
3E	Set vectors for interrupts 3B-3F, clear Post Fail bit in CMOS RAM, home the cursor, display any error messages, clear MSW of 32-bit registers (ISC Unix).
3F	Invoke INT 19 to boot operating system.

TANDY

Uses OEM version of Phoenix BIOS.

WYSE

Uses OEM version of Phoenix BIOS.

ZENITH

LEDs on system board to indicate the status of various stages of boot-up. All will light up first of all, then go out in sequence when the test concerned is completed. Zenith computers may also use an AMI (Plus, normally) or a Phoenix BIOS.

Post Procedures

Procedure	Meaning
CPU	Perform a read/write test on the internal register. Check for defective CPU or clock generator.
ROM BIOS	Check the CRC value stored in ROM against the computed value of this test. Check the BIOS or I/O circuitry.
RAM	Check first 64K of memory to see that data can be stored in it so the BIOS can use it later.
DMA	Test the register functions of the DMA chips.

PIT/PIC	Perform tests on the main support chips and enable the appropriate interrupts when completed. Check also for AC ripple.
RTC/CMOS	Check the validity of the CMOS RAM and compare value in CMOS with appropriate devices. The BIOS will use the values from the CMOS to set up appropriate IRQ routines for disk and other I/O access. Check for defective CMOS/battery/adapter or CMOS setting.
Video Display	Attempts will be made to initialise video to a mono screen very early on so error messages can be displayed. This test is for initialising upper video modes available with EGA/VGA.
Test/Boot to Diskette	Check the floppy subsystem and prepare the drive for boot if there is a bootable floppy in the A: drive.
Boot to Fixed Disk	Initialise any fixed disks in the CMOS and give control to the first one if a bootable floppy has not been detected previously. Check for corrupt boot code if not a hardware error.

POST Codes

Code	Meaning
01	VGA check
02	MDA initialise
03	Initialise video
05	Set hard reset
07	Check ROM at E000
08	Check ROM shadow at F000
09	Remap video to E000
0B	Keyboard controller test
0C	CMOS/8042 test
0D	DMA test
0E	DMA page register
0F	Test 64K memory
10	Test base memory
11	Second VGA unit
12	Mono initialisation
13	RTC/CMOS test
15	CPU register test
16	CPU add test
17	RTC/8042 test
18	Enter protected mode
19	Testing memory
1A	Testing extended memory
1B	Leaving protected mode
1C	Testing system board
1D	Testing system board
1E	Testing system board
1F	Bus sizing
20	Set BIOS data area
21	Testing DMA
22	Checking C800 for ROM
24	Testing base memory
25	8042 test

26	8042 test
27	8042 test
28	Memory parity test
29	PIT test
2A	Testing floppy disk
2B	Testing FDC/drives
2C	Testing HDC/drives
2D	Checking CMOS settings
2E	Soft configuration
30	Checking adapter ROM
31	Checking CMOS settings
32	Enabling interrupts
33	Soft configuration
34	Soft configuration
35	Jump to boot code
00	Boot to OS

Orion 4.1E—1992

Checkpoints 00h-1Fh and F0h-FFh are displayed after the indicated function is completed.

Code	Meaning
02	Cold Boot, Enter Protected Mode
03	Do Machine Specific Initialization
F0	Start of Basic HW Initialization for Boot
F1	Clear CMOS Pre-Slush Status Location
F2	Starting CLIO Initialization
F3	Initialize SYSCFG Register
F4	DXPI Initialization for Boot Block
F5	Turning OFF Cache
F6	Configure CPU Socket Pins
F7	Checking for 387SX
F8	82C206 DEFAULT Initialization
F9	Superior Default Initialization
FF	End of Machine-specific Boot Block
04	Check Flash Checksum
05	
06	Reset or Power-Up
07	CLIO Default init command
08	SYSCFG REG initialised
09	CMOS Pre-slush error words initialisation
10	SCP initialised
11	DRAM autosizing complete
12	Parity check enabled. Enable Memory Parity (EMP) LED turned off
13	Start of slushware test
14	Slushware at 000F0000h OK
15	BIOS ROM copied to slushware
16	Back in Real Mode
17	ROM BIOS Slushing is finished. CPU LED Turned off
18	Video ROM (C0000 Slushware Test

19	Internal Video ROM Slushed
1A	Back in Real Mode
1B	Internal video hardware enabled.
1C	CPU clock frequency determined
1E	BIOS RAM cleared

20-EF are displayed before the indicated function has been attempted. 20-2A indicate restart after system shutdown, usually to return to real mode from protected mode. The CMOS RAM shutdown byte (0F) will contain a value indicating the reason for the shutdown.

Code	Meaning
20	RESET (CMOS 0)
21	Continue after Setting Memory Size (CMOS 0F=1)
22	Continue after Memory Test (CMOS 0F=2)
23	Continue after Memory Error (CMOS 0F=3)
24	Continue with Boot Loader Request (CMOS 0F=4)
25	
26	Continue after Protected Mode Test Passed (CMOS 0F=6)
27	Continue after Protected Mode Test Failed (CMOS 0F=7)
28	Continue after Extended Protected Mode Test (CMOS 0F=8)
29	Continue after Block Move (CMOS 0F=9)
2A	
2B	Reserved
2C	Reserved
2D	Reserved
2E	Reserved
2F	Reserved
30	Exit from Protected Mode
31	TEST-RESET passed (80386). Warm Boot
32	Check the ROM Checksum. ROM LED Turned Off
33	Clear the Video Screen On
34	Check System DRAM Config Update CMOS-TOTAL-MEM-SIZE Value
35	Pro-load CMOS if CMOS is
36	Turn Off the UMB RAM
37	Turn Parity Generation
38	Initialize System Variable
39	Check for errors in POWER
3A	Initialize SCP MODE
3B	Test CMOS Diag. Power Reset
3C	Test CPU Reset 80386 & Determine State Number
3D	Save CPU ID & Processor-T
3E	Init the Video & Timers
3F	Init DMA Ports, Clear Page
40	Set Speed too Fast for Now
41	Test EEPROM Checksum
42	Enable/Disable Superior's Parallel, FDC & HDC Per CMOS
43	Slush External Video BIOS if on CMOS
44	Turn Cache off for Memory
45	Test Extended RAM (1-16Mb)

46	Test BASE RAM (0-64 OK). RAM LED turned off by Base RAM Test
47	Determine Amount of System
48	Set WARM-BOOT Flag if RES Indicates Cold Boot
49	Clear 16K of Base RAM
4A	Install BIOS Interrupt Vector
4B	Test System Timer. INT LED turned off if CLOCK Test passes
4C	(Re)Initialize Interrupt
4D	Enable Default Hardware Initialization
4E	Determine Global I/O Configuration
4F	Initialize Video
50	Init WD90C30 Scratchpad
51	Check for Errors before Boot
52	Reserved
53	Test (Ext Only) and Initialize
54	Reserved
55	Initialize the Keyboard Processor
56	Initialize the PS/2 Mouse
57	Configure CLIO for Mouse
58	Configure CLIO for LAN
59	Configure CLIO for SCSI
5A	Configure CLIO for WAM
5B	
5C	Init System Clock TOD, Enable
5D	Test, Init Floppy Drive Sensor. Disk LED Turned off
5E	Check for Z150 Style Disk
5F	Init Winchester Subsystem
60	Set Default I/O Device Parameters
61	Get LAN ID Info from LAN
62	*Install ROMs at 0C8000h
63	*Install ROMs at 0E000h
64	Initialize SCSI Interface
65	Run with A2O off in PC Mode
66	Really turn off the SCP
67	Set Machine Speed using CMOS
68	Turn on Cache
69	Calibrate 1ms Constants
6A	*Enable Non-Maskable Interpreter
6B	Reserved
6C	Clear the warm-boot flag
6D	Check for Errors before Boot
6E	Boot

191 BIOS -1992

Code	Meaning
0	Start of Slush Test
1	Processor Test
2	CACHE and CLIO
3	ISP Defaults Set

4	Into Protected Mode
5	Memory SIMMs Count
6	Memory Controller
7	Preped to Test Block
8	First 1Mb of Ram
9	Checksum OEM ROM
10	Low Flash ROM Checks
11	F000 ROM Checks
12	Aurora VIDEO ROM
13	F000 ROM Slushed
14	Sep Initialized
15	Language Slushed
16	Do VIDEO Specific tests
17	Done Slushing
32	Point Interrupt Vectors
33	Turn on Parity Generation
34	Initialize System Variables
35	Init Interrupt Controllers
36	Check Error that Occurred
37	Reinitialize SCP Warm Boot
38	Test CMOS Diag, Power, Reset
39	Reserved, or DDNIL status flag check
3A	Test CPU Reset (80386)
3B	Save the CPU ID in GS
3C	Slush Video ROM to C0000
3D	Init the Video and Timers
3E	Init CMA Ports, Clear Page
3F	Set Speed too Fast for now
40	Checksum the Nonvolatile RAM
41	Initialize Configuration
42	Init Expansion Boards from VRAM
43	Turn Cache off for Memory Test
44	Init Memory Ctrlr, test Extd Memory
45	Test Base RAM
46	Determine amount of System RAM
47	Test and Init Cache if installed
48	Test System Timer Tick
49	Initialize the Write queues
4A	Initialize Monitor RAM
4B	Clear 16K of Base RAM
4C	Install BIOS Interrupt Vectors
4D	Enable Default Hardware Initialization
4E	Determine Global I/O configuration
4F	Reserved
50	Initialize Video
51	Init WD90C30 Scratchpad register
52	Initialise the keyboard processor
53	Turn off IRQ 12 if mouse is off

54	Wait for user to enter correct password
55	Init System Clock Time of Day
56	Test, Init Floppy System, Track Seeks
57	Init Winchester subsystem, Messages
58	Install ROMs starting at C80000H
59	Install ROM starting at E0000H
5A	Initialise SCSI interface
5B	Set default I/O Device Parameters
5C	Init the cache speed and clock
5D	Always tell System ROM 'Cold
5E	Run with A20 off in PC Mode
5F	Really turn off the SCP
60	Set machine speed using CFG
61	Turn on cache if machine halt
62	Calibrate 1ms constants
63	Enable NMI
64	Test for errors before boot
65	Boot

17 Chipsets

BIOS PART NUMBERS AND CHIPSETS

AWARD

Part Number	Chipset
2A5KBxxx	Ali 1449/61/51
2A4KCxxx	Ali 1439/45/31
2ARKDxxx	Ali 1489
2A5KE000	Ali 1511
2A4H2xxx	Contaq 82C596-9
2A499xxx	Intel Aries
2A597xxx	Intel Mercury
2A59Axxx	Intel Neptune ISA
2B59Axxx	Intel Neptune EISA
2A498xxx	Intel Saturn II
2A59Cxxx	Intel Triton
2A59Fxxx	Intel Triton II (430 HX)
2B69Dxxx	Intel Orion
2A5UIxxx	Opti 82C822/596/597
22A5UMxxx	Opti 82C822/546/547
2A5ULxxx	Opti 82C822/571/572
2A5UNxxx	Opti Viper 82C556/557/558
2C4I8xxx	SiS 471B/E
2A5IAxxx	SiS 501/02/03
2A4IBxxx	SiS 496/497
2A4X5xxx	UMC 8881/8886
2A5X7xxx	UMC 82C890
2A4L6xxx	VIA 496/406/505
2C4L2xxx	VIA 82C486A

CHIPSET MANUFACTURERS

ACC MICROELECTRONICS
(408) 980 0622

Chip	Function
82010	PC/AT 286/386 Systems
2000	Integrated peripheral controller
2100	System controller
2210	Data Bus Buffer
2220	Address Bus Buffer
82020	Hi-Speed 286/386 Chip Set
2000	Integrated peripheral controller
2120	Enhanced system controller
2210	Data Bus Buffer
2220	Address Bus Buffer
2300	Page Interleaved Memory Controller
2500	System Controller
2030	Single chip 286 System Controller
2035	Single chip 386SX System Controller
2036	486SLC/386SX/286 Single Chip AT Controller with write-back cache support
2036LV	486SLC/386SX Low Voltage Single Chip AT Controller
2046	486/386 Single Chip AT Controller
2046NT	486/386 Single Chip AT Controller with Master Mode Local Bus
2046LV	486/386 Low Voltage Single Chip AT Controller
2086	486/386 Super Chip
2168	486/386 Single Chip AT Controller
2168DT	486/386 Single Chip AT Controller with Master Mode Local Bus
3201	Floppy Disk Formatter/Controller for AT and XT
3221SP	Data Processor, 100 PQFP
3221DP	Data Processor, 128 PQFP
3221EP	Data Processor, 144 PQFP
16C451	Multifunction I/O controller for AT and XT
16C452	Multifunction I/O controller for AT and XT
2020	Power Management Chip

ACER LABORATORIES INC (ALI)

(408) 434 0190

The **M1487/1489** chips are used in 486 systems, as is the **Finali**. Watch for slow cache controllers. The **Aladdin** chipset is used in Pentium systems. The **Genie** is for multiprocessing systems. If able to handle the Cyrix 6x86MX at 233 MHz, can run the bus at 75 MHz, keeping the peripherals at 33 MHz.

Chip	Function
M5105	Super I/O
M1207	Single Chip AT Controller with LIM 4 support
M1209	Single Chip 386sx PC/AT Controller
M1401/M1403	Dual Chip 386 Controller with cache control
M1385DX	High Performance cache controller for DX processors
M1385SX	cache controller for SX systems
A90	Notebook System Controller

AUSTEK

(408) 988 8556

Chip	Function
A38202SX	Cache controller
A38403	Cache controller

CHIPS & TECHNOLOGIES

(408) 434 0600

Chip	Function
82A235	Single Chip AT (SCAT)
82C836	Single Chip AT (SCAT SX)
84025	Data Buffer
84021	Bus/DRAM Controller
CS8221	Neat Chip Set
82C211	System Controller/Extended CMOS RAM Control Logic
82C212	I/O and memory decode
82C215	Parity Logic and Address & Data Bus Buffer
82C206	Integrated Peripheral Controller (high failure rate; no booting)
CS8223	Leap Chip Set
82C421	CPU/Bus, Page/Interleave, EMS Controller and laptop support
82C242	Data/Address Buffers and Bus Conversion Logic
82C631	Data Buffer
82C636	Power Control Unit with Slow Refresh Control
82C206	Integrated Peripheral Controller
82C601	Multifunction Controller, 1 parallel and 2 serial.
82C455	VGA compatible flat panel controller
82C765	Floppy Disk Controller
CS8230	Chip Set

Chipsets

82C201	System Controller, Clock Generation, Reset/Ready Synchronisation, Command and Control Signal Generation, Conversion Logic, Wait State Control, DMA and Refresh Logic, Coprocessor Control, NMI and Error Logic.
82C202	RAM/ROM Decoder, I/O Controller, Parity Error Detection Logic, I/O Decode Logic
82C303	High Address Bus Buffer and Port B Chip, High Address Bus Buffer for A17-A23, Memory and I/O Read/Write Signal Buffer, Port B Status (61h)
82C404	Low Address Bus Buffer and Refresh Counter, Provides Drive and Buffering for A1-A16, Provides Drive for MA0-MA7, Provides Refresh Counter SA0-SA7
82A205	Data Bus Buffer/Parity Generator Chip, provides Data Bus Buffer and Driver for D0-D15 >SD0-SD15 >MD0-MD15, ENHLB DIRHLB-Byte Conversion Logic, Parity Gen/Check Logic
CS8233	PEAK 386/AT Chip Set
82C311	CPU, cache, DRAM Controller
82C316	Peripheral Controller
82C315	Bus Controller
82C452	Super VGA Controller
82C601	Single Chip Peripheral Controller
82C765	Single Chip Floppy Disk Controller
CS82235	NEAT Chip Set
82C100	System Controller
82C202	Memory Controller
82C205	Data Buffer
82A203	Address Buffer
82A204	Address Buffer
82C322	Memory Controller
82C325	Data Buffer
82C223	DMA Controller
82C321	CPU Controller (MCA)
82C302	System Controller
82A305	Data Buffer
82A303	Address Buffer
82A304	Address Buffer
82C307	Cache/DRAM Controller

CONTAQ

The 82C599 is used in 486s with VL Buses.

ELITE

(408) 943 0500

Chip	Function
88C311	CPU/Cache/DRAM Controller
88C312	Data Controller

FARADAY (WD)

Chip	Function
FE 3600B	Chip Set
FE 3001	System Controller
FE 3010	Peripheral Controller
FE 3021	Address Bus and Memory Control Logic
FE 3031	Parity and Data Bus Controller

G-2 INC/HEADLAND

(408) 743 3355

Chip	Function
GC 102	Data/Address Buffer
GC 131	Peripheral Controller
GC 132	CPU/Memory Controller
GC 133	Bus Controller

HEADLAND

Chip	Function
HT 10	Super XT Controller
HT 11/12	Super AT Controller
HT 15	Single Chip Controller
HT 216	VGA Controller
HT 21/22	Single Chip Controller
HT 101SX	Peripheral Controller
HT 102	Data Buffer
HT 113	Memory Manager
HT 131	Peripheral Controller
HT 132	CPU/Memory Controller
HT 133	Bus Controller

INTEL

(408) 765 8080

www.intel.com

The **Aries** chipset is for 486s, typically used where VL Bus and PCI live together (the VL Bus is attached to a PCI-CPU bridge). Watch for problems with zero wait state operation.

The **Saturn** is for the 486, up to DX/4 and maybe the P24T. With earlier versions, any problems are dealt with by turning the high performance features off! ZX identifies the Saturn II. The **Ariel** is for notebooks, similar to Triton, with advanced power management.

The **Mercury** is for 60/66 MHz Pentiums (P5s – socket 4), and the **Neptune** for 75/90/99 MHz ones (Socket 5).

The **T I/II/III** (Triton is apparently a trademark of some company in Germany) chipsets are for Pentiums. They support bus mastering IDE, with software written by Triones (check your local BBS). Parity is not checked, and neither is the cache interleaved.

Chipsets

The **T I** (430 FX) has only one bus, or timing register set, between two IDE channels, so only one device may be active at a time, even on separate channels. The data bus is also shared with ISA functions, so if you have your serial or parallel ports on the ISA bus (as one does), COM or LPT activity (or any on the ISA bus) will be multiplexed with the two ATA interfaces on the same set of signals from the T I chip.

The Triton chipset also derives timing from the PCI clock, for a minimum (fastest) cycle of 5 clocks. The maximum transfer rates achievable, in terms of Mb/sec, are:

PCI Clock	Transfer Rate
25 MHz	10 Mb/s
30 MHz	12 MB/S
33 MHz	13.3 MB/S

You might get data corruption when the Triton is configured to run Mode 4 (16.7 Mb/s) drives over approximately 11 Mb/s. About 10% slower than the HX/VX. **T II** (430 HX) is apparently a redesign of the **Neptune** chipset, and **TIII** (430 VX) supports faster cache timing and SDRAM. The HX chipset has faster memory timings than the FX, and can handle non-Intel processors, but watch out for cheaper motherboards that cut corners with degraded Tag RAM chips. The VX is between the FX and HX in terms of performance, as it has a lack of CPU-PCI buffers.

Intel's chipsets are now numbered; the Pentium/MMX uses the **430FX/VX/HX/MX** and **TX**, which is a 2-chip set building on VX/HX, adding support for ACPI and Ultra DMA, and eventually replacing them, although it appears to have timing problems with SDRAM that detract somewhat from its promised performance, though it is stable at higher speeds. Performance-wise, TX and HX chipsets are about the same, as the HX has better buffers. The TX and VX can only cache 64 Mb RAM.

The **Mars** is for the P6, similar to T I/II, but supports parity checking. The **Natoma** (440FX/KX/GX) is also for the P6, competing with Orion (450GX), which supports more processors (4, not 2). L2 cacheing is taken care of by the CPU, helping with one bottleneck, but there is no support for SDRAM.

The 440 LX (for Pentium II) supports AGP, SDRAM, PC/97 and Ultra DMA, being a combination of the best of the 430 TX and 440 FX in one chip.

	430VX	430TX	430HX	430FX	Neptune	440FX	Orion
Max RAM	128Mb	256Mb	512Mb	128Mb	512Mb	1Gb	1Gb
Max cacheable RAM	64Mb	64Mb	512Mb	64Mb	512Mb	1Gb	1Gb
Max SIMM slots	4	6	8	6	8	8	8
Max CPUs	1	1	2	1	2	6	4
ECC DRAM support	No	No	Yes	No	Parity	Yes	Yes
SDRAM support	Yes	Yes	No	No	No	No	No
Disk Support	PIIX3	PIIX4	PIIX3	PIIX2	?	PIIX3	PIIX3

Chip	Function
82093AA	I/O, for 2-processor designs only.
82371SB	PCI/ISA IDE accelerator
82442FX	Data bus accelerator
82441FX	PCI and memory controller
82371SB	IDE controller (T III)
82439HX	System Controller (T II)
82371SB	IDE controller (T II)
82437FX	System controller (T I/III)
82438FX	Data Path (T I/III)
82371FB	PCI ISA IDE accelerator (T I)
83434NX	PCI/cache/memory controller (Neptune)
83433NX	Local bus extension devices (Neptune)
823781B-G	System I/O bridge (Neptune)
823783B	System I/O bridge (Neptune)
82351	Local I/O EISA Controller
82352	Address Buffer
82353	Data Bus Controller
82357	Integrated System Peripheral Controller
82358	EISA Bus Controller
82359	DRAM Controller
82385	Cache Controller

OPTI

The **Viper** supports IDE busmastering and Type F DMA in Pentium systems, plus power management. The Viper UMA also supports BEDO and UMA. An N suffix means *Notebook*.

The **Viper** supports IDE busmastering and Type F DMA in Pentium systems, plus power management. The Viper UMA also supports BEDO and UMA. An N suffix means *Notebook*.

SAMSUNG

Chip	Function
82C822	PCI bridge
82C556	Data Buffer controller
82C206	Integrated Peripheral Controller
82C281	Memory Controller
82C283	Page Interleave Memory Controller
82C291	Memory Controller
82C381	System and Cache Memory Controller
82C382	Direct Mapped Page Interleaved Memory Controller
82C391	System Controller

82C392	Data Buffer Controller
82C491	486 System Controller with Write-Back cache controller
82C492	Data Buffer
82C493	System Controller
82C498	CPU/Cache/DRAM and System Controller.

Chip	Function
KS82C531	Cache and RAM controller

SIS (Silicon Integrated Systems)

The 486 chipset uses the 85C496 and 85C497. Watch for unstable caches and slow PCI performance, as the PCI bus is bridged to the VL-Bus. The **5570X/5571X** is for Pentium systems. If able to handle the Cyrix 6x86MX at 233 MHz, can run the bus at 75 MHz, keeping the peripherals at 33 MHz. Not much power saving.

Suntac

(0587) 55 3331 (Japan)

Chip	Function
ST62C203	System Controller
ST62C241	Bus/Memory Controller
ST62C251	Bus/Memory Controller
ST62303	System Controller
286	
ST62C201	System Bus Controller
ST62C202	Memory Controller
ST62C008	Integrated Peripheral Controller
ST62C010	Address Bus Controller
ST62BC001	System Controller
ST62BC002	High Address Buffer
ST62BC003	Low Address Buffer
ST62BC004	Data Buffer
ST62C005	I/O Control/DMA Page Register
ST62C006	Integrated Peripheral Controller
286/386SX	
GS62C101	System/Data Bus/Timer and Interrupt Controller
GS62C102	Memory/DMA and I/O Controller

Symphony Labs

(408) 986 1701

The **Rossini** chipset is for Pentium systems, a low-cost alternative to the Triton.

Chip	Function
SL82C551	Cache/memory controller
SL82C555	System I/O controller
SL82C522	Data path controller
SL82C361	System Controller

SL82C362	Bus Controller
SL82C365	Cache Controller
SL82C461	System Controller
SL82C465	Cache Controller
SL82C471	Cache/DRAM Controller
SL82C472	EISA Bus Controller
SL82C473	DRAM Controller

TEXAS INSTRUMENTS

Chip	Function
83441	Data Path Unit
83442	Memory Control Unit
TACT83443	AT Bus Interface Unit

UMC (UNITED MICROELECTRONICS)

8881/8886 chips are used in 486s.

VIA

(510) 683 3300

www.fic.com.tw

Early versions with the VT82C505 are not terribly stable. The **Apollo** is used in Pentium systems, and the **Apollo Pro** with the P6. If able to handle the Cyrix 6x86MX at 233 MHz, can run the bus at 75 MHz, keeping the peripherals at 33 MHz (VPX/97). The VP2/97 is licensed by AMD as the AMD 640, and is synchronous – arguably the best Socket 7 solution. The VP3 supports AGP with double CPU-DRAM write buffers.

Chip	Function
VT82C685	Super I/O controller
VI82C695	System/PCI controller
VT82C575M	
VT82C576M	
VT82C577M	
VT82C416	
82C486	cache/memory controller + VLB to ISA bridge
82C482	VLB to ISA bridge
82C483	DRAM controller
VT82C505	PCI to VLB bridge

VLSI

The **Wild Cat** chipset is used in Pentiums and is allegedly in between the Neptune and Triton in terms of performance.

Chipsets

chapter

18 Fixed Disk Parameter Tables

ACER v1.00

Type	Mb	Cyls	Hds	Secs	Prec	LZ
1	10.1	306	4	17	128	305
2	20.4	615	4	17	300	615
3	30.6	615	6	17	300	615
4	62.4	940	8	17	512	940
5	46.8	940	6	17	512	940
6	20.0	615	4	17	-1	615
7	30.6	462	8	17	256	511
8	30.4	733	5	17	-1	733
9	112.0	900	15	17	-1	901
10	20.4	820	3	17	-1	820
11	35.4	855	5	17	-1	855
12	49.6	855	7	17	-1	855
13	20.3	306	8	17	128	319
14	65.0	733	7	26	-1	733
16	20.3	612	4	17	0	663
17	40.5	977	5	17	300	977
18	56.7	977	7	17	-1	977
19	59.5	1024	7	17	512	1023
20	31	733	5	17	300	732
21	44	733	7	17	732	732
22	31	733	5	17	300	733
23	10	306	4	17	0	306
24	20	612	4	17	305	663
25	10	306	4	17	-1	340
26	20	612	4	17	-1	670
27	42	698	7	17	300	732
28	42	976	5	17	488	977
29	10	306	4	17	0	340
30	20	611	4	17	306	663
31	44	732	7	17	300	732
32	44	1023	5	17	-1	1023
38	42	981	5	17	-1	981
39	85	981	10	17	-1	981
40	121	761	8	39	-1	761
41	42	980	5	17	-1	980
42	112	832	8	33	-1	832
43	159	683	12	38	-1	683
44	159	512	16	38	-1	513
45	104	776	8	33	-1	776
46	212	683	16	38	-1	683
47	84.0	832	6	33	-1	832

ALR FlexCache "Z" 33 MHz

Type	Mb	Cyls	Hds	Secs	Prec	LZ
1	10.1	306	4	17	128	305
2	20.4	615	4	17	300	615
3	30.6	615	6	17	300	615
4	62.4	940	8	17	512	940
5	46.8	940	6	17	512	940
6	20.0	615	4	17	-1	615
7	30.6	462	8	17	256	511
8	30.4	733	5	17	-1	733
9	112.0	900	15	17	-1	901
10	20.4	820	3	17	-1	820
11	35.4	855	5	17	-1	855
12	49.6	855	7	17	-1	855
13	20.3	306	8	17	128	319
14	65.0	733	7	26	-1	733
16	20.3	612	4	17	0	663
17	40.5	977	5	17	300	977
18	56.7	977	7	17	-1	977
19	59.5	1024	7	17	512	1023
20	136.6	823	10	34	-1	823
21	42.5	733	7	17	300	732
22	61.0	971	5	26	-1	971

365

23	40.0	820	6	17	-1	820
24	119	1024	7	34	-1	1024
25	20.4	615	4	17	0	615
26	34.0	1024	4	17	-1	1023
28	68.0	1024	8	17	-1	1023
29	31.2	615	4	26	612	615
30	103.0	1160	7	26	-1	904
31	41.0	989	5	17	128	989
32	127.0	1020	15	17	-1	1024
33	76.0	1024	9	17	-1	1024
34	144.3	966	9	34	-1	966
35	128.2	966	8	34	-1	966
36	42.5	1024	5	17	512	1024
37	65.0	1024	5	26	-1	1024
38	300.7	611	16	63	-1	612
39	20.0	615	4	17	128	664
40	40.8	615	8	17	128	664
41	114.1	917	15	17	-1	918
42	127.3	1023	15	17	-1	1024
43	68.3	823	10	17	512	823
44	40.0	820	6	17	-1	820
45	68.0	1024	8	17	-1	1024
46	91.0	1024	7	26	-1	1024
47	141.0	288	16	63	-1	1224

ALR FlexCache 25386/dt

Type	Mb	Cyls	Hds	Secs	Prec	LZ
1	10	306	4	17	128	305
2	20	615	4	17	300	615
3	30	615	6	17	300	615
4	62	940	8	17	512	940
5	620	1630	15	52	-1	1630
6	20	615	4	17	-1	615
7	331	1630	8	17	-1	1630
8	30	733	5	17	-1	733
9	112	900	15	17	-1	901
10	20	820	3	17	-1	820
11	35	855	5	17	-1	855
12	49	855	7	17	-1	855
13	120	953	7	34	-1	953
14	65	733	7	26	-1	733
16	80	953	5	34	-1	953
17	40.5	977	5	17	300	977
18	56	977	7	17	-1	977
19	59	1024	7	17	512	1023
20	136	823	10	34	-1	823

21	42	733	7	17	300	732
22	61	971	5	26	-1	971
23	40	820	6	17	-1	820
24	119	1024	7	34	-1	1024
25	120	1022	7	34	-1	1024
26	34	1024	4	17	-1	1023
27	42	1024	5	17	-1	1023
28	68	1024	8	17	-1	1023
29	31	615	4	26	612	615
30	103	1160	7	26	-1	904
31	41	989	5	17	128	989
32	127	1020	15	17	-1	1024
33	76	1024	9	17	-1	1024
34	144	966	9	34	-1	966
35	504	1024	16	63	-1	1630
36	42	1024	5	17	512	1024
37	65	1024	5	26	-1	1024
38	300	611	16	63	-1	612
39	330	654	16	63	-1	1630
40	330	642	16	63	-1	1778
41	114	917	15	17	-1	918
42	127	1023	15	17	-1	1024
43	1768	823	1	23	05	128
44	40	820	6	17	-1	820
45	68	1024	8	17	-1	1024
46	91	1024	7	26	-1	1024
47	141.0	288	16	63	-1	1224

AMI

Type	Mb	Cyls	Hds	Secs	Prec	LZ
1		306	4	17	128	305
2		615	4	17	300	615
3		615	6	17	300	615
4		940	8	17	512	940
5		940	6	17	512	940
6		615	4	17		615
7		462	8	17	256	511
8		733	5	17		733
9		900	15	17		901
10		820	3	17		820
11		855	5	17		855
12		855	7	17		855
13		306	8	17	128	319
14		733	7	17		733
16		612	4	17	0	663
17		977	5	17	300	977

Type	Cyls	Hds	Secs	Prec	LZ
18	977	7	17		977
19	1024	7	17	512	1023
20	733	5	17	300	732
21	733	7	17	300	732
22	733	5	17	300	733
23	306	4	17	0	336
24	925	7	17	0	925
25	925	9	17		925
26	754	7	17		754
27	754	11	17		754
28	699	7	17	256	699
29	823	10	17		823
30	918	7	17		918
31	1024	11	17		1024
32	1024	15	17		1024
33	1024	5	17		1024
34	612	2	17	128	612
35	1024	9	17		1024
36	1024	8	17	512	1024
37	615	8	17	128	615
38	987	3	17		987
39	987	7	17		987
40	820	6	17		820
41	977	5	17		977
42	981	5	17		981
43	830	7	17	512	830
44	830	10	17		830
45	917	15	17		918
46	1224		17		1223

Type	Mb	Cyls	Hds	Secs	Prec	LZ
16	21	612	4	17	0	663
17	42	977	5	17	300	977
18	59	977	7	17		977
19	62	1024	7	17	512	1023
20	31	733	5	17	300	732
21	44	733	7	17	300	732
22	31	733	5	17	300	733
23	10	306	4	17	0	336
25	21	615	4	17	0	615
26	35	1024	4	17	-1	1024
27	44	1024	5	17	-1	1024
28	71	1024	8	17	-1	1024
29	35	512	8	17	256	512
30	10	615	2	17	615	615
31	43	989	5	17	0	989
32	133	1020/4*	15	17	-1	1024
35	80	1024	9	17	1024	1024
36	44	1024	5	17	512	1024
37	72	830	10	17	-1	830
38	71	823	10	17	256	824
39	21	615	4	17	128	664
40	17	615	8	17	128	664
41	119	917	5	17	-1	918
42	133	1023	15	17	-1	1024
43	71	823	10	17	512	823
44	42	820	6	17	-1	820
45	41	589	8	17	97	619
46	72	925	9	17	-1	925
47	42	699	7	17	256	925

AMSTRAD 2286 v1.10/1.11*

Type	Mb	Cyls	Hds	Secs	Prec	LZ
1	10	306	4	17	128	305
2	21	615	4	17	300	615
3	32	615	6	17	300	615
4	65	940	8	17	512	940
5	49	940	6	17	512	940
6	21	615	4	17		615
7	32	462	8	17	256	511
8	31	733	5	17		733
9	117	900	15	17		901
10	21	820	3	17		820
11	37	855	5	17		855
12	52	855	7	17		855
13	21	306	8	17	128	319
14	44	733	7	17		733

AST

Type	Mb	Cyls	Hds	Secs	Prec
1	615	4	17	300	615
2	615	6	17	300	615
3	940	8	17	512	940
4	940	6	17	512	940
5	615	4	17	N/A	615
6	462	8	17	256	511
7	733	5	17	N/A	733
8	900	15	17	N/A	901
9	1023	10	17	ALL	1024
10	968	14	17	ALL	969
11	1023	14	17	N/A	1024
12	968	16	17	ALL	969
13	733	7	17	N/A	733
14	0	0	0	0	0

15	612	4	17	ALL	663
16	977	5	17	300	977
17	1223	14	17	N/A	1224
18	1024	7	17	512	1024
19	733	5	17	300	733
20	733	7	17	300	733
21	782	4	27	N/A	782
22	805	4	26	N/A	805
23	1053	3	28	N/A	1053
24	1053	7	28	N/A	1053
25	968	7	34	ALL	969
26	1023	7	34	N/A	1024
27	1223	7	34	N/A	1224
28	1223	11	34	N/A	1224
29	1223	13	34	N/A	1224
30	989	5	17	ALL	989
31	969	9	34	ALL	969
32	1023	5	34	ALL	1024
33	1223	15	34	N/A	1224
34	1024	9	17	1024	1024
35	745	4	28	N/A	745
36	824	8	33	N/A	824
37	823	10	17	256	824
38	1631	15	48	N/A	1632
39	615	8	17	128	664
40	917	15	17	N/A	918
41	1023	15	17	N/A	1024
42	776	8	33	N/A	776
43	820	6	17	N/A	820
44	1024	8	17	N/A	1024
45	925	9	17	N/A	925
46	1024	5	17	N/A	1024

AWARD 1.10/3.0B

Type	Mb	Cyls	Hds	Secs	Prec	LZ
1	10	306	4	17	128	305
2	21	615	4	17	300	615
3	32	615	6	17	300	615
4	65	940	8	17	512	940
5	49	940	6	17	512	940
6	21	615	4	17		615
7	32	462	8	17	256	511
8	21	940	5	17		733
9	117	900	15	17		901
10	21	820	3	17		820
11	37	855	5	17		855

12	52	855	7	17		855
13	21	306	8	17	128	319
14	44	733	7	17		733
16	21	612	4	17	0	663
17	42	977	5	17	300	977
18	59	977	7	17		977
19	62	1024	7	17	512	1023
20	31	733	5	17	300	732
21	44	733	7	17	300	732
22	31	733	5	17	300	733
23	10	306	4	17	0	336
24	21	612	4	17	305	663
25	10	306	4	17	-1	340
26	21	612	4	17	-1	670
27	42	698	7	17	300	732
28	42	976	5	17	488	977
29	10	306	4	17	0	340
30	21	611	4	17	306	663
31	44	732	7	17	300	732
32	44	1023	5	17	-1	1023

AWARD 3.0*/3.03/3.04 (3.0 ONLY TO 4.1)

Type	Mb	Cyls	Hds	Secs	Prec	LZ
1	10	306	4	17	128	305
2	20	615	4	17	300	615
3	30	615	6	17	300	615
4	65	940	8	17	512	940
5	49	940	6	17	512	940
6	21	615	4	17		615
7	32	462	8	17	256	511
8	31	733	5	17		733
9	117	900	15	17		901
10	21	820	3	17		820
11	37	855	5	17		855
12	52	855	7	17		855
13	21	306	8	17	128	319
14	44	733	7	17		733
16	21	612	4	17	0	663
17	42	977	5	17	300	977
18	59	977	7	17		977
19	62	1024	7	17	512	1023
20	31	733	5	17	300	732
21	44	733	7	17	300	732
22	31	733	5	17	300	733

Type	Mb	Cyls	Hds	Secs	Prec	LZ
23	10	306	4	17	0	336
24	42	977	5	17		976
25	80	1024	9	17		1023
26	74	1224	7	17		1223
27	117	1224	11	17		1223
28	159	1224	15	17		1223
29	71	1024	8	17		1023
30	98	1024	11	17		1023
31	87	918	11	17		1023
32	72	925	9	17		926
33	89	1024	10	17		1023
34	106	1024	12	17		1023
35	115	1024	13	17		1023
36	124	1024	14	17		1023
37	17	1024	2	17		1023
38	142	1024	16	17		1023
39	70	918	15	17		1023
40	42	820	6	17		820
41	42	1024/615*	5/8*	17	512/-15*	1023/615*
42		809	6	26	128	852
43		809	6	17	128	852
44		776	8	26		775

Type	Mb	Cyls	Hds	Secs	Prec	LZ
17	40	977	5	17	300	977
18	56	977	7	17		977
19	59	1024	7	17	512	1023
20	30	733	5	17	300	732
21	42	733	7	17	300	732
22/22***	31/49	733/751	5/8	17	300/0	733/752
23/23***	10/100	306/755	4/16	17	0	336/756
24	40	977	5	17		976
25	76	1024	9	17		1023
26	71	1224	7	17		1223
27	111	1224	11	17		1223
28	152	1224	15	17		1223
29	68	1024	8	17		1023
30	93	1024	11	17		1023
31	83	918	11	17		1023
32	69	925	9	17		926
33	85	1024	10	17		1023
34/34***	106/40	1024/965	12/5	17		1023/966
35/35***	115/80	1024/965	13/10	17		1023/966
36/36***	124/114	1024/814	9	17		1023/815
37/37***	17/160	1024/968	2/10	17/34		1023/969
38/38***	142/19	1024/873	16/13	17/36		1023/874
39	114	918	15	17		1023
40	40	820	6	17		820
41	42	1024	5	17	512	1023
42	65	1024	5	26	128	1023
43	40	809	6	17	128	852
44/44***	64/61	820/809**	6	26	-1**	852**
45	100	776	8	33	-1	775
46/**/***	203	684	16	38	-1	685
47/**/***	30	615	6	17	-1	615

AWARD
3.05/3.06*/3.06C**/3.10/3.12/3.13/3.14/3.16*/3.20/3.21/3.22/4.00***

User defined drive types started with 3.10.
*Made for OEMs.

Type	Mb	Cyls	Hds	Secs	Prec	LZ
1	10	306	4	17	128	305
2	20	615	4	17	300	615
3	30	615	6	17	300	615
4	62	940	8	17	512	940
5	46	940	6	17	512	940
6	20	615	4	17		615
7	30	462	8	17	256	511
8	30	733	5	17		733
9	112	900	15	17		901
10	20	820	3	17		820
11	35	855	5	17		855
12	49	855	7	17		855
13	20	306	8	17	128	319
14	42	733	7	17		733
16	20	612	4	17	0	663

AWARD 4.5

Type	Mb	Cyls	Hds	Secs	Prec	LZ
1	10	306	4	17	128	305
2	20	615	4	17	300	615
3	30	615	6	17	300	615
4	62	940	8	17	512	940
5	46	940	6	17	512	940
6	20	615	4	17	None	615

Fixed Disk
Parameter Tables

7	30	462	8	17	256	511
8	30	733	5	17	None	733
9	112	900	15	17	None	901
10	20	820	3	17	None	820
11	35	855	5	17	None	855
12	49	855	7	17	None	855
13	20	306	8	17	128	319
14	42	733	7	17	None	733
16	20	612	4	17	0	663
17	40	977	5	17	300	977
18	56	977	7	17	None	977
19	59	1024	7	17	512	1023
20	30	733	5	17	300	732
21	42	733	7	17	300	732
22	30	306	5	17	300	733
23	10	977	4	17	0	336
24	40	1024	5	17	None	976
25	76	1224	9	17	None	1023
26	71	1224	7	17	None	1223
27	11	1224	11	17	None	1223
28	15	1024	15	17	None	1223
29	68	1024	8	17	None	1023
30	93	918	11	17	None	1023
31	83	925	11	17	None	1023
32	69	1024	9	17	None	926
33	85	1024	10	17	None	1023
34	102	1024	12	17	None	1023
35	110	1024	13	17	None	1023
36	119	1024	14	17	None	1023
37	17	1024	2	17	None	1023
38	136	1024	16	17	None	1023
39	114	918	15	17	None	1023
40	40	820	6	17	None	820
41	42	1024	5	17	None	1023
42	65	1024	5	26	None	1023
43	40	809	6	17	None	852
44	61	809	6	26	None	852
45	100	776	8	33	None	775
46	203	684	16	38	None	685

COMMODORE

Type	Mb	Cyls	Hds	Secs	Prec	LZ
1	10	306	4	17	128	305
2	20	615	4	17	300	615
3	30	615	6	17	300	615
4	62	940	8	17	512	940

5	46	940	6	17	512	940
6	20	615	4	17		615
7	30	462	8	17	256	511
8	30	733	5	17		733
9	112	900	15	17		901
10	20	820	3	17		820
11	35	855	5	17		855
12	49	855	7	17		855
13	20	306	8	17	128	319
14	42	733	7	17		733
16	20	612	4	17	0	663
17	40	977	5	17	300	977
18	56	977	7	17		977
19	30	1024	7	17	512	1023
20	30	733	5	17	300	732
21	42	733	7	17	300	732
22	30	733	5	17	300	733
23	10	306	4	17	0	336
24	40	805	4	26	0	820
25	100	776	8	33	0	800
26	49	751	8	17	0	800
27	100	755	17	17	0	800
28	40	965	5	17	0	1000
29	80	965	10	17	0	1000
30	41	782	4	27	0	800
31	20	782	2	27	0	782
32	202	683	16	38	0	683
42	38	925	5	17	0	926
43	46	925	6	17	0	926
44	53	925	7	17	0	926
45	61	925	8	17	0	926
46	69	925	9	17	0	926
47	202	1526	16	17	0	1600

COMPAQ DESKPRO 386/25/33(27)/20E(37)

Type	Mb	Cyls	Hds	Secs	Prec	LZ
1	10	306	4	17	128	305
2	20	615	4	17	128	638
3	30	615	6	17	128	615
4	71	1024	8	17	512	1023
5	49	805	6	17	N/A	805
6	30	697	5	17	128	696
7	32	462	8	17	256	511
8	40	925	5	17	128	924
9	117	900	15	17	N/A	899
10	42	980	5	17	N/A	980

Type	Mb	Cyls	Hds	Secs	Prec	LZ
11	56	925	7	17	128	924
12	72	925	9	17	128	924
13	42	612	8	17	256	611
14	34	980	4	17	128	980
16	21	612	4	17	ALL	612
17	42	980	5	17	128	980
18	42	966	5	17	128	966
19	72	754	11	17	N/A	753
20	31	733	5	17	256	732
21	44	733	7	17	256	732
22	42	524	4	40	N/A	524
23	64	924	8	17	N/A	924
24	117	966	14	17	N/A	966
25	134	966	16	17	N/A	966
26	124	1023	14	17	N/A	1023
27	84	832	6	33	N/A	832
28	319	1222	15	34	N/A	1222
29	151	1240	7	34	N/A	1240
30	31	615	4	25	128	615
31	62	615	8	25	128	615
32	104	905	9	25	128	905
33	112	832	8	33	N/A	832
34	117	966	7	34	N/A	966
35	134	966	8	34	N/A	966
36	151	966	9	34	N/A	966
37	84	966	5	34	N/A	966
38	315	611	16	63	N/A	611
39	190	1023	11	33	N/A	1023
40	267	1023	15	34	N/A	1023
41	259	1023	15	33	0	1023
42	527	1023	16	63	0	1023
43	42	805	4	26	N/A	805
44	21	805	2	26	N/A	805
45	101	748	8	33	N/A	748
46	75	748	6	33	N/A	748
47	61	966	5	25	128	966

Type	Mb	Cyls	Hds	Secs	Prec	LZ
8	40	925	5	17	128	924
9	117	900	15	17	N/A	899
10	42	980	5	17	N/A	980
11	56	925	7	17	128	924
12	72	925	9	17	128	924
13	42	612	8	17	256	611
14	34	980	4	17	128	980
16	21	612	4	17	ALL	612
17	42	980	5	17	128	980
18	50	966	5	17	128	966
19	72	1023	8	17	-1	1023
20	32	733	5	17	256	732
21	44	733	7	17	256	732
22	42	805	6	17	-1	805
23	64	924	8	17	N/A	924
24	117	966	14	17	N/A	966
25	134	966	16	17	N/A	966
26	125	1023	14	17	N/A	1023
27	84	966	10	17	-1	966
28	104	748	16	17	-1	748
29	64	805	6	26	-1	805
30	32	615	4	25	128	615
31	63	615	8	25	128	615
32	104	905	9	25	128	905
33	104	748	8	34	-1	748
34	117	966	7	34	N/A	966
35	134	966	8	34	N/A	966
36	151	966	9	24	N/A	966
37	84	966	5	34	N/A	966
38	315	611	16	63	N/A	611
39	190	1023	11	33	N/A	1023
40	267	1023	15	34	N/A	1023
41	260	1023	15	33	0	1023
42	528	1023	16	63	0	1023
43	43	805	4	26	N/A	805
44	21	805	2	26	N/A	805
45	101	748	8	33	N/A	748
46	76	748	6	33	N/A	748
47	62	966	5	25	128	966

COMPAQ 386/20

Type	Mb	Cyls	Hds	Secs	Prec	LZ
1	10	306	4	17	128	305
2	21	615	4	17	128	638
3	31	615	6	17	128	615
4	71	1024	8	17	512	1023
5	49	940	6	17	N/A	939
6	30	697	5	17	128	696
7	32	462	8	17	256	511

COMPAQ PORTABLE III

Type	Mb	Cyls	Hds	Secs	Prec	LZ
1	10	306	4	17	128	305
2	20	615	4	17	128	638
3	30	615	6	17	128	615
4	71	1024	8	17	512	1023

Type	Mb	Cyls	Hds	Secs	Prec	LZ
5	49	940	6	17	512	939
6	30	697	5	17	128	696
7	32	462	8	17	256	511
8	40	925	5	17	128	924
9	117	900	15	17	N/A	899
10	42	980	5	17	N/A	980
11	56	925	7	17	128	924
12	72	925	9	17	128	924
13	42	612	8	17	256	611
14	34	980	4	17	128	980
16	21	612	4	17	ALL	612
17	42	980	5	17	128	980
18	42	966	5	17	128	966
19	72	754	11	17	N/A	753
20	31	733	5	17	256	732
21	44	733	7	17	256	732
22	42	825	6	17	-1	805
23	64	924	8	17	N/A	924
24	117	966	14	17	N/A	966
25	134	966	16	17	N/A	966
26	124	1023	14	17	N/A	1023
27	84	966	10	17	-1	966
28	104	748	16	17	-1	748
29	64	805	6	26	-1	805
30	31	615	4	25	128	615
31	62	615	8	25	128	615
32	104	905	9	25	128	905
33	104	748	8	34	-1	748
34	117	966	7	34	N/A	966
35	134	966	8	34	N/A	966
36	151	966	9	34	N/A	966
37	84	966	5	34	N/A	966

COMPAQ SLT/286

Type	Mb	Cyls	Hds	Secs	Prec	LZ
1	10.65	306	4	17	128	305
2	21.41	615	4	17	128	638
3	32.12	615	6	17	128	615
4	71.30	1024	8	17	512	1023
5	42.04	805	6	17	-1	805
6	30.33	697	5	17	128	696
7	32.17	462	8	17	256	511
8	40.26	925	5	17	128	924
9	117.50	900	15	17	-1	899
10	42.65	980	5	17	-1	980
11	56.36	925	7	17	128	924
12	72.46	925	9	17	128	924
13	42.61	612	8	17	256	611
14	34.12	980	4	17	128	980
16	21.31	612	4	17	0	612
17	42.65	980	5	17	128	980
18	42.04	966	5	17	128	966
19	72.19	754	11	17	-1	753
20	31.90	733	5	17	256	732
21	44.66	733	7	17	256	732
22	42.93	524	4	40	-1	524
23	64.34	924	8	17	-1	924
24	117.71	966	14	17	-1	966
25	134.53	966	16	17	-1	966
26	124.66	1023	14	17	-1	1023
27	84.34	832	6	33	-1	832
28	325.03	872	14	52	-1	872
29	151.10	1240	7	34	-1	1240
30	31.49	615	4	25	128	615
31	62.98	615	8	25	128	615
32	104.26	905	9	25	128	905
33	112.46	832	8	33	-1	832
34	117.71	966	7	34	-1	966
35	134.53	966	8	34	-1	966
36	151.35	966	9	34	-1	966
37	84.08	966	5	34	-1	966
38	315.33	611	16	63	-1	611
39	190.13	1023	11	33	-1	1023
40	267.13	1023	15	34	-1	1023
41	651.36	1631	15	52	-1	1631
42	527.97	1023	16	63	-1	1023
43	42.86	805	4	26	-1	805
44	21.43	805	2	26	-1	805
45	101.1	748	8	33	-1	748
46	75.83	748	6	33	-1	748
47	61.82	966	5	25	128	966
49	651.76	816	30	52	-1	816
50	121.41	760	8	39	-1	760
51	212.62	683	16	38	-1	683
53	42.65	548	4	38	-1	548
54	21.41	615	4	17	-1	615
55	60.70	760	4	39	-1	760
56	84.34	528	8	39	-1	528
57	325.14	629	16	63	-1	629
58	121.41	624	10	38	-1	624
59	31.91	410	4	38	-1	410
60	63.82	820	4	38	-1	820
61	510.42	989	16	63	-1	989

Type	Mb	Cyls	Hds	Secs	Prec	LZ
62	510.59	1696	12	49	-1	1696
63	340.11	659	16	63	-1	659
64	170.05	659	8	63	-1	659
69	242.57	940	8	63	-1	940
70	363.85	705	16	63	-1	705
71	485.13	940	16	63	-1	940
72	679.18	658	32	63	-1	658
73	679.18	1316	16	63	-1	1316
74	2037.55	987	64	63	-1	987
75	2037.55	3948	16	63	-1	3948
76	727.70	705	32	63	-1	705
77	727.70	1410	16	63	-1	1410
78	776.21	752	32	63	-1	752
79	776.21	1504	16	63	-1	1504
80	2716.73	658	12	63	-1	658
81	2716.73	526	16	63	-1	5264
82	970.26	940	32	63	-1	940
83	970.26	1880	16	63	-1	1880
84	424.75	823	16	63	-1	823
85	636.86	617	32	63	-1	617
86	636.86	1234	16	63	-1	1234
87	849.49	823	32	63	-1	823
88	849.49	1646	16	63	-1	1646
90	1018.77	987	32	63	-1	987
91	1018.77	1974	16	63	-1	1974
92	3059.42	741	12	63	-1	741
93	3059.82	5928	16	63	-1	5928
94	1273.72	617	64	63	-1	617
95	1273.72	2468	16	63	-1	2468
96	1358.36	658	64	63	-1	658
97	1358.36	2632	16	63	-1	2632
98	4079.22	988	12	63	-1	988
99	4079.22	7904	16	63	-1	7904
100	1698.99	823	64	63	-1	823
101	1698.99	3292	16	63	-1	3292
102	1529.71	741	64	63	-1	741
103	1529.71	2964	16	63	-1	2964

DTK

Type	Mb	Cyls	Hds	Secs	Prec	LZ
1		306	4	17	128	305
2		615	4	17	300	615
3		615	6	17	300	615
4		940	8	17	512	940
5		940	6	17	512	940
6		615	4	17	N/A	615
7		462	8	17	256	511
8		733	5	17	N/A	733
9		900	15	17	N/A	901
10		820	3	17	N/A	820
11		855	5	17	N/A	855
12		855	7	17	N/A	855
13		306	8	17	128	319
14		733	7	17	N/A	733
15		0	0	0	0	0
16		612	4	17	ALL	663
17		977	5	17	300	977
18		977	7	17	N/A	977
19		1024	7	17	512	1023
20		733	5	17	300	732
21		733	7	17	300	732
22		733	5	17	300	733
23		306	4	17	ALL	336
24		698	7	17	300	732
25		615	4	17	ALL	615
26		1024	4	17	N/A	1023
27		1024	5	17	N/A	1023
28		1024	8	17	N/A	1023
29		512	8	17	256	512
30		820	6	26	N/A	820
31		820	4	26	N/A	820
32		615	4	26	300	615
33		306	4	17	ALL	340
34		976	5	17	488	977
35		1024	9	17	1024	1024
36		1024	5	17	512	1024
37		830	10	17	N/A	830
38		823	10	17	256	824
39		615	4	17	128	664
40		615	8	17	128	664
41		917	15	17	N/A	918
42		1023	15	17	N/A	1024
43		823	10	17	512	823
44		820	6	17	N/A	820
45		1024	8	17	N/A	1024
46		925	9	17	N/A	925
47		699	7	17	256	700

EPSON

Type	Mb	Cyls	Hds	Secs	Prec	LZ
1	10	306	4	17	128	305
2	21	615	4	17	300	615
3	32	615	6	17	300	615
4	65	940	8	17	512	940
5	49	940	6	17	512	940
6	21	615	4	17	N/A	615
7	32	462	8	17	256	511
8	31	733	5	17	N/A	733
9	117	900	15	17	N/A	901
10	21	820	3	17	N/A	820
11	37	855	5	17	N/A	855
12	52	855	7	17	N/A	855
13	21	306	8	17	128	319
14	44	733	7	17	N/A	733
16	21	612	4	17	ALL	663
17	42	977	5	17	300	977
18	59	977	7	17	N/A	977
19	62	1024	7	17	512	1023
20	31	733	5	17	300	732
21	44	733	7	17	300	732
22	31	733	5	17	300	733
23	10	306	4	17	ALL	336
24	21	612	4	17	305	663
25	10	306	4	17	-1	340
26	21	612	4	17	-1	670
27	42	698	7	17	300	732
28	42	976	5	17	488	977
29	10	306	4	17	0	340
30	21	611	4	17	306	663
31	44	732	7	17	300	732
32	44	1023	5	17	-1	1023
41	88	1022	5	34	-1	1022
42	94	1022	5	36	-1	1022
43	71	1024	8	17	512	1023
44	144	828	10	34	-1	828
45	44	1024	5	17	512	1023
46	42	615	8	17	128	618

FERRANTI

Type	Mb	Cyls	Hds
1	977	5	17
2	615	4	17
3	615	6	17
4	940	8	17
5	940	6	17
6	615	4	17
7	462	8	17
8	733	5	17
9	900	15	17
10	820	3	17
11	855	7	17
12	855	7	17
13	306	8	17
14	733	7	17
15	1024	9	17

GOLDSTAR

Type	Mb	Cyls	Hds	Secs	Prec	LZ
1	10	306	4	17	128	305
2	21	615	4	17	300	615
3	32	615	6	17	300	615
4	65	940	8	17	512	940
5	49	940	6	17	512	940
6	21	615	4	17		615
7	32	462	8	17	256	511
8	31	733	5	17	N/A	733
9	117	900	15	17	N/A	901
10	21	820	3	17	N/A	820
11	37	855	5	17	N/A	855
12	52	855	7	17	N/A	855
13	21	306	8	17	128	319
14	44	733	7	17	N/A	733
16	21	612	4	17		663
17	42	977	5	17	300	977
18	59	977	7	17	N/A	977
19	62	1024	7	17	512	1023
20	31	733	5	17	300	732
21	44	733	7	17	300	732
22	31	733	5	17	300	733
23	10	306	4	17		336
24	65	820	6	26	544	819
25	21	615	4	17		615
26	35	1024	4	17	N/A	1023

27	44	1024	5	17	N/A	1023
28	71	1024	8	17	N/A	1023
29	35	512	8	17	256	512
30	10	615	2	17	615	615
31	43	989	5	17	0	989
32	133	1020	15	17	-1	1024
33	44	642	8	17	128	664
34	49	615	6	26	10	614
35	80	1024	9	17	1024	1024
36	44	1024	5	17	512	1024
37	72	830	10	17	N/A	830
38	71	823	10	17	256	824
39	21	615	4	17	128	664
40	42	615	8	17	128	664
41	42	615	8	17	128	664
42	119	917	15	17	-1	918
43	133	1025	15	17	-1	1024
44	71	823	10	17	512	823
45	42	820	6	17	N/A	820
46	71	1024	8	17	N/A	1024
47	72	925	9	17	N/A	925
48	42	699	7	17	256	700

22	42	739	4	28	-1	745
23	43	820	4	26	-1	820
24	85	636	2	33	-1	636
25	54	776	8	17	-1	776
26	41	965	5	17	-1	965
27	83	965	10	17	-1	965
28	65	948	5	27	-1	948
29	32	615	6	17	-1	615

IBM

Type	Mb	Cyls	Hds	Secs	Prec	LZ
1	10	306	4	17	128	305
2	21	615	4	17	300	615
3	32	615	6	17	300	615
4	65	940	8	17	512	940
5	49	940	6	17	512	940
6	21	615	4	17	N/A	615
7	32	462	8	17	256	511
8	31	733	5	17	N/A	733
9	11	900	15	17	N/A	901
10	21	820	3	17	N/A	820
11	37	855	5	17	N/A	855
12	52	855	7	17	N/A	855
13	21	306	8	17	128	319
14	44	733	7	17	N/A	733
16	21	612	4	17	ALL	663
17	42	977	5	17	300	977
18	59	977	7	17	N/A	977
19	62	1024	7	17	512	1023
20	31	733	5	17	300	732
21	44	733	7	17	300	732
22	31	733	5	17	300	733
23	10	306	4	17	ALL	336
24	21	612	4	17	305	663
25	10	306	4	17	N/A	340
26	21	612	4	17	N/A	670
27	42	698	7	17	300	732
28	42	976	5	17	488	977
29	10	306	4	17	ALL	340
30	21	611	4	17	306	663
31	44	732	7	17	300	732
32	44	1023	5	17	N/A	1023

GOUPIL

Type	Mb	Cyls	Hds	Secs	Prec	LZ
1	10	306	4	17	128	305
2	10	615	4	17	300	615
3	42	977	5	17	-1	977
4	42	615	8	17	128	664
5	40	925	5	17	128	940
6	44	1024	5	17	-1	1024
7	43	898	5	17	-1	1024
8	42	820	6	17	-1	820
9	88	1022	5	34	-1	1022
10	71	823	10	17	128	823
11	72	925	9	17	128	940
12	80	1024	9	17	-1	1024
13	71	1024	8	17	-1	1024
14	151	969	9	34	-1	969
16	146	1024	8	35	-1	1024
17	32	615	4	26	300	615
18	65	615	8	26	128	664
19	65	989	5	26	128	989
20	65	820	6	26	-1	820
21	42	804	4	26	-1	805

Fixed Disk
Parameter Tables

PS/2

Type	Mb	Cyls	Hds	Secs	Prec	LZ
33		614	4	17	0	663
34		775	2	17	0	900
35		922	2	17	0	1000
36		402	4	17	0	460
37		580	6	17	0	640
38		845	2	17	0	1023
39		769	3	17	0	1023
40		531	4	17	0	532
41		577	2	17	0	1023
42		654	2	17	0	674
43		923	5	17	0	1023
44		531	8	17	0	532

MR BIOS

Type	Mb	Cyls	Hds	Secs	Prec	LZ
1	10.7	306	4		128	305
2	21.4	615	4		300	615
3	32.1	615	6		300	615
4	65.5	940	8		512	940
5	49.1	940	6		512	940
6	21.4	615	4		None	615
7	32.2	462	8		256	511
8	31.9	733	5		None	733
9	117.5	900	15		None	901
10	21.4	820	3		None	820
11	37.2	855	5		None	855
12	52.1	855	7		None	855
13	21.3	306	8		128	319
14	44.7	733	7		None	733
15	0.0	0	0		None	0
16	21.3	612	4		0	663
17	42.5	977	5		300	977
18	59.5	977	7		None	977
19	62.4	1024	7		512	1023
20	31.9	733	5		300	732
21	44.7	733	7		300	732
22	21.9	733	5		300	733
23	10.7	306	4		0	336
24	42.9	805	4		None	805
25	72.5	925	9		None	925
26	104.9	776	8		None	776
27	44.6	1024	5		512	1024
28	71.3	1024	8		None	1023
29	71.6	823	10		None	823
30	159.8	1224	15		None	1223
31	98.0	1024	11		None	1024
32	133.7	1024	15		None	1024
33	44.6	1024	5		None	1024
34	10.7	612	2		128	612
35	80.2	1024	9		None	1024
36	71.3	1024	8		512	1024
37	42.8	615	128		615	17
38	71.6	823	10		256	823
39	42.2	809	6		128	809
40	42.8	820	6		None	820
41	42.5	977	5		None	977
42	42.7	981	5		None	981
43	71.6	823	10		512	823
44	72.2	830	10		None	830
45	119.7	917	15		None	917
46	User					

NIMBUS PC386 4.21A

Type	Mb	Cyls	Hds	Secs	Prec	LZ
1	10	306	4	17	128	305
2	21	615	4	17	300	615
3	32	615	6	17	300	615
4	65	940	8	17	512	940
5	49	940	6	17	512	940
6	21	615	4	17	N/A	615
7	32	462	8	17	256	511
8	31	733	5	17	N/A	733
9	11	900	15	17	N/A	901
10	21	820	3	17	N/A	820
11	37	855	5	17	N/A	855
12	52	855	7	17	N/A	855
13	21	306	8	17	128	319
14	44	733	7	17	N/A	733
16	21	612	4	17	ALL	663
17	42	977	5	17	300	977
18	59	977	7	17	N/A	977
19	62	1024	7	17	512	1023
20	31	733	5	17	300	732
21	44	733	7	17	300	732
22	31	733	5	17	300	733
23	10	306	4	17	ALL	336
24	21	612	4	17	305	663
25	10	306	4	17	N/A	340
26	21	612	4	17	N/A	670

Type	Mb	Cyls	Hds	Secs	Prec	LZ
27	42	698	7	17	300	732
28	42	976	5	17	488	977
29	10	306	4	17	ALL	340
30	21	611	4	17	306	663
31	44	732	7	17	300	732
32	44	1023	5	17	N/A	1023
33	50	830	7	17	-1	830
34	72	830	10	17	-1	830
35	44	1024	5	17	-1	1024
36	71	1024	8	17	-1	1024
37	42	615	8	17	128	615
38	42	615	8	17	-1	615
39	72	925	9	17	-1	925
40	80	1024	9	17	-1	1023
41	65	820	6	26	-1	920
42	32	615	4	26	-1	614
43	59	750	6	26	600	749
44	68	1024	5	26	768	1023
45	41	771	4	26	128	810
46	41	771	4	26	128	810
47	49	615	6	26	-1	614

Type	Mb	Cyls	Hds	Secs	Prec	LZ
24	117	966	14	17	-1	966
25	134	966	16	17	-1	966
26	124	1023	14	17	-1	1023
27	84	966	10	17	-1	966
28	72	754	11	17	383	754
29	110	830	10	17	512	830
30	65	615	8	17	384	664
31	62	615	8	17	128	615
32	72	830	10	17	512	830
33	21	1023	16	26	-1	1023
34	117	966	7	34	-1	966
35	134	966	8	34	-1	966
36	142	1023	16	17	-1	1023
37	84	966	5	34	-1	966
38	201	1024	8	48	-1	1023
39	377	1024	15	48	-1	1023
40	133	1024	15	17	-1	1023
41	267	1024	15	34	-1	1023
42	196	1024	11	34	-1	1023
43	124	1024	7	34	-1	1023
44	142	1024	8	34	-1	1023
45	42	820	6	17	-1	820
46	65	820	6	26	-1	820
47	42	615	8	17	128	664

NIMBUS VX386 V155A

Type	Mb	Cyls	Hds	Secs	Prec	LZ
1	10	306	4	17	128	305
2	21	615	4	17	300	615
3	32	615	6	17	300	615
4	65	940	8	17	512	940
5	49	940	6	17	512	940
6	21	615	4	17	N/A	615
7	32	462	8	17	256	511
8	31	733	5	17	N/A	733
9	11	900	15	17	N/A	901
10	21	820	3	17	N/A	820
11	37	855	5	17	N/A	855
12	52	855	7	17	N/A	855
13	21	306	8	17	128	319
14	44	733	7	17	N/A	733
16	21	612	4	17	ALL	663
17	42	977	5	17	300	977
18	59	977	7	17	N/A	977
19	62	1024	7	17	512	1023
20	31	733	5	17	300	732
21	44	733	7	17	300	732
22	31	733	5	17	300	733
23	10	306	4	17	ALL	336

OLIVETTI V3.27

Type	Mb	Cyls	Hds	Secs	Prec	LZ
1	30	697	5	17	0	696
2	21	612	4	17	256	700
3	21	612	4	17	612	663
4	10	306	4	17	128	305
5	42	612	8	17	128	664
6	42	820	6	17	256	819
7	42	820	6	17	820	819
8	71	823	10	17	512	822
9	42	981	5	17	128	980
10	42	615	8	17	512	614
11	71	1024	8	17	1024	1023
12	80	1024	9	17	1024	1023
13	45	872	6	17	872	871
14	21	612	4	17	128	656
15	21	612	4	17	128	663
16	10	306	4	17	128	305

Fixed Disk
Parameter Tables

OLIVETTI M380C

Type	Mb	Cyls	Hds	Secs	Prec	LZ
1	10	306	4	17	128	305
2	21	615	4	17	300	615
3	40	925	5	17	128	924
4	30	697	5	17	128	696
5	80	1024	9	17	-1	1023
6	42	820	6	17	256	819
7	42	615	8	17	128	664
8	42	981	5	17	-1	980
9	42	981	5	17	128	980
10	53	1024	6	17	-1	1023
11	56	925	7	17	128	924
12	71	1024	8	17	-1	1023
13	72	925	9	17	128	924
14	44	1024	5	17	-1	1023
16	21	612	4	17	128	656
17	21	612	4	17	-1	663
18	42	820	6	17	-1	819
19	45	872	6	17	0	871
20	21	612	4	17	128	663
21	65	820	6	26	-1	819
22	65	820	6	26	128	819
23	65	615	8	26	384	664
24	142	820	10	34	-1	822
25	142	1021	8	34	-1	1023
26	71	1021	4	34	-1	1023
27	71	823	10	17	512	622
28	42	615	8	17	512	614
29	65	615	8	26	512	65
30	65	981	5	26	-1	980

PHILIPS 2.24

Type	Mb	Cyls	Hds	Secs	Prec	LZ
1	10	306	4	17	128	306
2	20	615	4	17	300	615
3	30	615	6	17	300	615
4	68	1024	8	17	512	1024
5	43	874	6	17	650	872
6	25	512	6	17	256	615
7	34	512	8	17	256	512
9	20	615	4	17	128	663
10	25	1024	3	17	512	1024
11	42	1024	5	17	512	1024
12	59	1024	7	17	512	1024

13	43	754	7	17	65535	754
14	68	754	11	17	65535	754
16	20	782	2	27	65535	862
17	41	782	4	27	65535	862
18	20	745	2	28	65535	820
19	40	745	4	28	65535	820
20	43	868	3	34	65535	0
21	72	868	5	34	65535	0
22	100	868	7	34	65535	0
23	100	776	8	33	65535	776
24	40	745	4	28	65535	0
25	41	539	6	26	65535	0
26	40	979	5	17	65535	0
27	0	0	0	0	0	0
28	0	0	0	0	0	0
29	0	0	0	0	0	0
30	31	615	4	26	128	636

PHOENIX 1.1 16.H0

Type	Mb	Cyls	Hds	Secs	Prec	LZ
1	10	306	4	17	128	305
2	21	615	4	17	300	615
3	32	615	6	17	300	615
4	65	940	8	17	512	940
5	49	940	6	17	512	940
6	21	615	4	17	-1	615
7	32	462	8	17	256	511
8	31	733	5	17	-1	733
9	117	900	15	17	-1	901
10	21	820	3	17	-1	820
11	37	855	5	17	-1	855
12	52	855	7	17	-1	855
13	21	306	8	17	128	319
14	44	733	7	17	-1	733
15	0	0	0	0	0	0
16	21	612	4	17	0	663
17	42	977	5	17	300	977
18	59	977	7	17	-1	977
19	62	1024	7	17	512	1023
20	31	733	5	17	300	732
21	44	733	7	17	300	732
22	31	733	5	17	300	733
23	10	306	4	17	0	336
24	110	830	10	26	-1	830
25	21	615	4	17	0	615
26	35	1024	4	17	-1	1023

27	44	1024	5	17	-1	1023
28	71	1024	8	17	-1	1023
29	35	512	8	17	256	512
30	10	615	2	17	615	615
31	43	989	5	17	0	989
32	133	1020	15	17	-1	1024
33	0	0	0	0	0	0
34	0	0	0	0	0	0
35	80	1024	9	17	1024	1024
36	44	1024	5	17	512	1024
37	72	830	10	17	-1	830
38	71	823	10	17	256	824
39	21	615	4	17	128	664
40	42	615	8	17	128	664
41	119	917	15	17	-1	918
42	133	1023	15	17	-1	1024
43	71	823	10	17	512	823
44	42	820	6	17	-1	820
45	71	1024	8	17	-1	1024
46	72	925	9	17	-1	925
47	42	699	7	17	256	700

20	37	733	5	17	300	732
21	51	733	7	17	300	732
22	37	733	5	17	0	732
22	37	733	5	17	0	732
23	10	306	4	17	0	336

PHOENIX 3.00

Type	Mb	Cyls	Hds	Secs	Prec	LZ
1	10	306	4	17	128	305
2	21	615	4	17	300	615
3	32	615	6	17	300	615
4	65	940	8	17	512	940
5	49	940	6	17	512	940
6	21	615	4	17	-1	615
7	32	462	8	17	256	511
8	31	733	5	17	-1	733
9	117	900	15	17	-1	901
10	21	820	3	17	-1	820
11	37	855	5	17	-1	855
12	52	855	7	17	-1	855
13	20	306	8	17	128	319
14	44	733	7	17	-1	733
16	20	612	4	17	0	663
17	42	977	5	17	300	977
18	59	977	7	0	-1	977
19	62	1024	7	17	512	1023
20	31	733	5	17	300	733
21	44	733	7	17	300	733
22	31	733	5	17	300	733
23	10	306	4	17	0	336
36	41	1024	5	17	512	1024
37	72	830	10	17	-1	830
38	71	823	10	17	256	824
39	21	615	4	17	128	664
40	42	615	8	17	128	664
41	119	917	15	17	-1	918
42	133	1023	15	17	-1	1024
43	72	823	10	17	512	823

PHOENIX 1.64

Type	Mb	Cyls	Hds	Secs	Prec	LZ
1	12	306	4	17	128	305
2	25	615	4	17	300	615
3	37	615	6	17	300	615
4	75	940	8	17	512	940
5	56	940	6	17	512	940
6	25	615	4	17	65535	615
7	37	462	8	17	256	511
8	37	733	5	17	65535	733
9	136	900	15	17	65535	901
10	25	820	3	17	65535	820
11	43	855	5	17	65535	855
12	60	855	7	17	65535	855
13	24	306	8	17	128	319
14	51	733	7	17	65535	733
16	24	612	4	17	0	633
17	49	977	5	17	300	977
18	68	977	7	17	65535	977
19	72	1024	7	17	512	1023

PHOENIX 3.10 01

Type	Mb	Cyls	Hds	Secs	Prec	LZ
1	10	306	4	17	128	305
2	21	615	4	17	300	615
3	32	615	6	17	300	615
4	65	940	8	17	512	940

5	49	940	6	17	512	940
6	21	615	4	17	-1	615
7	32	462	8	17	256	511
8	31	733	5	17	-1	733
9	117	900	15	17	-1	901
10	21	820	3	17	-1	820
11	37	855	5	17	-1	855
12	52	855	7	17	-1	855
13	21	306	8	17	128	319
14	44	733	7	17	-1	733
16	21	612	4	17	0	663
17	42	977	5	17	300	977
18	59	977	7	17	-1	977
19	62	1024	7	17	512	1023
20	31	733	5	17	300	732
21	44	733	7	17	300	732
22	31	733	5	17	300	733
23	10	306	4	17	0	336
24	21	612	4	17	305	663
25	10	306	4	17	-1	340
26	21	612	4	17	-1	670
27	42	698	7	17	300	732
28	42	976	5	17	488	977
29	10	306	4	17	0	340
30	21	611	4	17	306	663
31	44	732	7	17	300	732
32	44	1023	5	17	17	1023
33	31	614	4	25	-1	663
34	44	1024	5	17	512	0
35	44	642	8	17	128	664
36	0	0	0	0	0	0
37	45	872	6	17	650	0
38	0	0	0	0	0	0
39	59	750	6	26	300	750
40	42	805	4	26	-1	0
41	103	776	8	33	-1	0
42	43	782	4	27	-1	0
43	49	615	6	26	-1	0
44	42	820	6	17	-1	820
45	0	0	0	0	0	0
46	43	539	6	26	-1	0

PHOENIX 3.10 08A

Type	Mb	Cyls	Hds	Secs	Prec	LZ
1	10	306	4	17	128	305
2	20	615	4	17	300	615
3	30	615	6	17	300	615
4	62	940	8	17	512	940
5	46	940	6	17	512	940
6	20	615	4	17	-1	615
7	30	462	8	17	256	511
8	30	733	5	17	-1	733
9	112	900	15	17	-1	901
10	20	820	3	17	-1	820
11	35	855	5	17	-1	855
12	49	855	7	17	-1	855
13	20	306	8	17	128	319
14	42	733	7	17	-1	733
16	20	612	4	17	0	663
17	40	977	5	17	300	977
18	56	977	7	17	-1	977
19	59	1024	7	17	512	1023
20	30	733	5	17	300	732
21	42	733	7	17	300	732
22	30	733	5	17	300	733
23	10	36	4	17	0	336
25	20	615	4	17	0	615
26	34	1024	4	17	-1	1023
27	42	1024	5	17	-1	1023
28	68	1024	8	17	-1	1023
29	34	512	8	17	256	512
30	10	615	2	17	615	615
31	41	989	5	17	0	989
32	127	1020	15	17	-1	1024
35	76	1024	9	17	1024	1024
36	42	1024	5	17	512	1024
37	68	830	10	17	-1	830
38	68	823	10	17	256	824
39	20	615	4	17	128	664
40	40	615	8	17	128	664
41	114	917	15	17	-1	918
42	127	1023	15	17	-1	1024
43	68	823	10	17	512	823
44	40	820	6	17	-1	820
45	68	1024	8	17	-1	1024
46	69	925	9	17	-1	925
47	40	699	7	17	256	700

Phoenix 3.4

Type	Mb	Cyls	Hds	Secs	Prec	LZ
1	10	612	2	17	306	611
2	20	612	4	17	100	611
3	0	0	0	0	0	0
4	42	615	8	17	-1	614
5	31	615	6	26	-1	614
6	42	805	4	26	-1	805
7	42	979	5	17	-1	979
8	59	997	7	17	-1	997
9	104	776	8	33	-1	776
10	121	931	15	17	-1	931
11	20	615	4	17	-1	615
12	42	980	5	17	-1	980
13	212	683	16	38	-1	683

Phoenix 3.40

Type	Mb	Cyls	Hds	Secs	Prec	LZ
1	42	862	2	48	-1	862
2	121	931	15	17	-1	931
3	41	1024	2	40	-1	1024
4	42	695	7	17	-1	695
5	84	695	14	17	-1	695
6	45	667	4	33	-1	667
7	42	977	5	17	-1	977
8	0	0	0	0	0	0
9	42	695	7	17	-1	695
10	84	695	14	17	-1	695
11	42	980	5	17	-1	980
12	42	981	5	17	-1	981
13	85	981	10	17	-1	981

Phoenix 3.63T

Type	Mb	Cyls	Hds	Secs	Prec	LZ
1	10	306	4	17	128	0
2	20	615	4	17	300	0
3	30	615	6	17	300	0
4	62	940	8	17	512	0
5	46	940	6	17	512	0
6	20	615	4	17	0	0
7	30	462	8	17	256	0
8	30	733	5	17	0	0
9	111	900	15	17	0	0
10	20	820	3	17	0	0

Type	Mb	Cyls	Hds	Secs	Prec	LZ
11	35	855	5	17	0	0
12	49	855	7	17	0	0
13	20	306	8	17	128	0
14	42	733	7	17	0	0
16	20	612	4	17	0	0
17	40	977	5	17	300	0
18	56	977	7	17	0	0
19	59	1024	7	17	512	0
20	30	733	5	17	300	0
21	42	733	7	17	300	0
22	30	733	5	17	300	0
23	10	306	4	17	0	0
24	20	612	4	17	305	0
25	10	306	4	17	0	0
26	20	612	4	17	0	0
27	40	698	7	17	300	0
28	40	976	5	17	488	0
29	10	306	4	17	0	0
30	20	611	4	17	306	0
31	42	732	7	17	300	0
32	42	1023	5	17	0	0
100	40	820	6	17	0	0
101	76	1024	9	17	0	0
102	40	615	8	17	128	0
103	42	1024	5	17	512	0
104	67	1024	8	17	512	0
105	24	987	3	17	0	0
106	41	989	5	17	0	0
107	57	987	7	17	0	0
108	67	1024	8	17	0	0
109	83	918	11	17	0	0
110	114	918	15	17	0	0
111	42	1024	5	17	0	0
112	50	1024	5	17	0	0
113	59	1024	7	17	0	0
114	38	925	5	17	0	0
115	53	925	7	17	0	0
116	69	925	9	17	0	0
117	10	615	2	17	0	0
118	25	754	4	17	0	0
119	43	754	7	17	0	0
120	68	754	11	17	0	0
121	28	699	5	17	0	0
122	40	699	7	17	0	0
123	68	823	10	17	0	0
124	20	830	3	17	0	0
125	34	830	5	17	0	0

126	41	830	6	17	0	0
127	48	830	7	17	0	0
128	68	830	10	17	0	0
129	40	981	5	17	0	0
130	56	981	7	17	0	0
131	127	1024	15	17	0	0
132	40	987	5	17	0	0
133	18	731	3	17	0	0
134	30	731	5	17	0	0
135	42	731	7	17	0	0
136	36	872	5	17	650	0
137	43	872	6	17	650	0
138	50	872	7	17	650	0
139	127	1024	15	17	0	0
140	41	989	5	17	128	0
150	80	969	5	34	0	0
151	112	969	7	34	0	0
152	144	969	9	34	0	0
153	68	823	5	34	0	0
154	81	823	6	34	0	0
155	95	823	7	34	0	0
156	136	823	10	34	0	0
157	67	1024	4	34	0	0
158	84	1024	5	34	0	0
159	101	1024	6	34	0	0
160	118	1024	7	34	0	0
161	135	1024	8	34	0	0
162	254	1024	15	34	0	0
163	68	830	5	34	0	0
164	96	830	7	34	0	0
165	137	830	10	34	0	0
166	209	903	14	34	0	0
167	80	1216	4	34	0	0
168	161	1216	8	34	0	0
169	242	1216	12	34	0	0
170	142	1224	7	34	0	0
171	162	1224	8	34	0	0
172	223	1224	11	34	0	0
173	243	1224	12	34	0	0
174	142	1225	7	34	0	0
175	223	1225	11	34	0	0
176	144	1243	7	34	0	0
177	226	1243	11	34	0	0
178	79	1600	3	34	0	0
179	106	1600	4	34	0	0
180	132	1600	5	34	0	0
181	159	1600	6	34	0	0
182	216	1632	8	34	0	0
183	263	1224	13	34	0	0
184	284	1224	14	34	0	0
185	304	1224	15	34	0	0
186	304	1225	15	34	0	0
187	309	1243	15	34	0	0
188	404	1624	15	34	0	0
189	406	1632	15	34	0	0
190	145	1249	7	34	0	0
191	145	1250	7	34	0	0
192	633	1632	15	53	0	0
193	644	1661	15	53	0	0
216	29	615	4	25	128	0
217	59	615	8	25	128	0
218	35	966	3	25	0	0
219	38	756	4	26	0	0
220	19	756	2	26	0	0
221	38	768	4	26	0	0
222	19	768	2	26	0	0
223	58	966	5	25	128	0
224	61	805	6	26	0	0
225	99	905	9	25	128	0
226	30	611	4	26	0	0
227	15	611	2	26	0	0
228	31	615	4	26	128	0
229	31	615	4	26	0	0
230	46	615	6	26	0	0
231	41	820	4	26	0	0
232	62	820	6	26	0	0
233	37	987	3	26	0	0
234	62	987	5	26	0	0
235	87	987	7	26	0	0
236	64	1024	5	26	0	0
237	116	1024	9	26	0	0
238	103	1166	7	26	0	0
239	40	745	4	28	0	0
240	99	776	8	33	0	0
241	41	782	4	27	0	0
242	40	805	4	26	0	0
243	34	834	3	28	0	0
244	199	1348	8	38	0	0
245	191	816	15	32	0	0
246	107	832	8	33	0	0
247	225	1747	5	53	0	0
248	105	906	7	34	0	0
249	316	1747	7	53	0	0

PHOENIX 3.06/3.07

Type	Mb	Cyls	Hds	Secs	Prec	LZ
1		306	4	17	128	305
2		615	4	17	300	615
3		615	6	17	300	615
4		940	8	17	512	940
5		940	6	17	512	940
6		615	4	17		615
7		462	8	17	256	511
8		733	5	17		733
9		900	15	17		901
10		820	3	17		820
11		855	5	17		855
12		855	7	17		855
13		306	8	17	128	319
14		733	7	17		733
16		612	4	17	0	663
17		977	5	17	300	977
18		977	7	17		977
19		1024	7	17	512	1023
20		733	5	17	300	732
21		733	7	17	300	732
22		733	5	17	300	733
23		306	4	17	0	336
25		615	4	17	0	615
26		1024	4	17		1023
27		1024	5	17		1023
28		1024	8	17		1023
29		512	8	17	256	512
30		615	2	17	615	615
31		989	5	17	0	989
32		1020	15	17		1024
35		1024	9	17		1024
36		1024	5	17	512	1024
37		830	10	17		830
38		823	10	17	256	824
39		615	4	17	128	664
40		615	8	17	128	664
41		917	15	17		918
42		1023	15	17		1024
43		823	10	17	512	823
44		820	6	17		820
45		1024	8	17		1024
46		925	9	17		925
47		699	7	17	256	700

PHOENIX 3.10

Type	Mb	Cyls	Hds	Secs	Prec	LZ
1		306	4	17	128	305
2		615	4	17	300	615
3		615	6	17	300	615
4		940	8	17	512	940
5		940	6	17	512	940
6		615	4	17		615
7		462	8	17	256	511
8		733	5	17		733
9		900	15	17		901
10		820	3	17		820
11		855	5	17		855
12		855	7	17		855
13		306	8	17	128	319
14		733	7	17		733
16		612	4	17	0	663
17		977	5	17	300	977
18		977	7	17		977
19		1024	7	17	512	1023
20		733	5	17	300	732
21		733	7	17	300	732
22		733	5	17	300	733
23		306	4	17	0	336
25		615	4	17	0	615
26		1024	4	17		1023
27		1024	5	17		1023
28		1024	8	17		1023
29		512	8	17	256	512
30		615	2	17	615	615
31		989	5	17	0	989
32		1020	15	17		1024
35		1024	9	17		1024
36		1024	5	17	512	1024
37		830	10	17		830
38		823	10	17	256	824
39		615	4	17	128	664
40		615	8	17	128	664
41		917	15	17		918
42		1023	15	17		1024
43		823	10	17	512	823
44		820	6	17		820
45		1024	8	17		1024
46		925	9	17		925
47		699	7	17	256	700

PHOENIX 1.00 ABIOS

Type	Mb	Cyls	Hds	Secs	Prec	LZ
1		306	4	17	128	305
2		615	4	17	300	615
3		615	6	17	300	615
4		940	8	17	512	940
5		940	6	17	512	940
6		615	4	17		615
7		462	8	17	256	511
8		733	5	17		733
9		900	15	17		901
10		820	3	17		820
11		855	5	17		855
12		855	7	17		855
13		306	8	17	128	319
14		733	7	17		733
16		612	4	17	0	663
17		977	5	17	300	977
18		977	7	17		977
19		1024	7	17	512	1023
20		733	5	17	300	732
21		733	7	17	300	732
22		733	5	17	300	733
23		306	4	17	0	336
25		615	4	17	0	615
26		1024	4	17		1023
27		1024	5	17		1023
28		1024	8	17		1023
29		512	8	17	256	512
30		615	2	17	615	615
31		989	5	17	0	989
32		1020	15	17		1024
33		615	4	26		615
34		820	6	26		820
35		1024	9	17		1024
36		1024	5	17	512	1024
37		1024	5	26	512	1024
38		823	10	17	256	824
39		615	4	17	128	664
40		615	8	17	128	664
41		917	15	17		918
42		1023	15	17		1024
43		823	10	17	512	823
44		820	6	17		820
45		1024	5	17		1024
46		925	9	17		925
47		699	7	17	256	700

SAMSUNG

Type	Mb	Cyls	Hds	Secs	Prec	LZ
1	10	306	4	17	128	305
2	21	615	4	17	300	615
3	32	615	6	17	300	615
4	65	940	8	17	512	940
5	49	940	6	17	512	940
6	21	615	4	17	-1	615
7	32	462	8	17	256	511
8	31	733	5	17	-1	733
9	117	900	15	17	-1	901
10	21	820	3	17	-1	820
11	37	855	5	17	-1	855
12	52	855	7	17	-1	855
13	21	306	8	17	128	319
14	44	733	7	17	-1	733
16	21	612	4	17	0	663
17	42	977	5	17	300	977
18	59	977	7	17	-1	977
19	62	1024	7	17	512	1023
20	31	733	5	17	300	732
21	44	733	7	17	300	732
22	31	733	5	17	300	733
23	10	306	4	17	0	336

SPERRY PC/IT

Type	Mb	Cyls	Hds	Secs
1	20	610	4	17
2	20	615	4	17
3	30	615	6	17
4	42	960	5	17
5	72	920	9	17
6	70	1000	8	17
7	118	900	15	17
8	42	960	5	17
9	26	604	5	17
10	42	960	5	17
11	21	614	4	17
12	44	1000	5	17
13	21	600	4	17
14	40	924	5	17

TANDON 001-2.24 000-10

Type	Mb	Cyls	Hds	Secs	Prec	LZ
1	10.65	306	4	17	128	305
2	21.41	615	4	17	300	615
3	32.12	615	6	17	300	615
4	65.45	940	8	17	512	940
5	49.09	940	6	17	512	940
6	21.41	615	4	17		615
7	32.17	462	8	17	256	511
8	31.90	733	5	17		733
9	117.50	900	15	17		901
10	21.41	820	3	17		820
11	37.21	855	5	17		855
12	52.09	855	7	17		855
13	21.31	306	8	17	128	319
14	44.66	733	7	17		733
16	21.31	612	4	17	0	663
17	42.52	977	5	17	300	977
18	59.53	977	7	17		977
19	62.39	1024	7	17	512	1023
20	31.90	733	5	17	300	732
21	44.66	733	7	17	300	732
22	31.90	733	5	17	300	733
23	10.65	306	4	17	0	336
28	124.78	1024	14	17		1024
29	31.96	612	6	17		612
30	42.82	615	8	17		615
31	71.30	1024	8	17		1024
32	32.12	615	6	17		615
33	98.04	1024	11	17		1024
34	72.46	925	9	17		925
35	42.25	809	6	17		852
36	71.37	820	10	17		820
37	27.19	781	4	17		805
38	57.10	820	8	17		820
39	28.03	805	4	17		805
40	44.56	1024	5	17		1024
41	71.30	1024	8	17		1024
42	80.22	1024	9	17		1024
43	42.82	820	6	17		820
44	75.20	960	9	17		960
45	72.24	830	10	17		830
46	133.69	1024	15	17		1024
47	42.69	981	5	17		981

TANDON 3.61

Type	Mb	Cyls	Hds	Secs	Prec	LZ
1	10	306	4	17	128	305
2	20	615	4	17	128	615
3	30	615	6	17	300	615
4	62	940	8	17	512	940
5	46	940	6	17	512	940
6	20	615	4	17	615	615
7	30	462	8	17	256	511
8	30	733	5	17	733	733
9	112	900	15	17	900	901
10	20	820	3	17	820	820
11	35	855	5	17	855	855
12	49	855	7	17	855	855
13	20	306	8	17	128	319
14	42	733	7	17	733	733
15	0	0	0	0	0	0
16	20	612	4	17	0	663
17	40	977	5	17	300	977
18	56	977	7	17	977	977
19	59	1024	7	17	512	1023
20	30	733	5	17	300	732
22	30	733	5	17	300	733
23	10	306	4	17	0	336
24	0	0	0	0	0	0
25	0	0	0	0	0	0
26	105	904	14	17	904	904
27	107	861	15	17	861	861
28	119	1024	14	17	1024	1024
29	30	612	6	17	612	612
30	40	615	8	17	615	615
31	68	1024	8	17	512	1024
32	30	615	6	17	615	615
33	93	1024	11	17	1024	1024
34	69	925	9	17	925	925
35	40	809	6	17	809	852
36	68	820	10	17	128	820
37	25	781	4	17	781	805
38	54	820	8	17	820	820
39	26	805	4	17	805	805
40	42	1024	5	17	1024	1024
41	68	1024	8	17	1024	1024
42	76	1024	9	17	1024	1024

43	40	820	6	17	820	820
44	71	960	9	17	960	960
45	68	830	10	17	830	830
46	127	1024	15	17	1024	1024
47	40	981	5	17	981	981

TOSHIBA 1.0

Type	Mb	Cyls	Hds	Secs	Prec	LZ
1	21	615	4	17	-1	615
2	21	581	2	36	-1	581
3	42	980	5	17	-1	980
4	42	791	3	35	-1	791
5	31	411	4	38	-1	411
6	64	823	4	38	-1	823
12	21	615	4	17	-1	615
13	21	581	2	36	-1	581
14	21	653	2	32	-1	653

VICTOR AT 3.01

Type	Mb	Cyls	Hds	Secs	Prec	LZ
1	10	306	4	17	128	305
2	21	615	4	17	300	615
3	31	615	6	17	300	615
4	65	940	8	17	512	940
5	49	940	6	17	512	940
6	21	615	4	17	-1	615
7	32	462	8	17	256	511
8	31	733	5	17	-1	733
9	117	900	15	17	-1	901
10	21	820	3	17	-1	820
11	37	855	5	17	-1	855
12	52	855	7	17	-1	855
13	21	306	8	17	128	319
14	44	733	7	17	-1	733
15	0	0	0	0	0	0
16	21	612	4	17	0	663
17	42	977	5	17	17	300
18	59	977	7	17	-1	977
19	62	1024	7	17	512	1023
20	31	733	5	17	300	732
21	44	733	7	17	300	732
22	31	733	5	17	300	733
23	22	306	4	17	0	336
24	23	440	6	17	256	440
25	30	615	4	24	0	616

26	71	1024	8	17	-1	1024
27	41	1024	5	17	-1	1024
28	44	640	8	17	250	641
29	80	1023	9	17	-1	1023
30	42	820	6	17	-1	820
31	119	918	15	17	-1	918
32	44	642	8	17	128	664
33	42	980	5	17	-1	980
34	40	965	5	17	0	965
35	84	965	10	17	0	965
36	41	1024	5	17	512	1024
37	120	814	9	32	0	814
38	168	968	10	34	0	968
39	209	873	13	36	0	873
40	49	750	5	26	600	750
41	59	750	6	26	600	750
42	69	750	7	26	600	750
43	41	1023	2	40	-1	1023
44	42	820	6	17	-1	820
45	0	0	0	0	0	0
46	32	616	4	26	0	615
47	42	699	7	17	256	700

WANG

Type	Mb	Cyls	Hds	Secs	Prec	LZ
1		306	4	17	128	305
2		615	4	17	300	615
3		615	6	17	300	615
4		940	8	17	512	940
5		940	6	17	512	940
6		615	4	17	N/A	615
7		462	8	17	256	511
8		733	5	17	N/A	733
9		900	15	17	N/A	901
10		820	3	17	N/A	820
11		855	5	17	N/A	855
12		855	7	17	N/A	855
13		306	8	17	128	319
14		733	7	17	N/A	733
16		612	4	17	ALL	663
17		977	5	17	300	977
18		977	7	17	N/A	977
19		1024	7	17	512	1023
20		733	5	17	300	732
21		733	7	17	300	732
22		733	5	17	300	733

Type	Cyls	Hds	Secs	Prec	LZ
23	306	4	17	ALL	336
24	0	0	0	0	0
25	615	4	17	ALL	615
26	1024	4	17	N/A	1023
27	1024	5	17	N/A	1023
28	1024	8	17	N/A	1023
29	512	8	17	256	512
30	612	2	17	128	612
31	0	0	0	0	0
32	0	0	0	0	0
33	0	0	0	0	0
34	0	0	0	0	0
35	1024	9	17	1024	1024
36	1024	5	17	512	1024
37	830	10	17	N/A	830
38	823	10	17	256	824
39	615	4	17	128	664
40	615	8	17	128	664
41	917	15	17	N/A	918
42	1023	15	17	N/A	1024
43	823	10	17	512	823
44	820	6	17	N/A	820
45	1024	8	17	N/A	1024
46	925	9	17	N/A	925
47	699	7	17	256	700

Type	Mb	Cyls	Hds	Secs	Prec	LZ
11	37	855	5	17	N/A	855
12	52	855	7	17	N/A	855
13	21	306	8	17	128	319
14	45	733	7	17	N/A	733
16	21	612	4	17	ALL	663
17	43	977	5	17	300	977
18	60	977	7	17	N/A	977
19	63	1024	7	17	512	1023
20	32	733	5	17	300	732
21	45	733	7	17	300	732
22	32	733	5	17	300	733
23	10	306	4	17	ALL	336
24	10	612	2	17		611
25	32	615	4	17	ALL	615
26	32	462	8	17	256	511
27	21	820	3	17		820
28	60	981	7	17		986
29	72	754	11	17		754
30	120	918	15	17		918
31	43	987	5	17		987
32	43	830	6	17	400	830
33	24	697	4	17		696
34	21	615	4	17		615
35	21	615	4	17	128	663
36	80	1024	9	17		1024
37	45	1024	5	17	512	1024
38	43	820	6	17		910
39	21	615	4	17	306	684
40	73	925	9	17		924
41	71	1024	8	17	512	1023
42	45	1024	5	17	1024	1023
43	43	615	8	17	300	615
44	43	989	5	17		988

ZENITH

Type	Mb	Cyls	Hds	Secs	Prec	LZ
1	11	306	4	17	128	305
2	21	615	4	17	300	615
3	30	699	5	17	256	710
4	65	940	8	17	512	940
5	49	940	6	17	512	940
6	21	615	4	17	N/A	615
7	43	699	7	17	256	710
8	32	733	5	17	N/A	733
9	117	900	15	17	N/A	901
10	40	925	5	17	N/A	926

19 | **Memory Chips**

The speed is indicated by the last number of the ID, typically after a hyphen, like -70, which means 70 nanoseconds. There may or may not be a leading zero.

Numbering on a chip is split into two, although it never looks like that. The first part indicates complexity, and the second the data path size, or how many bits can be read or written at the same time. To find capacity, multiply the first part by the second, divide by 8 and throw away the remainder:

>   banks of 256, meaning 1 Mb
>
>   bank of 1 Mb, meaning 1 Mb
>
>   banks of 1 Mb, meaning 4 Mb

You might see a date looking like this:

>   8609=9th month of 86.

SIMMS

SIMM stands for *Snap-In Memory Module* (or *Single In-line*). It is a small circuit board a few inches long on which are soldered some memory chips, vertically or horizontally.

A 256K chip on a SIMM has connections on all sides. If there are nine on each side, it is parity memory. Nine of these on a SIMM makes a 256 K SIMM with parity.

A 1 Mb chip has 10 on each side, in two groups of 5, or 13 on each side.

A 4 Mb chip is mostly about 20% wider than a 1 Mb, also with 10 leads in two groups of 5, or 14 on each side. The latter will be slightly taller.

SIMMs can identified with chip ID (see above) and placement, e.g. whether horizontal, vertical, on both sides, etc., and resistors, which are often used to tie the presence detect pins, 67-70, to ground.

If you really want to show off, you can ID 72-pin SIMMs by checking the resistance of those pins against 72, which is ground (if the notch is on the left, 72 is the one on the far right). For example, this table refers to IBM products:

70	69	68	67	Size speed and part no
I	I	I	I	Not valid
I	I	I	C	1 Mb 120 ns
I	I	C	I	2 Mb 120 ns
I	I	C	C	2 Mb 70 ns 92F0102
I	C	I	I	8 Mb 70 ns 64F3606
I	C	I	C	Reserved
I	C	C	I	2 Mb 80 ns 92F0103
I	C	C	C	8 Mb 80 ns 64F 3607
C	I	I	I	Reserved
C	I	I	C	1 Mb 85 ns 90X8624
C	I	C	I	2 Mb 85 ns 92F0104
C	I	C	C	4 Mb 70 ns 9F0105
C	C	I	I	4 Mb 85 ns 79F1002
C	C	I	C	1 Mb 100 ns 8 Mb 80 ns 79F1004
C	C	C	I	2 Mb 100 ns
C	C	C	C	4 Mb 80 ns 92F33372 Mb 85 ns 79F1003

30 PIN

There are two types, so-called "3-chip" or "9-chip". You may as well include "2-chip" or "8-chip" if you ignore the parity bit. In theory, software can't tell the difference, but Windows has been known to work better on the 9-chip variety; there are cost and refresh timing differences between the two, and some motherboards work with one but not the other.

72 PIN

These come as a longer circuit board with fine edge connectors and a notch in between. Some manufacturers, such as IBM, move the notch so the SIMM will only fit into one machine, or rather that their machine will only take one type of SIMM (guess whose?). They are 32 bits wide (or 36 with parity). The 4 extra bits in a 36-bit SIMM can be used for ECC instead, where single-bit errors will be corrected and not halt the machine, unlike parity which will merely report the error and halt it. Multiple-bit errors are reported with a halt.

SIMMs have address lines and a select line—a chip will respond when its select line is active. Motherboards that can only accept single-sided SIMMs have only one select line, so will not read the two select lines on a double-sided SIMM.

1Mb, 4Mb, 16Mb and 64 Mb SIMMs are generally single-sided, and 2Mb, 8Mb, and 32Mb SIMMs double-sided. They all load the chipset equally, as they use 4 x chips, except for one version of the 64 Mb, which uses 4 x 16 Mb ones, although the others are becoming available. It is not recommended to use the "conventional" 16 Mb SIMM (4 x 16) with the Triton II, and only use 2 SIMMs maximum with the Natoma. Note that electrically "single-sided" SIMMs may look double sided; they just have chips on both sides. Motherboards use these in different ways; some may treat a double-sided SIMM as two singles, and some may take two double sided or four single sided. You can't use a double sided as a "64-bit" chip in a Pentium based machine; they can still only be accessed 32 bits at a time.

There are two types of 36-bit SIMMs; those with logic parity, and those with true parity. A logic parity chip is programmed to answer "yes" if the computer checks for parity. If you use one in a machine that does more than just query for parity, it will complain loudly (e.g. Gateways), as it adds extra loading to the memory bus and the parity bit is computed later, so it also runs slower. Non-parity chips can be used in machines that either don't use parity (Macs) or allow you to turn off parity checking in the BIOS.

DIMMS

These are 64/72 bit modules, so you only need one for Pentiums. They use one set of contacts and chips for each side of the circuit board, have 168 pins and run at 3.3 and 5.0V. They are 5π inches wide and range from 1-1∫" in height.

VIDEO

The RAM on a video card is called the *frame buffer*, which holds a complete frame and defines the colour of each pixel. It follows that the greater the frame buffer (or the more memory there is on your card) the greater the resolution and/or colour depth you get.

How much video memory you need depends on what resolution you are trying to run, plus the colour depth and refresh rate. At 60 MHz refresh rates at 800 x 600, the controller is drawing dots on the screen at 40 MHz to keep up. For 256 colours, one byte is needed for each one.

With 24-bit colour at 72 KHz, 103, 680, 000 bytes are being written to the screen every second, without you making any changes! 24-bit colour uses 3 bytes per dot, 16-bit 2, and 1 colours only .5.

For a particular resolution, multiply the horizontal pixels by the vertical; 1024 x 768 = 786,43, for example. 256 colours needs 1 byte per dot, so in this case you need 768 K of RAM. 800 x 600 needs 469 K and300 is needed for 640 x 480.

MANUFACTURERS

AMI prefer chips from manufacturers in this order: Hitachi, Fujitsu, Micron, NEC, Samsung and Toshiba, although others are typically OK.

AEP

Number	Capacity	Notes
SS 4K32		128K (4Kx32)
SS 8K32		256K (8Kx32)
SS 64K8		512K (64Kx8)

SS 256K8	2 Mb (256Kx8)	
SS 256K9	2 Mb (256 x 9)	44 pin SIP
SS 128K8	1 Mb (128K x 8)	
SS 32K16	512K (32K x 16)	
SS 128K16	2 Mb (128Kx16)	

ARRAY TECHNOLOGY

Number	Capacity	Notes
AT 212SZ		
AT 212		
AT 612CP		40 pin DIP
AT 656CP	256K (16K x 6)	40 pin DIP

CYPRESS MULTICHIP

Number	Capacity	Notes
CYM 1240HD	1 Mb (256K x 4)	28 pin DIP
CYM 1420HD	1 Mb (128K x 8)	32 pin
CYM 1421HD	1 Mb (128K x 8)	32 pin DIP
CYM 1422PS	1 Mb (128K x 8)	30 pin SIP
CYM 1441PZ	2 Mb (256K x 8)	60 pin ZIP
CYM 1460PS	4 Mb (512K x 8)	36 pin SIP
CYM 1461PS	4 Mb (512K x 8)	36 pin SIP
CYM 1464PD	4 Mb (512K x 8)	32 pin DIP
CYM 1540PS	2 Mb (256K x 9)	44 pin SIP
CYM 1541PD	2 Mb (256K x 9)	44 pin DIP
CYM 1610HD	256K (16K x 16)	40 pin DIP
CYM 1621HD		
CYM 1622HV		
CYM 1623HD	1 Mb (64K x 16)	40 pin DIP
CYM 1624PV	1 Mb (64K x 16)	40 pin DSIP
CYM 1626PS	1 Mb (64K x 16)	40 pin SIP
CYM 1641HD	4 Mb (256K x 16)	48 pin DIP
CYM 1821PZ	512K (16K x 32)	64 FR-4 ZIP
CYM 1822HV	512K (16K x 32)	88 pin DSIP
CYM 1830HD	2 Mb (64K x 32)	60 pin DIP
CYM 1831PZ	2 Mb (64K x 32)	64 pin ZIP

Number	Capacity	Notes
CYM 1831PM	2 Mb (64K x 32)	64 pin SIMM
CYM 1832PZ	2 Mb (64K x 32)	60 pin ZIP
CYM 1840HD	8 Mb (256K x 32)	60 pin DIP
CYM 1841PZ	8 Mb (256K x 32)	64 pin ZIP
CYM 1841PM	8 Mb (256K x 32)	64 pin SIMM

DENSE-PAC

Number	Capacity	Notes
DPS 16X5	80K (16K x 5)	28 pin SIP
DPS 16X17	256K (16K x 16)	36 pin DSIP
DPS 257	256K (16K x 16) (32K x 8, 64K x 4)	40 pin DIP
DPS 1024	1 Mb (256K x 4) (128K x 8, 64K x 16)	42 pin DIP
DPS 1026	1 Mb (256K x 4) (128K x 8, 64K x 16)	40 pin DIP
DPS 1027	1 Mb (256K x 4) (128K x 8, 64K x 16)	40 pin DIP
DPS 2516	4 Mb (256K x 16)	44 pin DIP
DPS 4648	512K (64K x 8)	32 pin DIP
DPS 5124	2 Mb (512Kx4 256Kx8)	54 pin DIP
DPS 6432	2 Mb (64K 32)	60 pin DIP
DPS 8M612		
DPS 8M624		
DPS 8M656	256K (16K x 6)	40 pin DIP
DPS 10241	1 Mb (1024K x 1)	30 pin SIP
DPS 40256	256K (32K x 8)	28 pin DIP
DPS 41257	256K (32K x 8)	28 pin DIP
DPS 41288	1 Mb (128K x 8)	32 pin DIP
DPS 45128	4 Mb (512K x 8)	48 pin DIP
DPS 45129	4 Mb (256K x 16)	48 pin DIP
DPS 512S8	4 Mb (512K x 8)	32 pin DIP
DPS 3232V	1 Mb (32K x 32)	66 pin HIP
DPE 3232V	1 Mb (32K x 32)	66 pin HIP

EDI

Number	Capacity	Notes
8M1664C		
8M16256C	4 Mb (256K x 8)	48 pin DIP
8M16257C	4 Mb (256K x 16)	40 pin DIP
8F3254C	2 Mb (64K x 32)	60 pin DIP
8M32256C	8 Mb (256K x 32)	60 pin DIP
8M4257C	1 Mb (256K x 4)	28 pin DIP
8M8128C	1 Mb (128K x 8)	32 pin DIP
8M8130C	1 Mb (128K x 8)	32 pin DIP
8M8130P	1 Mb (128K x 8)	32 pin DIP
8M8256C	2 Mb (256K x 8)	32 pin DIP
8F8257C	2 Mb (256K x 8)	32 pin DIP

8F8258CMSC	2 Mb (256K x 8)	36 pin SIP
8M8512C	4 Mb (512K x 8)	32 pin DIP
8M864C	512K (64K x 8)	32 pin DIP
EDH81H256C	256K (256K x 1)	24 pin DIP
EDH816H16C	256K (16K x 16)	36 pin DSIP
EDH84H64C	256K (64K x 4)	24 pin DIP
EDH8808	64K (8K x 8)	28 pin SIP
EDH8832C	256K (8K x 8)	28 pin DIP
8F1664C	1 Mb (64K x 16)	40 pin DIP

MB 85410	512K (64K x 8)	60 pin ZIP
MB 85411	512K (64K x 9)	70 pin ZIP
MB 85414	512K (16K x 32)	64 pin ZIP
MB 85415	512K (16K x 36)	70 pin ZIP
MB 85420	2 Mb (256K x 8)	60 pin ZIP

GOLDSTAR

Number	Capacity	Notes
GM 71C1000J	1 Mb	72 pin
GMM 794000S	4 Mb	30 pin

HARRIS

Number	Capacity	Notes
HM 8808	64K (8K x 8)	28 pin DIP
HM 8816	128K (16K x 8)	28 pin DIP
HM 92560	256K (32K x 8) (16K x 16)	48 pin DIP synch

FUJITSU

SIMM

Number	Capacity	Notes
MB 85301A	1 Mb (256K x 8)	30 pin
MB 85306A	1 Mb (256K x 9)	30 pin
MB 85331	1 Mb (256K x 32)	72 pin 32 bit
MB 85336	1 Mb (256K x 36)	72 pin 36 bit
MB 85376	1 Mb (256K x 40)	72 pin 40 bit
MB 85332	1 Mb (512K x 32)	72 pin 32 bit
MB 85337	1 Mb (512K x 36)	72 pin d/s 36 bit
MB 85377	1 Mb (512K x 40)	72 pin d/s
MB 85230	1 Mb (1M x 8)	30 pin 8 chip
MB 85235	1 Mb (1M x 9)	30 pin
MB 85303	4 Mb (1M x 8)	30 pin
MB 85308	4 Mb (1M x 9)	30 pin
MB 85341	4 Mb (1M x 32)	72 pin
MB 85346	4 Mb (1M x 36)	72 pin
MB 85378	4 Mb (1M x 40)	72 pin
MB 85342	4 Mb (2M x 32)	72 pin
MB 85347	4 Mb (2M x 36)	72 pin
MB 85379	4 Mb (2M x 40)	72 pin d/s
MB 85280	4 Mb (4M x 8)	30 pin
MB 85290	4 Mb (4M x 8)	30 pin
MB 85285	4 Mb (4M x 9)	30 pin
MB 85295	4 Mb (4m x 9)	30 pin

DRAM

Number	Capacity	Notes
MB 8264	64K x 1 bit	DRAM
MB 85402	256K (16K x 16)	36 pin DSIP
MB 85403	2 Mb (256K x 8)	44 pin SIP

HITACH

Number	Capacity	Notes
HM 4864	64K x 1	DRAM
HB 56A25640BR	1 Mb (256K x 40)	72 pin 40 bit
HB 56A51240BR	1 Mb (512K x 40)	72 pin d/s 40 bit
HB 56G25632B	1 Mb (256K x 32)	72 pin 32 bit
HB 56G25636B	1 Mb (256K x 36)	72 pin 36 bit
HB 56G51232SB	1 Mb (512K x 32)	72 pin 36 bit
HB 56G51236SG	1 Mb (512 x 36)	72 pin d/s 32 bit
HM 514400AS	1 Mb	72 pin
HB 56A18B	1 Mb (1M x 8)	30 pin
HB 56A19B	1 Mb (1Mb x 9)	30 pin
HB 56G18B	4 Mb (1M x 8)	72 pin
HB 56G19B	4 Mb (1M x 9)	30 pin
HB 56D132SBR	4 Mb (1M x 32)	72 pin
HB 56D136SBR	4 Mb (1M x 36)	72 pin
HB 56D136SBS	4 Mb (1M x 36)	72 pin
HB 56A140BR	4 Mb (1M x 40)	72 pin
HB 56A232SBT	4 Mb (2M x 32)	72 pin d/s
HB 56D236SBS	4 Mb (2M x 36)	72 pin d/s
HB 56A240BR	4 Mb (2M x 40)	72 pin d/s
HB 56A48BR/AR	4 Mb (4M x 8)	30 pin

HB 56A48ATR	4 Mb (4M x 8)	30 pin
HB 56A49BR/AR	4 Mb (4M x 9)	30 pin
HB 56A49ATR	4 Mb (4M x 9)	30 pin low prof
HB 56A432SB	16 Mb (4M x 32)	72 pin
HB 56D436SBR	16 Mb (4M x 36)	72 pin
HB 56A440B	16 Mb (4M x 40)	72 pin d/s
HB 56A832SB	16 Mb (8M x 32)	72 pin d/s
HB 56D836SB	16 Mb (8M x 36)	72 pin d/s
HB 56A840B	16 Mb (8M x 40)	72 pin d/s
HB 56A168B	16 Mb (16M x 8)	30 pin d/s
HB 56A169B	16 Mb (16M x 9)	30 pin d/s
HM 66203(L)	1 Mb (128K x 8)	32 pin DIP
HM 66204	1 Mb (128K x 8)	32 pin DIP
HM 62256(L)P	256K (32K x 8)	28 pin DIP

HYUNDAI

Number	Capacity	Notes
HYM 591000AM	1 Mb	72 pin
HYM 514400ALJ	4 Mb	72 pin
HYM 536100AM	4 Mb	72 pin
HYM 594000M	4 Mb	30 pin
HYM 536410M	16 Mb	72 pin

IBM

Number	Capacity	Notes
57G8887	4 Mb	30 pin

INOVA

Number	Capacity	Notes
S 128K8(L)	1 Mb (128K x 8)	32 pin DIP
S 32K8	256K (32K x 8)	JEDEC 28 pin DIP

LOGIC DEVICES

Number	Capacity	Notes
LMM 4016	4 Mb (256K x 16)	48 pin DIP
LMM 624	1 Mb (64K x 16)	40 pin DIP
LMM 824	1 Mb (128K x 8)	32 pin DIP
LMM 456	256K (64K x 4)	28 pin SIP

MICRON

BEDO DRAMs

Number	Capacity
MT4LC4M4G6	4 M x 4
MT4LC16M4D7	16 M x 4
MT4LCl6M4D9	16 MX4
MT4LC2M8F4	2 M x 8
MT4LC8M8W4	8 M x 8
MT4LC8M8W5	8 M x 8
MT4LC1 M16H5	1 M x 16
MT4LC4M16U2	4 M x 16
MT4LC4M16U6	4 M x 16

EDO DRAMs

Number	Capacity
MT4C4007J (L)	1 M x 4
MT4LC4M4E8 (L)	4 M x 4
MT4LC16M4G3	16 M x 4
MT4LC16M4H9	16 M x 4
MT4LC2M8E7 (L)	2 M x 8
MT4LC8M8P4	8 M x 8
MT4LC8M8C2	8 M x 8
MT4C16270	256K x 16
MT4LC1M16E5 (L)	l M x l6
MT4LC4M16N3	4 M x 16
MT4LC4M16R6	4 M x 16

FPM DRAMs

Number	Capacity	Notes
MT4C1004J (L)	4 M x 1	
MT4C4001J (L)	1 M x 4	72 pin
MT4LC4M4B1 (L)	4 M x 4	
MT4LCl6M4A7	16 M x 4	
MT4LCl6M4T8	16 M x 4	
MT4LC2M8B1 (L)	2 M x 8	
MT4LC8M8E1	8 M x 8	
MT4LC8M8B6	8 M x 8	
MT4C16257 (L)	256K x 16	
MT4LC1M16C3 (L)	1 M x 16	
MT4LC4M16K2	4 M x 16	
MT4LC4MI6F5	4 M x 16	

SGRAM

Number	Capacity
MT41LC256K32D4 (S)	256K x 32

DRAM SIMMs

Number	Capacity
MT2D25632	256K x 32
MT4D51232	512K x 32
MT8D132 (X)	1 M x 32
MT2D(T)132 (X)(B)	1 M x 32
MT16D232 (X)	2 M x 32
MT4D(T)232 (X)	2 M x 32
MT4D232 B	2 M x 32
MT8D432 B	4 M x 32
MT8D432 (X)	4 M x 32
MT16D832 (X)	8 M x 32
MT12D436	4 M x 36
MT24D836	8 M x 36

DRAM DIMMs

Number	Capacity
MT2LDT132H (X)(L)	1 M x 32
MT4LDT232H (X)(L)	2 M x 32
MT8LDT432H (X)(L)	4 M x 32
MT16D164	1 M x 64
MT4LD(T)164 (ABX)	1 M x 64
MT8D264 (X)	2 M x 64
MT8LD264 (ABX)	2 M x 64
MTI6LD464 (ABX)	4 M x 64
MT9LD272(ABX)	2 M x 72
MT18LD472 (ABX)	4 M x 72
MT36LD872 (X)	8 M x 72

Assorted

Number	Capacity	Notes
MT 4264	64K x 1 bit	DRAM
MT 8C16256	4 Mb (256K x 16)	48 pin DIP
MT 8C3216	512K (16K x 32)	64 pin ZIP
MT 8C3264	2 Mb (64K x 32)	64 pin ZIP
MT 8C32256	8 Mb (256K x 32)	64 pin ZIP
MT 85C8128		
MT 85C1632		
MT 85C1664		
MT 9D136M	4 Mb	72 pin

MITSUBISHI

Number	Capacity	Notes
M5 4164	64K x 1 bit	
M5K 4164	64K x 1	DRAM
M5M 4256P		DRAM
MH 25632BJ/XJ	1 Mb (256K x 32)	72 pin
MH 25636XJ	1 Mb (256K x 36)	72 pin
MH 51232BJ/SXJ	1 Mb (512K x 32)	72 pin d/s
MH 51236SXJ	1 Mb (512K x 36)	72 pin d/s
MH 1M08B0J	1 Mb (1M x 8)	30 pin
MH 1M9B0DJA	1 Mb (1M x 9)	30 pin 9 chip
MH 1M08A0AJ	4 Mb (1M x 8)	30 pin
MH 1M09A0AJA	4 Mb (1M x 9)	30 pin
MH 1M32ADJ	4 Mb (1M x 32)	72 pin
MH 1M36ADJ	4 Mb (1M x 36)	72 pin
MH 1M36EJ	4 Mb (1M x 36)	72 pin
MH 2M32EJ	4 Mb (2M x 32)	72 pin d/s
MH 2M36EJ/AST	4 Mb (2M x 36)	72 pin d/s
MH 2M40AJ	4 Mb (2M x 40)	72 pin d/s
MH 4M08A0J	4 Mb (4M x 8)	30 pin
MH 4M09A0J/DJA	4 Mb (4M x 9)	30 pin
MHIM 36BNDJ	4 Mb	72 pin
M5M 44100AJ	4 Mb (4M x 1)	8 chip
M5M 444000AJ33ISH15 (MH2M365EJ)	8 Mb	72 pin
MH 4M36ANXJ	16 Mb	72 pin
MH 4M36AJ	16 Mb (4M x 36)	72 pin d/s
MH 16M08	16 Mb (16M x 8)	30 pin d/s
MH 16M09	16 Mb (16M x 9)	30 pin d/s
MH 12808TNA		
MH 12908TNA		
MH 25608S1N	2 Mb (256K x 8)	35 pin SIMM
MH 25608TNA	2 Mb (256K x 8)	32 pin DIP
MH 51208SN	4 Mb (512K x 8)	64 pin SIMM

MOSAIC

Number	Capacity	Notes
MS 1256CS	256K (256K x 1)	25 pin SIP
MS 1664BCX	1 Mb (64K x 16)	40 pin DIP
MS 3216RKX	512K (16K x 32)	JEDEC 40 pin DIP
MS 3264FKX	2 Mb (64K x 32)	60 pin DIP
MS 3264RKX	2 Mb (64K x 32)	JEDEC 64 pin ZIP
MS 32256FKX	8 Mb (256K x 32)	60 pin ZIP
MS 32256RKX	8 Mb (256K x 32)	64 pin ZIP
MS 8128SLU	1 Mb (128K x 8)	32 pin DIP
MS 8256RKL	2 Mb (256K x 8)	32 pin SIP
MS 8512	4 Mb (512K x 8)	32 pin DIP
PUMA 2S1000	1 Mb (32K x 32)	66 pin HIP
PUMA 2E1000	1 Mb (32K x 32)	66 pin HIP

MOSEL

Number	Capacity	Notes
MS 88128	1 Mb (128K x 8)	32 pin DIP

MOSTEK

Number	Capacity	Notes
MK 4564	64K x 1 bit	DRAM

MOTOROLA

Number	Capacity	Notes
MCM 3264	2 Mb (64K x 32)	64 pin ZIP
MCM 6665	64K x 1 bit	DRAM
MCM 8256	2 Mb (256K x 8)	60 pin ZIP
SCM 91781		DRAM

NATIONAL

Number	Capacity	Notes
MN 4164	64K x 1 bit	DRAM

NEC

Number	Capacity	Notes
D 41256		
D 4164C	64K x 1	DRAM
PD 4164	64K x 1 bit	DRAM
SM 591000A	1 Mb	72 pin

Number	Capacity	Notes
MC 120	1 Mb (128K x 8)	32 pin DIP
MC 42256A36	1 Mb (256K x 36)	72 pin
MC 42512A36	1 Mb (512 x 36)	72 pin d/s
MC 42512AA40	1 Mb (512K x 40)	72 pin d/s
MC 421000A8	1 Mb (1M x 8)	30 pin
MC 421000A9	1 Mb (1M x 9)	30 pin
MC 421000A36BE	4 Mb (1M x 36)	72 pin
MC 421000A40	4 Mb (1M x 40)	72 pin
MC 422000A32B	4 Mb (2M x 32)	72 pin d/s
MC 422000A36B	4 Mb (2M x 36)	72 pin d/s
MC 422000AA40	4 Mb (2M x 40)	72 pin d/s
MC 424000AB	4 Mb (4M x 8)	30 pin
MC 424100A9	4 Mb (4M x 9)	30 pin
MC 424000A36BE	16 Mb	72 pin

OKI

Number	Capacity	Notes
MSM 3764	64K x 1 bit	DRAM
M 514400B	1 Mb	72 pin
MSC 2328B	1 Mb (256K x 8)	30 pin
MSC 2332B	1 Mb (256K x 9)	30 pin
MSC 2327B	1 Mb (256K x 32)	72 pin
MSC 2320B	1 Mb (256K x 36)	72 pin
MSC 2333B	1 Mb (512K x 32)	72 pin d/s
MSC 2321B	1 Mb (512K x 36)	72 pin d/s
MSC 2322B	1 Mb (512K x 40)	72 pin d/s
MSC 2313B	1 Mb (1M x 8)	30 pin
MSC 2312B	1 Mb (1M x 9)	30 pin
MSC 23109	4 Mb (1M x 9)	30 pin
MSC 23108	4 Mb (1M x 8)	30 pin
MSC 2316B	4 Mb	72 pin
MSC 23132	4 Mb (1M x 32)	72 pin
MSC 23136	4 Mb (1M x 36)	72 pin
MSC 23S136	4 Mb (1M x 36)	72 pin
MSC 23140	4 Mb (1M x 40)	2 pin
MSC 23232	4 Mb (2M x 32)	2 pin d/s
MSC 23236	4 Mb (2M x 36)	72 pin d/s
MSC 23408	4 Mb (4M x 8)	30 pin
MSC 23409	4 Mb (4M x 9)	30 pin
M 5114100A	4 Mb	30 pin SIMM, 9-chip
M 514900	4 Mb	72 pin

SAMSUNG

Number	Capacity	Notes
KMM 366S203AT	(2M x 64)	SDRAM
KMM 532512BW	2 Mb	72 pin
KMM 5361003C	4 Mb	72 pin
KMM 594000B	4 Mb	30 pin
KMM 5364100A	16 Mb	72 pin
KMM 5368103AK	32 Mb	72 pin

SHARP

Number	Capacity	Notes
LH 6764	64K x 1	DRAM

SIEMENS

Hyundai?

Number	Capacity	Notes
HYB 41256		DRAM
HYB 4164	64K x 1	DRAM
HYB 514256A	256K x 4	DRAM

TEXAS INSTRUMENTS

Number	Capacity	Notes
TMS 4164	64K x 1	DRAM

TOSHIBA

SIMMs

BS/AS=SIMM
BL/AL=SIPP

Number.	Capacity	Notes
THM 82500BS/AS	1 Mb (256K x 8)	30 pin, 2 chip
THM 92500BS/AS	1 Mb (256K x 9)	30 pin, 3 chip
THM 85100BS/AS	1 Mb (512K x 8)	30 pin 4 chip
THM 81000BS/AS	1 Mb (1M x 8)	30 pin 8 chip
THM 81020BL/AL	1 Mb (1M x 8)	30 pin 8 ch d/s
THM 322500BS/AS	1 Mb (256K x 32)	72 pin 32 bit
THM 3225B0BS/AS	1 Mb (256K x 32)	72 pin 2 ch 32 bit

THM 91000BS/AS	1 Mb (1M x 9)	30 pin 9 chip
THM 91020BL/AL	1 Mb (1M x 9)	30 pin 9 chip
THM 91010BSG/AS	1 Mb (1M x 9)	30 pin
THM 91050BS/AS	1 Mb (1M x 9)	30 pin
THM 362500BS/AS	1 Mb (256K x 36)	72 pin 36 bit
THM 362570BS/AS	1 Mb (256K x 36)	72 pin 9 ch 36 bit
THM 36250B0BS	1 Mb (256K x 36)	72 pin 2 ch 36 bit
THM 402500BS/AS	1 Mb (256K x 40)	72 pin 10 ch 40 b
THM 402510BS/AS	1 Mb (256K x 40)	72 pin 10 ch 40 b
THM 325120BS/AS	1 Mb (512K x 32)	72 pin d/s 32 bit
THM 3251C0BS	1 Mb (512K x 32)	72 pin 4 ch d/s 32 b
THM 325140BSG	1 Mb (512K x 32)	72 pin 32 bit
THM 325180BS/AS	1 Mb (512K x 32)	72 pin 32 bit
THM 365120BS/AS	1 Mb (512K x 36)	72p 36 bit d/s
THM 365140BSG	1 Mb (512K x 36)	72p 36 b d/s
THM 365160BD/AS	1 Mb (512K x 36)	72p 36 b d/s
THM 3651C0BS	1 Mb (512K x 36)	72p d/s 36 b
THM 405120BS/AS	1 Mb (512K x 40)	72p d/s 40 b
THM 405140BS/AS	1 Mb (512K x 40)	72p d/s 40 b
THM 81070BS/AS	4 Mb (1M x 8)	30 pin 2 chip
THM 91070AS/AL	4 Mb (1M x 9)	30 pin 3 chip
THM 161000BS/AS	4 Mb (1M x 16)	72 pin 4 chip
THM 181000AS	4 Mb (1M x 18)	72 pin
THM 181010AS	4 Mb (1M x 18)	72 pin 6 chip

THM 84000BS/AS	4 Mb (4M x 8)	30 pin 8 chip
THM 84020BL/AL	4 Mb (4M x 8)	30 pin 8 ch d/s
THM 321000BS/AS	4 Mb (1M x 32)	72 pin 8 ch 32
THM 321090BS/AS	4 Mb (1M x 32)	72 pin
THM 331000BS/AS	4 Mb (1M x 33)	2 pin 8 ch 33
THM 94000BS/AS	4 Mb (4M x 9)	30 pin
THM 94020AL	4 Mb (4M x 9)	30 pin 9 ch
THM 361000AS	4 Mb (1M x 36)	72 pin
THM 361020AS	4 Mb (1M x 36)	72 pin d/s
THM 361010AS	4 Mb (1M x 36)	72 pin 36 bit
THM 361070BS/AS	4 Mb (1M x 36)	72 pin 36 bit 9 ch
THM 401000BS/AS	4 Mb (1M x 40)	72 pin JEDEC
THM 401010BS/AS	4 Mb (1M x 40)	72 pin
THM 88020B/ATS	4 Mb (8M x 8)	30 pin d/s
THM 164020BS/AS	4 Mb (4M x 16)	72 pin d/s
THM 322020BS/AS	4 Mb (2M x 32)	72 pin d/s
THM 322080BS/AS	4 Mb (2M x 32)	72 pin
THM 98020B/ATS	4 Mb (8M x 9)	30 pin d/s
THM 184020BS/AS	4 Mb (4M x 18)	72 pin d/s
THM 184040BS/AS	4 Mb (4M x 18)	72 pin d/s
THM 362020AS	4 Mb (2M x 36)	72 pin d/s
THM 362040AS	4 Mb (2M x 36)	72 pin d/s
THM 362060BS/AS	4 Mb (2M x 36)	72 pin d/s
THM 402020BS/AS	4 Mb (2M x 40)	72 pin d/s
THM 402040BS/AS	4 Mb (2M x 40)	72 pin d/s
THM 324080BS/AS	4 Mb (4M x 320)	72 pin
THM 334080BS/AS	4 Mb (4M x 33)	72 pin

THM 364080BS/AS	4 Mb (4M x 36)	72 pin d/s
THM 3225B0BS	4 Mb (256K x 32)	
THM 3625B0BS	4 Mb (256K x 36)	
THM 3251C0BS	4 Mb (512K x 32)	
THM 3651C0BS	4 Mb (512K x 36)	
THM 324000S	16 Mb (4M x 32)	72 pin
THM 364020S	16 Mb (4M x 36)	72 pin d/s
THM 364060SG	16 Mb (4M x 36)	72 pin
THM 81620S	16 Mb (16M x 8)	30 pin d/s
THM 91620S	16 Mb (16M x 9)	30 pin d/s
THM 404020SG	16 Mb (4M x 40)	72 pin d/s
THM 328020S	16 Mb (8M x 32)	72 pin d/s
THM 368020S	16 Mb (8M x 36)	72 pin d/s
THM 368060S	16 Mb (8M x 36)	72 pin d/s
THM 408020S	16 Mb (8M x 40)	72 pin d/s

DRAM

Number	Capacity	Notes
THM 82500BS/AS	1 Mb (256K x 8)	30 pin, 2 chip
THM 92500BS/AS	1 Mb (256K x 9)	30 pin, 3 chip
THM 85100BS/AS	1 Mb (512K x 8)	30 pin 4 chip
THM 81000BS/AS	1 Mb (1M x 8)	30 pin 8 chip
THM 81020BL/AL	1 Mb (1M x 8)	30 pin 8 ch d/s
THM 322500BS/AS	1 Mb (256K x 32)	72 pin 32 bit
THM 3225B0BS/AS	1 Mb (256K x 32)	72 pin 2 ch 32 bit
THM 91000BS/AS	1 Mb (1M x 9)	30 pin 9 chip
THM 91020BL/AL	1 Mb (1M x 9)	30 pin 9 chip
THM 91010BSG/AS	1 Mb (1M x 9)	30 pin

THM 91050BS/AS	1 Mb (1M x 9)	30 pin
THM 362500BS/AS	1 Mb (256K x 36)	72 pin 36 bit
THM 362570BS/AS	1 Mb (256K x 36)	72 pin 9 ch 36 bit
THM 36250B0BS	1 Mb (256K x 36)	72 pin 2 ch 36 bit
THM 402500BS/AS	1 Mb (256K x 40)	72 pin 10 ch 40 b
THM 402510BS/AS	1 Mb (256K x 40)	72 pin 10 ch 40 b
THM 325120BS/AS	1 Mb (512K x 32)	72 pin d/s 32 bit
THM 3251C0BS	1 Mb (512K x 32)	72 pin 4 ch d/s 32 b
THM 325140BSG	1 Mb (512K x 32)	72 pin 32 bit
THM 325180BS/AS	1 Mb (512K x 32)	72 pin 32 bit
THM 365120BS/AS	1 Mb (512K x 36)	72p 36 bit d/s
THM 365140BSG	1 Mb (512K x 36)	72p 36 b d/s
THM 365160BD/AS	1 Mb (512K x 36)	72p 36 b d/s
THM 3651C0BS	1 Mb (512K x 36)	72p d/s 36 b
THM 405120BS/AS	1 Mb (512K x 40)	72p d/s 40 b
THM 405140BS/AS	1 Mb (512K x 40)	72p d/s 40 b
THM 81070BS/AS	4 Mb (1M x 8)	30 pin 2 chip
THM 91070AS/AL	4 Mb (1M x 9)	30 pin 3 chip
THM 161000BS/AS	4 Mb (1M x 16)	72 pin 4 chip
THM 181000AS	4 Mb (1M x 18)	72 pin
THM 181010AS	4 Mb (1M x 18)	72 pin 6 chip
THM 84000BS/AS	4 Mb (4M x 8)	30 pin 8 chip
THM 84020BL/AL	4 Mb (4M x 8)	30 pin 8 ch d/s
THM 321000BS/AS	4 Mb (1M x 32)	72 pin 8 ch 32
THM 321090BS/AS	4 Mb (1M x 32)	72 pin
THM 331000BS/AS	4 Mb (1M x 33)	2 pin 8 ch 33

THM 94000BS/AS	4 Mb (4M x 9)	30 pin
THM 94020AL	4 Mb (4M x 9)	30 pin 9 ch
THM 361000AS	4 Mb (1M x 36)	72 pin
THM 361020AS	4 Mb (1M x 36)	72 pin d/s
THM 361010AS	4 Mb (1M x 36)	72 pin 36 bit
THM 361070BS/AS	4 Mb (1M x 36)	72 pin 36 bit 9 ch
THM 401000BS/AS	4 Mb (1M x 40)	72 pin JEDEC
THM 401010BS/AS	4 Mb (1M x 40)	72 pin
THM 88020B/ATS	4 Mb (8M x 8)	30 pin d/s
THM 164020BS/AS	4 Mb (4M x 16)	72 pin d/s
THM 322020BS/AS	4 Mb (2M x 32)	72 pin d/s
THM 322080BS/AS	4 Mb (2M x 32)	72 pin
THM 98020B/ATS	4 Mb (8M x 9)	30 pin d/s
THM 184020BS/AS	4 Mb (4M x 18)	72 pin d/s
THM 184040BS/AS	4 Mb (4M x 18)	72 pin d/s
THM 362020AS	4 Mb (2M x 36)	72 pin d/s
THM 362040AS	4 Mb (2M x 36)	72 pin d/s
THM 362060BS/AS	4 Mb (2M x 36)	72 pin d/s
THM 402020BS/AS	4 Mb (2M x 40)	72 pin d/s
THM 402040BS/AS	4 Mb (2M x 40)	72 pin d/s
THM 324080BS/AS	4 Mb (4M x 320	72 pin
THM 334080BS/AS	4 Mb (4M x 33)	72 pin
THM 364080BS/AS	4 Mb (4M x 36)	72 pin d/s
THM 3225B0BS	4 Mb (256K x 32)	
THM 3625B0BS	4 Mb (256K x 36)	
THM 3251C0BS	4 Mb (512K x 32)	
THM 3651C0BS	4 Mb (512K x 36)	
THM 324000S	16 Mb (4M x 32)	72 pin
THM 364020S	16 Mb (4M x 36)	72 pin d/s
THM 364060SG	16 Mb (4M x 36)	72 pin
THM 81620S	16 Mb (16M x 8)	30 pin d/s

THM 91620S	16 Mb (16M x 9)	30 pin d/s
THM 404020SG	16 Mb (4M x 40)	72 pin d/s
THM 328020S	16 Mb (8M x 32)	72 pin d/s
THM 368020S	16 Mb (8M x 36)	72 pin d/s
THM 368060S	16 Mb (8M x 36)	72 pin d/s
THM 408020S	16 Mb (8M x 40)	72 pin d/s

VALTRONIC

Number	Capacity	Notes
TC 511000BJ/AJ	1M x 1	No parity
TC 5116100J		
TC 5117400J		
TC 51256		
TC 5141000		
TC 514256AJ		256K x 8
TC 514260BJ		
TC 514280BJ		
TC 514400ASJ		
TMN 4164	64K x 1	DRAM

VITAREL

Number	Capacity	Notes
M 107	1 Mb (64K x 16)	40 pin DIP

Number	Capacity	Notes
VMS 10A24	1 Mb (64K x 16) (128K x 8) (64K x 8)	40 pin DIP
VMS 32K8	256K (32K x 8)	28 pin DIP
VMS 128K8M	1 Mb (128K x 8)	28 pin DIP

WHITE TECHNOLOGY

Number	Capacity	Notes
WS 128K8	1 Mb (128K x 8)	32 pin DIP

ZYREL

Number	Capacity	Notes
Z 108	1 Mb (128K x 8)	32 pin DIP
Z108	1 Mb (128K x 8)	32 pin DIP

SRAM

ALLIANCE

Number	Capacity	Notes
AS 7C256	32K x 8	
AS 7C3256	32K x 8	3.3V

AT&T

Number	Capacity	Notes
ATT 7C167	16K x 1	
ATT 7C168	4K x 4	
ATT 7C171	4K x 4	
ATT 7C172	4K x 4	
ATT 7C116	2K x 9	
ATT 7C187	64K x 1	
ATT 7C164	16K x 4	
ATT 7C166	16K x 4	
ATT 7C165	16K x 4	
ATT 7C185	8K x 8	
ATT 7C195	64K x 4	
ATT 7C199	32K x 8	
ATT 7C106	256K x 4	
ATT 7C109	128K x 8	
ATT 7C180	4K x 4	Tag
ATT 7C174	8K x 8	Tag

CYPRES

Number	Capacity	Notes
CY 7C106	256K x 4	
CY 7C109	128K x 8	
CY 7C178	32K x 18	Burst Pent
CY 7C167(A)	16K x 1	
CY 7C168(A)	4K x 4	
CY 7C169(A)	4K x 4	
CY 7C171(A)	4K x 4	
CY 7C172(A)	4K x 4	
CY 7C128(A)	2K x 8	
CY 7C187(A)	64K x 1	
CY 7C164(A)	16K x 4	

CY 7C166(A)	16K x 4
CY 7C185(A)	8K x 8
CY 7C186(A)	8K x 8
CY 7C195	64K x 4
CY 7B195	64K x 4
CY 7C198	32K x 8
CY 7C199	32K x 8
CY 7B198	32K x 8
CY 7B199	32K x 8
CYC 1399	32K x 8 3.3v

EDI

Number	Capacity
EDI 8164	64K x 1
EDI 8416	16K x 4
EDI 8417	16K x 4
EDI 8808CB	8K x 8
EDI 8466CA	64K x 4
EDI 8466CB	64K x 4
EDI 8833C/P/L	32K x 8
EDI 8834C/A	32K x 8
EDI 84256CS	256K x 4
EDI 84256LPS	256K x 4
EDI 88130C/LP	128K x 8

Fujitsu

Number	Capacity
MB 81C67	16K x 1
MB 81C68A	16K x 1
MB 81C69A	4K x 4
MB 81C71	64K x 1
MB 81C71A	64K x 1
MB 81C74	16K x 4
MB 81C75	16K x 4
MB 81C78A	8K x 8
MB 82B78	8K x 8
MB 81C84A	64K x 4
MB 82B85	64K x 4
MB 8298	32K x 8
MB 82B88	32K x 8
MB 82B005	256K x 4
MB 82B008	128K x 8

Hitachi

Number	Capacity
HM 6267	16K x 1
HM 6268	4K x 4
HM 6716	2K x 8
HM 6287	64K x 1
HM 6787	64K x 1
HM 6288	16K x 4
HM 6788	16K x 4
HM 6289	16K x 4
HM 6789	16K x 4
HM 6709A	64K x 4
HM 62832H	32K x 8
HM 624256A	256K x 4
HM 628127H	128K x 8

IC Works

Number	Capacity	Notes
ICW 73B586A	32K x 18	Burst Pent
ICW 73B586B	32K x 18	Burst Pent

Inmos

Number	Capacity
IMS 1403	16K x 1
IMS 1423	4K x 4
IMS 1600	64K x 1
IMS 1605	64K x 1
IMS 1620	16K x 4
IMS 1625	16K x 4
IMS 1624	16K x 4
IMS 1629	16K x 4
IMS 1630	8K x 8
IMS 1635	8K x 8

Logic

Number	Capacity	Notes
L 7C167	16K x 1	
L 7C168	4K x 4	
L 7C171	4K x 4	
L 7C172	4K x 4	
L 6116	2K x 8	
L 7C187	64K x 1	
L 7C164	16K x 4	

L 7C166	16K x 4	
L 7C165	16K x 4	
L 7C185	8K x 8	
L 7CL185	8K x 8	
L 7C195	64K x 4	
L 7C199	32K x 8	
L 7CL199	32K x 8	
L 7C180	4K x 4	Tag
L 7C174	8K x 8	Tag

MT58LC32K36C5	32K x 36
MT58LC32K36D8	32K x 36
MT58LC32K36G1	32K x 36
MT58LC64K36C5	64K x 36
MT58LC64K36D8	64K x 36
MT58LC64K36F1	64K x 36
MT58LC64K36G1	64K x 36
MT58LC128K36C5	128K x 36
MT58LC128K36D8	128K x 36
MT58LC128K36F1	128K x 36
MT58LC128K36G1	128K x 36

MICRON SYNCBURST PIPELINED SRAMs

Number	Capacity
MT58LC64K16C5	64K x 16
MT58LC64K16D8	64K x 16
MT58LC128K16C5	128K x 16
MT58LC128K16D8	128K x 16
MT58LC128K16F1	128K x 16
MT58LC128K16G1	128K x 16
MT58LC256K16F1	256K x 16
MT58LC256K16G1	256K x 16
MT58LC64K18C5	64K x 18
MT58LC64K18D8	64K x 18
MT58LC64K18C4	64K x 18
MT58LC64K18D7	64K x 18
MT58LC128K18C5	128K x 18
MT58LC128K18D8	128K x 18
MT58LC128K18F1	128K x 18
MT58LC128K18G1	128K x 18
MTS8LC256K18F1	256K x 18
MT58LC256K18G1	256K x 18
MT58LC32K32C4	32K x 32
MT58LC32K32D7	32K x 32
MT58LC32K32C5	32K x 32
MT58LC32K32D8	32K x 32
MT58LC32K32G1	32K x 32
MT58LC64K32C5	64K x 32
MT58LC64K32D8	64K x 32
MT58LC64K32F1	64K x 32
MT58LC64K32G1	64K x 32
MT58LC128K32C5	128K x 32
MT58LC128K32D8	128K x 32
MT58LC128K32F1	128K x 32
MT58LC128K32G1	128K x 32
MT58LC32K36C4	32K x 36
MT58LC32K36D7	32K x 36

Syncburst Flow--Through SRAMs

Number	Capacity
MT58LC64K16B2	64K x 16
MT58LC64K16B3	64K x 16
MT58LC128K16B3	128K x 16
MT58LC128K16E1	128K x 16
MT58LC256K16E1	256K x 16
MT58LC64K18B2	64K x 18
MT58LC64K18B3	64K x 18
MT58LC128K18B3	128K x 18
MT58LC128K18E1	128K x 18
MT58LC256K18E1	256K x 18
MT58LC32K32B2	32K x 32
MT58LC32K32B3	32K x 32
MT58LC64K32B3	64K x 32
MT58LC64K32F1	64K x 32
MT58LC128K32B3	128K x 32
MT58LC128K32E1	128K x 32
MT58LC32K36B2	32K x 36
MT58LC32K36B3	32K x 36
MT58LC64K36B3	64K x 36
MT58LC64K36E1	64K x 36
MT58LC128K36B3	128K x 36
MT58LC128K36E1	128K x 36

Synchronous SRAM Module

Number	Capacity
MT3L5T3264	32K x 64
MT3LST3264P	32K x 64
MT5LST6464	64K x 64
MT5LST6464P	64K x 64

Assorted

Number	Capacity	Notes
MT 5C1601	16K x 1	
MT 5C1604	4K x 4	
MT 5C1606	4K x 4	
MT 5C1607	4K x 4	
MT 5C1608	2K x 8	
MT 5C6401	64K x 1	
MT 5C6404	16K x 4	
MT 5C6405	16K x 4	
MT 5C6408	8K x 8	
MT 5C2565	64K x 4	
MT 5C256B	32K x 8	
MT 5C2568	32K x 8	
MT 5LC2568	32K x 8	3.3v
MT 5LC2568	32K x 8	3.3v
MT 5C1005	256K x 4	
MT 5C1008	128K x 8	

MITSUBISHI

Number	Capacity
M5M 21C67	16K x 1
M5M 21X68	4K x 4
M5M 5187A	64K x 1
M5M 5187B	64K x 1
M5M 5188A	16K x 4
M5M 5188B	16K x 4
M5M 5189A	16K x 4
M5M 5189B	16K x 4
M5M 5178	8K x 8
M5M 5259B	64K x 4
M5M 5278	32K x 8
M5M 51004	256K x 4

MOTOROLA

Number	Capacity	Notes
MCM 6268	4K x 4	
MCM 6287B	64K x 1	
MCM 6288	16K x 4	
MCM 6290	16K x 4	
MCM 6264C	8K x 8	

Number	Capacity	Notes
MCM 6209	64K x 4	
MCM 6206	32K x 8	
MCM 62V06	32K x 8	3.3v
MCM 6306D	32K x 8	3.3v
MCM 6229	256K x 4	
MCM 6226	128K x 8	
MCM 67B518	32K x 18	Burst Pent
MCM 67M518	32K x 18	Burst Power PC
MCM 67H518	32K x 18	Burst Pent

NEC

Number	Capacity
uPD 4311	16K x 1
uPD 4314C	4K x 4
uPD 4361	64K x 1
uPD 4362	16K x 4
uPD 4363	16K x 4
uPD 4368	8K x 8
uPD 43253	64K x 4
uPD 43258	32K x 8
uPD 431004	256K x 4
uPD 431008	18K x 8

PARADIGM

Number	Capacity	Notes
PDM 41298	64K x 4	
PDM 41256	32K x 8	
PDM 41028	256K x 4	
PDM 41024	128K x 8	
PDM 44258	32K x 18	Burst Pent

PERFORMANCE

Number	Capacity
P4C 168	4K x 4
P4C 1681	4K x 4
P4C 1682	4K x 4
P4C 116	2K x 8
P4C 187	64K x 1

P4C 188	16K x 4	
P4C 198	16K x 4	
P4C 164	8K x 8	
P4C 1298	64K x 4	
P4C 1256	32K x 8	

QUALITY

Number	Capacity	Notes
QS 8768	4K x 4	
QS 8761	4K x 4	
QS 8762	4K x 4	
QS 8888	16K x 4	
QS 8886	16K x 4	
QS 8885	16K x 4	
QS 86446	64K x 4	
QS 83280	32K x 8	
QS 83280	32K x 8	
QS 812880	128K x 8	
QS 8780	4K x 4	Tag
QS 83291	32K x 9	Burst 486

SAMSUNG

Number	Capacity	Notes
KM 6165	64K x 1	
KM 6465	16K x 4	
KM 6466	16K x 4	
KM 64B67	16K x 4	
KM 6865	8K x 8	
KM 64258	64K x 4	
KM 68257	32K x 8	
KM 688V257	32K x 8	3.3v
KM 641001	256K x 4	
KM 681001	128K x 8	

SGS

Number	Capacity	Notes
MK 41H67	16K x 1	
MK 41H68	4K x 4	
MK 41H87	64K x 1	

MK 41H80	4K x 4	Tag
Mk 41S80	4K x 4	Tag
MK 48S74	8K x 8	Tag

SHARP

Number	Capacity
LH 5267A	16K x 4
LH 52253	64K x 4
LH 52258	32K x 8
LH 52258	32K x 8
LH 521002	256K x 4
LH 52100	128K x 8

SONY

Number	Capacity
CXK 5164	64K x 1
CXK 5464A	16K x 4
CXK 5466	16k x 4
CXK 5465/7	16K x 4
CXK 5863	8K x 8
CXK 58258	32K x 8
CXK 541000	256K x 4
CXK 581120	128K x 8

TEXAS INSTRUMENTS

Number	Capacity
TM 6716	2K x 8
TM 6787	64K x 1
TM 6788	16K x 4
TM 6789	16K x 4

TOSHIBA

Number	Capacity	Notes
TMM 2018	2K x 8	
TC 5561	64K x 1	
TC 5562	64K x 1	
TC 55416(-H)	16K x 4	
TC 55417(-H)	16K x 4	
TC 5588	8K x 8	
TC 55465	64K x 4	
TC 55328	32K x 8	
TC 55B328	32K x 8	
TC 55V328	32K x 8	3.3v

American Megatrends (AMI)

6145-F North Belt Parkway

Norcross GA 30071

Tel: (770) 246 8600

Fax: (770) 246 8790

Tech Support: (770) 246 8645

www.megatrends.com

AMI (UK) Ltd

01342 410410

Award Software

777 East Middlefield Road

Mountain View CA 94043

Tel: (800) 800 BIOS

Fax: (415) 968 0274

www.unicore.com

Chips & Technologies

2950 Zanker Road

San Jose CA 95134

Tel: (408) 434 0600

www.chips.com

Chips & Technologies (UK)

01734 880237

01734 884874 (F)

DTK

(818) 810 0098

(818) 333 6548 BBS

Epson UK

01442 227478

01442 227353 (F)

01442 227479

Epson

787 6300

(310) 782 5350 (F)

(408) 782 4531 BBS

Eurosoft (UK) Ltd

3 St Stephens Road

Bournemouth

Dorset BH2 6JL UK

Tel: 44 (0)1202 297315

Fax: 44 (0)1202 297280

www.eurosoft-uk.com

General Software

320-108th Avenue NE, Suite 400

Bellevue WA 98004

Tel: (206) 454 5755

Fax: (206) 454 5744

IBM

3039 Cornwallis Road

Research Triangle Park NC 27709

Tel: (919) 543 4328

Fax: (919) 543 3518

www.ibm.com

Intel

5200 NE Elam Young Parkway

Hillsboro OR 97124

Tel: (503) 696 8080

Fax: (503) 645 8181

www.intel.com

Komputerwerk

(412) 782 0384

Micro Firmware

3330 West Gray Street, Suite 170

Norman, OK 73069

Tel: (405) 321 8333

Fax: (405) 321 8342

www.firmware.com

Microid Research

1538 Turnpike Street

North Andover MA 01845

Tel: (800) 800 BIOS

Fax: (508) 683 1630

www.unicore.com

Opti

(408) 980 8178

Phoenix

411 East Plumeria Drive

San Jose CA 95134

Tel: (408) 570 1000

www.ptltd.com

Silicon Pacific

44 1491 638275

SystemSoft

2 Vision Drive

Natick MA 01760-2059

Tel: (508) 651 0088

www.systemsoft.com

Unicore

1538 Turnpike Street

North Andover, MA 01845

Tel: (800) 800 BIOS

www.unicore.com

Upgrades Etc

(800) 541 1943

Xetal Systems

Makers of the POSTmortem™ card

Box 32602

9665 Bayview Avenue

Richmond Hill

ON L4C 0A2 Canada

Tel: (416) 410-3883

ulf@problem.tantech.com

21 Index

Phil Croucher provides technical writing and training services, and the books and courses are the result of several years experience of free-lance network management, system building and repairs.

Clients include (or have included): The Ministry of Defence, Barnardo's, Esselte Letraset Ltd., Rank Hovis, Royal Mail, Enterprise Oil plc., Line-Up Aviation Personnel, Triton Chemicals, Erith College, South Thames College, Kingsway College, Executive Airlines, Martini Airfreight Services and numerous small businesses.

He has been involved with computing since 1986, starting off with a variation of Acorn's BBC computer, the Torch, using its own version of CP/M, called CPN. From there he has fond memories of the Sirius and the Macintosh, but has mostly been involved with IBM compatibles of all shapes and sizes, specializing in Concurrent DOS and its later versions, including REAL/32. He has a regular column in *Computer Shopper* (UK) and is the resident technical expert for the AM1290 Talk Radio show *Experts On Call.*

Phil is also qualified to fly helicopters and aeroplanes, having over 6500 hours on 32 types of aircraft. He has at various times been a Chief Pilot and General Manager of several companies, including a third level airline in the UK. He is the author of *The Professional Pilot's Manual* (Airlife), and *Operational Flying.*

He can be contacted at **paco@advicepress.com**

Electrocution Technical Support Services

UK: Unit 7c Stonefield Park Chilbolton SO20 6BL

This edition of **The BIOS Companion** is the latest edition of this title originally published by Phil Croucher that are now known as the "engineers editions." Updates to the material published in the book will be made available on our website, *www.advicepress.com* on a regular basis as well as further information and links of interest.

Readers can also register their interest in similar titles and other information through the website or by mailing to companion@advicepress.com. Our fax number for registrations is (650) 321-2199.

Other Books by Phil Croucher

The **Hard Disk Companion**, ISBN 1-889671-21-5, January 1999 (US$29.95) a companion volume to this book, the hard disk companion documents over 6500 disk drives from over 267 manufacturers. Included are CMOS and jumper settings wherever obtainable as well as jumper settings of popular expansion cards, printer switches and printouts. This is the largest single documentation collection of hard drive settings published to date.

The **Motherboard Companion**, ISBN 1-889671-24-X, March 1999 (US $49.95) the third in the series, this title covers over 600 motherboards. The largest reference for most current motherboards available. Written with the system integrator and home system builder in mind, this title is a valuable reference for those building computer systems for both business and personal use.

Availability and Ordering

The titles and other books by ADVICE Press are available from your local bookstore or through your favorite online bookseller. If you can't find these books at your preferred store, please let us know and we will contact them or ask your bookseller to contact us. We certainly appreciate your feedback and support.

ADVICE Press
480 California Avenue Suite 104
Palo Alto, CA 94306

(650) 321-2197
(650) 321-2199 fax

info@advicepress.com
www.advicepress.com